Advance praise for .

D0850915

"Can we really understand celibacy or mistresses without consi̶d̶e̶r̶i̶n̶g̶ ̶m̶a̶r̶r̶iage, the socio-sexual bond that convention tells us is the heart of love? Elizabeth Abbott's new volume of accessible social history completes a sparkling trilogy about human intimacy. Her writing is as witty and informative as ever, her tone as wry and wise, and the value to understanding ourselves as profound. No thoughtful person—married, celibate, unfaithful or otherwise—should be without this book." —Mark Kingwell, author of *Concrete Reveries* and *Extraordinary Canadians: Glenn Gould*

"Whether you consider marriage a prison or a paradise, an outmoded institution or the culmination of all your white lacy dreams, Elizabeth Abbott's probing history deftly shows how this always fragile, yet always resilient institution has evolved. It's not always a pretty picture, but it's a fascinating one." —Judith Timson, author of *Family Matters*

"I love this book. Elizabeth Abbott is an engaging story-teller. She wisely recognizes that we can only understand the changing meanings of marriage if we also appreciate that what it means to live single has changed dramatically, too." —Bella DePaulo, author of *Singled Out*

"Elizabeth Abbott has penned a masterpiece ... *A History of Marriage* is a wide-ranging account of how the social intersects with many forms of the personal. An outstanding work that deserves as many readers as can be found." —Ahmad Saidullah, author of *Happiness and Other Disorders*

"With her genius for the apt example and her characteristic wit and warmth, Elizabeth Abbott expertly illuminates the lived experience of marriage past and present, discovering, in the process, some surprising parallels between the way we were and the way we are today, and offering suggestions to help bolster tomorrow's unions. Wide-ranging yet cohesive, sharply observed yet hopeful, *A History of Marriage,* like the institution it animates, rewards commitment." —Susan Olding, author of *Pathologies: A Life in Essays*

"Fascinating and utterly engrossing, Elizabeth Abbott's book is crammed full of delicious morsels of information about nuptials past and present. What we take for granted as the immutable, eternal rituals of romance and marriage aren't that at all. You should see how they did it in the past. Romance? Forget it." —Maureen Jennings, author of the Detective Murdoch series

"Like any marriage, this book is full of surprises. Elizabeth Abbott's take on the ties that bind so many of us is lively and intelligent. A must-read." —Catherine Dunphy, author of *Morgentaler: A Difficult Hero*

Praise for Elizabeth Abbott's other books

"Ambitious ... Her research is detailed and thorough. She is gifted at relating not just the triumphs and tragedies of those who lived centuries ago but also in giving a sense of their daily lives. She makes us ... hungry to know more about them." —*The Columbus Dispatch*

"Elizabeth Abbott mixes anthropology with history in her confection of insights ... The pages of Abbott's lucid, exciting book throb with both life and its denial ... It is a strength of her moving and dazzling achievement that Abbott is never conventional, preachy or platitudinous. Like all good history, her book is a signpost to the strangeness of a world that has such deviance in it." —*The Guardian*

"Entertaining, fascinating, and frequently disturbing." —*The Gazette* (Montreal)

"Ambitious and wide-ranging." —*The New Yorker*

"A rich, dramatic, fascinating history." —*The Globe and Mail*

"Here is history with a human face, effective, moving, written with surprising and admirable restraint." —*Kirkus Reviews* (starred)

"This book is powerfully composed with a dense rush of events and documentation, the passion of personal feeling, an outrage expressed in bitter irony." —*Los Angeles Times*

"Splendid, passionate ... Elizabeth Abbott portrays a depth of misery and exploitation which, it might be said without disrespect to Graham Greene, he was only able to hint at." —*Newsday*

"Manag[es] to be both academic and entertaining." —*Evening Standard*

"Abbott presents a fascinating panoply of characters ... [her] extensive research is impressive." —*Edmonton Journal*

"A juicy, brilliantly insightful survey—as readable as it is intellectually sophisticated, alternately witty and moving." —*Village Voice Literary Supplement*

"Once you begin this astonishing book, you are not likely to put it down ... She is an extraordinarily brave woman with the talent to match her bravery." —Eugene D. Genovese, author of *Roll, Jordan, Roll: The World the Slaves Made*

PENGUIN CANADA

A HISTORY OF MARRIAGE

ELIZABETH ABBOTT is a writer and historian with a special interest in social justice and women's issues, the treatment and lives of animals, and the environment. She has a doctorate from McGill University in nineteenth-century history and is a Research Associate at Trinity College, University of Toronto, where from 1991 to 2004 she was Dean of Women. She is the author of several books that have been translated into sixteen languages, and include the bestselling *A History of Celibacy* and *A History of Mistresses.* In 1991 Abbott won a National Magazine Award for Environmental Writing. Her book *Sugar: A Bittersweet History* was short-listed for the 2009 Charles Taylor Prize for Literary Non-Fiction.

Abbott is also a book reviewer and lectures on topics related to her books and on the art of writing literary non-fiction.

Abbott is a mother and expectant grandmother. She lives with three dogs and two cats in Toronto and is a dog rescuer.

Elizabeth Abbott's website is www.elizabethabbott.ca.

Also by Elizabeth Abbott

Sugar: A Bittersweet History
A History of Mistresses
A History of Celibacy
Chronicle of Canada (general editor)
Haiti: The Duvaliers and Their Legacy
Tropical Obsession

ELIZABETH ABBOTT

A
HISTORY OF
MARRIAGE

PENGUIN
CANADA

PENGUIN CANADA

Published by the Penguin Group

Penguin Group (Canada), 90 Eglinton Avenue East, Suite 700, Toronto,
Ontario, Canada M4P 2Y3 (a division of Pearson Canada Inc.)

Penguin Group (USA) Inc., 375 Hudson Street, New York, New York 10014, U.S.A.
Penguin Books Ltd, 80 Strand, London WC2R 0RL, England
Penguin Ireland, 25 St Stephen's Green, Dublin 2, Ireland
(a division of Penguin Books Ltd)
Penguin Group (Australia), 250 Camberwell Road, Camberwell, Victoria 3124,
Australia (a division of Pearson Australia Group Pty Ltd)
Penguin Books India Pvt Ltd, 11 Community Centre, Panchsheel Park,
New Delhi – 110 017, India
Penguin Group (NZ), 67 Apollo Drive, Rosedale, North Shore 0745, Auckland,
New Zealand (a division of Pearson New Zealand Ltd)
Penguin Books (South Africa) (Pty) Ltd, 24 Sturdee Avenue, Rosebank,
Johannesburg 2196, South Africa

Penguin Books Ltd, Registered Offices: 80 Strand, London WC2R 0RL, England

First published 2010

1 2 3 4 5 6 7 8 9 10 (WEB)

Copyright © Elizabeth Abbott, 2010

All rights reserved. Without limiting the rights under copyright reserved above, no
part of this publication may be reproduced, stored in or introduced into a retrieval
system, or transmitted in any form or by any means (electronic, mechanical, photo-
copying, recording or otherwise), without the prior written permission of both the
copyright owner and the above publisher of this book.

Manufactured in Canada.

LIBRARY AND ARCHIVES CANADA CATALOGUING IN PUBLICATION

Abbott, Elizabeth
A history of marriage / Elizabeth Abbott.

ISBN 978-0-14-301714-1

1. Marriage--History. I. Title.

HQ503.A22 2010   306.8109   C2009-906007-8

Visit the Penguin Group (Canada) website at **www.penguin.ca**

Special and corporate bulk purchase rates available; please see **www.penguin.ca/
corporatesales** or call 1-800-810-3104, ext. 2477 or 2474

To the memory of my father, Bill Abbott, who never doubted that he had hit the jackpot when he married Marnie Griggs, my mother.

And to my beloved son and daughter-in-law, Ivan and Dina, for the joy of sharing your lives and for making me a grandmother.

Contents

Acknowledgments

During my thirteen years as Dean of Women at the University of Toronto's Trinity College, I wrote *A History of Celibacy* and *A History of Mistresses*. In 2004, I left my deanship to become a full-time writer. I detoured in subject matter, and *Sugar: A Bittersweet History* appeared in 2008. I resumed my narrative trajectory and, with *A History of Marriage*, have completed my historical relationship trilogy. Dreams can come true, and I am most grateful to everyone who helped me realize them.

Andrea Magyar, editorial director of Penguin Canada, reined me in and gave *Marriage* its North American orientation, for which I thank her. I thank her as well for putting me into the editorial hands of Helen Smith, whose energy and enthusiasm are contagious. And the droll animal images she implants in emails always make me laugh, assuaging the stress of editorial demands and deadlines.

For twenty-three years my agent, Heide Lange, has supported my writing goals and sold my books worldwide. I treasure our collaboration and am proud to be one of her authors.

I loved the rigour and excellence of copy editor Shaun Oakey's work on *Sugar* and am delighted that he agreed to take on *A History of Marriage* as well. The "track changes" dialogue between us added another dimension to the revision process.

Production editor David Ross has been wonderfully patient and understanding of my vision of a narrative enhanced by images.

Dr. David Reed, Professor Emeritus of Pastoral Theology at Wycliffe College, University of Toronto, gave generously of his time and expertise to critique several chapters.

Tim Cook, a historian at the Canadian War Museum in Ottawa and winner of the 2009 Charles Taylor Prize, did a critical reading of chapter 8 and provided supplementary sources; thank you so much, Tim.

Rev. William Craig, what would I do without you to turn to for that emergency Latin translation or that theological nicety? Thank you, Bill!

Listening to and questioning the manuscript's focus group was endlessly interesting, revelatory, and often cathartic. Carol, Carolyn,

Catharine, Elaine, Emily, Heather, Laura, LaTanya, Vivian, and everyone else who joined us: you are great readers and talkers, and I learned so much from each of you! Viv, your lawyerly perspective was invaluable.

Karl Jaffary was a solo reader and gave valuable feedback.

Yves Pierre-Louis, my brother of the heart, read, critiqued, and directed me to new sources. Louise Abbott, my flesh-and-blood sister, provided the images of our parents' wedding and of Mom as a tot.

My son, Ivan, and my daughter-in-law, Dina, walked hand-in-hand with me throughout the research and writing, even as they became engaged, planned their Big Fat Greek Wedding, married, honeymooned, and settled into newlywed domestic life. We will celebrate their third wedding anniversary cradling their newborn, due to be born just after this book is.

Heather Conway never wilted under the onslaught of TIFF and JPG files (and terrible deadlines); once again she worked her technological magic and transformed them into the wonderful images I knew they could become.

Pegi Dover and Philip Jessup enriched this book with their family photograph. Carol McPhee and Jon Bankson helped me illustrate the intricacies of modern marriage with their joyous wedding portrait.

Carlton Abbott was always encouraging, and his faith in me made me stronger.

LaTanya, Ashiyah, and Tyanna Abbott pitched in and made a scrapbook of the images I was considering; thank you!

Emily Griggs made time to help me with the bibliography; many thanks.

Thanks to Elaine Wong, Mehran Ataee, Mera Nirmalan-Nathan, Puja Karmaker Mullins, Rehaana Manek, Sophie Chung, Stephanie Creighton, and Vizarath Ali for helping with research.

Lastly, I owe a huge debt of gratitude to the patrons of the Charles Taylor Prize for Literary Non-Fiction (2009). Through their graciousness and generosity in publicizing the short-listed books, they made good on their promise that all three of us were winners.

Part 1

Marriage in History

The Way We (Really) Were

It is August 2009, and sunshine warms Nathan Phillips Square, the concrete piazza in front of Toronto's City Hall that, on this autumnal August afternoon, is also a bridal path. The wedding party is small: bride Heather and Greg her groom, their parents, one aunt, two uncles, a cousin with his fiancée, and a single friend. To the brisk beat of a duo of rappers entrancing their audience of clapping children, the celebrants stroll in pairs and trios past *The Archer*, Henry Moore's masterful sculpture, up to the solid block of doors that usher them into the subdued stillness of weekend City Hall.

The party squeezes into one elevator and exits on the third floor, into the milling throng of another wedding party anxiously awaiting late-comers who are delaying their ceremony. That bride is young and in full white regalia, her deep blue and blood-red shoulder tattoos a startling contrast to her floor-length strapless satin gown and pale floral bouquet. After the elevator disgorges two high-heeled, miniskirted women pushing babies in strollers, the group races into the wedding chamber, and Heather and Greg's party sink into the vacated chairs.

Heather glows in a shimmering grey sleeveless summer dress accessorized with a shawl, several pinkish necklaces and a silver bag (all borrowed), and new Payless slippers. Greg, florid with emotion and heat, wears a darker grey suit with a pink-striped tie. They chat with their guests, and Greg remarks, sotto voce, that this is the first time in over a decade that he has seen his mother and father in the same room.

*After fourteen years of a marriage of true minds, Heather
and Greg formalize their union with a city hall wedding.*

Everyone is relaxed and happy as they wait—not for long—until the
previous wedding ends and one more new husband-and-wife file past to
the elevator.

Inside the chamber, to the strains of recorded classical music,
Heather's father and mother walk her up the narrow passageway that
doubles as an aisle. The justice of the peace, imposing and priest-like in
academic gown, begins the brief but touching service that includes
inquiring of the assembly whether they will help Heather and Greg
fulfill their marriage vows. Everyone nods and sits up straighter. They
are no longer just witnesses. They have just been inducted into the ceremony as participants.

Greg faces Heather and, with a catch in his voice, recites his vows.
"When I was a kid, my little sister had a T-shirt of a brontosaurus with
a little girl riding on his neck and a caption that read: 'He followed me

home, can I keep him?' I'm like that brontosaurus and I followed you home. And, my love, I'm glad you kept me."

Heather responds, her words thick with held-back tears: "You're good with words. I'm good with pictures. So I won't say anything, and I'll paint you a picture instead." The picture she describes is a panorama of their fourteen years together, and includes two brown boxes filled with months of back-and-forth letters; a huge Thunder Bay sky filled with bubbles and lollipops; a skinny Victorian house full of nail holes and groceries; two hound dogs at a beach with shared ice cream; Las Vegas flamingos and enormous Chicago meals; duelling laptops playing favourite songs in a city backyard; a newspaper with a hidden love note; an early bird and a night owl; hand-holding, quick smooches, and spooning.

And then, her voice stronger, Heather completes her vows: "I'll paint a plane flying to an unknown country to find an unknown child. I'll paint a happy past, a wonderful present, and an exciting future. I'll paint fourteen years of loving a man who is my husband and my best friend. And with all that together, I'll be painting you and me."

I weep (for I am the friend honoured to share this ritual), and around me so do most of the others. Soon after, the justice smiles and waves us off. "That's it," he declares. "Now you're really married."

We leave, and in a convoy of taxis proceed to the Victorian house where Heather and Greg plan to love and raise the unknown child from an unknown country that, their adoption agency has advised them, releases its orphans only to formally married couples. There, in their spacious garden lit by candles in wrought-iron lanterns, they also welcome neighbours and friends invited to celebrate this most tradi-tional of occasions: a marriage rooted in their mutual longing to raise children together.

During the several years I have been working on this book about marriage, I have attended several weddings: my son's, my brother's, former students', and most recently Heather and Greg's. Our society's constant lament that marriage is a doomed institution is at odds with the reality that, at some point, most of us marry, and often remarry. As I researched and organized my material, I was constantly struck by how much has changed over the years—and even more so by how much more remains unchanged.

A History of Marriage is the third of the trilogy that *A History of Celibacy* introduced and *A History of Mistresses* continued, the sweeping story of how men and women have related to each other over the centuries. But unlike *A History of Celibacy* and *A History of Mistresses, A History of Marriage* is restricted to the North American historical experience and its mostly European antecedents. In this book I also strive to explain and contextualize the state of marriage today, and to identify and discuss the issues most important to how it is developing. The subtext of *A History of Marriage*, in other words, is the connection between the past and the present, where we've been and where that has led us.

Heather and Greg epitomize this subtext. At the time of their marriage, they had lived together for fourteen years, for the last ten of those in a spacious, leaf-shaded Victorian home in a neighbourhood rich in dogs, including their two hounds, and children. They see their happy and fulfilling relationship as a marriage of true minds that transcends mere law. They have careers, hobbies, friends, family, and each other. But, unable to procreate and longing for children, they are hoping to adopt and, to improve their prospects, they have decided to wed. Today as in the past, children—wanted and unwanted—have always been at the heart of marriage.

People argue about and cry over and celebrate marriage because on a multitude of interlocking levels, emotionally, logistically, socially, and financially, it matters. *A History of Marriage* traces its evolution as an institution in terms of law, custom, and religion. It also explores the realities of marriage as individuals lived it in the context of love and duty, sex and loyalty, child-rearing and cohabiting, shared finances, and social recognition.

These real-life experiences are presented in their wider historical context: What were a couple's alternatives to staying together? How long was the average marriage until death ended it? What were the realities of daily life for trousered husbands and their skirted wives? How pervasive was the double standard that empowered men while it denied women the right to vote, to control their own money, to win custody of their children, to commit adultery with impunity? What were housekeeping standards and practice? How was food prepared? How were children raised? What divorce laws existed when divorce was rare? Did spouses separate without legally divorcing (in which case they were still considered married)? Crucially, what were the differences between the experiences of wealthier and poorer spouses, between, for example, the marriages of Martha Coffin Wright and the unnamed immigrant woman—let's call her Marta—who locked her children out of their tenement apartment on a bitterly cold March afternoon in 1911?

Both Martha and Marta had four children and husbands whose earnings they needed to supplement: Martha wrote articles and Marta did textile piecework. Martha was a fervent abolitionist and women's rights advocate who, with her husband's cooperation, hid fugitive slaves in her

A seven-year-old girl cares for her siblings in their New York City tenement hallway. Their mother has locked them out of their apartment while she delivers finished piecework to her employer.

house and, in full-bellied pregnancy, entertained the historic Seneca Falls Women's Rights Convention of 1848 with her newspaper article "Hints for Wives—and Husbands," about the tedious, interminable "treadmill" of housework and caring for "the fallen little sons and daughters of her Adam." But Martha's droll address belied her near despair at the toll exacted by her daily grind and how, unlike her "liege lord," she rose "weary & unrefreshed, again to go through the same routine."

Marta left far fewer traces of her existence. Had social justice observer Elizabeth C. Watson not happened upon her children, crying and huddled together for warmth in their tenement hallway because Marta had locked them out of their apartment on a bitterly cold and snowy winter day, there might be no traces at all. When she returned home and Watson demanded to know what had happened, Marta silenced her with this unanswerable query: "What I must do? I maka the coats, my man he no gotta job. He walk this day for work. I lock a children in, they burn up. I lock a children out, they cry. What I must do?"

Like most other pieceworkers in her teeming tenement, Marta was overworked and under intolerable pressure. Unlike Martha's children, Marta's did not enjoy endless supplies of homemade gingerbread and stew; they survived on pushcart fast food or their own culinary efforts, leaving them malnourished and often hungry. Their living quarters were overcrowded, with pieces of the coats Marta stitched together from early morning until late at night stashed in every nook and cranny. Even when her man found work she had to supplement his wages with piecework, and her older children had to pitch in as well.

That daily struggle in that tenement and those children provided the framework for Marta and her underemployed husband's marriage, just as the daily grind, the children, her loving husband, and their personal circumstances provided the framework for Martha and her husband's marriage. Individuals like Martha and Marta people this book, and their stories bring to life the realities and particularities of historical marriage.

Part 1 of *A History of Marriage* examines the role of romantic and erotic love as it developed over the centuries and how it was affected by marriage's other dimensions, notably how spouses were chosen. For example, the hundreds of seventeenth-century women encouraged and dowered by the French state—the *filles du roi*, or king's daughters—who sailed to New France to become the wives of bachelors under official orders to marry them had quite different priorities and prospects than nineteenth-century debutantes armed with dowries, social connections, and skills that included competency in music, embroidery, and sketching, and perhaps conversational French or Italian.

Part 1 also considers how spouses learned what marriage meant and demanded of them, the parameters of its rules and guidelines, its purpose and its rewards. It traces the evolution of weddings and the married state (not always synonymous). In the chapter "Marriage from within Four Walls," it delves into realities of daily life that constituted and shaped the marital experience, for example Martha and David Wright's. "Go Forth and Multiply" focuses on every aspect of child-rearing and discusses contraception, childbirth, nursing, training and teaching, loving and disciplining, putting to work, and mourning. The special and contentious role of step-parents is identified as one of the most important threads that link the past, when death ended so many young marriages, and today, when divorce plays the same role. "When Things Went Wrong" surveys the various ways spouses have responded to marital dissension—bigamy, separation, even murder—but concentrates on the complex institution of divorce with its concomitants of custody and division of property.

By identifying the core values and realities of historical marriage, including the social and individual contexts in which it operated, part 1 of *A History of Marriage* provides a lens onto the present and even the future of marriage, as the experiences of millions of historic spouses lend perspective and sometimes lessons to today's North Americans. One crucial lesson is to avoid romanticizing historical marriage, because, as the great realist writer Gustave Flaubert observed, "Our ignorance of history causes us to slander our own times." Our own times are extraordinarily interesting, and part 2 will tell their story as new chapters in marriage's long history.

Chapter 1

Husbands and Wives— Who Were They?

Making Matches

On November 10, 1670, Jean Talon, the Intendant, or district administrator, of Quebec City, wrote to France's minister of finance: "All the king's daughters sent to New France last year are married, and almost all are pregnant or have had children, a testament to the fertility of this country. I strongly recommend that those who are destined for this country [next year] be in no way unattractive or have anything repugnant in their appearance, that they be healthy and strong, for the work of the country, or at least have some skill in household chores.... It is good to have them accompanied by a certificate from their Pastor or a local Judge who can vouch for their being free and marriageable."[1]

The ambitious matchmaking program described in this letter succeeded in recruiting 737 women, known as *les filles du roi*, or the king's daughters, to leave France and set sail for the fledgling fur-trading colony of New France, where men heavily outnumbered women, and soldiers, settlers, and fur traders were desperate for wives. Most of *les filles* came from modest backgrounds and more than half were orphans. With the king's dowry (except when the royal treasury was empty) of at least 50 livres to supplement their good looks, household talents, and, often, literacy and accounting skills, they quickly found husbands.

Typical among *les filles* were nineteen-year-old Catherine Paulo, from LaRochelle, who married Etienne Campeau, a twenty-six-year-old mason and farmer, and went on to have fifteen children. Another, Mathurine Thibault, was twenty-nine when she arrived and married the recently widowed Jean Milot, a master toolmaker with whom she had six children.

A tiny number of women disappointed their sponsors and misbehaved. One offender was Catherine Guichelin, who led a scandalous life and was once charged with prostitution. She gave birth to several illegitimate children, and instead of raising the son and daughter she had with one husband, she adopted them out to other families. Despite her notoriety, though, even Catherine had no trouble finding husbands, annulling two marriage contracts, and marrying a third time.

Les filles were as healthy and capable as Talon and French officials intended, and so prolific that millions of today's French Canadians are

A group of king's daughters arrives in Quebec in 1667. Officials greet the higher-ranked women while hopeful bachelors gaze at the newcomers waiting in line.

descended directly from them. Against a checklist of qualities and skills, each of these women established her worth and her eligibility in the marriage market of man-heavy seventeenth-century French-Canadian colonial society. In turn, *les filles* exercised their right to evaluate prospective husbands. Their primary concern, according to Marie de l'Incarnation, the Ursuline Mother Superior who chaperoned them, was whether a man had a house. They knew from the experience of earlier arrivals that, without proper lodgings, a new bride would endure great discomfort until a proper home was built.

As in New France, all societies have criteria for selecting spouses, and any exploration of marriage, in any time or place, should begin by identifying the men and women who married: Who were they? What characteristics did they share? What was expected of them, and why did they choose—or how were they chosen—to marry each other?

It might seem frivolous to note that the most basic qualification for both bride and groom was to be living beings—except when we learn that in rare cases, desperation and grief overcame even that obstacle. In China, *minghun*, or afterlife marriage, weds dead sons to dead daughters, sparing them the eternal torment of their unmarried states. In France even today, the president's approval is enough to legitimize weddings between the living and the dead.

The "rule" that marriages join only spouses of opposite sex has also been practised in the breach. In ancient Rome, for example, Emperor Elagabalus married Zoticus, a male athlete from Smyrna; he also referred to Hierocles, his blond slave, as his husband. The Roman historian and biographer Suetonius described how Emperor Nero "castrated the boy Sporus and actually tried to make a woman of him; and he married him with all the usual ceremonies, including a dowry and a bridal veil … and treated him as his wife." Contemporary Roman literature speaks about lesbian relationships but not marriages, likely because women lacked the influence and power to bring them about.

Same-sex unions did not survive antiquity, and early European visitors were astonished and repelled by North American Native versions of them. The Crow people, for example, recognized a third gender, or

The earliest known photograph of a North American berdache is titled "Squaw Jim and his Squaw." Jim is an enlisted scout honoured for his bravery after he saved the life of a tribesman in the Battle of the Rosebud, June 17, 1876.

berdache, understood by Natives as "two spirit" people possessed of both maleness and femaleness and, in many tribes, permitted to marry partners of the same sex. The polygamous Aleut and Cheyenne permitted male berdaches to be co-wives of a man alongside single-spirit women. Whether they married monogamously or polygamously, berdaches had to observe traditional kinship rules for marriage. "Strange country this," observed fur trader Edwin T. Denig in 1833, "where males assume the dress and perform the duties of females, while women turn men and mate with their own sex!"[2] In Europe and colonial North America, meanwhile, the reality of same-gender sexual attraction continued to pass unnoticed or to be suppressed and even criminalized, and spouses had to be of opposite sex for a marriage to take place.

Age at First Marriage

One issue that affected all marriages was the age of the newlyweds, especially the brides. As historian Brent D. Shaw explains, the age of brides is "one of the most important factors in determining the overall rates of fertility in a given population, and hence its general demographic profile. It also affects a whole range of social institutions of reproduction, above all the 'shape' of the family, the relationships between the mother and her children, between husband and wife, and the ways in which property can be redistributed through inheritance."[3] The age of brides reflected as well women's status and the roles their society expected them to play.

In much of the world, even babies could be married off. In traditional China, the practice of *t'ung yang-hsi*—raising a daughter-in-law from childhood—involved giving away or selling a baby girl as young as weeks or months old as the future wife of the son whose family would raise her. It was believed this practice was conducive to raising submissive, obedient, and hardworking brides perfectly familiar with their in-laws' domestic routines and personal needs and—always a worry—less likely to run away than wives married at an older age. *T'ung yang-hsi* dated from at least the Sung dynasty (960–1279) and, as late as the twentieth century, accounted for about 20 percent of marriages in China.

In India, where Hinduism revered marriage as "a sacrament of transcendental importance" that families arranged under the influence if not the inspiration of divine guidance, little girls could also be married.[4] Indian families, like Chinese, appreciated the malleability of the very young bride whose husband and in-laws could train and mould. Child marriage was so widespread that in the single decade between 1921 and 1931, the number of child wives rose from 8,565,357 to 12,271,595. However, the custom of *gauna*—keeping the preadolescent bride in her parents' home until she matured sexually—made many child marriages a two-step process. The first was the wedding. The second was the *gauna* ceremony, after which the bride was sent to live with her husband's family.

Among the upper classes of western Europe, the situation was not unlike the Asian. Parents so often married off their daughters at or before puberty that the words *nubile* and *marriageable* were synonymous. Pushing a young girl to marry guaranteed against the disgrace of her having a bastard baby and thereby destroying her chances of consolidating or improving her family's status and fortune through marriage.

In the twelfth century, Pope Alexander III tried to bring a measure of protection to these young brides through a canon law that specified that the minimum age for "present consent," without which a marriage could be annulled, was twelve for girls and fourteen for boys. Some parents among the elites circumvented this restriction by interpreting "twelve" to mean the twelfth year, and married off their daughters at eleven. Other parents simply ignored the law or applied for papal dispensations to marry off even younger children.[5]

Often, young spouses were betrothed in infancy or early childhood, despite a twelfth-century papal decree setting seven as the minimum age for betrothal. (Betrothal was akin to marriage except that the death of one partner did not mean widowhood.) This was the fate of Marguerite, who was only two when her father, the French king Louis VII, betrothed her to five-year-old Henry, son of Henry II of England. Two years later, after Marguerite's mother, Constance, died in childbirth, and Louis waited a mere five weeks before remarrying, Henry II responded to the diplomatic implications of these events with an immediate celebration of little Marguerite and Henry's marriage.

Most betrothed girls lived at home until they were deemed old enough to marry. But as in China and India, some were brought up by their future in-laws. These girls learned their new home's customs, culture, language, and idiosyncrasies. Countess Agnes of Essex, betrothed at three years to Geoffrey de Vere, was six when she was handed over to Geoffrey's brother, the Earl of Oxford. Seven-year-old Matilda, daughter of Henry I of England, betrothed to Holy Roman Emperor Henry V, twenty-one years her senior, was entrusted to Henry's court to "learn the language and customs and laws of the country, and all that an empress ought to know, now, in the time of her youth."[6] To ensure her immersion in the Germanic court, the emperor dismissed her English caretakers.

The first time they married, husbands tended to be close in age or a few years older than their wives, though it was neither uncommon nor illegal for a man of sixty to marry a child four or five decades younger. Sixteenth-century British translator Angel Day, for example, denounced a greedy father's plan to marry off his "young and dainty" daughter to a repulsive miser of "filthy tawny deformed and unseemly hue ... so wretched and ill favoured a creature" as "repugnant to reason, or any manner of considerate and sage advisement."[7]

What was it like for a small child to be betrothed or married and delivered into the hands of strangers? Mohandas Gandhi, betrothed at seven and wed at thirteen, later condemned child marriage as a "cruel custom" and added, "Little did I dream then that one day I should severely criticize my father for having married me as a child."[8]

A Korean girl gazes for the first time at the bridegroom she will soon wed in an arranged marriage, ca. 1920.

Rassundari Devi, a nineteenth-century Bengali mother of eleven, likened herself as a child bride to "the sacrificial goat being dragged to the altar, the same hopeless situation, the same agonized screams."[9] Most of the once child wives and grooms have left no traces, certainly not testaments. And although some may not have minded being married so young, we can reasonably extrapolate that a great many women were wretched, and the laws against child marriage reflect a bitter awareness of their ill treatment and unhappiness. Even if well treated, they were deprived of childhood.

Once ensconced in their new homes, these children were not always well looked after. Some girls were raped by impatient husbands or callous in-laws. And both boys and girls were vulnerable to their in-laws' vengeance if the alliances they had helped forge changed, or the fortunes they commanded were lost. After her father lost his wealth, Countess Agnes of Essex was confined to a tower and maltreated. Even those who were not unkindly treated suffered the loss of their parents, families, and homes, all replaced by new people expecting the newcomer, almost always a girl, to be modest and obedient, soft-spoken and submissive, and virginally pure in word and deed.

Yet however difficult the transition, however onerous the demands, however unnatural for mere children to be cast in the role of apprentice spouses, few girls were subjected to sexual relations until they reached physical maturity, usually menarche or an age between twelve and fourteen, commonly the legal age of consent and the age most societies considered suitable for marriage, at least for girls from privileged families. Non-elite girls and boys had quite different experiences. In ancient Athens, most women married at between fourteen and eighteen years, very soon after menarche, to men usually a decade or more older. The consequence of this age discrepancy was that the brides' fathers, by then at least in their mid-forties and aware of their own mortality, were eager to arrange their daughters' futures while they could. (Their sons married as adults, and so were deeply involved in arranging their own marriages.) Marriage pre-empted premarital pregnancy and its attendant disgrace. It also freed young women to engage in the marital sex then thought to cure gynecological problems, including the hormonal imbalances of puberty.

In keeping with its militaristic culture, ancient Sparta prepared its *parthenoi*—unmarried girls—for their future duties as the mothers of strong warriors with a rigorous training regimen that set them apart from their sisters in other Greek city states. Muscular, conditioned, and fit, the *parthenoi* were at least eighteen before they married. Marriage put an abrupt end to this relatively unbridled life as the bride took up residence with her husband or his parents. But if her groom was under thirty, he continued to live in communal military barracks and could visit his wife only "under cover of darkness, in conspiratorial secrecy from his messmates and even from the rest of his household," even as the couple proceeded to produce little Spartans.[10] Family life, known to encourage relaxation, was suppressed for as long as possible to avoid eroding the militaristic infrastructure that permeated Spartan culture from top to bottom.

As in Greece, most girls in ancient Rome married in their late teens to early twenties. Many scholars now believe that there, too, only girls from the propertied class were married off at younger ages, to men usually in their mid-twenties. Upper-class marriages were therefore characterized by a wider age gap between husband and wife, with all the implications that had for marital relations, reproduction, widowhood, remarriage, and the transfer of property.[11] Centuries later in western Europe, non-elite brides tended to marry in their mid- to late teens to early twenties. This is necessarily a generalization about such vastly different nations and cultures, but it provides a useful rule of thumb and is the basis for scholarly interpretations of the dynamics and nature of marriage, as the following examples show.[12]

In Germany during the second half of the sixteenth century, trades-men were prohibited from marrying until they passed the exams that transformed journeymen into masters. But as economic constraints made it more difficult for even a master to afford marriage, there arose a significant class of men whose financial situation made them unmar-riageable. Engagements stretched from months to years, forcing some couples to petition for exemption from the rules, usually because of pregnancy or, as one urgent petition phrased it, "weighty reasons." Despite critics who argued that marriage prevented giving in to lust, that newlyweds should welcome financial hardship as a divine challenge, and that in any case God would provide, the rules were so stringently applied that the average age of marriage rose, with many would-be spouses remaining single.

Other examples suggest wide variations in the age at first marriage. In 1864, in the northern and southern Portuguese provinces of Viana do Castelo and Faro, 15.5 percent and 42.7 percent respectively of women between twenty and twenty-four were married; 37.8 percent and 11 percent of women between fifty and fifty-four remained single. In 1880, in the Belgian *arrondissements* of Tielt and Charleroi, the average age of marriage was 28.4 and 25 respectively; 30.5 percent of fifty-year-old Tielt women remained unmarried compared to only 9.2 percent in Charleroi.[13] In England and Wales between the 1840s to the 1870s, more than two-thirds of men and women in their mid-twenties had not yet married, and 12 percent of women in their fifties remained unmarried.[14]

By the nineteenth century, North Americans tended toward the western European practice of later marriage or lifelong celibacy, or at least singleness. In Upper and Lower Canada (now Ontario and Quebec), men and women married almost as late as western Europeans, though fewer remained unmarried. In Lower Canada, more widowers than widows remarried. In Upper Canada, however, with its ratio of 145 males to 100 women aged fifteen to thirty-nine, widows were likely to remarry. In 1871 in Nova Scotia, especially in Scottish-settled counties, women often married in their mid- to late twenties, usually to men a few years older. Though some women married before their twenty-first birthdays, men rarely did.[15] In 1880, in Philadelphia, Irish immigrant women, many working as domestics, married at an average 26.4 years (Irish men at 29.1), German women at 23.9 years (men at 25.9), and American-born white women at 25.4 years (and the men at 28 years).[16]

Patterns of Marriage

A wealth of studies exploring the details and dynamics of marriage has allowed scholars to postulate the existence of marriage models. In historic Europe, three are evident: the Western, Eastern, and Mediterranean models. Each is linked to the age of spouses at their first marriage and is best understood in the context of environmental, economic, and demographic conditions. These marriage models help make sense of the past, particularly in understanding the effect that age at first marriage had on individual spouses, on their families and societies, and on the kind of household they lived in as a married couple.

In the Western model, both men and women married at relatively later ages, usually no more than a few years apart, and formed a new, usually nuclear household. Few households were multi-generational or comprised more than one family. For example, French peasants in the four centuries before the Revolution married later because of rules ingrained in their culture. One such rule was that spouses did not cohabit with parents after they married. Another was that establishing one's own home and hearth was essential. Western households, in other words, seldom included extended families or any sort of polygamous arrangement, although a variant Western marriage model incorporated domestic servants or labourers into the household.

The Eastern model was almost the opposite of the Western. Most people married at a young age and joined an existing household, usually the groom's, instead of establishing a new one. These joint households included more than one married couple who were usually related to each other, as well as other relatives such as unmarried siblings or widowed elders. One result of this model was that few people lived alone or with unrelated people. (In the Far East, establishing new households was actually forbidden.)

The Mediterranean model was characterized by young brides married to older husbands. As in Eastern marriages, the new couple seldom established a new household but instead took over, joined, or split an existing household. The result was a society in which most households comprised more than one generation and family, and included extended family members.

What primarily distinguished the Mediterranean from the Eastern model was the age at first marriage, with its very different social, cultural, and economic implications. For one thing, older husbands were less likely to have living fathers, which significantly affected their income and livelihood. Upon his father's death, for example, a man gained legal and social independence, which changed his position and role in society and in his extended family; usually the oldest male was the head of the household. In ancient Rome, more than three-quarters of males and half of females had lost their fathers by the time they married, greatly reducing the influence of the *patria potestas*—the Roman father's life-and-death power over his family.[17] Yet another marriage model was polygamy. Usually polygamy was reserved for wealthy men. In China, men could marry more than one wife as well as taking concubines into their houses. One extraordinary consequence of this marriage system was that today, one and a half million Chinese men are directly descended from Giocangga, the Ch'ing dynasty's founder's grandfather, through his descendants' many wives and concubines. The average monogamously married Chinese man, on the other hand, has an average of only twenty descendants.

The Bible, too, describes the several wives of many Old Testament notables, among them Abraham, David, and King Solomon, the latter having seven hundred wives and three hundred concubines. King Philip of Macedon and his son Alexander the Great both had multiple wives, and polygamy was not uncommon among nobles and other privileged men. As Christianity developed, the church gradually turned against polygamy, in part because Greco-Roman culture prescribed monogamy. "Now indeed in our time, and in keeping with Roman custom, it is no longer allowed to take another wife," Saint Augustine observed.

The new religion of Islam, however, did not ban polygamy. Instead, its Quran restricted Muslim men to four wives, and the Prophet advised a man with eleven wives to divorce seven of them. "If you fear that you shall not be able to deal justly with the orphans," the Quran advises, "marry women of your choice, two or three or four; but if you fear that you shall not be able to deal justly with them, then only one." Unlike the Chinese system, in which a principal wife held sway over secondary wives, Islam decreed that all wives were equal.

Meanwhile Christian Europe struggled for centuries to stamp out polygamy, which many theologians regarded as less morally repellent than divorce. When Henry VIII wished to divest himself of his first wife, Catharine of Aragon, Pope Clement VII and his advisers at one point proposed that the king marry a second wife instead, averting the sin of divorce and granting legitimacy to the male heir that she might deliver.

Reformation leader Martin Luther, who could find no scriptural condemnation of polygamy, held similar views; this was reflected in his advice to the adulterous Philip of Hesse. After Philip pleaded that the sexual wasteland of his arranged marriage to Christine of Saxony had driven him to defile his marriage vows, Luther advised him to take a second wife, keeping the marriage secret to avoid both scandal and the risk of execution, which was then the penalty for bigamy. (After news of Philip's marriage to Margarete von der Saale leaked out, Luther urged him to deny it.) In early nineteenth-century North America, the Church of Jesus Christ of Latter-day Saints, popularly referred to as Mormons, revived the mostly moribund practice of "plural marriage," or polygamy, after founder Joseph Smith received a divine revelation that some elders should take more than one wife. As this practice spread, so did public outrage. Yet it was not polygamy that sealed Smith's fate but his 1844 declaration that he was a candidate for the U.S. presidency, which led to his arrest on charges of treason and conspiracy. A mob of about a hundred and fifty armed men charged the jail where Smith was being held and shot him dead.

Smith's murder did nothing to stop the debate about Mormon polygamy. By the time of his death in 1877, Smith's successor, Brigham Young, had entered "sealings," or marriages, with fifty-six women, sixteen of whom bore him fifty-seven children. The rest, he said, were "old ladies whom I regard rather as mothers than wives," whom he had "sealed" to protect, a Mormon variant of a common practice in many tribal societies that stipulate that a widow must marry her brother-in-law.

Seven widows of Mormon leader Brigham Young pose in 1899, two decades after their husband's death. On the right at the back is Amelia, who married Young when she was twenty-four and he was sixty-one. She was his favourite wife.

In 1878, after the U.S. Supreme Court ruled against Mormon George Reynolds's right to plural marriage, polygamists were subjected to severe penalties. To save the church, its fourth president, Wilford Woodruff, officially abandoned polygamy in an 1890 manifesto. Some diehard polygamists fled to remote communities in the United States and Canada, and the Church of Latter-day Saints ceased to acknowledge them as members. In 1892, Canada also criminalized polygamy, which ran counter to the legal definition of marriage as articulated in the 1866 English case of *Hyde v. Hyde:* "the voluntary union ... of one man and one woman to the exclusion of all others."

(Polyandry, in which women marry more than one husband, has no North American history. Polyandry is almost always the product of, or perhaps the logical response to, an environment so harsh that the land cannot sustain an ever growing population: the Himalayas are a good example. It enables men to share rather than forgo fatherhood, and provides a social structure in which hard-scrabbling people can survive and perpetuate themselves.)

Besides Mormons and breakaway Mormons, North American utopias such as the Oneida Community, founded in 1848, practised "complex marriage," with every member theoretically married to every other member and encouraged to have "interviews"—that is to say, sex—with other community members. To avoid pregnancies, which were supposed to be pre-approved by a sort of eugenics committee, Oneidan men practised coitus interruptus. But by 1879, the Oneidans abandoned complex marriage in favour of monogamy, and in 1880, over seventy of them married traditionally.

In North America and Europe, monogamy has developed as the only legal form of marriage, and apart from pockets of resistance, polygamy has been mostly stamped out. When North Americans marry, they are choosing a single mate whose qualities will not be supplemented or complemented by another one.

This convention is rooted in the strict regulations about bloodlines that in all societies define acceptable spouses and prohibit incestuous mating. Most ban marriage with close blood relatives—sisters with brothers, mothers with sons, fathers with daughters—but permit or even encourage cousins to marry. Marrying cousins was a common Greek and Eastern strategy for reuniting property that had been divided among heirs.[18] So was marrying uncles with nieces, which Jewish canon law, for example, permitted. In India, marrying relatives was common, and in some parts remains so today.[19]

Incest taboos identify those we are forbidden to marry. Rules about lineage, exquisitely complex statements about the nature of blood relationships, identify those we are permitted or even supposed to marry. The levirate system, for example, required men to marry their brothers' widows. Among the ancient Hebrews, levirate operated among members of a household when the deceased had no male heir; it ensured his continuity by acknowledging him as the father, rather than the uncle, of his living brother's child. (That living brother could procreate again, guaranteeing that his bloodline did not die out.)

Rules about appropriate marriage partners stem from each society's view of itself and its people. The nature of descent—matrilineal, patrilineal—is of paramount importance. (A few small societies use variations on these primary lineage systems: Hawaii's ambilineality, which traces lineage through either mother or father; or unilineality, by which the Iroquois trace lineality through either their mother's or father's descent.) Exogamous marriage, the union of blood-unrelated people, involves different financial considerations, often in the form of a bride price or other arrangement. Endogamy, on the other hand, was the custom of marrying within a social class, religion, or ethnicity. Endogamy served to preserve minority cultures and to prevent assimilation into or dilution by (or of) the dominant culture. Aristocrats married aristocrats and peasants married peasants; Christians married Christians and Jews married Jews; whites married whites and non-whites married non-whites. In India, with its intrinsically endogamous caste system that permits marriage only between members of castes of equal or similar rank, Brahmins married Brahmins and dalits, or untouchables, married dalits.

In North America, the familiar European rules sometimes ceded place to urgent circumstances. In New France, where the economic interests of the fur trade were paramount, officials overlooked racial differences and encouraged colonists to marry Natives as a means of facilitating the fur trade and ensuring loyalty toward France. In the Thirteen Colonies and later the United States, on the other hand, the racialism that stoked black slavery so permeated social consciousness that forty-one states passed anti-miscegenation laws outlawing white–black marriage and, for good measure, often white–Native and white–Asian as well. For three centuries, until the U.S. Supreme Court struck them down as unconstitutional, these laws reflected and supported white supremacy and the twentieth-century notion of white purity, and defined interracial marriage as the crime of miscegenation.

Though race was not an issue in homogenous European societies, complex rules narrowed down the hunt for a suitable bride or groom. Among the privileged classes, political, commercial, and social considerations were paramount to parents selecting their children's mates.

Nobles and royals contended as well with complicated diplomatic issues, betrothing their young sons and daughters to form or reinforce alliances they hoped would still be advantageous when the marriage eventually took place.

Less privileged people, the great majority, had different concerns, but for them as well, marrying off children had serious financial implications for the entire family. It was not enough to ensure that the married-into family were people of means. Parents, usually fathers, were responsible for negotiating the best deal possible and then for ensuring that all parties honoured it.

If a potential bride was attractive, apparently healthy and chaste, and unburdened with hopelessly unmarriageable older sisters or disgraced relatives, her family could expect a substantial commitment from a future husband. Depending on his family's social class, this could be anything from a job to a substantial inheritance, future or already in hand. In societies with primogeniture, which kept land holdings intact by bequeathing them to one son, usually the oldest, these sons were valued marital candidates. Their siblings, however, were much less so.

The same was true wherever inheritance favoured first sons. Among the nobility in Poitou, France, from the twelfth to the fourteenth centuries, 77 percent of oldest sons but only 30 percent of younger ones married. In one Portuguese province in the fifteenth and sixteenth centuries, 80 percent of first-born sons married, compared with only 39 percent of fourth-born sons. Norway's nineteenth-century inheritance laws were so strict that they left about a quarter of all males without the means to marry and support a family.

BRIDAL ENDOWMENTS

Brides were also expected to bring property, money, or other valuables to the union, usually in the form of a dowry. Without a dowry, most women could not have married. But the dowry also offered some measure of protection to the woman in her new world, especially if her parents paid it in instalments, encouraging her husband to treat her better than he might have without the promise of further payments.

Furthermore, if he died, the dowry was returned to her; though her father-in-law managed her dowry, she remained its legal owner. If it included land, she had to consent to any sales.

Maristella Botticini's detailed study of dowries in fifteenth-century Tuscany, which examined both wealthy and humble households, illustrates how dowries worked.[20] In Tuscany, the dowry was a prerequisite for marriage, regardless of class. Even orphan girls reared in charities received small dowries, provided by the charities or by townspeople's bequests. In Florence, parents could even invest money in the Monte delle Doti, or dowry fund, which offered a good return for the dowries their daughters would inevitably need.

Dowries involved substantial transfers of wealth. In the decades between 1415 and 1436 in the city of Cortona, when the average annual salary for an urban worker was only 14 florins, dowries averaged an impressive 125.5 florins. The size of dowries depended on several factors. After searching out a suitable candidate for their daughter, parents offered a dowry based on the work she would do in the house and, sometimes, the field, and how many children she would bear and raise. An older bride, "a less valuable product" who would cost her family more in keep and then offer fewer child-bearing and housework years to her future husband, would require a bigger dowry to persuade the groom to accept her. (This category included women marrying for the second time.) A younger daughter, with more years of work and child-bearing to offer, could be married off with a smaller dowry.

Social mobility also determined the size of dowries. Tuscan girls marrying down (for example, from the mercantile class to the peasantry) were given larger dowries than those marrying up (from the peasantry to the professional class). Botticini interprets this as evidence that caring parents thereby enabled their daughters to maintain a standard of living similar to their birth family's. Compared to girls with smaller dowries, girls with larger ones tended to produce more children, likely because they were better fed and treated.

The dowry system, however, also spawned much sadness. Because societies that greatly valued males over females regarded endowing a daughter as a drain on the family finances, countless unloved, unattractive, inconvenient, orphaned, or just plain unlucky girls got married off to patently undesirable men or were interred in convents, because both accepted smaller than usual dowries.

In colonial North America, the importance of dowries was leavened by the dearth of marriageable women. This was the case in seventeenth-century New France, where, among a population of three thousand, men outnumbered women five to one—and many of those women were nuns. Though some fur traders, adventurers, and colonial servants entered unions with Native women and a few married them, most bachelors faced such gloomy marital prospects that King Louis XIV and Jean-Baptiste Colbert, his finance minister, developed a program that prepared robust young women to immigrate to New France and marry settlers.

This chapter introduced a couple of the 737 *filles du roi*, most of whom ranged in age from fifteen to the late twenties. Most had urban backgrounds, and more than half were orphans raised in the Hôpital Général du Paris, which trained them in domestic skills that qualified them to work in bourgeois homes or to marry men eager for such capable wives. Six percent of *les filles* were of impoverished noble or bourgeois stock, welcomed into the program because, as Intendant Talon remarked in his report to Finance Minister Colbert, "Three or four girls of high birth and distinguished by quality would perhaps be useful to unite in marriage with Officers whom nothing holds to the country except their appointment and their land grants." In France, a coterie of well-born, well-endowed women signed on to marry these officers. Like their *consoeurs*, they were adventurous women game to make better lives in New France than Old France could offer.

Dowries played an important role and were substantial: from 50 livres to as much as 3,000 livres provided by the families of higher-ranked women who expected to marry military officers and whose households needed more finery. (The royal treasury provided at most 100 to 200 livres for these gentlewomen.) Among such women were Marguerite Chabert de la Carrière and Judith de Matras, each with substantial dowries of 3,000 livres. Marguerite married Troop Captain Jacques Du Mesnil-Heurry, and Judith married a seigneur, Charles-

Pierre Le Gardeur. Catherine de Belleau, with 1,000 livres, married another seigneur, Jean-Baptiste Morin de Belleroche.

Les filles also received trousseaus of ordinary clothing and such useful items as needles, thread, scissors and pins, a comb, stockings, gloves and a bonnet, 2 livres for spending money and (subject to the fluctuations of the royal treasury) 50 livres to stock their future households.[21]

At least 95 percent married and seemed to fare well in their marriages, managing to withstand the harshness of Canadian winters. Observers praised their homes, conduct, and fertility—about 90 percent had children. After a decade, New France's gender imbalance greatly lessened and its marriage rate increased. The *filles du roi* program was discontinued, a victim of its own success. Most of that success was due to its French overseers' clever matching of paired bachelor-colonists under orders to marry with dowered and trained women well prepared for what awaited them, including the likelihood of having to marry outside their social class.

PARENTAL PRESENCE AND PRESSURE

Unlike *les filles*, who were under the tutelage of the French state, many young women in both Europe and North America had parents who took an active interest in their marital arrangements, although high mortality rates meant that a significant number had at least one step-parent or guardian instead. Katarina von Bora, for example, was five when her mother died and her father sent her to a Benedictine boarding school; soon after, he remarried and never brought Katarina back to live with him. In adolescence, she was consigned to the convent, which she later fled in search of a husband and a family life. On the other hand, American Mary Westcott's stepmother was devoted to her and, with her husband, was deeply involved in Mary's marriage planning.

After the financial and other issues had been duly considered, many parents took pains to investigate the characters of both the potential spouse and the in-laws. First-time brides were expected to be virgins, though first-time husbands did not need to be. Good looks, good character, and good health were important and, in the marriage market, openly discussed. Pity the pockmarked, bucktoothed, bowlegged, or cross-eyed, who were mercilessly described and demeaned to force up (or down) the dowry or bride price.

Where beauty had its price, subterfuge had its place. Where light skin was valued, so were powder, sunbonnets, and bleaches. Juiced lemons and rhubarb lightened dark hair. By the sixteenth century, makeup from powder, rouge, and mascara recast faces. Bad teeth could be (temporarily) concealed behind sombre expressions or shy smiles. Odours could be masked—or at least diluted—by powder.

Mothers had a duty to produce presentable daughters who conformed to the beauty standards of their time and place. In 1609, Ben Jonson described various duplicities a woman should employ to counteract her flaws. Among them: "If she be short, let her sit much, lest, when she stands, she be thought to sit.... If a sour breath, let her never discourse fasting, and always talk at her distance. If she have black and rugged teeth, let her offer the less at laughter, especially if she laugh wide and open."[22]

In eras of high mortality, good health was at least as important as good looks, and a robust constitution desirable. The pale skin that was an asset among patricians was a disability among ruddy-faced peasants; the calloused palm that made aristocrats shudder indicated an experienced field hand.

The terrible and permanent consequences of serious error made selecting a mate a demanding task fraught with anxiety. Some families preferred not to rely solely on their own impressions and hired special detectives to investigate.

In the late nineteenth century, young Edma Griggs, daughter of Detroit Alderman Stephen Adelbert Griggs (and the author's great-aunt), fell in love and accepted a proposal of marriage. As the wedding preparations proceeded, so did a discreet investigation by a detective hired by Edma's father. Belatedly, after the invitations had been printed, the detective discovered that the young man already had a wife. Edma's parents cancelled the wedding and packed their heartbroken daughter off on a European tour to recover. She returned to live with them and, after their death, a paid companion. She never married, and her broken engagement entered family lore as a muted tragedy.

An exhibit at the Jewish Museum in Berlin details a happier premarital investigation by the detective agency Salamonski & Co, hired by nineteen-year-old Anne Schmidt's parents after twenty-eight-year-old Paul Benedick asked for her hand in marriage. For 40 Deutschmarks— the same amount Paul paid each month for his rented room— Salamonski investigated such questions as: What is Paul's uncle Siegmund's profession? Where does Paul's family come from? How is his family's business doing? What did Paul inherit from his family? Who is Paul's aunt married to? What can be found out about Paul's mother? How much does Paul earn? Is he able to support a family? What type of person is he? How much rent does he pay for his lodging? What does he like about life in the big city? Is he able to father healthy children and will he raise them as Jews? Happily, Salamonski & Co. uncovered nothing untoward and, in 1928, Anne and Paul were married.

Les filles du roi would have understood why Anne's parents hired Salamonski & Co. and they almost certainly could have provided the detectives with a list of similar questions. They would also have sympathized with Edma Griggs when her fiancé's true marital status was revealed, because Jean Talon and local priests shared the same concerns and suspicions about certain French immigrants to New France—and indeed about a few of *les filles.*

Throughout history, choosing marriage partners has been a complex and, especially in the case of nobles and royals, often convoluted procedure. Before a deal was struck, a host of considerations were weighed, and usually family needs and obligations took priority over individual preferences. Nonetheless, future spouses were necessarily at the heart of their own marriages, and had to be personally prepared for what was to come.

Chapter 2

Learning Marriage, Rites of Passage

THE MARRIAGE STAKES

In the late 1820s, Caroline Sheridan was officially introduced into London high society. As she danced, flirted, and chatted at Almack's Assembly Rooms, she never lost sight of her mission: to find a husband in a single social "season." Caroline's chances appeared bright. She was named one of Almack's twelve prettiest debutantes, and she and her sisters, Helen and Georgiana, were referred to, approvingly, as "the Three Graces," a nickname inspired by their beauty and breeding, and because they lived in a grace-and-favour apartment at Hampton Court, beneficiaries of a charitable gesture to honour their grandfather, the playwright Richard Brinsley Sheridan.

The stakes were high for the sisters. Their father had died young, leaving his widow with four sons, three daughters, and only a small pension to support them. Marrying well seemed the only way out for the girls, and because they had no dowries, they had to rely on their personal qualities: Helen's charm, Caroline's wit, and Georgiana's great beauty. They had to abide as well by the convention that sisters should marry, or at least be engaged, in descending order of age. This meant that Helen and Caroline had to weigh the cost that refusing proposals would have on Georgiana, their beauteous little sister, already courted by several bachelors.

Countess Lieven, the Russian ambassador's wife, waltzes at the high-society social club Almack's in this 1813 sketch by George Cruikshank. Almack's was considered the best marriage mart for the elite.

Helen capitulated first and, though she did not love him, married Captain Price Blackwood, heir to the Irish peer Lord Dufferin. Blackwood overlooked her lack of a dowry and his family's disapproval because he loved her so much, and before long, Helen grew to love him as well. Caroline, next oldest, had no proposals from the men she met during her season, perhaps because of her confident intellectuality, and so the Honourable George Norton's pursuit of her became an urgent matter. Norton, brother of Lord Grantley, had been enamoured of Caroline since she was sixteen. Her mother had advised him to wait until she was eighteen and a debutante; he did so, and once again asked for her hand in marriage.

By then Caroline was in her second social season, terrified of "living and dying a lonely old maid" and deeply affected by her mother's plea that she sacrifice her personal qualms and accept Norton's proposal for its apparent financial benefits. Reluctantly, she agreed to marry "a man she did not love; whom she did not profess to love; for certain advantages—to avoid certain pressing miseries."[1] On June 30, 1827, nineteen-year-old Caroline wed twenty-six-year-old George Norton and was trapped for nearly a lifetime in a marriage soon notorious for her legal helplessness as an abused wife. After her failure to attract a suitor during nearly two London social seasons, the English gentlewoman's rite of passage from maiden to woman, Caroline had taken a (mis)calculated risk and accepted the only proposal she had, thereby—she thought— ensuring her financial future and freeing her younger sister, Georgiana, to marry in her turn.

Marriage has always been a serious business that ushered spouses into a new stage of life, and in most societies, rites of passages helped prepare them for the transition from childhood to their future lives as wives and husbands. Menarche, marking sexual maturation, is a rite of passage in itself and is often the occasion for ceremonies. Many North American Native peoples, for example, confined menstruating girls to a menstrual hut where their mothers cared for them and taught them what it was to be a woman.[2]

Rites of passage involving feats of daring, courage, or skill often propelled adolescent boys into the next stage of life. Some rituals, like scarification, tattooing, or circumcision, forced them to suffer pain "manfully"—that is, in silence. Circumcision, which underscored sexual maturity, also encouraged male bonding, and marked the passage between boyhood and young manhood. Other kinds of rites, such as Native American vision quests, sent young men (and sometimes women) alone into nature, fasting and awaiting a supernatural vision to guide their future.

In ancient Rome, a boy surrendered the purple-bordered *toga prae- texta* that was a symbol of childhood and donned the pure white toga of a Roman man. He also dedicated his *bulla*, a locket-like piece of jewellery containing a talisman, to the *lares*, the household gods. Then a public procession led to the Forum, where the no-longer boy was formally enrolled as a citizen. Fathers would decide when this rite of passage would take place, usually when their sons were fourteen to sixteen years old and physically developed enough for military service. Afterward, the new citizen began a year's training with a prominent civilian or military man his father had selected to care for him.

In Europe and Euro-North America, breeching—dressing boys in breeches or trousers at the age of six or seven—was an important ritual passage that ended "infancy" and corresponded to the age of reason as most societies understood it. After breeching, fathers assumed more control over their sons' education or training. This included arranging for schools or tutors or instructing them personally, including about their roles and responsibilities in society.

Religious rites of passage such as Protestant confirmation and Jewish bar and (since 1922) bat mitzvahs emphasized statements of faith and knowledge of theology, and conveyed a sense of the celebrant's responsibilities upon entry into religious and social maturity. This maturity has been reflected in laws that, by specifying legal ages of consent for sexual activity, transfer personal responsibility from parents to their children.

Whereas rites of passage mark the arrival of maturity, parents and other married adults have always been the principal instructors about the realities of domestic married life. From early childhood, girls "helped" their mothers with household work, cooking and baking, dusting and scrubbing, mending, darning and sewing, tending gardens, poultry, and small animals, and minding younger children. They accompanied mothers to market and helped or watched them buy and sell. Like their brothers, who learned how to be men by assisting and imitating their fathers, their upbringing constituted an apprenticeship in adulthood and in the married life most expected would be part of it.

Aristocratic girls learned different skills: literacy in English, and enough arithmetic to keep household account books and even conduct or understand business ventures. They were also expected to master household and estate management, including supervising servants, and to be competent at fine needlework, weaving, herbal medicine, and playing musical instruments such as the lute and virginal.

But a girl's most essential skill, learned by observing her mother and the adult women in other households, was to obey her male relatives, including her brothers, without being meek—what historian J. Barbara Harris calls "subordinate agency," a term that reflects the contradictions built into their position.[3] Excluding girls from studying Latin, the language of legal and official documents such as land transactions,

Vermeer's Lady Seated at a Virginal, *ca. 1673. Playing the virginal and other instruments was an important skill for elite women.*

manorial accounts, and court rolls, reinforced their dependence on males.

In addition to parental "apprenticeships," societies had other, more direct methods, such as ritual storytelling, to teach youth about marriage. Books, especially sacred texts, laid down rules. In Europe and North America, the Old and New Testaments and their interpretations were especially important marriage manuals that described patriarchal husbands who honoured their obedient and submissive wives fashioned, as the Book of Genesis explained, from their very ribs. The balance of power was clearly set out: "Wives, be subject to your own husbands, as to the Lord. For the husband is the head of the wife, as Christ also is the head of the church, He Himself being the Saviour of the body. But as the church is subject to Christ, so also the wives ought to be to their husbands in everything" (Ephesians 5:22–24). At the same time, a good wife was "far more precious than jewels," and won her husband's life-long trust (Proverbs 31:10–11).

The ideal biblical marriage was usually monogamous (despite polyg-amous characters in the Old Testament) and permanent (though divorce existed). Marital sex was designed to conceive children and to express mutual love, and wives had sex only with their husbands, who might also have sex with their concubines.

More practically, marriage was an economic and domestic unit that formed the core of society. The "excellent wife" worked in and outside her home, earned money, and increased her family's property. As chate-laine and entrepreneur, she "rises while it is yet night and provides food for her household and portions for her maidens. She considers a field and buys it, with the fruit of her hands she plants a vineyard.... She seeks wool and flax, and works with willing hands.... She perceives that her merchandise is profitable." The excellent wife seldom rests; "her lamp does not go out at night" as she spins, weaves, and "makes linen garments and sells them; she delivers sashes to the merchant." She is charitable, and gives to the poor and needy. Her reward is that her chil-dren call her blessed, and her husband praises her above all other women (Proverbs 31:13–29).

Marriage manuals almost exclusively centred on religious texts and their interpretations, simplified for popular edification. They varied greatly in content and context, reflecting changing attitudes. Usually they were practical how-to guides predicated on an ideal version of marriage, but they also offered advice on how to deal with the often difficult realities of life together.

A fourteenth-century to-do (and to-be) list directed to the Italian bride advocated suppressing all tastes, interests, and habits that displeased the groom, including forthright speech and curiosity. Francesco Barbaro's highly influential essay "On Wifely Duties," published in 1415, prescribed a marriage lovingly unified by wifely submission to husbandly control. Such advice was in part a response to the fear that elite women were undermining their patriarchal society by using dowries to favour daughters over sons.

In 1523, Desiderius Erasmus's popular and much-translated colloquy "Marriage" considered the horrors, in an era in which divorce was unknown, of a drunken and brutal husband whose stepmother hated his long-suffering wife. Erasmus advised her to resist the temptation to dump a full chamber pot on his head (clearly not all abused women resisted this temptation) and to employ sexual ploys to appeal to the brute's good nature, however minuscule that might be.

The marriage manuals directed to Protestant wives in Germany, England, and North America between 1500 and 1700 also defended male dominance as divinely decreed but did introduce the notion of mutuality between spouses. In the much-republished *A Godly Form of Household Government*, Puritan pastors John Dod and Robert Cleaver exhorted spouses to love each other, husbands to exercise wisdom and restraint, and wives to remember their multitudinous duties: housekeeping, not wasting household money, holding their tongues, and presiding over an orderly home. Men had to earn money, obtain needed goods, conduct business, and act as family spokesperson. "The duty of the husband is to be lord of all; and of the wife, to give account of all," they advised. Dod and Cleaver also painted a dramatic picture of homes made wretched by slovenly or sottish wives, or by husbands heedless of their wives' capacity for revenge.

The influential clergyman William Gouge stressed women's inferiority and subjection to her husband but at the same time counselled mutuality. "Of all other inferiors in a family, wives are far the most excellent, and therefore to be placed in the first rank," he wrote conciliatorily. However, "among all other parties of whom the Holy Ghost requireth subjection, wives for the most part are most backward."[4]

Other popular essays on marriage denounced what must have been seen as common wifely behaviour: laughing, flirting, dressing immodestly, speaking out of turn, reading unsuitable books, eating too much, even reading letters without their husband's permission. A widely read sixteenth-century writer described the ideal wife as one who leapt early from bed "to start on the housework, without combing her hair and putting on stockings, with her shirtsleeves rolled up and her arms bare, getting the servants to work and giving the children their clothes to put on. What a joy to see her do the laundry, wash the sheets, sift flour, make bread, sweep the house, fill the lamps, get lunch going, and then pick up her sewing needle. I don't think those women are any good who do nothing but to sleep at midnight and arise at noon, telling dirty stories all evening."[5]

A sixteenth-century wedding play extolled the ideal peasant wife as one who knew how to stoke the fire and wash pots and pans, make good noodles, mill grain and fatten oxen, guide pigs to market, and, once there, buy and sell shrewdly.

From the Reformation and to this day, the sermons and writings of Martin Luther, the great Reformation theologian, have shaped the development of marriage and family life. His towering stature and (at the time) controversial marriage to former nun Katharina von Bora inspired an insatiable interest in his life and produced a wealth of Luther-centric literature. In addition to his voluminous other writings, *Table Talk*, the memoirs of the many boarders and guests who regularly dined at his table ("Make a note of this!" Luther would exclaim. "Write it down!") has provided endless material for admirers and detractors alike. Revered or reviled, the union of the former religious was an important and exciting marriage guide.

Table Talk had no startling revelations but rather described the relationship between two intelligent and extremely busy people who seemed much like other men and women. Martin respected and trusted Katharina but scolded her for chattering too much during meals—she was well educated, spoke Latin, and enjoyed the men's spirited discussions—because like his contemporaries, he believed that women were less rational than men. Their broad hips, he pointed out, were evidence of their child-bearing destiny and so what little schooling girls needed should focus on housekeeping and pious motherhood. The male and female spheres were separate and divinely ordained, with husbands earning money and women running the household.

Table Talk, however, also describes how much the Luther family reality deviated from these "principles." For one thing, Luther delegated much of the paid work to Katharina, who rose at four every morning to give her enough time to manage not just the Black Cloister, which was both family home and boarding house, but also a brewery, stables, and several gardens, including one outside the city limits. Katharina also supervised the Luther family's farms.

But even in face of Katharina's masterful administration of most of the couple's income-producing activities, Luther reserved his husbandly right to ultimate control: "In the household I concede to you the governance, saving only my right," he told her. "For the rule of women never accomplished anything good. God made Adam the lord of all creatures so that he might rule all living things. But when Eve persuaded him that he was a lord above God, he thereby spoiled it all. We have that to thank you women for ..."[6]

Lady Sarah Pennington's immensely popular and much-reprinted *An Unfortunate Mother's Advice* (1761) described difficult relationships and offered women practical advice to deal with them. What to do, she asked, if your husband is a chronic complainer, happy only when criticizing, and less intelligent to boot? Her response: remember your duty and your promise to love, honour, and obey. She added one caveat: if your husband demands an unchristian act, it is your duty to disobey him. Like Pennington's, Victorian and post-Victorian marriage guides tended to focus more on marital strategies.

In the nineteenth and twentieth centuries, many marriage guides painted cautionary portraits of what marriage could be. Though many marriages were perfect unions of kindred spirits, others were between "unmatched souls ... held in hateful contiguity by a legal bond, but divided in heart by a torrent of passionate aversion."[7] An American writing in 1871 decried "modern" women's fashions: "A big hump, three big lumps, a wilderness of crimps and frills, a hauling up of the dress here and there, an enormous hideous mass of false hair or bark piled on the top of her head ... while the shop windows tell us all day long, of the paddings, whalebones, and springs, which occupy most of the space within that outside rig.... How is a man to fall in love with such a compound, doubled and twisted, starched, comical, artificial, touch-me-not, wiggling curiosity?"[8]

In *Modern Marriage: A Handbook* (1925), Paul Popenoe, known as the father of North American marriage counselling, found men equally

repulsive: "What pimply-faced, hollow-chested, greasy, flabby speci-
mens many of them are; saturated with the products of constipation,
flavored with nicotine and fusel oil, peppered with the germs of gonorrhea! Is it any wonder a superior girl looks over these fellows, thinks of
being tied to one for life and having children like him, and shudders?"[9]
(A eugenics expert who believed that blacks were racially inferior,
Popenoe argued against intermarriage and for regulating human reproduction for the good of society. He also wrote the *Ladies' Home Journal*'s
long-lived and wildly popular "Can This Marriage Be Saved?" column,
based on case histories.)

In *Eve's Daughters; or Common Sense for Maid, Wife, and Mother*
(1882), Marion Harland presented marriage from the perspective of the
disillusioned newlywed bride who must tolerate everything, including
infidelity, "the heavy cross appointed for you to carry" that is a sadly
common "crime" that women have to bear "because they must!" And
through all marriage's trials and tribulations, a woman must remember
always: better to lose his affection than his respect.[10]

By the early twentieth century, Dr. Sylvanus Stall's classics *What a
Young Wife Ought to Know* and *What a Young Husband Ought to Know*
emphasized mutual interests and suggested that a pre-nuptial camping
trip would be an excellent test of compatibility. The homemaker wife
and mother and the provider husband and father together form a
complete unit, each sex superior in its own sphere. Moderation in everything was the key: not too much sexual intercourse, not too many children, no extreme clothing such as corsets or high heels.

Novels, devoured by the literate minority, provided intimate portraits
of fictional marriages and, by the late 1820s, supplanted marriage
manuals in popularity. By the Victorian era, this genre proliferated, with
the stories usually structured to preach moral messages contextualized
within lifelike stories "on the 'There but for the Grace of God'
combined with the 'How like my life' principles," according to historian
Judith Rowbotham in *Good Girls Make Good Wives*.[11] The ubiquity and
influence of novels prompted La Rochefoucauld-Doudeauville, in his
Family Guide, to advise mothers to warn their daughters against reading
novels, which, he warned, encouraged them to believe in a kind of

happiness that does not exist, thereby weakening their moral fibre.[12] In the United States, the Reverent Daniel Wise, author of *The Young Lady's Counselor* (1857), commented caustically about "the multitude who form their notions of love and marriage from sickly novels, from theatrical performances, and from flippant conversation."[13]

HOPE CHESTS AND COMING OUT

Most western European and North American girls expected to marry, and all the literature influenced their expectations. And they were keenly aware of the domestic dimensions of marriage and the need to establish their own households. Their female relatives helped out by contributing to a hope chest, the name itself an acknowledgment of the very real possibility that not all girls would find these hoped-for husbands. The hope chest was a sturdy box—though it could also be a drawer or part of a closet—dedicated to the accumulation of linens, silverware, and other essential household items. Hope chests originated in medieval European peasant cultures and, by the last decades of the nineteenth century and the first of the twentieth, were an established tradition among both peasant and middle-class girls in both Europe and North America.

Hope chests were common in North American homes until recent decades. As late as 1967, a study of university students found that 38 percent were assembling a hope chest. "In a sense," the study concluded, "the hope chest represents on a symbolical level a young woman's aspirations and on a reality level her concrete investment in the marital estate prior to its onset."[14] The annual birthday spoon, Christmas tea cup, and Easter pillowcase inculcated in the growing girl her community's values and expectations, and framed marriage in essentially domestic terms.

The privileged classes had different priorities, chief among them the snaring of socially and financially suitable spouses. After the Industrial Revolution created a bourgeoisie so wealthy that its members could aspire to marrying into the aristocracy, a marketplace in which to introduce and match eligible young men and women was needed. The social "coming out" of debutantes provided both venue and ritual. These debutantes, usually seventeen or eighteen years old, were launched into adult society during the social season of balls, dinners, and formal visiting. In England, young belles were presented in one of the drawing rooms at the Court of St. James's; elsewhere, the ceremony was held at royal courts, grand ballrooms, or hotels.

The debutantes required a facility for dancing, singing, or playing a musical instrument, an understanding of society's rules and customs, and a modicum of beauty or at least handsomeness. These attributes were, of course, offered within the context of her parents' social status, reputation, and wealth, and the dowry and connections she would bring to her marriage.

Debutantes had one season to find a husband, April to August in England and usually from November to January in North America. In the United States, as early as 1748, fifty-nine families in Philadelphia held "Dancing Assemblies" that introduced young women to polite society and, hopefully, to their future husbands. Failure to make a match was a disappointment for both the young woman and her parents. She could still marry but, shopworn and eclipsed by each season's newcomers, she had to lower her sights as her prospects worsened.

In the antebellum American South, teenaged girls left their schooldays behind to come out into society, meet and enchant a suitable beau, and afterward marry him and devote the rest of their days to keeping house and raising children, just as their mothers had. That was, as diary after diary reveals, the problem: though they flung themselves into the social round that coming out involved, revelling in the chance to dress fashionably and to show off their cultivated young beauty, "they proved remarkably resistant to the intended purpose of this stage of life: finding a husband," writes historian Anya Jabour in *Scarlett's Sisters*.[15]

One such resister was North Carolinian Penelope Skinner, who staved off marrying by flirting, attracting then rejecting one suitor after another: in three years, she sent thirty suitors packing. In Washington, D.C., Laura Wirt declined three proposals and declared, "I do not fall

Debutantes at the Tidal Basin, Washington, D.C.

*A delighted debutante
in her designer evening
gown, ca. 1916.*

*Debutantes in 1923, likely before they began a dance
rehearsal that included the Charleston. Their accompanist
is playing from popular songbooks.*

in love."[16] Like most other eligible young women, Penelope and Laura eventually married, but only after years of indulged freedom as unattached "belles" still "on the Carpet."

When Penelope finally fell in love with and married Thomas Warren, a physician whose work often took him away from home, she suffered greatly from loneliness. "I have nothing to do but to think on my sorrows—while you have your business to attend to & young companions to associate with," she complained. "Being absent from you has the same effect on me that sickness has—it perfectly subdues me—makes me as meek & gentle as possible."[17] Laura married Thomas Randall and, heartsick at leaving her family ("My heart falters ... dies within me ... I kill myself by dwelling on this")—moved with him to a Florida homestead.[18]

Penelope Warren became pregnant almost at once, and concentrated on taking great care of herself: in letters to her husband, she described her healthful diet, "loose" clothes, "troublesome" but "hardly at all painful" hemorrhoids, and determinedly cheerful spirits. In January 1841 she gave birth to a daughter and, in sad justification of her dread of childbirth, died shortly after.[19]

Laura Wirt Randall did not die but, despite a white nurse and several slave women, was exhausted by repeated pregnancies and nursing infants: "I declare if I tho't I was to be thus occupied for the rest of my life, I wd—I was going to say—*lie down & die*. It wd be a slavery beyond that of all the galleys—& for a lifetime too!" Laura was even unhappier about her marriage and husband, whom she no longer loved. "I am now, as my husband declares 'the most miserable, poor, good-for-nothing woman he ever saw."[20]

In patrician England, where money and status weighed more heavily than love, expectations were correspondingly different. In the 1870s, debutante Alice Catherine Miles navigated the season and kept a frank account of it in her diary. Alice's family was too large to allow her a good income, and even at seventeen, she knew that she could satisfy her expensive tastes only by parlaying her connections and beauty into marrying a man with at least £5,000 per year. At the same time, her modest means put very rich men, like flirtatious young Henry Charles Keith Petty-Fitzmaurice, 5th Marquess of Lansdowne—he had inherited an estate of 140,000 acres in Britain and Ireland—out of bounds, so that paying attention to his advances wasted precious time (though he was scarcely serious; she was too poor for consideration). Alice understood that she could never compete with the likes of Miss Harriet Ives Wright, "rather a pretty little heiress ... who I suspect will put us all in the shade from the mere fact of her possessing £4,000 a year."[21]

Typical of her society, Alice was obsessed with income and real estate. As her cousin introduced her to eligible bachelors, he provided "a rapidly whispered enumeration of their possession and social standing: "Beauty Campbell, Captain, Guards, splendid place in the North, £20,000 a year:—Captain Campbell—Miss Miles." Alice made short shrift of one would-be suitor, Sir Samuel, "as I had previously ascertained he has only £4,000 a year," well below her minimum.[22]

Alice's pursuit of a suitable marriage was astute and calculated. Her family's inability to provide an adequate dowry seriously handicapped her, but they had tried to counter this with her excellent personal preparation for the marriage market. Toward the end of 1869, twenty-year-old Alice identified a suitable prospect: George Duppa, a sheep rancher thirty-three years her senior who had made a fortune in New Zealand. She had few illusions about the nature of their union, though she believed that George's wealth would offset the age difference and any personal incompatibility. But what truly mattered was that she had achieved her long-time goal of securing a moneyed bridegroom.

Chapter 3

Weddings and the Married State

The Mystery of Weddings

It is 1434, and a handsome young couple stands, hands clasped in contented intimacy, in their sun-drenched bedroom. Giovanni di Arrigo Arnolfini, a merchant from Lucca who frequently visited Bruges, and Giovanna Cenami are richly clothed, he cloaked in fur, she in an ermine-trimmed green gown. As he holds her slender hand he gazes forward and points slightly; she rests her fingers on her swelling stomach and gazes toward the hand that holds hers. A tiny terrier stands beside her, close to her trailing gown, eyes alert and tail high.

Giovanni and Giovanna are sharing a tender moment that the great portrait painter Jan Van Eyck immortalizes in glazed layers of oil paint. If Giovanna tires of posing, she can lounge on the bed behind her. But it is much more likely that she relaxes on the chair beneath which her shoes lie askew. Giovanni's wooden clogs are still beside him, as if he has shucked them off where he stands.

What does this portrait mean? Why, more than half a millennium later, do scholars still engage in passionate debate about *The Arnolfini Portrait*? Are Giovanna and Giovanni already married, marrying, or pledging their troths? Or does their joint portrait signify something else altogether? Is she pregnant? Is she even—alive?

Van Eyck's Arnolfini Portrait, *painted in 1434.*

The mystery has its origins in the vagaries of marriage as much as in artistic metaphor.[1] One interpretation is that the painting is actually a marriage licence. Clandestine marriages required only the spouses' consent, and Giovanni's raised hand indicates his pledging an oath that he and Giovanna had just recited, while their joined hands were a traditional element in ancient marriage. The dog, symbol of fidelity, and the likeness of Saint Margaret, patron saint of childbirth, carved into the bed reinforce this hypothesis. Van Eyck's image reflected in the mirror, and his stylized signature on the wall over it, seem to confirm that he was witness to a marriage, and that his painting doubled as a marriage licence.

On the other hand, Van Eyck might be painting an already married couple, comfortably posed in their lavishly furnished house alongside their cherished little dog. After all, why would such obviously wealthy people resort to a clandestine marriage rather than the ostentatious wedding that would impress the groom's guests and prove his worth?

Or perhaps the painting records a betrothal ceremony, an alliance designed like a business contract between two prominent and affluent Italian families. But Giovanna's hair, styled like a wife's rather than worn long, in the manner of a virgin, contradicts this. So does her presence in the portrait, because in Tuscan betrothals only male relatives attended.

No, the painting is a legal document validating Giovanna's right to Giovanni's power-of-attorney when he travels on business, as he so often does; he is, after all, a major textile supplier to the Burgundian court. The double portrait flatters both husband and wife, and the symbols— faithful dog, round belly, and blossoming cherry tree—suggest faithfulness, fertility, and a strong marriage. Even when he is absent, the painting proclaims, Giovanna has her husband's full confidence.

Yet all the above may be wrong, even their names. Arnolfini is not Giovanni Arrigo—Arrigo married thirteen years after the portrait was painted, and six years after Van Eyck's death—but Giovanni di Nicolao, his cousin, and Van Eyck's painting is a memorial to his wife, Costanza Trenta, who by 1434 had already died, likely in childbirth, at the age of twenty. But why, in an era when women were not valued as individuals but for their lineage, was a dead woman memorialized? Precisely because of her lineage, which was the basis for the alliance her marriage had cemented.

The evidence for this theory is persuasive. Costanza's blue-lined green dress symbolizes faithfulness and the state of being in love; Giovanni's sombre garb expresses his grief at losing her. Costanza is deathly pale; he is in sad shadows. The little dog at her feet will be her companion in the afterlife, as are so many other dogs in funeral portraits of laid-out women. She died childless, and so her rounded belly hints at a pregnancy that she, like so many other women, did not survive. The single carpet and the two silver candlesticks signify that the bed behind her is the bed in which she will lie-in—and die in. Even the carved Saint Margaret is subdued, sorrowing rather than proudly besting the dragon. And Costanza's hand is not folded into Giovanni's but rather lies limply, fingers already slipping away.

Nearly six centuries after Van Eyck painted his masterpiece, its meaning and layered dimensions remain baffling. Art historians steeped in the history of fifteenth-century marriage interpret the painting's rich details in the light of law and custom, and their many versions of what it means are testimony to the complex nature of weddings and their relationship to marriage, and to the social, economic, and legal foundations of individual marriages.

THE WEDDING PROCESS

Van Eyck's cryptic painting is living testimony to the mysteries of marriage. At what precise moment did men and women make the transition from the unmarried to the married state? Was it after a religious or civil authority made his final pronouncement? Was it the moment the ink was dry on the deed of marriage? Was it, as in the Catholic tradition, when a man and woman agreed between them that they were married, even if no witnesses were present?[2] Was it as soon as the spousal partners had, through sexual intercourse, consummated, and thereby legitimized, their marriage? Was it when a bloodstained sheet testified that the bride had been a virgin? There is no single answer because around the world, marriage has always been a complex process that involved parents, relatives, and the community as much as the marrying couple.

Parents exercised so much control over their children's marriages that the children were often excluded from the arrangements. In 1413, in Derbyshire, an English father negotiated a marriage contract but reserved the right to decide at a later date which one of his two daughters would be the bride.[3] Marriage contracts often specified the names of siblings who would wed in place of the bride or groom should one die before the wedding. In Reformation Germany, after the bride's parents accepted the groom or his representatives' proposal and agreed on property and inheritance issues, the couple was formally engaged and referred to as "bride and groom." Traditionally, they were introduced only after both sets of parents agreed to the provisions of the contract.

France took a different path from the rest of Europe. In France, the church and the state waged ferocious battles to control marriage. The church saw marriage as a sacrament that a consenting man and woman conferred on each other and that was also confirmed sexually and blessed by church nuptials. Clandestine marriages, however, meant secret promises, and so the church's clerics, lawyers, judges, and courts strove to regulate them through exacting penance and by re-enacting the alleged or clandestine marriage. The French state, on the other hand, claimed that marriage was primarily "a public act transmitting family property, sanctioned by the state, and tied to the public good."[4] Clandestine marriage, often the fruit of abduction, seduction, or sexual passion, violated the "natural law" of honouring parents and abiding by the French civil law; as such, these marriages were illegal and challenged French state authority.

A series of edicts reinforced France's position against the church. The first French marital edict, in 1557, set the tone. It required minors to obtain both parents' consent and raised the age of majority from twenty to thirty for men, and from seventeen to twenty-five for women, effectively trapping young adults in childhood. The edict allowed parents to legally disinherit "children" who married clandestinely, thereby forfeiting their right to a dowry and an inheritance. It also directed judges in civil courts to determine penalties.

The 1579 Ordinance of Blois strengthened the edict of 1557. It removed clandestine marriage cases from church court jurisdiction by making clandestinity a capital crime, and capital crimes could be heard only in civil court. (In practice, most judges opted to impose fines, banishment, or imprisonment rather than the death penalty.) It also extended the clandestinity charge to majors (men over thirty, women over twenty-five) and to all levels of society, from the highest to the lowest. The ordinance established France's official standard for marriage: before a priest officiated at a wedding, he had to obtain proof of age and parental consent for minors, publish marriage banns, and ensure the presence of four witnesses.

The marriage of Pierre Houlbronne and Elisabeth Pallier tested France's commitment to the French Marital Law Compact, unique in Europe and fiercely defended as a cornerstone of national sovereignty. Since 1587, Elisabeth, a widow, had lived with Pierre, who fathered her children, all of whom had died. In 1595, a church judge moved to re-enact their clandestine marriage. When Pierre resisted, the judge had him arrested and thrown into prison. When at last the unwilling bridegroom capitulated, church guards escorted him to his wedding.

Later, Pierre began a new job in the Palais de Justice. It made him a marital catch who, his parents felt, could do much better than Elisabeth. They found a more suitable candidate and petitioned to have his marriage annulled on the grounds that they had not consented to it though Pierre had been a minor. Enraged, Elisabeth lodged a complaint at a church court that Pierre planned to abandon her for another woman his parents had arranged for him to marry. The court ruled that, despite the lack of banns and parental consent, the re-enacted wedding had legitimized the marriage.

Pierre's parents appealed this judgment to the Parlement of Paris. In 1601, French civil judges ruled against the decision of the church court because church officers had intimidated Pierre into consenting, and the ensuing wedding lacked the banns and parental consent necessary to authenticate it. Their decision transformed Pierre into a bachelor and Elisabeth into an unwed mother, albeit childless. The case underscored the church's determination to re-enact clandestine marriages between minors and those of age, to bully couples (or individual spouses) to submit, and to place canon law above French civil law.

Elsewhere in Europe, parental consent, published banns, two witnesses, and written records of marriages were merely recommended. In their absence, however, the couple's "wedding" could be re-enacted and thereby validated.

Until the fifteenth century, marriage forced by rape or kidnapping was also practised in England. (It was also common in Central and parts of Southeast Asia, Turkey, the rainforests of the Philippines, Central and South America, and parts of Africa.) As well as violating the property rights and the pride of the fathers and male relatives of the victim, such an assault instantly eroded her bride price and made her a social pariah. Usually such marriages were rooted in violence and pain, and could exist only in societies that held women in low regard and valued their virginity as a fragile commodity owned by the father. (A persistent legend holds that honeymoons are relics of marriage by capture, when a new "husband" hid out with his wife hoping to impregnate her so that her relatives would no longer plan retaliatory attacks.)

But there was a way out: the abducted bride could negate her disgrace by staying with her husband. And sometimes she wanted to. Indeed, some young couples defied their parents' disapproval—or alternative marriage arrangements—by staging bogus kidnappings that effectively disguised elopement as bride capture and forced parents shamed by a daughter's "rape" to agree to an otherwise unacceptable groom.

MARRIAGE CONTRACTS

Marriage contracts, agreed to by the spouses' parents, included a trousseau and dowry, and even the poorest girl's parents tried to supply a bed. In Augsburg as elsewhere, a civic dowry fund helped poor couples equip themselves. In many parts of England, Wales, Lutheran Germany, and German-speaking Switzerland, the community collected household goods for the couple and money for their wedding celebrations.

The contract and the bride and groom's exchange of marriage promises were publicly proclaimed, sometimes on church property. Then, in keeping with the custom for completing deeds of sale, the couple shared a celebratory drink and shook hands to confirm the agreement. A wealthy groom might also present jewellery. They were now engaged, and called each other bride and groom.

What was the significance of an engagement? What, besides sexual urgency and social pressure, drove men to marry? (Unlike men, women seldom had a choice about marrying.) The answer, for the merchant, trade, and professional classes, was that marriage was the key to achieving social, financial, and political adulthood. For example, a journeyman or tradesman who had completed his apprenticeship and could now support a wife endeavoured to coordinate the transition to master by marrying. "Marriage marked the boundary between the guild of masters, who had to have wives, and the journeymen, who ought not to, and weddings enacted the rites of passage between these two states," explains historian Lyndal Roper.[5] Some other advantages for men (and women): non-patrician spouses gained patrician rights as long as their patrician spouses lived, and non-citizens acquired citizens' rights. (Though wives gained some control over their new household, they remained politically impotent and financially dependent on their husbands.)

Now followed weeks or months of wedding preparations interspersed with parties, and all of these together constituted the marriage. The wedding itself involved days of feasts and dances, culminating in either a ceremony at the church door or a bridal mass. Though the very devout and the very abstemious married in sedate privacy, for most people weddings were the occasion for exuberant celebration, drinking and feasting, boisterous pranks, and ostentatious display.

No other event, even such life passages as births or funerals, was worthy of such expenditure. The finer the jewels offered a bride, the more luxurious her apparel, the more extravagant the feasts offered, the more prestige accrued to the couple and their parents. Sumptuary rules, however, limited how much members of each social class might spend: in sixteenth-century Nuremberg, for example, no more than 150 gulden on rings for the brides of patricians, 75 for merchants, and 3 for ordinary citizens. (A trained midwife earned 2 to 8 gulden annually, a male barber-surgeon 10 to 25 gulden.) The poor struggled to compete, even pawning their meagre goods to raise money. Privacy was seldom an option. Weddings were public, and local chroniclers described the most impressive.

Sumptuary rules for weddings also limited the number of guests, although foreigners and churchmen were excluded from the count. Patrician petitions for extra guests were usually accepted, but those of less distinguished citizens were denied. To ensure compliance, civic officials queried guests and others about details of the wedding. The guests of the less well-off ate in taverns and paid out of their pockets, whereas the wealthy paid for their guests' food. The dishes they served were varied and abundant, and both church and secular officials urged, usually unsuccessfully, that the surplus be donated to the needy.

Staking out one's social position was a central function of weddings. Bachelors on horses carried patricians' invitations to guests; before they left, they enjoyed a wine-splashed wedding breakfast. Tradespeople paid

Hochzeitslader ("wedding inviters") to walk to the homes of those invited; poorer people managed without any such formalities.

As weddings became "pageants of the town's social structure, where each individual might read off his or her place in that society," and sexual definition was rigidly enforced, civic authorities even determined the order in which people walked to the church. In Augsburg, a 1571 decree dictated that bankrupt men should sit with the women at weddings—"a powerful denigration of their manhood at a moment when ritual rejoiced in the dissimilarity of the sexes." (At different times, sometimes only decades apart, and in different regions, and among different social classes, men and women were separated at weddings— but not always. "Throughout the wedding ritual, the mutually complete but distinct offices of husband and wife found non-verbal expression in gifts, clothes and action. Moving from single-sex celebrations to parties for men and women together, weddings constantly created and reflected on sexual difference.")[6]

In both religious and secular wedding rituals, bride and groom symbolically gave themselves to each other by sharing food and drink or by holding hands, and by exchanging rings and vows at the church door. This exchange of rings was integral to the ceremony. An early sixteenth-century marriage manual explained that the ring must be worn on the fourth finger of the left hand, where a vein connected to the heart, just as the couple was sexually and emotionally united. As a circle made of gold, the most precious of metals, the ring represented both fertility and the enduring nature of marriage. The matrimony rite in the English Book of Common Prayer described the ring as a "token and pledge" that, just as "Isaac and Rebecca lived faithfully together, so these persons may surely perform and keep the vow and covenant betwixt them made."

The bride typically wore a wreath on her flowing hair, symbolic of her virginity. She also presented the groom with a wreath at the time of their engagement and at the wedding, where her bridesmaids distributed wreaths to guests. (Brides known to have had sex with their grooms before marriage could be forced to wear a straw wreath open at the back.)

During the wedding ceremony, held at the church door or inside the church, sermons drummed home the message of wifely subservience to the husband who would keep and "rule her and the whole house in Christian earnest and by good example." But many women resorted to folkways to gain the marital upper hand, for example by putting mustard and dill in their shoes.

To an eighteenth- or nineteenth-century community, the wedding ceremony was not necessarily the defining moment that made the couple "married." More important was the custom of "going to church and street," the public processions to the church and then to the couple's new lodgings, all to the beat of pipe and drum. If the legitimacy of the marriage was later questioned, witnesses to those public processions, rather than church documents, constituted proof. At the same time, social as opposed to legal recognition of a marriage was more nebulous. One man described a woman he visited as "practically his wife or not far off it." Another said that "he has taken a wife ... but they have not held the wedding yet." A woman pledged to "go to church and streets, according to Christian custom, with my husband to whom I am now married."[7]

The public role in legitimizing marriages included reading the banns of marriage three times before the actual wedding. ("If any of you know cause, or just impediment, why these two persons should not be joined together in holy Matrimony, ye are to declare it.") Before the Reformation, the church had encouraged banns, though it also sanctioned a priestly pre-wedding "bridal examination" that effectively eliminated the likelihood that anyone would object to the marriage for reasons of kinship or prior engagement. Reformation Protestants, who defined marriage as secular rather than a sacrament, believed strongly that banns should be read before the congregation.

Some German cities levied hefty fines on those who married in *Winkelehen*, private or secret marriages or elopements without parental permission, though they still acknowledged them as legal. Community members, however, were inclined to act as if they were not, and often challenged the legitimacy of children born to privately married parents. In England, some clerics offered cut-rate prices for clandestine marriages devoid of banns and ritual. After these were outlawed by the

1753 Marriage Act, many poor English people emulated their European counterparts and simply lived together as man and wife.

The state of being married had the effect of implementing the terms of the marriage contract. The bride brought a trousseau and household goods, anything from a good bed, tin pans, and a cow to a small fortune in cash, while her groom brought the tools of the trade with which he would support the household, anything from carpentry to property, investments, or real estate. The bride also brought the dowry, which the groom afterward controlled. Should he die leaving no children, the dowry would revert to his widow.

These inheritance relationships, however, and also the "morning gift," a legal provision for supporting a wife should her husband predecease her, took effect only after a successful wedding night. In keeping with the public nature of marriage, the wedding night was the subject of intense public scrutiny. After the feasting, celebrating, dancing, and often ribald entertainment, guests watched as the bride and groom left for the bridal chamber. At that point the bride's virginal wreath was removed, her father or relatives handed her over to the groom, and, the wedding party hoped, her virginity would soon cease to exist. If this happened, the next morning she would receive her morning gift, a sum of money that remained in her possession. (Remarrying widows, having no virginity to give, were ineligible for a morning gift.)

The wedding night was fraught with danger from evil spirits, black magic spells cast by jealous ex-lovers, and impotence, the last a cause for annulling a marriage. Before the Reformation, Catholic cleansing rituals defused evil spirits. Afterward, various stratagems were employed, including, in France, marrying after dark. In Germany and elsewhere, wedding guests combated malevolent forces by drinking, singing, and shouting bawdily. Where permitted, the Catholic Church blessed both bed and bedroom.

On wedding nights, the local community gathered to celebrate or censure the newlyweds. In France, *charivaris* (transplanted to England and later Canada and the United States, where they are known as shivarees) could be raucous events, as jeering participants clanged pots and pans, heckling older women and old men who married youngsters, or impatient widows or widowers who married while still in mourning, and punishing them by keeping them up all night.

(British immigrant Susanna Moodie described her first Canadian *charivari* in 1834, a terrifying cacophony of clanking metal, horns, drums, and cracked fiddles, shrieking, and gunshots. A neighbour told her the *charivari* was "a queer custom" borrowed by English Canadians from the French, during which local idlers disguised themselves by blackening and masking their faces, and sporting clothes put on back to front and "grotesque caps ... adorned with cocks' feathers and bells."[8] As in Europe, *charivaris* could be fatal. After a runaway slave escaped to Canada and married an Irish woman, a mob that included the sons of prominent families broke into his house, dragged him from his bed, and rode him on a rail. Naked in the freezing night, the just-wed bride-groom died at their tormenting hands. In its early twentieth-century manifestation in Louisiana, an observer explained, "It is a matter of inequality, or lack of balance, that makes for *charivari*. A widower of fifty-eight takes a bride of eighteen. Ho-ho, he has a noise coming to him, that one. What you think, ahn?")

When the bride and groom were well matched, *charivaris* were crudely cheerful. In parts of rural France, the tradition was (and still is) for drunken bachelor wedding guests to break in, pull the couple out of bed, and dump them onto the floor. Then they offered a curious gift: a chamber pot full of champagne and chocolate, symbolizing urine and feces, which everyone devoured.[9] In earlier times, the pot would contain a roast chicken, eggs, and a doll, symbols of sex and fertility. This custom originated in the Middle Ages and sprang from the community's need to control the process of marriage, including the appropriateness of the spouses, and to ensure that sexual intercourse confirmed it. In England, revelling wedding guests escorted the couple to bed, played crude games, and, the next morning, woke the newlyweds with loud music and banter.

Post-wedding *charivaris* also humiliated spouses whose behaviour offended their community; favourite victims were husbands whose

The dissolute Tom Rakewell has wasted his inheritance, so he marries a rich old one-eyed woman he intends to bilk of her fortune. In this painting from Hogarth's "A Rake's Progress," Tom strains to look at his "bride's" maid. His abandoned fiancée, mother of his child, stands in the background with her mother, desperate to prevent the wedding. The two dogs symbolize the bizarre nature of the wedding.

wives beat them. Over a long period, as new notions of privacy spread, bourgeois newlyweds began to spend their wedding night in a secret location, alone.

CHURCH WEDDINGS: PORCH, YARD, OR INTERIOR

Marriage was the only one of seven sacraments that did not require priestly participation and religious invocation. The consent of the spouses alone was sufficient, although, after the mid-twelfth century, the mutual declarations "I take you as my husband" and "I take you as my wife" were also required. Throughout western Europe's sixteenth-century Reformation, church, state, and reformers waged battle over whether the nature of marriage was sacramental, spiritual, or civic. Though the overwhelming majority of people were unaware of it, the site of weddings and the liturgy were the battlegrounds. From the fourteenth to the sixteenth centuries, the public exchange of vows in the church porch was both the custom and the fashion. The Reformation, seeking to cleanse marriage of the sullying effects of blending economic interests with the religious ceremony, moved weddings from the church's porch to its holier interior.

The nature of betrothals, or spousals, slowly changed as well. Traditionally, betrothed couples had referred to each other as man and wife even though they did not *act* as if they were fully married, by having sex and cohabiting. But by the late seventeenth century, writes historian Christine Peters, spousals could be described as "in great measure worn out of use."[10] One reason was that, more and more, spousals did not precede church weddings.

Among prosperous English people, the wedding served as the vehicle for spouses to consent to their marriage, as spousals used to. Even then, the completion of the financial arrangements and cohabitation did not always immediately follow. Brides often returned to their parents, and the marriage was finalized only later, when their husbands brought them "home."

Although the Reformation clarified the boundaries between sacred and secular, people continued to celebrate marriage with weddings that mingled the religious with the secular as in pre-Reformation days, when priests sometimes blessed spousals or rings. They also bestowed religious meanings on formerly secular customs, as priests served wine in place of "love drinks," organ music replaced the pipes and drums, and wedding sermons taught both wifely subservience and the horrors of adultery.

A Protestant Wedding

Over the centuries, all these developments and refinements, to say nothing of regional, national, religious, and class variations, changed the

The Peasant Wedding *by Bruegel, 1568. The bride is depicted in the traditional
posture of modesty, in front of a dark green cloth beside crossed sheaves of wheat,
symbols of fertility. Her groom is not identified; he may be the man pouring out
beer or serving food. Bruegel, black-clad and red-bearded, sits on the far right,
chatting with a monk.*

religious and political meanings of marriage and, to a lesser extent, the
face of European and, later, North American weddings. The well-
documented mid-sixteenth-century courtship, wedding, and marriage
of Felix and Madlen Platter is an intriguing case study of how that
upwardly mobile professional-class Swiss Calvinist couple celebrated
their nuptials.[11]

Felix Platter's father, Thomas, an autodidact printer and boarding
schoolmaster, had first glimpsed Madlen Jeckelmann on a visit to her
surgeon father. Though Felix was only fifteen, Thomas decided that
Madlen, a very shy and pretty teenager, would be his bride. He and
Dr. Jeckelmann began to negotiate the terms of the marriage and
exchanged small gifts.

Felix was delighted to learn that he was engaged, and eagerly set out
to fulfill Dr. Jeckelmann's stipulation that he establish himself profes-
sionally. With Thomas's help, Felix enrolled in the world-renowned

medical faculty at the Université Montpellier and returned to Basel in 1557, with his bachelor's and master's degrees. But, because he and Madlen had not been formally introduced, Madlen fled whenever she happened upon him in the street. Felix respected her circumspection and the fact that her father insisted on strict observance of social niceties.

Emmanuel Le Roy Ladurie, the Platter family's biographer, divides the Platters' "campaign" to win Madlen's hand into three phases: the introduction, the marriage proposal, and the romance. They were officially introduced at a formal luncheon at Thomas Platter's country estate; Madlen's father attended along with her brother Daniel and his fiancée, Dorothea. After the post-prandial music and dancing, at which Felix played the lute and danced the galliard, an athletic dance much loved by Queen Elizabeth I, the group walked back to Basel. "When two young people are fond of each other and see each other frequently," Dorothea counselled Felix and Madlen, "they mustn't wait too long [to marry], for there can easily be a mishap." Madlen blushed at Dorothea's reference to sex. Felix, reflecting on the day's events, felt "like stone."

As the campaign entered its next phase, Felix and Madlen began to establish a personal relationship. They went cherry picking together with approved chaperones. They chatted in the privacy of her home though never in public. When Madlen complained because a much older widow was flirting with Felix, he broke off all contact with the other woman. Felix was by then madly in love and Madlen responded to his fervent declarations with shy warmth.

Dr. Jeckelmann was a more difficult conquest. He held out for better terms, demanding, among other things, that Felix obtain his doctorate. He worried so much about Thomas Platter's financial soundness that the intervention of various friends and relatives was required to convince him to clinch the deal. Felix's mentor, Professor Hans Huber, brought Dr. Jeckelmann Felix's formal proposal and reassured the physician that Thomas Platter's real estate was worth more than his notorious debts. He also made several promises. First, Thomas would close his student boarding house because Madlen would find it too noisy. Secondly, she would continue to manage her father's household as well as Felix's; Dr. Jeckelmann need not worry about losing his housekeeper. Lastly, Felix would complete all the requirements for his doctorate.

Felix, who was to become a noted physician and medical scholar, was up to the challenge. On September 20, 1557, before his twenty-first birthday, he was awarded his doctorate and appointed a professor at the university. On November 18, Dr. Felix Platter accompanied his father to Dr. Jeckelmann's to sign the marriage contract.

Dr. Jeckelmann had four witnesses; the Platters had three. The meeting, in a room off the kitchen where Madlen stood eavesdropping, was acrimonious and, for the rookie physician and his hopelessly indebted father, humiliating. Jeckelmann's proposed dowry was stingy and his financial demands were crushing. In desperation, Thomas pledged that, in lieu of a cash contribution, he would lodge and feed the young couple in his own home and, as promised, give notice to his

*Felix Platter in 1584, twenty-seven years after
his marriage to Madlen Jeckelmann.*

noisy student lodgers. The subdued and disheartened Platters, Dr. Jeckelmann, and the seven witnesses "celebrated" the signed contract.

From Dr. Jeckelmann's perspective, the deal had gone well. He considered Felix an accomplished man with a brilliant future and excellent connections. But Madlen had other suitors and, though her heart was set on Felix, her father would not compromise on his demands. He was sure he knew what was best for her, and he also factored in the cost of her wedding and the loss of her undivided attention to his domestic needs. Many other widowers, loath to lose their daughters' housekeeping skills, forbade them to marry.

Two days later, on November 20, 1557, one hundred and fifty people, among them merchants, artisans, medical men, Protestant clergymen, a few artists, and four nobles, were invited to the November 22 wedding. On Sunday, November 21, the Thomas Platter household frantically cleaned, cooked, and baked in preparation for the next day's festivities. They had to live up to their community's and their new in-laws' expectations.

Felix dressed in a close-fitting blood-red silk jacket set off by flesh-coloured breeches and a wedding shirt with a short ruff, gold pins, and collar; his head was covered with his velvet doctoral cap decorated with braided pearls and flowers. Madlen, less spectacular, wore a blouse that turned out to be the same colour as Felix's breeches. A printer led the wedding procession to the church. There, Dr. Jeckelmann gave Madlen away to Felix, who exchanged vows and rings with her. After the marriage sermon, everyone set out for the Platter house.

Fifteen tables had been set up throughout the house. Felix presided over the table for elite males in one room, Madlen over the table for elite females in another. The first of two substantial meals began. Appetizers included chopped fish, soup, meat, and chicken, followed by entrees of boiled pike, roast beef, pigeon, cock and goose, boiled rice, and liver in aspic, and after that Gruyère cheese and fruit. When the guests could eat no more, the entertainment—that fundamental element of celebrating weddings—began.

The guests may have expected the usual wild offerings provided by wandering musicians, clowns, rhymesters, and sometimes even prostitutes, as celebrants turned their backs on decorum, lost their inhibitions, and engaged in rowdy dances and obscene gestures and jokes. No number of decrees, rules, or ordinances could erase people's interest in the erotic possibilities and the sexual realities that marriage evoked. The Platter-Jeckelmann guests, however, were treated to a children's choir from Thomas Platter's school. Afterward, Felix performed a solo galliard. Madlen, too bashful to join him, looked on as her husband leapt, jumped, and hopped for his guests' edification.

Supper followed, a lavish meal that mostly observed the sumptuary rules. Chicken liver, tripe, meat soup, and chicken were succeeded by boiled carp and then roast, Black Forest game stew, and fish cakes; this time the dessert was pastries, even though the sumptuary rules mentioned only cheese and fruit.

Evening fell. The guests were stuffed and soused. It was time to end the wedding and begin the marriage. Felix now joined Madlen and served sugared claret to the matrons who had gathered around her to offer encouragement and advice. Then, amid the gleefully suggestive comments of their guests, the young couple retired to an attic room, where they sat at the edge of the bed, shivering in the November chill. They debated briefly: should they indulge in sexual intercourse right away or, like Felix's parents, wait several weeks? The coldness decided them. They crawled under the covers.

But they were not quite alone. Felix's mother, joyous that her son had finally succeeded in marrying Madlen, had tramped upstairs and now stood in the nearby privy, serenading them boisterously. A few feet away, in her wedding bed, Madlen roared with laughter.

The Platter-Jeckelmann union raises several questions that focus attention on some of the key issues in marriage's evolution. As they bartered hard about the marriage contract and exchanged vows and rings in their church, did these Protestants even consider the changed nature of post-Reformation marriage as a less economically driven union? Did Madlen resent or resist the patriarchal structure that granted her father the right not only to give her away but also to retain her housekeeping services despite the vastly increased workload this required of her? Why did Felix mention only the flesh-coloured blouse Madlen wore to their wedding, and neglect to describe the rest of her outfit? Why did this groom, who recorded the details of his own wedding wardrobe, seem so much less interested in his bride's? Were the wedding guests, segregated by sex and class, appreciative or apprehensive about the appearance of unsanctioned pastries?

NORTH AMERICA

In North America, marriages could be as difficult to define as those in Europe, and a great many were created without benefit of a wedding. As in the European custom, private vows between two consenting partners were often considered sufficient to constitute a marriage. Self-marriage, later known as common-law marriage, was widespread. (So was self-divorce.)

There were myriad reasons for self-marriage. Many people were unaware of the legislation that, over time, specified the need for wedding licences, banns, and ceremonies. They assumed that mutual consent legitimized a marriage and that, as in Europe, their community's witness to their relationship constituted proof of marriage. It was also a common belief that conceiving a child together constituted marriage. In 1728, a chaplain serving on the North Carolina and Virginia border was called on to christen more than a hundred children but not to marry any adults. "Marriage is reckon'd a lay contract in Carolina," his supervisor concluded.[12]

Self-marriage had other causes. Religious or secular authorities were often unavailable to perform the rites. In Texas, Catholics without access to a priest married "by bond" in improvised ceremonies. Non-Catholics without access to a pastor simply pledged themselves to each other in the presence of friends. In 1791, future president Andrew Jackson married his not-yet-divorced wife, Rachel Donelson Robards, in this simple way. Afterward, her first husband divorced her on the grounds of her adultery with Jackson.

Disavowing self-marriage, at least among whites, had such dire consequences, notably the bastardization of huge numbers of children, that it rarely happened. "The maxim *semper praesumitur pro matrimonio* (the assumption is always in favour of matrimony) directed and summed up judges' thinking," American historian Nancy Cott explains.[13] This assumption embraced even marriages created when one partner had been married to someone else, as long as that now extraneous spouse was divorced or dead. Some jurisdictions recognized marriage ceremonies held in circumstances later proved fraudulent, as long as the spouses had married in good faith.

In the United States, the great exception was interracial marriage. If a white person's spouse was revealed to be not entirely white, laws and outraged communities rushed to end the relationship with everything from fines and compulsory divorce to mob attacks. The Civil War and emancipation fuelled white terror of "amalgamation," and interracial marriage evoked hysterical and violent reactions.

To some extent this was also true of intermarriage between whites and Natives, which many jurisdictions and governing agencies such as the Hudson's Bay Company banned. In the fur-trading hinterland, Christian marriage was not an option for white men involved with Native women. Instead, these men had to follow *la façon du pays*—the custom of the country or Native rituals. The prospective husband had to obtain his would-be bride's parents' permission to marry—otherwise, as an elderly trader cautioned, "There is danger of having one's head broken if one takes a girl from this country without her parents' consent"[14]—and he had to negotiate a bride price, often as substantial as a horse. After he completed his payment, he smoked tobacco in a ceremonial pipe shared with her relatives or band members. Her relatives then prepared her for her role as a wife, cleansing her and dressing her in new clothes. Her groom—now her "squaw man"—escorted her home, united as a couple by Native rites.[15]

How valid were these marriages? Until the nineteenth century, many white husbands considered themselves legally bound, and English courts tended to agree. When their employers tried to force them to divest themselves of their embarrassing Indian wives, many refused and stoutly defended the legitimacy of their marriages. But when traders were company men rather than independent entrepreneurs, retirement often ended their relationships.

Some husbands dealt with white society's revulsion to their Native wives by staying put in Indian territory. Others resorted to "turning off"—marrying off their suddenly burdensome wives to new, woman-less arrivals. Others simply disappeared into the white world. A few fair-minded judges attempted to force white husbands into legal marriage with their Native wives, and to transfer to the wives one-third of the man's property. But this seldom happened, and the abandoned women packed up their mixed-blood children and returned to their tribes, which welcomed them back, stigmatizing neither.

In 1824, in Green Bay in the Michigan Territory, a grand jury summoned by newly arrived U.S. circuit court judge James Duane Doty

Sophia Tod, daughter of B.C.'s Chief Lolo, had seven children with her white husband, John Tod, who in 1863 formally married her after he learned that his wife in England had died.

indicted thirty-six townsmen for fornication and two for adultery. Most pleaded guilty and, to avoid paying a fine, married their Native wives in front of a justice of the peace. Two husbands countersued, arguing that they were guilty of nothing, being legally married in the Indian way to women with whom they had fathered many children.

John Lawe, however, refused to repent or amend his ways and continued to live with Therese Rankin until her death nearly two decades late. Lawe had chosen well: Sophia Therese Rankin, or Ne-kick-o-qua, was the granddaughter of a prominent Ottawa man whose policy was to marry his daughters and granddaughters to white fur traders and to settle a land grant on them. But, as Lawe lamented to a Metis friend, "the old times is no more that pleasant reign is over and never to return any more."[16]

In the American South, black slaves were forbidden legal marriage. They had no legal status as persons and were, therefore, legally incapable of consent. As well, their master's demands on them took precedence over other aspects of their life and made fulfilling marital obligations impossible. Indeed, white slave owners worried that consenting to a slave's legal marriage might even be interpreted as tantamount to manumission, in part because Christian rites implied that slaves had souls recognized by God.[17] They were also aware that slave marriages created complicated legal property issues, for example when slaves of different owners married, or a slave married a free black or person of colour. Unlike unmarried slaves, who could be sold or rented out without any problems, spouses would want to visit each other and would demand not to be sold away as so often happened. The ownership of their children could also cause tensions between the slave owners.

Nonetheless, slaves married, by choice or coercion, though these unions were neither registered legally nor sanctioned by the church. After courting, slaves requested permission to marry from their owners. If they had different masters, however, this became a complicated property issue. Some slave owners accommodated their slaves' pleas, as happened on the South Carolina plantation of Mary Boykin Chesnut. She writes, "When Dick married Hetty the Anderson house was next door. The two families agreed to sell either Dick or Hetty, whichever consented to be sold. Hetty refused outright, and the Andersons sold Dick that he might be with his wife." So far so good, but, as Chesnut's account makes plain, the Andersons had made a grievous sacrifice, "for Hetty was only a lady's-maid and Dick was a trained butler, on whom Mrs. Anderson had spent no end of pains in his dining-room education, and, of course, if they had refused to sell Dick, Hetty would have had to go to them. Mrs. Anderson was very much disgusted with Dick's ingratitude when she found he was willing to leave them."[18] Very few other slave owners inconvenienced themselves for slave lovers as the Andersons had done.

Slaves with different masters usually hoped at best for an "abroad" arrangement with visiting privileges, and asked someone else to intercede on their behalf. (Even more contentious was a slave's request to marry a freeman or freewoman.) If permission were granted, a ceremony might mark the union, often presided over by the master and sometimes capped by jumping or stepping over a broom, and usually held in agricultural down-time: the Christmas season or July.[19] A celebratory party in the quarters followed.

An estimated 10 percent of slaves were forced to marry against their will, matched up by large plantation owners or overseers desirous of increasing their slave stock through breeding. A former slave in Alabama, Penny Thompson, recalled that "mos times masters and misses would jus' pick out some man fo' a woman an' say 'Dis yo' man, an' say to the man 'Dis yo' woman.' Didn't make no difference what they want. Then they read some from the Bible to 'em an' say 'now you is husban' an wife.' "[20] Sometimes the male slave's preference clinched the deal if his master granted him permission to marry a woman who might not reciprocate his feelings. The woman had no say in the matter. West Virginia slave Lizzie Grant related how sometimes masters purchased slaves and "put us to live together to raise from just like you would stock today.... They never cared or thought about our feeling in the matter."[21]

But slave unions were also forged in deepest love. After Emancipation, former slave Laura Spicer managed to locate her husband, sold away from her and their children years earlier. Her husband responded with a profoundly sad love letter:

> *I love you just as well as I did the last day I saw you.... [Y]ou know it never was our wishes to be separated from each other, and it never was our fault.... I had rather anything to have happened to me most than ever have been parted from you and the children.... The woman is not born that feels as near to me as you do.... I thinks of you and the children every day of my life.... My love to you never have failed.... You feels and seems to me as much like my dear loving wife, as you ever did.*[22]

Thanks to slavery, slave unions were inherently unstable, and white owners ended two out of five by selling away one of the spouses. Historian Wilma Dunaway calculates that in the Upper South by the end of the Civil War, half of slave families had been affected by broken marriages, and many of these families were now headed by women. (Black households were complex mixtures of kin and non-kin, children from previous marriages, adopted orphans, and old people. Many incorporated at least two families.) The "structured absence of black fathers" through abroad marriages, hiring them out elsewhere, or sending them to distant work assignments eroded slave marriages. Separated spouses were often forcibly mated with new "spouses"; others voluntarily took new ones, as slave rescuer Harriet Tubman discovered when her husband, John, a free black, declined to join her in the North because he preferred to remain in the South with his new wife, Caroline, and their children. Laura Spicer's hopes of reunion were also smashed because, in his love letter, her husband explained that "I would come and see you, but I know you could not bear it.... I have go[t] another wife, and I am very sorry, that I am." Unable to leave his new family, Spicer told Laura sorrowfully, "please git married" and "send me some of the children's hair."[23]

During the Reconstruction that followed the Civil War, married freedmen flocked to legalize and register their marriages. "Weddings, just now, are very popular, and abundant among the Colored People," a

Union army chaplain commented.[24] Union army officers, missionaries, and officials presided over mass marriages. State legislators validated slave unions if husband and wife continued to cohabit. In 1866, in seventeen counties in North Carolina, for example, more than nine thousand couples registered their unions.

The nature of slavery and white manipulation of slave unions created a legal and moral quagmire: if slave unions could be retroactively validated, were people who had had more than one spouse bigamists? Which of multiple "marriages" was the most legitimate? "Whenever a negro appears before me with 2 or 3 wives who have equal claim upon him, I marry him to the woman who has the greatest number of helpless children who otherwise would become a charge on the Bureau," a Freedmen's Bureau agent reported.[25] Reconstruction judges, recognizing the extraordinary circumstances of such unions, often dealt leniently with African-American "bigamy" and were inclined to apply the test of continued cohabitation to determine if a marriage should be validated.

WEDDING RITUALS

Wedding rituals differed from era to era and from place to place, shaped and coloured by individual tastes and resources. There was little standardization. Until the late eighteenth or early nineteenth centuries, the common denominators were parental consent (required by law) and marriage licences. Banns of marriage were usually posted. From the mid-sixteenth century, most Christian wedding services included versions of the Church of England's Solemnization of Marriage from the Book of Common Prayer, the nearly identical vows adopted by Protestant churches, or the Roman Catholic marriage liturgy from which the others were derived.

By the mid-eighteenth century, weddings were growing in popularity. But cost was a huge consideration, and poorer people who did not opt for self-marriage could not always afford even the simplest wedding. Instead, they were often content to publish banns, mutual pledges, or both and then move in together. Wealthier people, meanwhile, hosted gala weddings, usually at home, to celebrate and to entertain in a manner befitting their positions and possessions.

Wedding garb ranged from the humblest to the most lavish, in accordance with the bride's family's ambitions, status, and means. In Europe, noble and patrician women wore spectacular dresses made of the costliest fabrics—velvet, damask silk, or satin, sometimes glimmering with interwoven gold or silver threads. They chose the deepest, richest colours—red, indigo, or black—that only the very wealthy could obtain. They disdained economical styles in favour of wide, gathered skirts, generous sleeves, and conspicuously lavish trains that trailed for yards. Fur trim and jewellery, often part of the dowry and, for the wedding, sewn right into the dress, completed the ensemble.

Wedding gowns had their own history, with royals and nobles establishing fashions and standards of taste. For her strategic marriage to Charles the Bold in 1468, Margaret of York's jewel-encrusted dress was so heavy she had to be carried into the church. Her coronet, nearly five inches high, was a magnificent creation of pearls and finely crafted enamelled white roses that symbolized the House of York. It featured her name in red, green, and white enamel, with lovers' knots and the golden initials C and M. (The coronet is still on display at Aachen Cathedral.)

The well-to-do woman emulated much wealthier brides by using extravagant amounts of fabric she trimmed with cheaper fox or rabbit fur, and by decking herself in her best jewellery. The less affluent bride made a dress of linen or wool, softer than the coarse, rough, homespun fabric she usually wore. She was limited to dying it a shade of affordable vegetable-based dye, but she aspired to a grander style: flowing sleeves and trains, impractical but beautiful, were particularly prestigious. For the frugal or financially constrained, a new dress that could serve as "best" for years to come was a calculated expense, and drab colours that would not show stains were the most practical. Grey was popular; white too wildly impractical. The truly impecunious simply made do with whatever they had.

Traditions that travelled across the Atlantic included superstitions about the choice of colours: blue, the colour of Roman bridal gowns and of the Virgin Mary, symbolized purity and fidelity; brides wore blue to ensure that their husbands would not stray. Pink was pretty but unlucky; red as scandalous as a scarlet letter. Yellow was in vogue in the eighteenth century, but green evoked fairies and the verdancy of rainfall that might drench the proceedings. Homespun brown was common if unloved; grey was popular and considered very smart and useful, especially for a bride in mourning. Ribbons tied into love knots made plain or shabby dresses special. At the ceremony's end, guests pulled off the ribbons and took them home as favours. By the nineteenth century, flowers had replaced ribbons. Brides wore them in their hair and carried them as bouquets.

By the late eighteenth century, the machine-made cloth of the Industrial Revolution and inexpensive, thin Indian muslins became the fabrics of choice for wedding gowns. By the end of the century, wedding white was coming into its own, though silver with white, topped by a coloured cape, remained classic. In her much-discussed May 1816 wedding, Princess Charlotte wore silver lamé over a silver slip, its hem embroidered in bells and flowers also in silver lamé. In 1840, Queen Victoria created the tradition of the white wedding dress in her lavish, ceremonious, and very public wedding to her beloved Albert. Despite a heavy downpour, thousands gathered hours early to watch the wedding procession into the Chapel Royal at St. James's Palace. At ten o'clock, a marching band's "Haste to the Wedding" reflected the impatience of many onlookers and ticketed spectators; the latter, waiting inside, were 2,100 strong. At noon, after a twenty-one-gun salute announced that Victoria had entered her carriage, the damp but determined multitude outside cheered lustily as the celebrants arrived. Prince Albert and his entourage arrived first, to the accompaniment of trumpet and drum, and after formally greeting royal and church dignitaries, they waited for the bride. To the strains of music, Victoria and her many attendants proceeded slowly into the chapel.

Victoria's dress was white silk satin trimmed with sweet-smelling orange blossoms. The train, about six yards of the same fabric, was carried by twelve bridesmaids. Her headdress was a simple

Queen Victoria's official wedding portrait, and portraits of her in her wedding gown, were much reproduced. The lavish ceremony influenced the style and culture of weddings throughout Europe and North America.

orange-blossom wreath; attached to it was a veil, one and a half yards of diamond-studded Honiton lace draped over her shoulders and back. (Sixty-one years later, Victoria would be buried in it.) The flounce of the dress was also Honiton lace, four yards of it, specially made in the village of Beer by over two hundred lace workers, at a cost of more than £1,000. Victoria's shoes were square-toed, leather-soled flats trimmed with a small bow and six bands of ribbon and, like the rest of her outfit, British-made. Victoria designed her bridesmaids' gowns; they were "dressed all in white with white roses, which had a beautiful effect," she wrote in her diary.[26] Prince Albert designed the gold brooches she gave each of them, eagle shaped and set with turquoise, pearls, rubies, and diamonds—setting off another tradition, of giving the bridesmaids gifts.

After an emotional ceremony that included the 67th Psalm, Victoria and Albert left the chapel and stepped into the sunshine that had broken through the fog and rain. The bride's eyes were "swollen with tears, but great happiness was seen in her countenance, and her look of confidence and comfort at the Prince when they walked away as man and wife was very pleasing to see," Dowager Lady Sarah Lyttelton recalled.[27]

These details were reported in hundreds of newspapers and magazines, and read and replicated, as perhaps never before, by hundreds of thousands of brides throughout and beyond the Empire. What this attention to the clothing, the music, the ceremony illustrates, though, is that the wedding itself gained in prominence, and, as it did so, people focused on the wedding rather than on the (supposed) lifetime institution of marriage. (Part 2 will discuss how today our culture blinds us to the realities and practicalities of marriage by stressing the wedding ceremony.)

Victoria's wedding inspired instant "traditions." She was not the first royal to marry in white, but her gown, seen by thousands and reproduced in newspaper sketches, fashion magazine colour plates, and a flood of popular engravings, became the model for brides and their parents everywhere. And so, despite family photos showing ancestral brides clutching modest bouquets over their dark-coloured outfits, and even though white was the traditional colour for royal mourning, and despite the fact that Victorian white, innocent of bleach, would today be classed as cream, white became *the* colour of wedding gowns.

Victoria's choice of orange blossoms, an ancient Chinese emblem of purity and fertility, inspired million of brides to wear them, and Victorian wedding etiquette manuals prescribed them as essential. Where the real, fragrant ones were unavailable, brides made do with wax replicas. Thanks to Victoria, these floral wedding accessories became so ubiquitous that the expression "to gather orange blossoms" became the euphemism for "to seek a wife."

The public splendour of Victoria and Albert's wedding, with its parade of train bearers, its pomp, ceremony, and music, and the grand slow march down the aisle transformed North American as well as European weddings; it injected them with drama and held brides up to a new standard of dress and presentation that became an almost instant tradition. The result, writes Stephanie Coontz, is that "thousands of middle-class women imitated her example, turning their weddings into the most glamorous event of their lives."[28]

Another wedding tradition, "Something old, something new, something borrowed, something blue," is often interpreted as representing family and past (old); the bride's future life (new); the shared happiness of the loved lender (borrowed); and the colour of the Virgin Mary, signifying purity and fidelity, and formerly a popular choice for wedding gowns (blue). Less known is that the source of this saying is actually a poem that ends, "And a silver sixpence in her shoe," a good-luck token especially if worn in the left shoe.

The bridegroom's attire also mattered, even to the point of competing with the bride's. Like her, he wore his best clothes, his suit (of wool, worsted, or even cashmere) and his shirt (of linen, cotton, or silk) reflecting his economic status. If he possessed a waistcoat or tie, he wore them too. The man who could afford special wedding attire sported strong colours of blue, green, or wine until the latter part of the nineteenth century, when the well-turned-out groom was more muted, in a black or navy coat worn over grey trousers cheered up by a white vest and tie.

*This young bride, ca. 1850, poses among studio props,
but the orange blossoms in her hair may be real.*

*Despite the devastation of the Civil War, Godey's published this ad for
extravagant and expensive gowns. The bride on the far right wears a
Victoria-inspired wreath of leaves and orange blossoms.*

Marnie and Bill Abbott, the author's parents, pose outside Hart House,
University of Toronto, after their wedding in 1940. Women were permitted into
the chapel at Hart House, but it was otherwise off limits to them. In wartime
austerity, Marnie chose to wed in a dressy suit. A year later, she graduated from
law school and articled with Bill.

Over the decades, male wedding fashion slowly evolved until, by
the 1930s, it embraced the dinner jacket, known in North America as
the tuxedo and until then regarded as suitable for less formal events.
(In 1866, tobacco heir Griswold Lorillard shocked fellow guests at the
Autumn Ball of the Tuxedo Park Country Club, in Tuxedo, New York,
by wearing a black, tail-less dinner jacket copied from one worn by the
Prince of Wales. The style became popular, and North Americans
called it the tuxedo.) The groom who lacked the resources (or the
desire) to buy one wore a dark suit instead. By the mid-twentieth
century, tuxedo rentals offered a thrifty way for men to indulge in
extravagant wedding attire.

In the centuries since Van Eyck tantalized the art world with his
hauntingly lovely but cryptic painting, weddings assumed greater

importance until they became the climactic event in the marriage process. And, just as wedding traditions were increasingly associated with notions of love—romantic, erotic, and eternal—so did the ideal of marriages rooted in love also evolve.

Chapter 4

Love and Sex in Marriage

LOVE AND AFFECTION

Who in the world knew more about love and marriage than Jane Austen? As one of eight children of an Anglican rector forced to supplement his income by farming and teaching student boarders, she understood very well the social and economic realities of her era, especially the narrow range of opportunities for women. In her personal life as in *Sense and Sensibility* (1811), *Pride and Prejudice* (1813), *Mansfield Park* (1814), *Emma* (1815), *Northanger Abbey,* and *Persuasion* (1817), she tackled the conflict between the new respect for love-based marriage and the old and often morally-fraught dilemma of women's economic and legal dependence.

Jane Austen had the happiest of home lives, rich in companionship and in intellectual stimulation. Her sister, Cassandra, was her closest friend. Her brothers were kind and committed. Her parents were affectionate and encouraging. She participated fully in her family's social life and was a favourite of her brothers' children. She was an exceptional seamstress and a virtuoso of the satin stitch. She played the pianoforte and sang. She read English and French books and drew. Secretively, she also wrote stories she shared only with her family, relying on a creaking swinging door in her writing den to warn her when domestics and visitors were approaching. In a world where men recoiled from too-clever women, nobody knew just how clever Jane Austen really was.

From her late teens, Jane was a candidate for the marriage market, the well-bred and accomplished daughter of a distinguished family. She was good-natured and very pretty; one young woman reported that "her Sister & herself are two of the prettiest Girls in England."[1]

Jane was particularly fond of dancing, and excelled at it, her favourite brother, Henry, remembered. In her family's social world, where financial constraints prevented parents with marriageable daughters from launching them as debutantes, regular socializing doubled as the locus for matchmaking. Dancing was often involved, either impromptu gigs after supper parties or at balls in the local assembly rooms. As a character remarks in *Pride and Prejudice*, "To be fond of dancing was a certain step towards falling in love."

This engraving of Jane Austen was inspired by a drawing by her sister, Cassandra. Thanks to Cassandra's modest artistic talents, Jane's reputed beauty has been lost to posterity.

This happened to Jane, who often attended Thursday-evening dances with her parents. During the Christmas season of 1795 to 1796, she had a brief, quasi romance with Tom Lefroy, her neighbour's nephew, visiting before he headed to London to study law. Jane's excitement about their relationship percolates through her letters to Cassandra: "I am almost afraid to tell you how my Irish friend and I behaved. Imagine to yourself everything most profligate and shocking in the way of dancing and sitting down together," she exclaimed in one.[2]

Their mutual joy was short-lived. Tom's family noticed the intensifying relationship and packed him off out of harm's way. The Lefroys had the greatest respect for Jane's lineage and character, but other considerations weighed more heavily. Tom had no money of his own and was dependent on a great-uncle to finance his education and, later, to help him establish his legal career. How then could he marry Jane, who had neither dowry nor inheritance prospects? Jane left no record of any pain and disappointment at Tom's departure; her biographer Deirdre Le Faye believes her feelings "were poised on the knife-edge between flattered amusement and the exciting apprehension of possible romantic commitment."[3]

There followed a second "stillborn romance" with a man whom Cassandra thought so charming, handsome, and elegant that if ever a man could win Jane's love, it would be this one. They met at a seaside vacation spot, and he declared before leaving that he would soon see them again. Shortly after, the sisters heard that he had suddenly died. "I believe that, if Jane ever loved, it was this unnamed gentleman," opined her nephew.[4]

The years went by, pleasant and rewarding, but Jane could never forget that her status as a spinster made her a financial burden to her family. She wrote a ditty that gently mocked the desperation of Maria, good humoured, handsome, and tall, "a middle-aged flirt" who, "having in vain danced at many a ball" and "for a husband was at her last stake," married "a Mr. Wake, whom, it was supposed, she would scarcely have accepted in her youth." In a more serious vein, Jane warned her niece that "single women have a dreadful propensity for being poor—which is one very strong argument in favour of Matrimony."[5]

For a single day, Austen succumbed to that argument. In December 1802, Harris Bigg-Wither proposed to her, and, though she did not love him, she accepted. Harris was a family friend she had known since childhood, "a large, plain-looking man who spoke little, stuttered when he did speak, was aggressive in conversation, and almost completely tactless." He was, however, heir to vast family estates, and as his wife, Jane could have provided comfortably for her parents, offered still-single Cassandra a permanent home, and even helped her brothers. But the day after accepting his proposal, she rejected it *because* she did not love him. She did not regret her decision, and years later begged her niece, then considering a marriage proposal, "not to commit yourself farther, & not to think of accepting him unless you really do like him. Anything is to be preferred or endured rather than marrying without Affection."[6]

When the Times Were Unloving

Since time immemorial, even in the most pragmatically created of marriages, passionate love could stir. Yet when it did, that love was disparaged as unseemly, equated with lust, and believed to corrode good marriages. "Nothing is more impure than to love one's wife as if she were a mistress," thundered the Roman thinker Seneca. In Rome in 184 BC, the politician, general, and writer Cato expelled a senator from the Senate for the shameful act of kissing his wife in broad daylight in full sight of their daughter.

Far from challenging the perception that love equalled lust, theologians of the new religion of Christianity reinforced it by teaching that women were intrinsically lascivious and fickle seductresses. For Saint Jerome, who struggled so hard against temptation, women were sexually insatiable, and if you extinguished their desire "it bursts into flame ... it enervates a man's mind, and engrosses all thought except for the passion which it feeds."[7]

The church's introduction of mutual consent as a feature of marriage did not alter this perception of "love" as a destructive feeling or sensation on which to base a union. Nor did the Black Death of 1348, which did not greatly reduce parental control over children's marriages, though it undermined the basis of feudal society by killing so many people. As long as property and financial considerations were paramount, they overrode the imperative of love as the basis for marriage. In the words of historian Brent Shaw, "The institution of marriage was inextricably bound up with a vocabulary of property, words which were not just coincidental metaphors."[8] Women as "chattel" and marriages as "contracts" are examples. Historian Amanda Vickery concurs: "The length of a man's rent-roll remained the ultimate aphrodisiac."[9]

The subordinate status of women largely accounts for the seeming immutability of love-based marriage. As long as men controlled family property, including women's earnings, as long as women had no legal status apart from their husband's, as long as legal *couverture*—covering—smothered wives with their husbands' identity, as long as husbands pledged to protect and support their wives and wives pledged to serve and obey their husbands, pragmatic marriage trumped marriage rooted in love. "The body of marriage was understood to rest on this economic skeleton as much as on sexual fidelity," writes legal scholar Nancy Cott.[10]

Poorer people shared similar marital perspectives. In France in 1700, for example, the prior of Sennely-en-Sologne wrote that his parishioners "get married out of financial interest rather than any other inclination. Most of them when looking for a bride only ask how many sheep she can bring in marriage. Women and girls who have lost their honour are not precluded from the search. It is a daily occurrence to see a man take a wretched bride, pregnant by someone else and adopt the child for a modest sum."[11]

Marriage was further protected from the ravages of love by the knowledge that mistresses, with whom husbands *could* share passions considered inappropriate in marriage, had few or no rights. Their children usually remained illegitimate, bastardized by a society intent on protecting marriage from the internal erosion love could inspire. A concomitant was that, despite Henry VIII's spectacular attempts, changing spouses or divesting oneself of them through divorce was an almost impossible endeavour. With mistresses, men could indulge in erotic passion without greatly damaging their marriages or their wives' status.

The sixteenth-century Protestant Reformation and the Catholic Counter-Reformation in response to it both encouraged radical changes in marriage. The new reformed Christian denominations rejected the long-held Roman Catholic doctrine that celibacy was a superior way of life. After years of forbidding clerical marriage, they permitted their priests and pastors to marry. This was a dramatic change after centuries of forcing legions of priests' de facto wives to live as lowly concubines and to raise children stigmatized as bastards. The most prominent cleric to marry was the great reformer and ex-monk Martin Luther, who in 1525, aged forty-two, married Katharina von Bora, a twenty-six-year-old former nun he had helped escape from a Cistercian convent by hiding her, along with eleven other nuns, in a wagon used to transport herring. One of his students reported wryly, "A wagon load of vestal virgins has just come to town, all more eager for marriage than for life. God grant them husbands lest worse befall."[12]

Luther's marriage legitimized clerical marriage as nothing else had. But it did not begin as a love match. As a former nun, Katharina had three choices: to go back to the convent she had fled, to return home to her family, or to marry. Desperate to avoid the first option, unwilling to return to the father who had sent her away to boarding school and afterward the convent, and who had remarried the year after her mother's death, she decided to marry. She fell in love with Hieronymus Baumgartner, but his noble and conservative family disapproved of his marrying a former nun and he became engaged to another woman. Afterward, Katharina implored Luther, who was busily finding husbands for the nuns he had encouraged to renounce their cloisters, not to marry her off to the one he had found for her, the (to her) miserly Pastor Kaspar Glatz. Instead, she said she would marry either Luther's friend Nicholas von Amsdorf or Luther himself.

Luther initially had not planned to marry, but in early 1525 surprised a friend by announcing, "If I can manage it before I die, I will still marry my Katie to spite the devil, should I hear that the peasants continue [to rebel]." (He also wished to please his father, who longed for a continuation of the male line.) Luther recalled later that "I never loved my wife but suspected her of being proud (as she is), but God willed me to take pity on the poor abandoned girl, and he has made my marriage turn out most happily."[13] The marriage was a small and private ceremony at Luther's residence, and so sudden that his close friend the theologian Philip Melanchthon complained, "Unexpectedly Luther married Bora, without even mentioning his plans to his friends." Two weeks later, the Luthers hosted a public celebration.

Not a romantic beginning, but the Luther marriage, which produced six living children, grew into an immensely satisfying union. "I wouldn't give up my Katie for France or for Venice," Luther confided to a friend. To another: "Katie, my dear rib … is, thanks to God, gentle, obedient, compliant in all things, beyond my hopes. I would not exchange my poverty for the wealth of Croesus." Katharina reciprocated, and after his death told her sister-in-law, "I am in truth so very saddened that I cannot express my great heartache to any person and do not know how I am and feel. I can neither eat nor drink. Nor again sleep. If I had owned a principality or empire I would have felt as bad had I lost it, as I did when our dear Lord God took from me … this dear and worthy man."[14]

The Luther marriage also had a powerful erotic dimension that Martin reconciled with his conviction that marital sex was a remedy against *worse* sin, because even Christian spouses performed the act of intercourse as if caught in the frenzy of epileptic seizures that made them impervious to thoughts of God. He warned that they should not disrobe and further agitate their senses, and certainly not turn the "unspotted marriage bed" into "a manure heap and a sow bath" with acrobatic or unusual positions.[15] He believed, however, that women needed sexual fulfillment as much as men did and, in his last months of life, regretted for Katharina's sake that he had become impotent.

One of their student boarders recalled that a dinner guest had once asked Katharina if she would like to return to the nun's life in her former convent. "No! No!" she exclaimed. Why not? the guest persisted. Martin jumped in, answering one question with another: "And, I wonder, why don't women choose to be made virgins?" The table was silent and all present sat smiling.[16] But Luther's great affection for Katharina—"my little love," "my beloved housewife," "preacher, brewer, gardener, and whatever else she can be"—did not change his conviction that marrying for love was unsound, and that parents had the right to stop their children from pursuing love marriages. When his own nephew became engaged without his family's consent, Martin promised to write a severe letter to the young woman's parents. At the same time, he denounced the custom of parents' forcing their offspring into arranged marriages with spouses they did not love.

This emphasis on what Luther called bridal love—that is, postmarital rather than premarital love—and on parental control over children's marriages endured in both western Europe and North America. Sermons described the love between husband and wife in terms that would today connote affection or great fondness. "People valued love in its proper place," writes Stephanie Coontz. "But it is remarkable how many people still considered it a dreadful inconvenience."[17]

For one thing, love could derail the balance of power between spouses, weakening lovelorn husbands and setting bad precedents for

Lucas Cranach the Elder was a court painter renowned for his realism.
He witnessed Martin Luther and Katharina von Bora's betrothal. He painted
this portrait of Luther in 1529 and that of Katharina in 1530.

other husbands. Love had little place in an institution in which wives who quarrelled with errant husbands were castigated as troublemakers rather than pitied as victims; a husband's philandering was a way of life, and reasonable women knew they had to swallow it. The same was true of wives who were beaten. They were supposed to accept their husbands' right or even duty to "correct" them, as long as the correction did not mutilate or kill them. "The potential for violence and cruelty in marriage can be glimpsed from the horrible complaints of the aggrieved minority who felt compelled to seek redress in the church courts, and from the depositions generated when noblemen sued their wives' lovers for financial compensation," writes historian Amanda Vickery.[18]

The Growth of Love

By the seventeenth century, just decades after Elizabeth I had declared, "Affection is false!" love—or affection—was considered a necessary component of marriage, and husbands and wives were counselled to "love one another." Most in the highest ranks of society ignored this advice; for them, dynastic considerations continued to prevail in choosing mates. Renowned jurist Sir Edward Coke demonstrated this when he tied his daughter to a bedpost and beat her until she consented to marry the man of his choice. The lesser gentry and the middle class, however, began to grant personal inclination or love a greater role.

In New France, Swedish traveller Peter Kalm was intrigued to hear girls leavening their housework with songs full of the words *amour* and *coeur*.[19] The expatriate *filles du roi*, too, gave *amour* a glance, though they had been recruited to marry quickly, and their future husbands had been warned that "all Voluntary Companions and other persons old enough to enter into marriage [had] to marry within fifteen days of the arrival of the ships carrying *les filles* under Pain of being deprived of the rights to any kind of fishing, hunting, and trading with the natives."[20] Yet official impatience did not stampede *les filles* into marriage, and, as historian Yves Landry's analysis of their marriage contracts and other documents reveals, they averaged five months, not the prescribed fifteen days, before they married.

After disembarking in New France, *les filles* were sent to various convents where nuns supervised them. Soon after, at a ceremony at the Governor's chateau hosted by senior colonial officials and society women, they met the bachelors. Ursuline Mother Superior Marie de l'Incarnation described approvingly how *les filles* evaluated the men, who were at least a decade older. Their first concern was whether the men had somewhere to live; "they acted wisely, because those men who were not established suffered a great deal before they could lead a comfortable life."[21] At the same time, *les filles* took into account the degree of their attraction to the men they were considering, and many cancelled hastily made betrothals because "there is no longer affection between them." Afterward, they betrothed themselves to a different man. A few changed their minds yet again, reneged on the new agreement, and later married someone else.[22] At the same time, they followed their hearts only if the men were otherwise satisfactory.

By the next century, Enlightenment philosophers were examining marriage through the lens of reason and the exciting new principle of the pursuit of happiness. Their ideas, trickling down into the popular consciousness, softened long-held perceptions about the role of love. In the 1770s in France, unhappily married spouses applied theory to their personal realities, and the percentage seeking to annul their marriages on the grounds of lovelessness rose from less than 10 percent in earlier decades to more than 40 percent. In England, too, love was gaining ground as a legitimate feature of marriage. Thomas Blundell, for example, told his daughter, Molly, "that I would not compel her to marry, much less to marry one she could not love and so to make her miserable as long as she lives.... All I require is that he be a gentleman of a competent estate, one of good character and a catholic."[23]

Yet until well into the eighteenth century there was strong resistance to giving love such importance. Young French aristocrat Geneviève de Malboissière's scathing remarks to her friend Adélaïde Méliand reflected the sophisticate's attitude to the proper place of love in and out of marriage. "Imagine," she wrote, "M. de Lavigny is still in love with his wife. What a lasting passion after ten months of marriage living together in proximity. They will be an example for posterity."[24]

English gentlewoman Elizabeth Parker, on the other hand, struggled between her longing to marry an unwealthy man she loved and her desire to obey her parents, who objected to him. "Every Parent takes utmost care to marry his child [where there] is Money," her lover mused, "not considering Inclination w[hi]ch is [the] only plea for Happiness."[25] It took Elizabeth seven years of strategizing and suffering to win her father's consent to her marriage.

Other women fought bitterly to avoid marrying men they did not love or who repelled them. Twenty-one-year-old Frances Burney wept inconsolably, stopped eating, and begged on her knees to be allowed to live with her father rather than the (to her) repulsive man he wished her to marry. Her father finally relented, and Frances later fell in love with and married an impoverished French exile, then staved off destitution with the proceeds of *Camilla, or a Picture of Youth*, her novel about frustrated love and impoverishment.

Anne and William Gossip's conventional marriage in England united their family fortunes but also inspired a deep love that lasted their lifetimes. Twenty-six years married, Anne described William as "you who I love a thousand [times] better than myself or anything in the world." William wrote her, "My heart will open itself towards the object of its desires."[26] But when their son and heir, George, secretly married a pretty but socially inferior woman, William disinherited him. Love was all very well, but only in the proper sort of unions. "Mutual affection which crowned an advantageous match was a welcome blessing, but immoderate passion leading couples to disregard other criteria was thought near-insane," writes historian Amanda Vickery.[27]

As the eighteenth century wore on, the notion of marrying for love crept into popular thinking, even if that love was not so much passion as strong affection and companionship that would provide emotional sustenance, and a cessation of the unkindness and violence that marked so many marriages. "The measure of a successful marriage was no longer how big a financial settlement was involved, how many useful in-laws were acquired, or how many children were produced, but how well a family met the emotional needs of its individual members," Stephanie Coontz writes.[28]

Mutuality and companionate marriage were becoming the new standards, but because wives remained financially and legally subservient to husbands, many caveats leavened the notion that love was all-important. In 1811, Jane Austen's financially embarrassed teenager, Marianne Dashwood, the younger sister in *Sense and Sensibility*, could not imagine marrying a man who had anything less than a "competence" of about £2,000 a year, to support "a proper establishment of servants, a carriage, perhaps two, and hunters."

Men were equally subject to these strictures. George Du Maurier, an impecunious artist and writer, was an example of a middle-class man prevented from marrying. In the early 1860s, Du Maurier had ended his courtship of the very suitable Emma Wightwick when her family's business collapsed. But, because he adored her, he soon resumed wooing her. They became engaged, with marriage to follow when he accumulated £1,000. Time passed, and he realized the impossibility of his raising the money. His health and mental stability deteriorated. His mother suggested he take a mistress to relieve his anxieties, but George declined, with the remark that "every woman but one is a gorilla."[29] Emma's father salvaged the situation by renegotiating the marital stake down to only £200. The discounted price restored George to health, and he and Emma were soon married.

As long as dowries and financial and social considerations dominated the process of marrying, and parental consent was paramount, love-based marriage developed more as a literary ideal than a reality. Alice Catherine Miles, whose enterprising pursuit of a husband was described in chapter 2, held attitudes typical of England's privileged class. As they manipulated the marriage market, Alice and her friends experienced love and discussed it frankly. "Love in a cottage overgrown with roses is a very fine thing in theory," Alice concluded, "but depend upon it, love in a palace is the pleasanter of the two.... Love is a charming thing in itself and gives undoubtedly a delicate flavour to life, not to be imparted by anything else, but as in a cunningly wrought sauce, you must have all the other ingredients as well. Otherwise it will be an utter failure." To her dear friend Aggie, Alice wrote, "Some love must of course enter into the compact, but like the scriptural leaven, a very little leaveneth the whole lump." When the "intensely" pretty Edith Wood agreed to a loveless marriage with "an old Essex bumpkin between 45 and 50, owner of a fine unencumbered property and £12,000 a year!" Alice was delighted for her friend.[30] In her view, £12,000 a year trumped love any day.

Among the North American bourgeois and upper classes, money, property, and financial expectations were also priorities, but a culture of careful socializing and common expectations allowed love a greater place in marriage making. The routine of family life included extensive socializing—visits, teas, dinners, dances, berry picking, picnics, sleigh rides, church, and benevolent activities—all within a highly regulated social network of kinsfolk, friends, and acquaintances.

Few strangers crashed these invisible gates, cemented solid by a shared concern to protect those inside, especially young people of courtship age. In a circle of compatible suitors and almost always in groups, couples flirted and developed special friendships without the need for close parental supervision. They seldom rushed, waiting instead for love to root and determine their final choice of mate.

In Virginia, for example, Elizabeth Gamble rejected William Wirt's first proposal ("I have struck, and—have been stricken down … alas me!" he confided to a friend), then his second (this time "so gently, so sweetly, so angelically"), and his third, until finally, admitting that he held a place "deep in her secret heart," she accepted him.[31] In Upper Canada, Mary Gapper agreed to marry Edward O'Brien only after concluding that she would gain "the possession of a heart capable of entering into all my views & feelings & attached to me with an affection so exactly suited to my humour that I sometimes fancy that I myself have dictated it."[32] The system worked so well that most found mates within their own communities and religious denominations. The rest cast their nets farther afield or never married.

In the American South especially, romantic love was seen as the lifeline to a decent life, a guarantee that in a patriarchal society, an otherwise vulnerable wife would be respectfully treated by her loving husband. So clear was this understanding of the role of love that a great many women resisted marrying until they inspired love in a prospective husband. "I see so many unhappy matches it almost discourages me," wrote one young woman. Another observed that in marrying, her friend "has taken the irrevocable step by which her future is decided. Her happiness is in another hand."[33]

One clever young belle identified only as Miss Toombs, courted and loved by one lovelorn suitor after another, devised a strategy to evaluate her own feelings. "So, as they sat by the lamp she would look at him and inwardly ask herself, 'Would I be willing to spend the long winter evenings forever after sitting here darning your old stockings?' Never, echo answered. No, no, a thousand times no. So, each [suitor] had to make way for another."[34]

When love and money were not both present, parents made it clear that financial resources took priority. Sometimes their offspring rebelled. In Montreal in 1817, Cécile Pasteur incurred the displeasure of both her mother and brother by "sacking" her rich but unloved suitor. "I will never give my hand without giving my heart," she declared.[35] In Texas, Lizzie Scott defied her parents to marry financially unsound Will Neblett.

Others voluntarily entered loveless but financially secure marriages. After her friend did so, Upper Canadian Mary Hallen lamented, "I can conceive of nothing more dreadful, but peoples tastes are not all the same & I have heard some people say that those sort of matches turn out happier than love marriages but I cannot fancy it & think it far too great an experiment to be tried."[36] Southerner Marry Shannon deplored the loveless nuptials of a Miss Georgiana to Mr. Brown "or rather his money bags." Another young woman vowed that "adversity can not drive me to the extremity of marrying for mammon."[37] Women who believed that love was an essential tool to empower them in an inherently unequal relationship struggled hard to identify and nurture it in potential husbands. Romantic novels also influenced their view that just as love was ennobling, marrying without love was degrading.

Love for the Upper Classes

American Mary Westcott and French-Canadian Amédée Papineau faced no financial hurdles after they fell in love, but their religious differences—she was Presbyterian, he Catholic—loomed large. Years elapsed before they married, and the story of their convoluted courtship illustrates the system's underlying values and how it served the elite of both countries. The common denominator was social status and the wealth at its core.

Mary Eleanor Westcott was the fetching and cultured only daughter and stepdaughter of widowed merchant James Westcott of Saratoga Springs, New York, and his second wife, Mary. Louis-Joseph Amédée Papineau was the oldest son of Louis-Joseph Papineau, lawyer, political leader, and seigneur, whose conservative economic and patrician social views conflicted with his anti-imperialist republicanism and his virulent anti-clericalism. After a *Patriote* military defeat in 1837, Papineau fled to Saratoga Springs, where Amédée, a law student also sought by the authorities for his complicity in the rebellions, joined him. Amédée, who was fluent in English, resumed his legal studies and supported himself by teaching French at the Wayland Academy for girls.

For the next two years Amédée moved in the same social circle as Mary and he developed a friendship with her family that included attending her twelve-year-old brother's funeral. But it was only on December 1, 1840, just as he was about to depart for France where his exiled family had settled, that Amédée realized that he had fallen in love with her. He was twenty-two, Mary nineteen. After a long farewell, the young couple made do with long letters and newspaper clippings until June 1843, when Amédée returned to Saratoga. Before he did, Mary clarified her feelings for him, and he rejoiced in his diary: "Oh! happy man that I am."[38]

But their Saratoga reunion was brief and, after they shocked James Westcott with the news of their mutual affection, difficult. Westcott's primary fear, shared by his wife, was that marriage to Amédée would force Mary to abandon her Presbyterian beliefs and practice, which the Catholic Papineaus would mock. He was also loath to see the daughter he was so close to move all the way to Montreal, especially after losing his son. He did not order the lovers to break up but he decreed that they wait four or five more years to test their love, and that they correspond only occasionally. Mary gave Amédée a lock of her hair and swore eternal love. She also warned him that she would not forgive any infidelities. "My soul is so sad," Amédée lamented. In a poem, "Farewell to Mary W.," he wrote, "I must seek in another land my lot,/And strive dear Mary, to love thee not."[39]

Back in Lower Canada, where his political past had been forgiven, Amédée worked as protonotary of the Court of Queen's Bench in Montreal.[40] Obedient to James Westcott's command, he made do with a sparse correspondence and expressed his longing for Mary in poetry. Mary, on the other hand, was so conflicted that she contemplated breaking off with him, primarily over their religious differences. She asked herself if she really loved him, and deciding that she did, agonized over the pain her marriage to a Catholic foreigner would cause her parents. Finally, with her father's reluctant assent, she committed herself to marrying Amédée.

"So my dear child," wrote her stepmother,

> *you have taken the most important step in woman's existence; I think him the most desirable man I have met in many years; as a man, and a gentleman he exactly hits my mark, … in fact if he had been my own son, I do not know that I could wish him to be other than he appears to be, <u>except in his religion</u>— … I think his education, and his information, is superiour my sincere wish and desire is that you may be happy…. You must try and establish yourself in the Protestant faith, make it your study you will need a strong bulwark against their incursions…. Mrs. P has a brother who is a Priest, and they are so stealthy, so cuning, they leave not stone unturned to make one prosolite—I said so to Mr. P—your family and friends will look upon Mary as a Heretick, how shall we feel do you think? … he said how mistaken you are my Parents, are very liberal they can have no such feelings or any of my family.*[41]

Her stepmother's letter goes a long way to explain why Mary had struggled so hard with her feelings. In a letter to Amédée she pleaded for understanding and tried to convey something of what she had experienced.

> *I was subject, it is true, to no open influences, yet forever feeling the effects of an influence more powerful and dangerous, constantly strug-gling between my own feelings and filial duty ... I dared not trust to a self-examination, and for months I communed not with my spirit. You may not understand me. I think no one could, who had not passed thro it. I wrote you I should immediately tell my parents of any state of feeling, but ... I could not speak the words that would have roused the lion in the hearts of those who love me.*[42]

If her stepmother's deep-rooted suspicions about Catholic priestly proselytizing and her evident ignorance about the Papineaus' anticleri-calism were not obstacles enough, Mary's father pulled out all the stops in his campaign of relentless emotional blackmail. When, after years of waiting on tenterhooks for Mary to accept his proposal, Amédée proposed an early wedding date, Westcott refused outright. "The contents of [your letter] cause me many, and painful emotions. The separation from my daughter at any time, would make my heart to bleed, but the time you mention, so close at hand, I cannot even give it a thought." He added, "Mary is my only one and I must for once exer-cise, decidedly, a control, which will soon, in the same sense, be mine no longer."[43] When Amédée—jealously? petulantly?—wondered if Mary loved him less than she did her father, she reproached him: "Had I sisters, were there others to take my place, I could act fearlessly and with independence, but it is otherwise. You cannot know how my Father depends upon me for daily enjoyment," she wrote.[44] Unsurprisingly, Amédée had to accede to James Westcott's decision that they delay the wedding for a year, until May 20, 1846.

In early May, Amédée made a brief trip to Saratoga Springs, where he and Mary, accompanied by several friends to act as witnesses, signed a marriage contract that kept them separate as to property. In the event one spouse died, the survivor would receive an annual income of $600. Soon after, Amédée returned to his job in Montreal.

On May 19, Amédée returned to Saratoga with his father and brother, Lactance. The wedding ceremony was simple. Amédée had failed in his attempt to obtain the bishop of New York's dispensation for a Catholic wedding, and so the Reverend A.T. Chester, a Presbyterian minister, officiated. The ceremony, held in the Westcott family parlour, was over in fifteen minutes. There was a brief recital of the marriage rites. Amédée gave Mary a ring, and they joined hands. A short prayer followed the sacrament, and the guests began to celebrate. Lactance, Amédée's groomsman, or best man, doled out slices of wedding cake. Mary distributed flowers to the women. The guests ate and drank, then bid the new couple and their families farewell. The wedding trip that was not a honeymoon began.

Many couples went straight from their weddings to their new lodgings to begin married life. Others stayed with relatives or visited friends who had been unable to attend the ceremony. A few opted for a honeymoon, with its implications of privacy and withdrawing from the world. But the notion of newlyweds travelling alone was alien to the worldview that in uniting individuals, marriage also united families. A wedding trip, on the other hand, allowed the couple to experience the married state and the public to identify them as spouses. Parents could forge deeper relationships with their child's new spouse and in-laws. And so Mary and Amédée, who shared these fundamental values, happily set out on their wedding trip in company with her parents and his father and brother.

The wedding party toured, sometimes together, sometimes splitting off. Amédée and James Westcott visited construction sites and conducted business, Louis-Joseph and Lactance Papineau made a brief side trip to New York City, Mary explored the sights and shopped, sometimes with Amédée, sometimes with her parents. During one such excursion, her father bought her a rosewood Chickering piano for the enormous sum of $450. The wedding trip ended with a farewell dinner and champagne toasts onboard a Montreal-bound steamboat. Then, wiping away tears, the Westcotts bade their daughter goodbye.

Amédée's diary entries portrayed the wedding trip as a series of sight-seeing excursions and meetings; despite his poetic bent, he did not see it as a romantic time. In letters to her parents, Mary described her heart-break at leaving them "to return no more" rather than her joy at marry-ing her loved one, but a romantic breakfast with Amédée's friends in St. John's quickly dried her tears. Then she focused on the anxiety—swiftly dispelled—of truly entering her new life as Mary Papineau.

Her letters home reassured her parents as she reported even the minutiae of her busy days. Compared to slow and stately Saratoga Springs, Montreal was vast and impressive. Julie Papineau thrilled her new daughter-in-law, who spoke excellent French, with her warm and affectionate greeting. "I never felt more at ease in my own dear home than in the family circle I have now entered," Mary enthused. "Every thing is so well understood & easily done that one feels at home at once."[45] A week of visitors—upwards of one hundred—introduced her to the Papineau world, followed by a ball honouring her marriage. To make sure that Mary would shine, Julie Papineau gave her a "splendid

*Five years into married life, Mary and Amédée pose together
with the serene confidence that characterized their union.*

Brocade silk dress" that, embellished with precious jewellery, would outdo everyone else's. The marital alliance of Mary Westcott and Amédée Papineau started off well, and would continue so until her death in 1890.

On one level, the Westcott–Papineau marriage was a love affair that began uncertainly, unfolded tortuously (if not torturously), and triumphed as a lifelong union. Certainly both Mary and Amédée related on that emotional and erotic sphere. But however powerful their love, it led to their marriage only because the couple came from compatible backgrounds. Saratoga Springs was one of New York's wealthiest and most urbane towns, and the Westcotts were among its leading citizens. The professional and seigneurial Papineaus were not only wealthy but socially and politically dominant. The two families shared social standards and cultural appreciation; they valued education, spoke each other's language, and dressed and decorated similarly. Politically, too, they were compatible, republicans who saw no contradiction between their reformist principles and their privileged lifestyles.

But there were differences. To the Westcotts, Amédée's Catholicism was a giant stumbling block; to the Papineaus, Mary's Presbyterianism less so, at least theologically, because Louis-Joseph had renounced the Catholicism he was born into, though he continued to believe in God. Despite Mary's stepmother's fears, the Papineaus did not proselytize, and both Amédée and Mary attended each other's church services, apparently without conflict. Their other principal difference was nationality and geographical location, which they overcame with frequent and lengthy family visits. And so, with love as the wildcard, the two young people merged their worlds that were so much more compatible than different. After that, it was in everyone's interests to work hard to make the new alliance function smoothly.

A CONFEDERATE WEDDING, SEPTEMBER 1861

In the secessionist American South, another marriage, also inspired by romantic love, was forged in the traditional context of the community's social network.[46] Rebecca "Decca" Coles Singleton was a Southern belle engaged to Alexander Cheves Haskell, a devout Christian soldier on the staff of Brigadier-General Maxcy Gregg. Decca and Alex, both from prominent families, conducted their courtship within the safety of their families' social milieu, and Mary Boykin Chesnut, whose husband, James, was also a Confederate brigadier general, described the progress of their wartime romance. "Decca was the worst in love girl she ever saw," and Alex a persistent suitor. In letter after letter he urged Decca to let him marry her at once because, Chesnut observed, "in war times human events, life especially, are very uncertain."

Decca cried for days. Then she agreed to marry Alex right away. The plans were made: the wedding ceremony, in Charlottesville, Virginia, would be followed by a luncheon at Decca's grandfather's, and then a "brief slice of honeymoon" in Richmond. "The day came," Chesnut wrote. "The wedding-breakfast was ready, so was the bride in all her bridal array; but no Alex, no bridegroom. Alas! such is the uncertainty of a soldier's life. The bride said nothing, but she wept like a water-nymph."

At dinnertime, Alex appeared with his best man and an explanation that dried Decca's tears: circumstances over which he had no control had delayed him. After the lovers returned from a brief post-prandial stroll, Decca told Mary Chesnut to fetch the minister. "I mean to be married to-day," she insisted. "Alex says I promised to marry him to-day." Mary objected that it was too late that evening, but Decca, "the positive little thing," responded: "I don't care. I promised Alex to marry him to-day and I will. Send for the Rev. Robert Barnwell." Chesnut capitulated, "found Robert after a world of trouble, and the bride, lovely in Swiss muslin"—the same dress she had worn on her engagement day—"was married."

That night Chesnut vacated her bedroom so that the newlyweds could sleep alone. At dawn the next day, they boarded the train for a few days in Richmond. "Such is the small allowance of honeymoon permitted in war time," Chesnut wrote.

A year later, Decca gave birth to a daughter. Days later, grieving because she was convinced Alex had died in battle—though saying she had had "months of perfect happiness"—she died, pressing several of his unopened letters to her breast. She was buried in "the little white frock" that had been her engagement-wedding gown.

LOVE FOR THE WORKING CLASSES

A thrice-married old farmer's ruminations about marrying first for convenience and afterward for love are pragmatic and tinged with cynicism. Sam's first wife, who was also his cousin, "was not very pretty, but she was good and industrious [and had inheritance prospects].... She was fond of me, and I thought I could not do better than to make her my wife. It is all very well to marry for love ... if a fellow can afford it; but a little money is not to be despised; it goes a great way towards making the home comfortable." After his wife died in childbirth, Sam fell passionately in love. "There was a devilish fine gall in our village, only she was a leetle flighty, or so. The lads said to me, when they saw what I was after—'Sam, you had better carry your pigs to another market. The lass is not right in the upper works.'" But Sam, "desperately in love," did not heed the warning. Three days after the wedding, his beautiful new wife slit her throat, preferring "killing herself to living comfortably with me." Though her suicide sullied his reputation with eligible women, Sam married again, for love, to "a good woman."[47]

Unlike Sam, women struggled with the new ideals of companionate marriage. Elinore, a young domestic helper, was stunned when a former workmate announced their marriage banns even though she had not consented to marry him. She "had no sort of love for him tho' she likes him well enough to marry him," her employer reported.[48] For Elinore, publicly and dramatically courted, a few days' reflection decided the matter. Fearing the gossip her suitor's boldness might generate if she declined him, and impressed by his determination, Elinore accepted his proposal.

Elinore and other working women—and the men most would marry—had much at stake. Like their more privileged compatriots, they were fully aware that society expected them to marry, indeed was structured with married families at its core; they were aware, too, of the growing emphasis on love in marriage. Their task, then, was to find suitable mates whom they loved and were loved by.

Increasingly, working-class men and women assumed more control over their lives as their parents' authority was gradually diluted. As burgeoning cities full of hungry factories and bourgeois families demanded more workers, those workers came, from the countryside as well as from cities, to work in factories, shops, and private homes. Waged day labour began to replace the apprenticeship system. Men no longer had to wait to inherit a field or to take over a business. Women who earned and managed their own money became less dependent on their parents. As they accumulated dowries in the form of household goods and a little nest egg, they could now make concrete plans for the future. Usually, marriage topped the list.

In the nineteenth century, young working women preferred factory jobs to even worse-paid domestic service. These sisters pose in a photographer's studio holding shuttles, used to weave cloth, just before they leave Montreal to work in a Massachusetts textile mill.

Most married within their communities or groups, the son or daughter of a family friend or neighbour suggested by their parents, or a colleague or tradesperson they met while working. Love or strong attraction was a consideration, though seldom the decisive factor. Young women, for example, were warned against mistaking "romance" and "irrational love" for the kind of enduring affection marriage demanded. Instead, they were urged to choose a spouse who would fulfill both their expectations of family life and their sense of their personal worth as wage earners.

The families they established were unlike the old model of the working-class family that strove to produce almost everything it consumed. In North America, among the better off, a stay-at-home wife gradually became a status symbol, testimony to her husband's earning capacity. Many poorer wives also stayed home because their homemaking—gardening, churning butter, sewing and mending clothes, pickling and canning, soap- and candlemaking—was worth more to their families than the small wages they could earn outside. The wages of children old enough to send out to work would later compensate for this arrangement.

The exigencies of the quotidian grind tested and sometimes obliterated the ideal of companionate marriage between mutually respectful and loving spouses. That is not to deny that marriages were grounded in love; some were. But the imbalance of power between men and women that essentially stripped wives of personal autonomy made many of these marriages "an exercise in raw power."[49] Plenty of women were the victims of physical and emotional abuse, and some died as a result. But when that happened, public opinion tended to blame the women, and so did the judicial authorities. As an often reprinted caution to a daughter warned in 1777, "In the fate of a woman, marriage is the most important crisis: it fixes her in a state, of all others the most happy, or the most wretched."[50]

These stark reminders of a wife's vulnerability kept the role of marital love in perspective even as the ideal of companionate marriage evolved in popular culture. In the self-consciously companionate marriage of Southerners Elizabeth and William Wirt, who corresponded extensively when he was absent on business, the responsibility for marital happiness was hers. As a wife, she was expected to hide any traces of unhappiness, but William worried that Elizabeth, who described herself as "exceedingly unhappy," needed to learn this. "I cannot repress an apprehension," he wrote, "that … you will be drawing comparisons between the liberty you once enjoyed … [and] the high bounding hopes of your young heart … and the reality which has put an end of those hopes.… 'And now' do you not say to yourself 'all this is over—I am a wife and a mother.'"[51]

In a society that deemed marriage as much a civic responsibility as a personal necessity, and therefore disdained singles, love coexisted with (and sometimes vied with) economic considerations and family pressures in the push to the altar; love was increasingly associated with marriage. As the stay-at-home wife married to the male breadwinner gradually became the marriage model, the home was idealized as a haven for weary husbands, a sanctuary presided over by women who offered "disinterested love … ready to sacrifice everything at the altar of affection."[52] Instead of, or as well as, workmates, wives and husbands expected to be each other's soulmates. In literature if not in life, marriage became a happy ending rather than a lifelong narrative. The perennial heroine Jane Eyre evokes this sentiment when, at the end of her harrowing story, she announces triumphantly, "Reader, I married him."

ANGEL IN THE HOUSE

As literature and popular culture sentimentalized home and linked it with marriage, "Home Sweet Home" epitomized an ideal way of life. A subculture developed as doyens of domesticity preached their visions of what a good homemaker should do, and how she should do it. Wifeliness, the narrative went, was a demanding combination of domestic skills and moral standards that made a house a home, and a woman who succeeded in transforming herself into the "angel in the house" was rewarded with her society's approval and her husband's praise and protection.

The treacly glorification of wives was epitomized by admiring poet-husband Coventry Patmore's very long poem *The Angel in the House* (1854), a mystical approach to love that gained a huge readership and saddled generations of women with its title. Felix Vaughan, the husband in the poem, reflects that love is divinely ordained through Nature's parting of "each thing into 'him' and 'her,'/And, in the arithmetic of life,/the smallest unit is a pair," and he calls his beloved Honoria his "oh, strange, sweet half of me."

At the same time, Felix makes it clear that he chose carefully before falling in love—"A dear, good Girl! she'd have/Only three thousand pounds as yet;/More bye and bye"—and he also made sure to follow convention by asking her father's permission for his darling Honoria's hand in marriage. Honoria's father permitted Felix to court her, but his consent to marriage was contingent on her growing to love her suitor. Nonetheless, as the father of three unmarried daughters, he was properly appreciative of Felix's substantial income, estate, and prospects.

By the end of the nineteenth century, increasing longevity cast love in a new light. In 1711 in England, men died at an average age of thirty-two. By 1831, that had risen to forty-four, and by the end of the century, to the late fifties. The consequence to marriages was in how long they lasted: in the eighteenth century, about fifteen years, and more than double that by the end of the nineteenth.

The same was true of marriages in North America, where life expectancy also soared, from twenty to thirty years during the Colonial period when diseases such as measles, smallpox, and dysentery were endemic in a population already debilitated by infections and parasites. By the late eighteenth century, improved public health gave ten-year-old white males a life expectancy of almost fifty-seven years. (At the same time, African-American males, many of them slaves, had an estimated life expectancy of twenty-three years, 40 percent lower than for whites.)

Thanks in large part to improved medical practices, diet, housing, public health, and personal hygiene, the twentieth century ushered in the most extraordinary rise in life expectancy in human history, to about seventy-four from forty-six years for men and to eighty from forty-eight years for women.

If spouses lived much longer, so did marriages. In an era of sentimentalized marriage, those years and often decades could feel like an eternity if they were spent in a loveless union.

Marriage and Sex

The sentimentalization of marriage and the sanctification of wifedom had many subtexts. An angelic woman was supposed to entrust her well-being to her husband; he, in return, acted on her behalf in the economic and political spheres—he voted and she did not, for example. In the case of recalcitrant or otherwise difficult husbands, her moral superiority would prevail; she was, for example, advised to feign giggly girlishness. (An intelligent woman "may be admired but she will never be beloved," one devoted father reminded his teenaged daughter, who had a passion for the classics.)[53]

But this simultaneous veneration and infantilization also desexualized the Angel: who, after all, lusts after someone so never-wrong, self-sacrificing, and passionless? So, with longer engagements and a double standard that enforced female but not male chastity, legions of men approached their wedding beds with sexual experience and expectations while their (usually) virginal wives waited quavering, either dreading the imminent violation or longing for this final consummation.

Sex was couched in contradictory terms that could confuse and appall as well as delight. Sex meant pleasure for men but pain for women. In an era of rampant prostitution, it spread venereal disease that crippled its victims and their children. It involved body parts otherwise associated with effluvia. It was a woman's moral and legal duty to submit to it. A husband could take legal action against a wife who managed to withhold sex, but a wife could not lay rape charges against a husband who forced sex on her.

This double standard also permitted men to indulge in extramarital sex, visiting prostitutes or, for the few who could afford it, taking mistresses. Women, however, had to remain chaste, because the legitimacy of their family bloodline was at stake. The consequence was that a Good Wife was supposed to tolerate sex without enjoyment, to satisfy her husband's sexual needs. Medical and popular literature justified this version of proper sexual relations, describing the female organism as colder and calmer than the male and, if not passionless, then at least less sexually motivated than the male. (It helped that the Good Husband tried not to shock his Good Wife with the kind of foreplay and sexual practices he associated with mistresses or even prostitutes.) If—to a Good Wife's surprise and shock—she responded to sex with unexpected arousal, she worried that she was morally degraded, and many husbands felt the same way. One confided to Marie Stopes, whose book *Married Love* was initially banned in the United States, that his wife's orgasm had frightened him because he "thought it was some sort of fit."[54]

As a result of this dissonant sexual culture, some husbands could scarcely bring themselves to have sex with their Good Wives. A man of Stopes's acquaintance, "after a loose life, met a woman whom he reverenced and adored. He married her, but to preserve her "purity," her difference from the others, he never had sexual relations with her."

In the American South, the issue had racial overtones rooted in slavery, as white males sought erotic satisfaction with women of colour rather than their wives. Until slavery ended, they followed the "tradition" of losing their virginity with a black woman, usually a slave. "Why, Sir, if you could only see [white men] slipping around at night, trying to get into negro women's houses, you would be astonished," a mulatto man testified just after emancipation.[55] Thereafter, white men sought out and forced themselves on women of colour, poisoning both the women's family lives and their own. Twentieth-century Mississippi-born writer Willie Morris was twelve before he realized that white women, too, were sexual beings. The white woman, one observer remarked, "was not supposed to know she was a virgin until she ceased to be one."[56]

During the slave era, some white wives fought back in myriad ways, including lashing or selling off slave women their husbands favoured. Most, however, preferred to feign ignorance of the paternity of their household's light-skinned children, including those born to slave concubines assigned to the Big House so they would always be sexually accessible. White wives accepted the double standards—gender and racial—entrenched in their culture, softened by a few associated "privileges," notably the laws that protected their wifely status and denied the legitimacy of any children born of a husband's illicit relationship. These laws, decreeing that the offspring of slaves inherited their mother's status, resolved the thorny issue of many mulattoes—12.5 percent of the African-American population by 1860—though they ran counter to English common law. (Some mulattoes were born to white mothers with black lovers or, rarely, black husbands.)

It would be easy to conclude that because of the sexual double standard and the repression of so many women, North America was teeming with sexually frustrated wives. Yet many wives unabashedly enjoyed marital sex as much as their husbands did. Robert and Eliza Hoyle, he a widower in his fifties with three children, and she thirty-eight, apparently enjoyed a satisfying (and fruitful) sex life she playfully referred to as "disturbing his repose." Confederate war bride Ellen Shackelford Gift teased her soldier husband: "I am so very glad that you were drugged or 'Shanghaied'"—their code word for sex—"on your last visit, & was it not a sweet little visit after all Darling?"[57] Another Confederate wife, Jane Goodwin, sent her soldier husband a letter so erotic it amounts to private pornography:

> *[Do] you ever suffer your mind to scan the scenes of love and pleasure of the first night's transactions, which was only witnessed and enjoyed by ourselves.... Think, James, my dear husband, [of] the night we first retired to the midnight couch, one by one to enjoy the highest streams of pleasure that the soul and body ever knows.... Soon did I feel my delicate form embraced by his gigantic and robust one for a pillow and the other fondling with anxiety over my small but firm breastworks ... you becoming more adventurous inclined your right downward you know where ... better to ascertain the position and strength of my noble and generous battery, which so often has given you relief and pleasure. Your remarks so singular as a Quaker: Jane, hoist thy linen, spread thy thighs abroad and receive the seed of Jacob in the name of the Lord. James ... procure a furlough.... I think a certain portion of it is necessary to life.... You would find only one difficulty in charging my battery—your ammunition might give*

out.... you need not fear ... reinforcements could be brought up every
twelve hours.... You have charged many times satisfactory to both of
us without even the amputation of a limb ... write soon.[58]

Jane Goodwin was by no means alone in luxuriating in sexual intercourse, and in using it to keep her absent husband connected to her. But
countless other women were terrified of yet another pregnancy or horrified when newlywed friends died in childbirth—in the antebellum
South, at twice the rate of northern women—and they conflated sex
with childbirth and potential death, a potent combination of negatives
that far outweighed intercourse's transitory joys. Lizzie Nesblett, who
had already borne five children, wrote to her husband in despair, "This
constant & never ceasing horror I have of childbearing constantly
obtrudes itself between me and & my desire & longing to see & clasp
you round the neck once more, & thus my longing wears a curb."[59]

Other women, with low expectations of enjoyment, kept silent, and
a contingent of white middle-class women, perhaps responding to the
popular perception of female arousal as a perversion, welcomed unsatisfying sex as evidence of their suitability as moral guardians. They
accepted that procreation, the purpose of marriage, must involve at least
some sex, but they shuddered at the moral implications of sex for pure
pleasure, or as a way to deepen intimacy.

When illnesses real or feigned kept spouses apart, some women
relished the respite from sexual intercourse. Harriet Beecher Stowe,
petite and worn out with the drudgery of child-rearing in straitened
circumstances, extended her stay at Brattleboro sanitarium, where, with
her sister, Catharine, she lodged in the aptly named Paradise Row, took
"water cures," exercised in the fresh air, and spent hours conversing with
other women. After one visit, Calvin Stowe railed against his sexual
deprivation and "the mean business of sleeping in another bed, another
room, and even another house, and being with you as if you were a
withered-up old maid sister instead of the wife of my bosom ... this
having the form of marriage and denying the power thereof is, to my mind,
of all contemptible things the most unutterably contemptible." He had
not slept with her since her last miscarriage, a year earlier, he

complained, and "it is enough to kill any man, especially a man such as I am." Harriet, unmoved by his pleas, stayed at Brattleboro for eighteen months. "Not for years, have I enjoyed life as I have here," she reflected.[60] Nine months after returning home, she gave birth to a son.

Some women avoided sex with men altogether, and remained unmarried, usually in their parents' home or with relatives. Others lived in quiet contentment with other women, expressing their feelings and yearnings behind closed doors, lesbians before the term was invented. Victorians approved romantic friendships among girls, who expressed their feelings for each other in the most extravagant language, and kissed and fondled each other. What were they, after all, but girlhood rehearsals for marriage, the great drama of a woman's life? (Henry Wadsworth Longfellow answered this rhetorical question in *Kavanaugh*.)

After Henry James observed in *The Bostonians* that adult versions of these friendships were very common in New England, they became known as Boston marriages. Boston marriages were committed, usually chaste love relationships between women, most of them unmarried working professionals. The difference between romantic friendships and Boston marriages was cohabitation, which in itself provoked no suspicions about possible homosexuality. North American spinsters and widows reliant on their own devices often pooled resources by living together. Especially after the American Civil War created so many spinsters and widows, the practicality of unrelated, unattached women sharing living quarters was recognized and accepted.

Cloaked in this social respectability, Boston marriages thrived. In the absence of a controlling male, they provided the structure and domestic context for women to achieve their personal goals. Some wanted just to go through life together. Others had professional or artistic aspirations. "Out of the darkness of the nineteenth century," writes Lillian Faderman, "they miraculously created a new and sadly short-lived definition of a woman who could do anything, be anything, go anywhere she please."[61]

Some Boston marriages stemmed from a refusal to endure the constraints of heterosexual marriage rather than from homosexual orientation. An artistic woman committed a "moral wrong" by marrying, wrote nineteenth-century sculptor Harriet Hosmer, because either her art or her household would suffer, making her a poor artist or a poor mother. "I urge eternal feud with the consolidating knot," she declared. But some women tied consolidating knots with each other.

Varieties and Vagaries of Married Sexuality

For wives, or for women who expected to marry, the notion of female sexual satisfaction was fraught. To admit that female orgasms were essential to sexual satisfaction implied that non-orgasmic women were unhappy, perhaps because their husbands were incompetent lovers. (It also meant that women had to know or learn what orgasms were.) And if sex was an integral part of the romantic love that was increasingly invoked as an important factor in marrying, then unsatisfied spouses had legitimate complaints. If they were legitimately unhappy, they might reasonably look at a wide range of solutions to end their unhappiness. This had such horrifying implications, notably divorce as the logical consequence of failed marital love, that it skewed discussions about sex and its meaning until the sexual revolution cut to the bones, simplifying, permitting, and forgiving.

Sexual fidelity was another area of contention. The double standard was tolerant of bachelors who had sex with prostitutes, less forgiving of husbands with extramarital adventures. But the man who had pressured his fiancée to have premarital sex could break off their engagement on the grounds that she was an impure woman, and any wife who cheated was furiously denounced. A primary reason for this double standard was that female fidelity guaranteed paternity, to say nothing of loyalty and obedience to a husband. (We know through DNA testing as well as anecdotal evidence that at least 10 percent of us are not our fathers' biological offspring. The laws, anticipating this possibility, awarded husbands the paternity of all children born in the marriage.)

A 1929 study details the attitudes of 2,200 women to marriage and sex. Almost all were educated white women of means, married and unmarried; because most of them were born before 1890, their responses reflected late- and post-Victorian attitudes and values, and were likely more open than those early in the nineteenth century.

Of the married women, 90 percent said their husband's sex drive matched or was stronger than theirs; only 3.3 percent claimed their own was stronger. Forty percent of wives and 64.8 percent of unmarried women masturbated, though two-thirds agreed that this was "morally degrading." The 12 percent who denied having any sexual feelings or experience claimed they were the happiest. Slightly more than half of the single women had had "intense emotional relations" with other women; of these, more than half described their behaviour as overtly homosexual.

To compile "an index of current feeling and thought, a reflection of the mores of today and yesterday" regarding sex, Davis asked single women the following questions:

Do you believe sex intercourse necessary for complete physical and mental health? (No: 61.2%)

Is a young man before marriage ever justified in having sex intercourse? (No: 79%)

Is a young woman before marriage ever justified in having sex intercourse? (No: 80.5%)

Is a husband ever justified in having sex intercourse with a woman or women other than his wife? (No: 75.8%)

Is a wife ever justified in having sex intercourse with a man or men other than her husband? (No: 79.2%)

Are married people justified in having intercourse except for the purpose of having children? (Yes: 84.6%)

The results of Davis's survey confirm the evidence of personal correspondence, memoirs, and contemporary accounts of nineteenth-century women's attitudes toward marital sex. Denying and repressing sexual urges was one of them. Female orgasms were particularly frightening. Marie Stopes, whose own five-year marriage was annulled on the grounds of non-consummation, likened women's sexual desire to "a rhythmic sex-tide" with a "Periodicity of Recurrence of Desire."[62]

The frequency of sex in marriage was another sensitive issue. Though even sexual moderates such as Martin Luther had suggested three times weekly for spouses in their prime, the North American moral purity movement, which dated from the 1830s, advocated sex no more than once a month, and only for procreation. Dr. John Harvey Kellogg, author of *Plain Facts about Sexual Life* (and creator of Kellogg's Corn Flakes, designed to be nourishing and so bland that they numbed all taste buds), described sex as "the reproductive act ... the most exhausting of all acts." Rather than risk that exhaustion, and despite being married, Kellogg practised lifelong celibacy and died a virgin.

Masturbation, the self-love that proved what marital sex so often did not—that women could reach, and revel in, orgasms—became an urgent social concern. Masturbating was condemned as immoral, perverted, and the cause of imbecility, insanity, consumption, blindness, cowardice, the inability to look people in the face, melancholy, split hair ends, constipation, epilepsy, apoplexy, paralysis, premature old age, even (probably welcome) death. A book describing masturbation as "man's sin of sins, vice of vices [causing] incomparably more sexual dilapidation, paralysis and disease, as well as demoralization, than all the other sexual depravities combined," sold more than half a million copies.[63] *Our Family Physician* (1871), a widely consulted and much-reprinted home health manual, warned that "there is probably no vice which is more injurious to both mind and body ... the whole man becomes a wreck, physically, morally and mentally."[64]

A vast market developed for devices and medications to control masturbation or nip it in the bud. (Even wet dreams were dangerous.) These included "erection alarms, penis cases, sleeping mitts, bed cradles to keep the sheets off the genitals and hobbles to keep girls from spreading their legs."[65] Some worried parents improvised by tying their children's hands behind their backs or to bedposts. The more fanatical resorted to straitjackets.

Astonishingly, or at least counterintuitively amid the century's "masturbation phobia," clinical, physician-administered masturbation emerged as a treatment for female "hysteria," the term used to describe many "female conditions," including the absence of orgasm.[66] In an era when the respected *British Medical Journal* debated, as it did in 1878, whether the touch of a menstruating woman's hand could spoil a ham and concluded that it could, female orgasms, like menstruation and menopause, were viewed as crises.

Rachel Maines, a historian of masturbation, estimates that at least half of women in Western cultures failed to reach orgasm during vaginal sex. But because male ejaculation during intercourse was "known" to satisfy both man and woman, and to suggest that a man was an inadequate lover was a heresy, women's symptoms—their failure to achieve orgasm or satisfaction, that is, their hysteria—were pathologized, medicalized, and treated.

The treatments included hydrotherapy, with strong jets of water pulsating onto the genitals, or having a physician perform "vulvular stimulation" that, by bringing (or trying to bring) a woman to climax, eased her hysteria. But physicians found these pelvic massages tiring and tedious, and many grumbled that a husband's penis should be doing the job instead. In 1880, Dr. Kelsey Stinner invented the first battery-operated vibrator for women to treat themselves at home (and to relieve his colleagues). Though the first vibrators were large, awkward, and expensive, "vibration therapy" became very popular and widely available. Luxury resorts in North America and Europe offered "musical vibrators, counterweighted vibrators, vibratory forks, undulating wire coils called vibratiles, vibrators that hung from the ceiling, vibrators attached to tables and floor models on rollers."[67]

In 1902, the Hamilton Beach company patented the first electric model for retail sale. The vibrator became the fifth electrified domestic appliance after the sewing machine, the fan, the teakettle, and the toaster, and preceded the vacuum cleaner and iron by a decade. Manufacturers disguised their vibrators' sexual connotations with medical terminology, describing them as appliances designed to produce not orgasms but "hysterical paroxyms" that relieved pathological hysteria. Advertisements in such popular women's magazines as *Needlecraft*, *Woman's Home Companion*, *Modern Priscilla*, and the Sears, Roebuck catalogue used the vocabulary of healthful self-help, promising rest, strength, rejuvenation, and, daringly, "release." These advertisements disappeared only in the 1920s, when vibrators began to be associated with pornography.

Learning how to use the vibrator, 1891. By 1900, vibrators were available for home use. Its erotic uses were euphemistically noted. Hamilton Beach's vibrator included six "special attachments" and a "300 page library bound book, profusely illustrated," instructing how to apply them.

Women were not the sole victims of sexual anxiety. Male impotence, sporadic or chronic, was a private embarrassment that sometimes became a public shame. In many jurisdictions, unconsummated marriages could be annulled, and the primary cause of non-consummation was male impotence. (In canon law, the impotent female was defined as "so narrow that she cannot be rendered large enough to have carnal relations with a man," but records do not indicate that anyone was ever prosecuted.) In the mid-sixteenth century, French churchmen aggrieved by the notion that in marrying, impotent men were attacking the church's authority, tracked them down and inspected their genitals for proof of erection and ejaculation. One accused's erection was rejected because of its "tension, hardness and duration." Others were invalidated as merely byproducts of an urgent need to urinate.

The French Revolution ended these humiliating trials but not the shame of impotence and its assumed association with infertility. In the words of popular writer John Marten, whose *Onania* (1712) sparked eighteenth-century Europe's anti-masturbation crusade:

> *For as the due Erection and Stiffness of the* Yard *is one main qualification for the performing the Office of a Husband, so no less is the regular ejaculation of the* Seed *thro' the* Yard *so erected. [The impotent man,] Unfruitful, and not able to Generate, ... is a useless Member to the Commonwealth in which he lives, and One, whom the Fair Sex would avoid, unless it were to look at him, Point and Laugh with their Fans before their Faces, as not fit for that Conversation, which they are so susceptible of, and take so much Delight and Pleasure in.*[68]

Impotence inspired much genuine and pseudo-medical literature and countless recipes and products to reverse it: Nervous Cordial and Botanical Syrup, Cordial Balm of Gilead, galvanic cures, and physicians' remedies such as cold bathing of genitals, bloodletting, purges, and painful injections or candle-like bougie probes into the urethra. In the eighteenth century, English surgeon John Hunter dismissed masturbation as a cause of impotence and declared that male pride—such as anxiety about deflowering a virgin—could bring it on. Men who had consorted with prostitutes, for example, could be rendered impotent by guilt at the thought of sex with their pristine and sexually unresponsive brides. (One such woman read during the sexual act, stopping only to inquire if her husband were through. A few books later, his erotic urges had withered to near impotency.)

Female prudishness and frigidity were also blamed for male impotence. A woman might feign sexual passivity to conceal what she feared was her overly bestial nature or, much more commonly, as a form of birth control. The ferocious female erotic appetite was equally a cause of male impotence. So were the sight and smell of a woman's body. As Charles Kingsley confided to his fiancée, Fanny, he would need to learn "to bear the blaze of your naked beauty. You do not know how often a man is struck powerless in body and mind on his wedding night."[69]

Conversely, ugliness, a "flabby vulva, or a very large vagina," to say nothing of menstrual blood, body odour, or false teeth, could erode a man's sexual power. This was the case for nineteenth-century writer John Ruskin, whose (still virginal) wife, Effie, won an annulment on the grounds that he was impotent. On their marriage bed, something about Effie's naked body had disgusted him: either that, unlike the Greek statutes he so loved, Effie had pubic hair or, more likely, that she was menstruating.

Or perhaps Effie's sin was that she failed to practise "feminine hygiene." Had she lived a few decades later, she might have read the July 1933 issue of *McCall's Magazine*—among hundreds of sources—and learned that "fewer marriages would flounder around in a maze of

Poor Mary did not know that her female odour and her ignorance of Lysol were standing between her and Dave. For decades Lysol was marketed and used as a vaginal douche and a contraceptive.

misunderstanding and unhappiness if more wives knew and practiced regular marriage hygiene." What she needed was to cleanse her vagina with Lysol, the douche that would appeal to her womanly fastidiousness and also stave off pregnancy. Used regularly and correctly—and the manufacturers promised to elaborate on this in a helpful booklet forwarded in a plain envelope—Lysol would ensure "health and harmony" throughout a marriage.[70] With this "power to please" within her grasp, indeed within her household cleaning supplies, the once flailing wife could banish the odoriferous aging process, rekindle the restorative air of romance—and stop contributing to her husband's impotence.

Unsavoury as their women might be, males were also to blame for their own flabby failings: alcohol, tobacco, evil thoughts, drugs, masturbation, overly spicy food. Husbands were bombarded with ads for Therapion, Dr. McLaughlin's Electric Belt, and Wood's Phosphodine. Marie and Pierre Curie's discovery of radioactivity in 1898 led enterprising charlatans such as William J.A. Bailey to market "radium therapy" for impotence and other medical issues. Bailey, a Harvard dropout earlier fined for promoting a strychnine pill as an aphrodisiac, changed directions and sold bottled radioactive water as Radithor, a cure for impotence and decreased sexual drive. But the company shut down after millionaire American amateur-golf champion, steel manufacturer, and socialite Eben M. Byers died in 1932 of dissolved bones after guzzling gallons of Radithor—"The Radium Water Worked Fine Until His Jaw Came Off," the *Wall Street Journal* sniped in a headline.

Despite Radithor's bad publicity, men (in the Roman poet Ovid's felicitous phrase) "as limp as yesterday's lettuce" continued to seek out potions and salves and penis splints, to no avail. (How much simpler and metaphoric earlier European folk cures had been: a husband peeing through his wife's wedding ring or through a church keyhole.) Respectable physicians offered treatment as well but only, warned Dr. Irvin S. Koll, after "the charlatan, faith healer, and Christian Scientist have also had their fling at him."

Koll's magisterial *Diseases of the Male Urethra Including Impotence and Sterility* (1918) is a grim reminder of what that treatment entailed.

Koll urged physicians to recognize the urgency of restoring male potency to make "barren marriages becom[e] fruitful and lessen the many instances of marital infelicity which are so appallingly due to sexual incapacity on the part of the afflicted male." Impotence was a "true pathology" that led to mental illness and even suicide, and—how comforting this would have been to cure-seekers—"patients should not be dismissed with an exhortation to 'forget it,' a so-called aphrodisiac pill, which is valueless, or possibly the passage of a urethral sound or a cold rectal irrigation."

Koll's recommendations echoed the Victorian era's regimen of cauterizing and injecting or probing the urethra. These "cures," rooted in the conviction that impotence was caused by masturbation, "the vicious habit of indulging in *coitus interruptus*," and other sexual excesses, pained and punished the sufferer. While one physician was masturbating the "hysterical" wife to orgasm, another was inserting endoscopes or syringes with caustic liquid into the impotent husband's penis, massaging his prostate through his rectum, administering rectal suppositories, and ordering hot sitz baths twice daily.

War injuries wounded or castrated thousands of men and accounted for a majority of the cases categorized as impotence in military records. In ground campaigns where combat soldiers knelt, sat, or lay prone during battle, they were often wounded in the buttocks or genitals, and the kidney, bladder, prostate, urethra, penis, testes, and spermatic cord could be perforated by bullets or bone fragments. Until the mid-nineteenth century, for example in the Crimean War, such injuries were more often fatal. But during the Civil War, American physicians began to save a much greater number of them.

One was a twenty-one-year-old private from the 8th Ohio Infantry retrieved from the field after the Battle of Cold Harbor, June 3, 1864: "Wounded by a ball in the left of the scrotum, passing backward and wounding the testis, urethra, and rectum.... Right testis gone; persistent urethral fistula; incontinence of urine and severe pain on exercise; occasional discharges of matter from urethra and rectum; disability total."[71]

During the Civil War, when thousands of such wounds were documented, sexual dysfunction after pelvic injuries was both common and untreatable, and the National Archives Pension files are filled with records "of impotence and depression related to loss of sexual function." The continued suffering, sadness, and frustration must have darkened many marriages as spouses attempted to cope with veterans' sexual wreckage.

It could not have helped that popular culture also stuck it to impotent men with its assumptions that impotence meant infertility, and that the might of an erection was the measure of a man. As historian Kevin J. Mumford writes, "advertising pitches for impotence remedies suggest that a new standard of male sexuality—'giant strength and power,' 'enlarged organs,' and 'sexual power'—was gradually emerging and becoming more and more central to constructions of masculinity."[72]

SEXUALIZED MARRIAGE

The new century hastened the transformation of marriage. The suffragette movement, rooted in nineteenth-century abolitionism, offered women different visions and priorities and exposed the inequality of domestic sexual politics. The Angel stormed out of her house to picket government offices and demand the right to vote. Wives and single women protested their political impotence.

Newspapers and magazines featured photographs and cartoons of policemen hauling respectable middle-class women to prison, and of guards force-feeding them during hunger strikes. Public outrage at their mistreatment won the suffragettes much support.

By the early 1900s, the sentimental ideal of separate, complementary male and female spheres was crumbling. World War I intensified the process of gender integration as women took over jobs vacated by servicemen and made their presence felt in their communities. Suffragettes, most middle class, often Protestant, and well educated, borrowed familiar rhetoric and shaped it to their goals, arguing that their moral superiority and motherly instincts would leaven the male political sphere just as they did the family. Giving women the vote, they

*Miss G. Brytton costumed as a gentleman, Montreal, 1895. Cross-dressing
became popular as women responded to the suffragette movement, to the demand
for more suitable garb for cycling, and to the introduction of (much-ridiculed)
bloomers. Other women cross-dressed so they could join the military or get jobs
restricted to men. Dress reform movements reflected women's great frustration with
restrictive fashion. The social aspects of cross-dressing were stronger than its
sexual connotations.*

declared, would strengthen both family and society through child
welfare, education and farm reform, temperance, moral purity, and
applied Christianity.

By the second decade of the twentieth century, North American
women began to win voting rights, Canadian women first in Manitoba,
in 1916, then federally in 1919 (though in 1917 women with close relatives in the military could vote on their behalf), and finally in Quebec,
in 1940. In the United States, Washington state granted voting rights in
1910 and the federal government in 1920, when the Nineteenth
Amendment was ratified.

Sexual liberation was also in the air. In 1916, Margaret Sanger opened the first birth control clinic. The family planning it provided had been unavailable to her mother, a devout Roman Catholic who endured eighteen pregnancies that produced eleven live births. Sanger also wrote popular books, such as *What Every Girl Should Know* (1916)—which dealt straightforwardly with menstruation and adolescent sexuality—and *What Every Mother Should Know* (1917), and founded and edited the monthly periodical *The Birth Control Review and Birth Control News.*

Sanger promoted birth control not as a means to facilitate indiscriminate sex but as a way to empower working women otherwise crushed by too much child-bearing. Women were so desperate for birth control information that, between 1921 and 1926, they bombarded Sanger with one million letters.

The New Woman of the 1900s had a more hedonistic interest in sex than Sanger did. This New Woman spoke openly about sexual passion and sometimes indulged in it. She wore less confining clothes than her mother had. After World War I, she donned flapper garb, bobbed or shingled her short hair, flattened her breasts with chest bands, wore short skirts and bare legs and arms, reddened her lips, rouged her cheeks, smoked cigarettes. She "dated" boys and sometimes necked and petted. She finished high school and sometimes went on to college or university. She could aspire to a professional job, though obtaining it was less likely. She valued self-realization and self-determination over selfless, moral loftiness. "Here she comes, running, out of prison and off the pedestal; chains off, crown off, halo off, just a live woman," the writer Charlotte Perkins Gilman enthused.

The New Woman criticized marriage as a bourgeois institution corroded by male tyranny, but she married anyway, hoping and expecting to find happiness and love. With birth control, she could control her fertility. If she were unhappy, she might divorce. But despite her rejection of Victorian gender segregation, the New Woman remained a wife dependent on her breadwinner husband. In fact, writes legal scholar Nancy Cott, "the economic bargain between a husband-provider and a wife-dependent had become the most important public stake in marriage."[73]

Nonetheless, many people feared that the institution of marriage was decaying. As august a person (and as ardent a lover) as Theodore Roosevelt was shocked that lovelessness could break up a marriage. Love, erotic as well as romantic, had become so integral to marriage that marriage was sinking under its weight.

When Roosevelt lost his beloved Alice, the passionate love they shared was increasingly common between spouses. More and more people resisted settling for pure convenience because, like Jane Austen, they believed that "anything is to be preferred or endured rather than marrying without Affection." After millennia, the centrality of love in marriage was strongly developing.

Chapter 5

Marriage from within Four Walls

HOUSING AND HOUSEKEEPING

"A very dangerous woman," Martha Coffin Wright's neighbours deemed her, and to people opposed to freedom for slaves and rights for women, she was indeed a menacing presence. She attended and chaired anti-slavery meetings at a time when they required armed defenders against pro-slavery mobs, and wrote reviews for political and abolitionist publications such as *The Liberator*. She welcomed black abolitionists into her home and hid fugitive slaves northward-bound via the Underground Railway; later she developed a close friendship with African-American slave rescuer Harriet Tubman. With her older sister, Lucretia Mott, Martha helped organize the historic Seneca Falls Women's Rights Convention of 1848, which she attended heavily pregnant with her seventh child.

Despite her fervour for social justice, Martha Wright was also a Good Wife governed by her society's conventions about homemaking. Even with her heavy volunteer commitments, she had to raise her four children (three others died), operate a household, and earn money. "The only way is to grub & work, & sweep & dust, & wash & dress children, & make gingerbread, & patch and darn," she wrote. Housework was endless. Unlike her husband at his place of work, the wife

amid incessant clamor, must renew the treadmill task of yesterday— must wash the same faces, make the same beds, sweep the same rooms;

must settle disputes in the Kitchen, & quarrels among the ... fallen little sons and daughters of her Adam: and amid all these occupations, must find occasional moments to "stitch-stitch-stitch" the innumerable garments needed in a family.

Let her look to it ... that she gets through this in time to clothe her harassed and worn visage in those "wreathed smiles" so indispensable toward maintaining the good humor of her liege lord. He too has had troubles to encounter ... but not of that petty, harassing kind that are wearing away the spirits & the life of the partner he has chosen.

The husband sleeps at night while his wife "rises weary & unrefreshed, again to go through the same routine."[1]

Martha was no malcontent; she was a much loved—and loving—wife: "I was not aware before of how much I loved you Dearest, but your absence leaves such a blank in my existence," David wrote her. (Her first husband, Peter Pelham, who died leaving her a nineteen-year-old widowed mother, had been more ardent: "I have never loved, until I knew you.... beauty united with wit & taste.") But even in the most loving, companionate relationship, and like countless other middle-class wives, Martha was "too busy to live."[2]

Though a hired domestic relieved a small part of her burden, Martha was perpetually exhausted, especially by her "vociferous and boisterous" children and by interminable, essential sewing. "There is only one day out of 7 that the baby sleeps long enough for me to take a needle in my fingers," she wrote to Lucretia. Yet somehow, she had to make all her family's clothes, make purses, knit socks and hats, and make most of the household linens. She commented about an acquaintance pregnant with her fifteenth child, "I should think she would commit suicide."[3]

When Martha visited Boston to help at the birth of her fourteenth grandchild and instead contracted a fatal case of typhoid pneumonia, her close friend and women's rights colleague Susan B. Anthony grieved: "I could not believe it; clear-sighted, true and steadfast almost beyond all other women!" Throughout her lifetime, Martha railed against society's expectations of the Good Wife, all the while fulfilling them,

Martha Coffin Wright and David Wright

and somehow managing to remain "a very dangerous woman" in pursuit of social justice.

As bride and groom began to forge a life together, their housing and housekeeping arrangements profoundly affected their marriage. Europeans, who would later remake North America in their own image, emphasized sociability over privacy. By the end of the late Middle Ages, city houses featured living quarters on upper floors with business conducted downstairs at street level. The custom of keeping livestock in adjacent outbuildings was dying out. Wood, fireplaces, and chimneys were replacing earthen floors, open hearths, and the roof holes that drew out smoke. Two-storeyed houses were becoming common. Windows were glazed. After the Great Fire of London, in 1666, those who could afford it built with brick and stone rather than wood.

Medieval families included as secondary members unrelated domestics and apprentices as well as boarders and "unfortunates"—orphans, old folk, invalids—placed in their care by local authorities. In the rare event that parents survived into old age, they too lived with their offspring. Apprentices and journeymen, even the children of gentry and nobles sent to other families to learn the dynamics of the world they would inhabit, lived and slept cheek by jowl with their masters.

As John Dod and Robert Cleaver taught in their much-reprinted *A Godly Form of Household Government: For the Ordering of Private Families, According to the Direction of God's Word* (1621), masters and mistresses were like fathers and mothers to their servants and apprentices, bound to provide good food, drink, and lodging; to comfort, relieve, and cherish them in sickness as in health; and to "correct" them when they erred.

In return, servants and apprentices owed their masters cheerful compliance, courtesy, and moral behaviour. They were to beg forgiveness if they spoke in anger. They were not to run away. They were to do anything asked of them unless it were "unhonest, unlawful, wicked, unjust, or ungodly, then they must in no wise obey it."

Residents of these mixed households functioned on levels of considerable intimacy. When nature called, they defecated and urinated in the chamber pots kept in most rooms, and breathed in each other's bad smells. They bathed infrequently, had unsavoury personal hygiene, seldom changed their clothing and—rich and poor—were riddled with lice and fleas. They had few possessions or furniture, except for dining tables. In prosperous families, younger children played in the kitchen and courtyard; older ones studied at the dining table.

In large homes, the rooms were multi-purpose. In smaller ones, one or two rooms accommodated all residents and all activities, including cooking, working, and sleeping. Beds, often curtained, were placed wherever they fit; as some people slumbered, others continued their activities in the same room. Beds were also shared space, and couples lay side by side with their children, unrelated household members, guests, or travellers.

This lack of privacy made marital intimacies difficult or impossible. Co-residents heard each other converse and squabble, and sometimes intervened, for example when a wife was being abused. They saw what their housemates did and who visited them. They were privy to other people's sexual encounters. Though some thinkers, for example the Puritan theologian William Perkins, had begun to teach that "the marriage-bed signifieth that solitarie and secret societie, that is betweene man and wife alone," privacy was rare.[4] Martin Luther's household included not just his wife, Katharina, and their six children but a constant supply of student boarders, his nephew Andraesel, and one of Katharina's nephews. In historian Philippe Ariès's words, "People lived on top of one another, masters and servants, children and adults, in houses open at all hours to the indiscretions of the callers. The density of society left no room for the family."[5]

Early European colonists transported this form of household to North America, where shared beds were common, children learned about sex by observing it, and one's personal life was laid bare to all the household members. When colonists travelled, they shared beds in roadside inns with fellow travellers, strangers to them until they bedded down side by side for the night.

British immigrant Mary O'Brien was forced to share her cramped Upper Canadian farmhouse with the domestic workers she spent her days supervising. Reluctantly, and grumbling that they did not "know their place," she followed the North American custom of having her "helps" take their meals at her family's table.

By the nineteenth century, new ideals of privacy had developed and, for those who could afford it, influenced home construction on both sides of the Atlantic. Large houses were now divided into four zones: the servants' quarters, the adult family's quarters, the children's quarters, and the great public rooms. Hallways, previously absent, allowed people to enter one room without first passing through another. A back staircase hid servants from family and guests as they hauled wood and coal. Bathrooms, or water closets, made elimination a private affair. Bell wires enabled servants to respond night and day even from a distance, so they no longer had to hover and sleep nearby. Adultery in bedrooms became less risky.

As architect Robert Kerr observed in 1840: "The family constitutes a community; the servants another. Whatever may be their mutual regard as dwellers under one roof, each class is entitled to shut its door upon the other and be alone. What passes on either side of the boundary shall be invisible and inaudible on the other. On both sides this privacy is highly valued."[6]

This was a typical sight in urban North America, as neighbourhood children and adults crowded together to work on piecework. In such overcrowded surroundings, personal privacy was difficult to imagine and seldom achieved.

A male frog courting a female frog, who notices that a frog voyeur is peering in the window. By 1876, cultural awareness of personal privacy was growing, and this humorous image implies that even in nature, privacy is important.

But the great majority of North American households could not incorporate privacy into their physical or operational structure. Rural families shared their homes with the usually female help whose wages consisted of a few dollars a month and room and board. In Upper Canada, as in much of rural North America, "when a girl arrived to take up her position, she immediately became an integral member of her employer's household," sharing their work, physical space, and living conditions. The relationship between employer and help was so intimate that it mirrored aspects of kinship.

Like the woman whose house they shared, the help saw themselves as homemakers who would one day have homes—and help—of their own. These homemakers-in-training held their employers to democratic North American standards; as British immigrant Anne Langton noted, "We ladies are as busy as the servants rubbing furniture.... you lose no respect in such exertions ... here one of our domestics would be surprised and perhaps consider herself a little ill-used if, in any extra bustle, we should be sitting in our drawing room. They are apt to think it quite right that we should be taking our due share."[7]

Privacy had little presence in these shared lives, and neither employer nor employed could conceal much of their lives, including the dynamics of their marriages, from each other. Spouses had no choice but to conduct themselves as best they could within these communal conditions.

In urban settings, a measure of privacy was easier to come by even though bourgeois homes usually had domestic helpers. Those who lived in had their own quarters to retire to when they were not on duty; those who worked in more modest homes lived out, returning at night to their own lodgings. Even in grander homes, privacy was sacrificed to such customs as paying trade or professional assistants in board and lodging as well as training. Until well into the nineteenth century, North Americans practised a modified form of European apprenticeship, with master artisans or craftsmen indenturing youngsters for four or five years of training. In return, the apprentices lived with them and usually performed some household chores as well.

In the American South, slaveholders neither valued nor practised the new notion of privacy. Early plantation houses, often modelled on colonial New England's traditional hall-and-parlour plan, incorporated a "lack of privacy [that] reflects in part the relatively informal relationship between family members, servants, and slaves in the late eighteenth and early nineteenth centuries," explains architect and scholar Gerald L. Foster.[8] Until the Civil War, many larger and more elegant plantation houses still retained this basic form.

In the nineteenth century, Elizabeth and William Wirt had five slaves in their house in Norfolk, Virginia. Elizabeth "rallied her captive assistants"—three women—to work alongside her spinning, weaving, and sewing, while two male slave coachmen tended the animals and gardens.[9] (William's legal clerks also lived with them until they became lawyers.)

Southern plantation houses overflowed with slaves—"they are in the parlor & in your rooms & all over," New Yorker Sarah Hicks Williams reported to her parents about North Carolina. Slaves lived and slept throughout the house, including on the floor of their white masters' and mistresses' bedrooms so they could be instantly at hand to fetch a glass of water, open or shut a window, swat a mosquito. One or two also had free access to the white family's bedrooms, which they entered to light the morning fire and do other chores without disturbing the inhabitants. The whites seldom bothered to censor what they said or did in their slaves' presence, their race and status as property rendering them invisible and unheeded.[10]

This lack of privacy had a sexual dimension. Like other North Americans, privileged white Southern families grounded their marriages in the conjugal domesticity that was replacing older marriage models. They were dotingly child-centred and strove to prepare their children for success, sending a high proportion of sons to college and many daughters to schools for young women. Yet the bonds between husband and wife, and their self-image as a nuclear family, were constantly tested by the husbands' infidelities committed on the bodies of black women.

"Like the patriarchs of old, our men live all in one house with their wives and their concubines; and the mulattoes one sees in every family partly resembled the white children," South Carolina planter's wife Mary Boykin Chesnut wrote. "Any lady is ready to tell you who is the father of all the mulatto children in everybody's household but her own. Those, she seems to think, drop from the clouds."[11] The daily presence of those children and their mothers was one of the most galling consequences of racism-honed sexual mores, and of the pervasive lack of privacy in Southern homes.

This enforced sociability extended to the quarters, the nearby hamlet of shanties where most slaves lived. The architecture of those squalid cabins, juxtaposed against a looming Great House, offered very different meanings of the nature of marriage and the purpose of children and family. The slave houses, puny and insignificant, were usually one room into which whites stuffed as many people as they could. "They warn't particular about how many they put in a room," former slave John Van Hook recalled. Another added that unrelated families were crammed "in the same cabin, just as many as could get in, men and women all together."[12] Slave spouses, whether their marriages had been voluntary or imposed, had to accommodate themselves to this utter lack of privacy.

THE CULT OF DOMESTICITY

In nineteenth-century North America's middle-class homes, notions of privacy were taking root and were reflected in new models of residential houses. These typically featured front porches, entrances and front parlour or drawing rooms to receive guests, who had to be kept away from the kitchen or any other "service" area, and bedrooms, usually upstairs. Larger homes might also have a nursery; a library, often with its own side entrance, for the husband; and a sitting room for the wife. Instead of the older notion of common bedrooms, children were provided with pleasant individual rooms to prevent them from seeking "pleasure and excitements neither so wholesome or refining as a fond parent would wish."[13]

The expansion of North American cities and the concomitant scarcity of land prompted the construction of housing even denser than the narrow townhouses that were popular in Philadelphia, New York, Montreal, and Toronto: apartments for the comfortable classes, tenements for the poorer. By the second half of the nineteenth century, even upper-class North Americans were living in European-influenced apartment buildings. Spacious and elegant, they maximized land use and provided gardens, storage, ground-floor commerce, the latest in plumbing and heating, and concierges to monitor the building's comings and goings. As in the townhouse, apartment dwellers embraced the gendered breadwinner-homemaker marriage model, and their housing reflected this with at least one room designed for the exclusive use of the stay-at-home wife ("non-working" but hard at work sewing, embroidering, and so on) and another for her husband.

The changing functions of society—schools that took over the education once provided in the home, factories and businesses that replaced the home as workplaces, and asylums and correctional institutes that handled social welfare—greatly influenced what went on inside North American homes. North American architecture, reflecting these changes, helped to shape the marriage model of male breadwinner and female homemaker, each with specific responsibilities. Women were expected to create a refuge for work-weary husbands and a delightful cocoon for children who might otherwise yearn for more exciting horizons. The meaning of interior, observed a French historian, "referred not so much to the heart of man as to the heart of the household, and it was there that one experienced happiness; similarly, well-being was now conditioned on 'comfort.'"[14]

These homes reflected as well the fundamental change away from sociability and toward intra-family privacy and gender segregation. Husbands and wives often had separate spheres. Family members respected each other's privacy by knocking on doors before entering. Fewer middle-class homes took in paying boarders, a time-honoured way for wives to supplement their family's income while confined to the domestic sphere. Upper-class American writer Edith Wharton valued privacy as "one of the first requisites of civilized life."[15]

Countless homes, however, were too small or wrongly divided to accommodate much privacy. Harriet Beecher Stowe was tormented by its lack and complained to her husband, "If I came into the parlor where you were, I felt as if I were interrupting you, and you know you thought so too."[16] Noise, too, limited privacy: Stowe's brood of children studied, played, practised piano, and were generally underfoot; if she tried to take a few minutes' respite, one of them would rattle the latch of her closed door. Stowe craved privacy and continually sought it, but as in so many other homes, reality fell far short of the ideal.

In this ideal, the new inward-looking home was also a wife's workshop, where she "she is to live, to love, but where she is to care and labor," as a contemporary noted. "Her hours, days, weeks, months and years are spent within its bounds, until she becomes an enthroned fixture, more indispensable than the house itself."[17] Wifedom had become house-, husband-, and child-centred, and was conducted in the familiar comfort of domestic privacy.

This new cult of domesticity recast middle-class wives as custodians of their homes, chaste and accomplished in the arts of homemaking and child care, Good Wives ruling their clean, cheerful, and segregated roosts. But though they did not go out to work to offices, factories, or fields to earn money, even privileged Good Wives worked at home, and "going into housekeeping" or setting up a household included earning as well as saving cash. In Virginia, for example, Elizabeth Wirt worked as her lawyer husband's clerical assistant on top of supervising a highly organized domestic assembly line that produced a wide range of preserved and fresh foodstuffs, linens, and clothing. Southerner Louise Winifred "Loula" Kendall forgot her third wedding anniversary because she was "busy doing up lard, and making sausage meat all day.... Farewell sentiment, poetry, beauty and flowers!" the once romance-obsessed belle added ruefully.[18]

Good Wives who did not manufacture their own cotton or linen or spin their own wool still sewed their family's clothes. An Upper Canadian dry-goods merchant remarked that he did not stock clothing as the women made it all themselves. Upper Canadian Eliza Hoyle, whose husband was often absent on business, was expected to "collect his debts, oversee his workmen at the mill, supervise the care of the livestock, see to it that the horses were properly watered and that the fences were kept in good repair, and [in times of anticipated scarcity] buy oats or hay."[19] Slaveholding women supervised or pitched in to dip candles, stuff sausages, sew mattresses, make soap, churn butter, and grow, harvest, and can fruits and vegetables.

Some women earned money in other ways, notably by writing. Harriet Beecher Stowe, whose anti-slavery novel *Uncle Tom's Cabin* prompted president Abraham Lincoln to call her "the little woman who wrote the book that made this great [Civil] war," was one of these scribbling sisters. She once explained to a fan, "As I married into poverty and without a dowry, and as my husband had only a large library of books and a great deal of learning ... when a new carpet or mattress was going to be needed, or when my accounts, like poor Dora's, wouldn't add up, then I used to say ... I'll write a piece, and then we'll be out of the scrape. So I became an author."[20]

Good Wives also contributed to their family's welfare and raised its standard of living through clever shopping, cooking, sewing, and cleaning. Historian Jeanne Boydston calculates that based on the weekly family food budget estimated by the *New York Tribune* in 1851 at $4.26, a thrifty wife who bought in bulk and dried and salted extra food could save from 40 cents to over $2 a week, 10 to 50 percent of her family's food budget. For example, keeping kitchen gardens or chickens and producing their own cheese saved 25 cents a week, the price of a bushel of potatoes.[21]

Good Wives were also targeted as important—and valued— consumers who wanted and needed the fruits of the new technological advances that had earlier revolutionized society with factories and that now produced stoves, vacuum cleaners, and a host of other labour-saving devices. But these labour-saving devices generated new demands and ever-higher standards, which, accompanied by the exodus of servants, made more work for Mother.

Women's diaries and memoirs testify to the fact that housekeeping had never been easy, as Boydston documents in *Home and Work*. Wives washed clothes on scrub boards, ironed with heavy flatirons, chopped firewood, baked bread, cooked meals, picked and preserved fruits and vegetables, spun wool, sewed and mended clothes, scoured floors and walls, shovelled coal, carried pails of water, emptied slop buckets, doctored and cared for children, taught morals, and recorded flashes of their life in letters or diaries.

New labour-saving devices eased or, in the case of toilets, eliminated some of these burdens. But except for the wealthiest women, all the nineteenth-century Angels in the House had to master standards of homemaking that would daunt Martha Stewart. "I am but a mere drudge," Harriet Beecher Stowe confided to a friend.[22] In author Louisa May Alcott's succinct words: "Housework ain't no joke!"

The new economic structure, with wage earners working in factories and offices and shops rather than at home, made midday dinner obsolete for most people. Men began to eat in restaurants that boasted quick and cheap meals and were near their places of work. In the evening, when family members gathered together, their dinner was the most important and elaborate meal of the day and included several dishes and dessert. (The exception was Sunday, when midday dinner followed church services.)

These complicated dinner menus arose in response to the view that women with stoves should no longer confine their offerings to the traditional one-pot stews and soups suitable to hearths. But the wondrous cast-iron coal- or wood-fired stove was extremely difficult to use. To get it going, the housewife had to clean out the ashes from the previous cooking session, replace them with kindling and paper, get going a new fire, and adjust the dampers and flues. Because the stove had no thermostat, she had to monitor its heat output, fiddling with the flues or adding fuel, responding to its capriciousness. The stove's appetite was voracious: about fifty pounds of coal or wood a day. On average, housewives devoted four hours a day to its maintenance, including rubbing it with the thick black wax that kept it from rusting, and emptying the ash box.

Martha Wright's stove was typical: "Whack! went the stove equal to a cannon & now both windows are open to let out the smoke," she grumbled to her sister. "Bang! Goes the *blamed* stove again I had got all the smoke out & closed the windows, and then raised the door to get the stove hot again—before it was too hot. I shut it nearly down & it *chosed* to *puff*."[23] Harriet Beecher Stowe observed wryly that the new airtight stove "has saved people from all further human wants, and put an end forever to any needs short of the six feet of narrow earth which are man's only inalienable property."[24]

Food preparation was also onerous; until the end of the nineteenth century, most food was unprocessed. The Campbell Soup Company, for example, invented condensed soup only in 1897. The housewife (working alongside her help if the family could afford any) had to slaughter, pluck, and gut chickens; scale fish; roast and grind coffee beans; pound loaves of sugar; sift flour and pick out insect larvae, twigs, and other impurities; shell nuts; and seed raisins. She had to plan, prepare, cook, and serve the meals her family expected from her, then dispose of kitchen slops. This could entail transporting them to a public collection area, throwing them to domestic pigs, or packing them for collection by a delivery service.

Inevitably, there were failures. Danish immigrant journalist Jacob Riis described his beloved wife Elisabeth's first attempt at roasting a chicken. "I cannot to this day imagine what was the matter with that strange bird.... The skin was all drawn tight over the bones like the covering on an umbrella frame, and there was no end of fat in the pan that we didn't know what to do with. But our supper of bread and cheese that night was a meal fit for a king." When a carefully prepared fruitcake refused to rise, Elisabeth "smuggled it out of the house; only to behold, with a mortification that endures to this day, the neighbor-woman ... examining it carefully in the ash-barrel next morning."[25]

Ruining food was one worry among many. The smoke from burning coal or wood fuel and from gas and kerosene lamps permeated the air and coated carpets, curtains, walls, and furniture in black soot. Though rich, dark-coloured wall paint concealed the worst of the omnipresent dirt, lamp globes needed to be wiped, wicks to be trimmed, and fuel to be added. Floors had to be washed, carpets beaten, and windows washed. In homes outside the cities, women had to fetch the water to cook and clean from wells or springs. In 1886, in North Carolina, for example, a typical housewife had to do this eight to ten times every day. This translated to 148 miles annually, carrying over 36 tons of water.

But as arduous as cleaning, cooking, water-carrying, and other household chores could be, nineteenth-century women particularly dreaded "the Herculean task" of laundry, which Nevada housewife Rachel Haskell described as "the great domestic dread of the household."[26] Laundry involved overnight soaking, scrubbing on a washboard, soaping with stinging lye, stirring in a vat of boiling water, rinsing, bluing, wringing out, and finally hanging out to dry. Some clothes were then ironed, and collars and crinolines starched. Housework expert Catharine Beecher advised: "*Tuesday* is devoted to washing, and *Wednesday* to ironing. On *Thursday*, the ironing is finished off, the clothes folded and put away, and all articles which need mending put in the mending basket, and attended to."[27] And this assumed that soap and starch were already made. (Beecher's hard soap recipe took four hours of frequent stirring, and further refinement the day after. Starch began with soaking unground wheat for several days, stirring and straining it, and drying it for several days in the sun.)

A Norwegian immigrant noted with astonishment that the North American housewife "must do all the work that the cook, the maid and the housekeeper would do in an upper class family at home. Moreover, she must do her work as well as these three together do it in Norway."[28] Expatriate European writer and educator Francis Grund, visiting the United States, believed that American wives generally suffered ill health because of "the great assiduity with which American ladies discharge their duties as mothers. No sooner are they married than they begin to lead a life of comparative seclusion; and once mothers, they are actually buried to the world."[29] Writer, abolitionist, and reformer Lydia Maria Child tallied a year's activities: 360 dinners, 362 breakfasts, sitting room and kitchen swept and dusted 350 times, lamps filled 362 times, and the chamber and stairs swept and dusted 40 times.[30]

This housework was integral to the housewife's marital duties and assumed great importance as advice books, cookbooks, newspaper and magazine columnists, and house-pattern books defined and described, literally, the correct way to manage a household. Though unmarried (her fiancé died in a shipwreck), Catharine Beecher produced, during the "manual mania" of 1840 to 1860, eleven manuals. Her masterpiece, the 1841 *Treatise on Domestic Economy*, was adopted by Massachusetts

"Do we look cheerful? Washing clothes is pretty hard work generally, but if you use Kirkman's Borax Soap according to directions, it's really wonderful how it lightens labor, and, besides, it makes the clothes as sweet as a rose and as white as snow." Laundry was notoriously onerous work. This 1891 ad used pretty young women and promises of relief from the thankless toil to pitch its product.

As more women protested their subordinate status and demanded change, cartoons mocked the New Woman and her emasculated husband. Laundry, the most dreaded chore, was often depicted. In this 1901 image, the woman's sense of entitlement is underscored by the feminist wall picture and magazine.

public schools, often reprinted, and informed generations of women about their duties as housewives.

Beecher's *Treatise* incorporated housekeeping instructions, terrifyingly comprehensive and relentlessly detailed, with a sweeping discourse on women's responsibilities as wives and mothers. Beecher dismissed discussions about male and female intellectual equality as frivolous and useless, but she challenged as "pernicious and mistaken" the widespread view that housework was a mindless pursuit. "No statesman, at the head of a nation's affairs, had more frequent calls for wisdom, firmness, tact, discrimination, produce, and a versatility of talent than a woman in charge of a large household," she wrote.[31] She also noted that women had to gear their housekeeping to their circumstances: a poorer woman with a large family could be forgiven for neglecting other aspects of housework, for she had to devote more effort to feeding and clothing her brood "than would be right were she in affluence and with a small family."[32]

Beecher considered the physical plan of houses so important to proper living that she included in her book a section "On the Construction of Houses" and in 1869 wrote *American Woman's Home* with her sister, Harriet Beecher Stowe, the consummate wife and mother who had written *Uncle Tom's Cabin* with one hand and baked beans and gingerbread with the other as children clung to her skirts and dogs ran underfoot. A too-large house meant excessive work for the housewife. To save her from traipsing up and down stairs, Beecher proposed eliminating the servants' staircase and the basement kitchen in favour of locating parlour, kitchen, and nursery on one floor. To observe the dictates of privacy, she urged women to forgo domestic help as much as possible by doing the work themselves and enlisting their children to help them.

The Angels in the House who became metaphors for the cult of domesticity that idealized them set the standard for women throughout North America. As well as being a sanctuary for their husbands and children, their perfectly run homes were a central feature of national prosperity and defined middle-class identity. The Angels' husbands, charged with the responsibility of providing for and protecting their families, felt

Alexander McGibbon poses in 1869 with his wife, Harriet, and five of their ten children. (They went on to have three more.) This Notman studio portrait (the dog is a stuffed prop) was commissioned to affirm Alexander's success as a grocer and Harriet's as a wife and mother. In other images, Alex posed in his grocery store wearing an apron and looking much more relaxed.

empowered by how the cult of domesticity assigned them authority over their households. This reciprocal arrangement inspired wives to strive for domestic perfection as a way of maintaining the husbandly love and respect that was their principal protection in a still-unequal world.

Wives in the cheaper and more spacious suburbs that proliferated in the late nineteenth century as railroads allowed people to commute from the city also tried to live up to the ideals of the cult of domesticity. Indeed, historian Margaret Marsh believes the cult was "centered firmly in the suburbs, represented family and community togetherness in the face of an urban society that promised individual achievement, anonymity, and excitement."[33] A subtext to the growth of suburbia was

Thomas E. Askew, Atlanta's first African-American photographer, created a richness of portraits, including successful African-American families posing outside their fine homes. Here an unnamed lawyer presides over his family, his wedding ring testifying to his married status. Such portraits represent what W.E.B. Du Bois called "the Talented Tenth," successful role models and leaders.

uneasiness about the immigrants and African Americans moving into the cities. Though they felt safe, suburban wives suffered more from loneliness and isolation than their city sisters. But their husbands, often alienated by their working environment, took comfort in the homes and garden plots that seemed like mini versions of the rugged agricultural past. By making them lords of these small manors, the cult of domesticity helped redefine the meaning of manliness.

It was much harder for rural middle-class women to hew to the Angel model. North Dakotan Emilie Schumacher, a typical rural stay-at-home Victorian-era North American wife, had to cook, bake, clean, wash, iron, mend, tend garden, preserve vegetables and fruits for winter, and entertain. She also had to gather and sell eggs, tend chickens and pigs, milk cows, separate cream, churn butter, render lard, and manage a large household.[34] After his mother died, Hamlin Garland of Iowa recalled "the cheerful heroism of her daily treadmill ... Visioning the long years of her drudgery, I recalled her early rising, and suffered with her the never-ending round of dishwashing, churning, sewing, and cooking, realizing more fully than ever before that in all of this slavery she was but one of a million martyrs. All our neighbors' wives walked the same round."[35]

Many farm women, and almost all their children, assisted with field and farm work. Children rose at or before dawn to light fires, empty chamber pots, clean boots, muck out stables, fetch wood and water, and weed the garden. These chores took precedence over everything else, even for children as young as five. "After the last bundle was threshed, and the last furrow turned, they could go to school, if they so desired," writes historian Elizabeth Hampsten in *Settlers' Children.*[36]

Family life on the North American farm was shaped by the relentless-ness of hard work and the spectre or thrall of poverty. Garland, for example, wrote, "I cannot recall a single beautiful thing about our house, not one." His mother, overwhelmed by the struggle to feed and clothe her children, "never expressed her deeper feelings. She seldom kissed her children."[37] Others showed more tenderness than Garland but, "work-weary" like her, spent most of their time working and super-vising rather than playing with or indulging the children. One woman recalled that children "were special" only on their birthdays.[38] Too often, the Angel in the House was plumb tuckered out.

CHALLENGING THE CULT OF DOMESTICITY

Charlotte Perkins Gilman wrote about women's work from an irreverent perspective quite different from her aunt Catharine Beecher's. Far from venerating the Good Wife's self-sacrifice, Gilman indicted it as "a primi-tive standard of domestic ethics" that corrupted marriage relations. Unpaid wives slyly rifled their husbands' pockets and stole from them because they had to, and though "the home has patience, chastity, indus-try, love.... there is less justice, less honour, less courage, less truth."[39]

Gilman envisioned "a pure, lasting, monogamous sex-union ... without bribe or purchase, without the manacles of economic dependence" as a solution to the economic dependency of wives trapped at home.[40] To end "this Cupid-in-the-kitchen arrangement" that forced dependent women to provide home-cooking, she proposed urban residential apartments with communal dining rooms and without kitchens in individual units. "Is it not time that the way to a man's heart through his stomach should be relinquished for some higher avenue? ... The heart should be approached through higher channels." Except for the rare case of "natural-born cooks," cooking should be left to trained experts. The kitchenless apartments would be cleaned by professional cleaners, sparing "woman, the dainty, the beautiful, the beloved wife and revered mother ... all that is basest and foulest ... Grease, ashes, dust, foul linen, and sooty ironware." Children would be cared for by professional nurses and teachers. Wives as well as husbands would daily sally forth to earn their livings and pursue their interests. They would live comfortably, in privacy, and marriage would evolve as a union in which woman stood "beside man as the comrade of his soul, not the servant of his body." Most women would choose work compatible with motherhood; few would persist in "being acrobats, horse-breakers, or sailors before the mast."[41]

A prominent social activist and a leading feminist, Gilman brought clarity and biting wit to her analyses of marriage and the family culture that was, by the late nineteenth and early twentieth centuries, well established throughout North America. There was no stampede to build kitchenless apartments and houses. But Gilman attracted a wide readership and provoked people to rethink much of what seemed immutable about marriages and family life.

And there were some middle-class couples who, from expediency or conviction, chose arrangements that in certain ways resembled Gilman's ideals; they boarded in residential "hotels" that included communal meals at set hours in the dining room. Mary and Amédée Papineau, for example, began married life in Montreal's Donegani Hotel, in a three-room suite that they furnished. They ate the hotel's meals sent up to their suite but found them so unappetizing that Amédée's mother often supplied finer fare. Before a year was up, the young couple had moved into their own house.

In these hotel-households, only husbands went out to work, while wives usually stayed in their rooms, washing, ironing, and sewing clothes. "I always observed that the ladies who boarded wore more elaborately worked collars and petticoats than any one else," remarked novelist and reformer Frances Trollope. Their husbands, however, seemed impervious to their wives' finery and spent little time in their room or in the common sitting room. Instead, Trollope observed, they found excuses to go out in the evening "on business" while their neglected wives were consigned to roles of "lamentable insignificance."[42]

Working-Class Marriages

Because wages were generally too low to support a family, the working-class version of the cult of domesticity did not centre on the male bread-winner/female homemaker model. It was geared instead to making the family financially secure, keeping it intact, and, where possible, improving the children's conditions and futures.

This translated into doing whatever work was required—by whomever had the opportunity to do it. Scavenging—a rag rug fetched 50 cents, an old coat several dollars, flour scooped from a broken barrel at the docks close to a dollar—could net $50 a year. Women took in paying boarders—Martha Wright's first love and husband was her widowed mother's boarder Peter Pelham—to net about $130 a year. They accepted home-based piecework; a needlewoman might earn about $2 weekly. When factory and sweatshop owners started recruiting women, albeit at lower wages than men earned, many of these women trooped out to work.

Children had to pitch in. Mothers trained them to assist with piece-work and to care for younger siblings. They were sent out to toil in factories, sweatshops, mills, and mines and as domestics—and at home handed over their wages; when social reformers fought to raise the legal age of employment, parents were the strongest opponents. Education seemed a remote gamble, but waged work, however miserably remunerated, put cash into the family's coffers.

Working-class living quarters had to be multi-functional. By day, dining tables functioned as work stations; at night the family cleared them off and ate around them. "Bedrooms" were anywhere: hallways, kitchens, living rooms; beds, for family and boarders, were stowed away by day, hauled out for use at night.

Tenements were the direst kind of housing. In his investigative exposé of tenements in New York City, *How the Other Half Lives* (1890), Jacob Riis described them as "the hot-beds of the epidemics that carry death to rich and poor alike; the nurseries of pauperism and crime that fill our jails and police courts; that throw off a scum of forty thousand human wrecks to the island asylums and workhouses year by year; that turned out … [a] half million beggars … that maintain a standing army of ten thousand tramps." Tenements "touch the family life with deadly moral contagion," Riis concluded. "This is their worst crime, inseparable from the system."

The first tenements were carved out of the large houses of middle-class homeowners who had moved away to leafy suburbs. Their "large rooms were partitioned into several smaller ones, without regard to light or ventilation" and, along with garrets and cellars, were rented out to immigrants desperate for lodging. Landlords gouged their tenants with relatively high rents in what the Society for the Improvement of the Condition of the Poor described as "crazy old buildings, crowded rear tenements in filthy yards, dark, damp [rat-infested] basements, leaking garrets, shops, outhouses, and stables converted into dwellings … scarcely fit to shelter brutes."[43]

These slums were so profitable that landlords added storeys, built over gardens, converted properties into ever-smaller units, and packed in tenants in ever-greater concentrations: ten families now lived where two once had. Riis visited one 12-by-19-foot room furnished only with two beds and shared by five families totalling twenty persons of both sexes. By the turn of the twentieth century, New York City's tenements made it the world's most densely populated district: 290,000 people to the square mile. Pigs roamed the streets where loads of their manure

Nine-year-old Jennie Rizzandi stayed home from school to help her mother and father finish piecework in their dilapidated New York City tenement. They earned about $2 a week. Mr. Rizzandi sometimes found work outside the home.

accumulated. Children died of air pollution; at least one child suffocated to death "in the foul air of an unventilated apartment."[44]

Elsewhere in American and Canadian cities, tenements shaped the marriages and family lives of their residences. Social reformer Margaret Byington described life in a two-room tenement in Pittsburgh:

The kitchen, perhaps 15 by 12 feet, was steaming with vapor from a big washtub set on a chair in the middle of the room. The mother was trying to wash and at the same time keep the older of her two babies from tumbling into the tub full of scalding water that was standing on the floor. On one side of the room was a huge puffy bed, with one feather tick to sleep on and another for covering; near the window stood a sewing machine; in the corner, an organ—all these besides the inevitable cook stove upon which in the place of honor was simmering the evening's soup. Upstairs in the second room were one boarder and the man of the house asleep. Two more boarders were at work, but

Photographer Lewis Wickes Hine noted that many fathers refused to participate in their family's piecework. His note about this image of a New York tenement family: "5:15 P.M. Father hanging around the home while family works on feathers. Said, 'I not work. Got some sickness. Dunno what.'" His wife and children, aged sixteen to five, all worked, the older ones until 9 or 10 p.m. Together they earned up to $6 a week. Hine added: "Dirty floor. Vermin abounded. Garbage standing uncovered near the work."

at night would be home to sleep in the bed from which the others would get up.[45]

Thanks to boarders, neighbours, thin walls, and shared toilets, tenement life was notoriously unprivate and startlingly similar to medieval living conditions. But unlike the fundamentally unprivate Middle Ages, tenement dwellers had at least inklings of ideals of privacy against which to measure their utter lack of it. And if they did not, middle-class public opinion did, in outraged complaints about the indecency and immodesty that resulted from families sharing rooms with unrelated lodgers. This egregious lack of privacy "breaks down the barriers of self-respect, and prepares the way for direct profligacy," reported the New York Association for Improving the Condition of the Poor.[46] During

The Arnao family, pictured here in 1910, are berry pickers. They came from Philadelphia to work in this Delaware berry field, and are moving on to New Jersey. The youngest child is three.

working-class divorce trials, for example, witnesses easily provided intimate accounts of behaviour that unhappily married middle-class spouses could keep under wraps.

Despite—perhaps oblivious to—the immensely difficult circumstances of the working class, reformers tried to impress upon them the values of the cult of domesticity and its associated values of efficiency, order, and self-discipline. They also promoted home ownership, a common dream of immigrants despite the obstacles to achieving it. A 1909 textbook *English for Foreigners* described the ideal American home: "This is the family, in the sitting-room. The family is made up of the father, the mother, and the children. That is the father who is reading. The father is the husband. That is the mother who is sewing. The

The unknown photographer noted only that this image included all members of an African-American family. They are standing in front of their house—former slave quarters in Savannah, Georgia—and likely worked together at farming and other activities.

mother is the wife. The father and the mother are the parents.... The family makes the home."[47]

By the end of the nineteenth century, wages for male workers rose with the demand for skilled industrial workers and the development of unions, and more working-class women remained at home. Their own wages (primarily in clerical and retail jobs) remained low, and many calculated that, after paying for child care, they made little profit. As increasing numbers of older children attended school or went (or were sent) to work themselves, they were unavailable to mind younger siblings. By shopping carefully and cooking and baking from scratch, a homemaker could provide her family with a higher standard of living, especially a more nutritious and tastier diet, without spending more money. If she feared or suffered marital violence, she could hope, as many women did, that a more comfortable home would reduce the likelihood of it. By becoming a homemaker, she could aspire to raise her husband's and family's status in society; having a parlour to preside over was a tangible symbol of success.

There were risks and dangers. The homemaker was dependent on her husband's wages and at the mercy of his temper, especially if he drank. In difficult economic times, she had no wages to supplement his. But with homemaking regarded as a worthy vocation, and her services difficult to replace, she had some influence and bargaining power in the marriage relationship. Among the working class as in the more advantaged, the cult of domesticity had taken root and was spreading.

Chapter 6

Go Forth and Multiply:
Children at the Heart
of Marriage

Marriage as Procreative Union

At dinnertime on November 30, 1809, the Emperor Napoleon
Bonaparte informed his Empress that he had decided to divorce her. He
had tolerated, even forgiven, her infidelities, her lies, her faked pregnancy, and her extravagances. But much as he loved his Josephine, he
wanted a wife who could give him children, and years earlier, Josephine
had become barren. As she heard the dread news she cried out in shock,
and then fainted.

At their divorce ceremony, Napoleon reiterated his love for his soon-
to-be ex-Empress: "Far from ever finding cause for complaint, I can to
the contrary only congratulate myself on the devotion and tenderness of
my beloved wife. She has adorned thirteen years of my life; the memory
will always remain engraved on my heart."

Josephine responded that because she could not give her "august and
dear husband … children who would fulfill the needs of his policies and
the interests of France, I am pleased to offer him the greatest proof of
attachment and devotion ever offered on this earth."

Josephine, the widowed mother of a son and a daughter, had for
years concealed from Napoleon that she had become barren, blaming

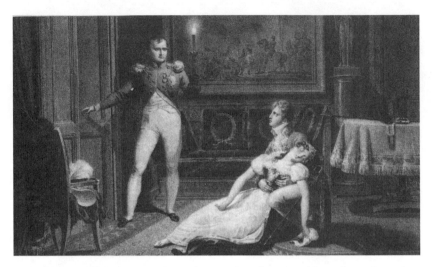

The Emperor Napoleon, in the Tuileries Palace, has just informed Josephine that he will divorce her, and Josephine faints at the devastating news. This image by French painter Bosselman, and engraved by Chasselat, is one of several portraying the major events of Napoleon's life.

him for her failure to conceive and feigning pregnancy and miscarriage. But the recent birth of Napoleon's son Charles, Count Léon, with his teenaged mistress Éléonore Denuelle was unanswerable proof that Josephine had lied.[1]

Her predicament was classic. Like countless others, she was victimized by the fact that having children was regarded as integral to marriage. Under France's Napoleonic law, barrenness was not grounds for divorce. From Napoleon's perspective, however, it was a compelling reason, so much so that as soon as he divorced Josephine, he married the Archduchess Marie Louise of Austria, eighteen years old and, as she was soon to prove, fertile.

Most cultures and religions assume that marriage should result in procreation. Judaism, Christianity, and Islam are rich with praise for the blessing of children: Genesis 22:17 promises patriarchs that their wives "will multiply your descendants as the stars of heaven and as the sand which is upon the seashore," and Deuteronomy 7:12–14 that "you shall be blessed above all peoples; there shall not be a male or female barren among you." The Prophet described "worthy offspring" as "a bunch of sweet-smelling flowers which God has distributed amongst his servants."

Children are begotten through sexual intercourse, which, most religions teach, should be preceded by marriage. Christianity's many sex-phobic theologians go further, declaring that spouses should indulge in sexual intercourse *only* for the purpose of procreation, and never to satisfy mere lust. As in the Roman Catholic Church it had broken away from, for example, the sixteenth-century Church of England listed procreation as the primary purpose of marriage, followed by restraint and remedy of sin, and last, companionship. The Orthodox Church, on the other hand, taught that the first purpose of marriage was reciprocal love and assistance, with sexual restraint and reproducing the human race secondary. In Saint John Chrysostom's words: "Marriage does not necessarily include [reproduction] ... the proof is to be found in the many marriages for which having children is not possible. This is why the primary reason for marriage is to regulate the sexual life, especially now that the human race has already populated the whole world."

The Puritans, whose theology and way of life so strongly influenced North America, also put mutual society, help, and comfort well before procreation. In *Matrimoniall Honour: or, the Mutuall Crowne and Comfort of Godly, Loyall, and Chaste Marriage* (1642), clergyman Daniel Rogers wrote: "Husbands and wives should be as two sweet friends, bred under one constellation, tempered by an influence from heaven whereof neither can give any reason, save mercy and providence first made them so, and then made their match; saying, see, God hath determined us out of this vast world for each other."[2]

CHILDBIRTH

By no means all spouses wanted children, and many wanted fewer than they conceived. Part of the reason was the experience of childbirth. As a French proverb warned, "A pregnant woman has one foot in the grave." Childbirth could be the straightforward delivery of a healthy infant. But until midwives and physicians grasped the implications of Louis

Pasteur's 1881 discovery that microbes caused infection, they handled their labouring patients with unscrubbed hands in filthy conditions, and so giving birth was often the death knell for mother, baby, or both. Seventeenth-century Englishwoman Elizabeth Joceline, typical of so many pregnant women, anticipated that childbirth would kill her and composed a letter-from-the-grave to her unborn child. Nine days after her daughter's birth, Joceline died. In the eighteenth century, the complications of childbirth killed one in five women aged twenty-five to thirty-four. In mid-nineteenth-century America, at least 4 percent of deceased Southern and 2 percent of Northern women had died in childbirth.[3]

The elite were not spared. In 1817, to the shock of English women, twenty-one-year-old Princess Charlotte, the only child of King George IV, died just five hours after delivering a stillborn son. The nation mourned, and three months later, Sir Richard Croft, her attending physician, shot himself.

Women's very real fear of death in childbirth reinforced the desire of many privileged Southern girls to postpone marriage for as long as they could. Laura Wirt, whose own mother had suffered greatly during her many pregnancies, was horrified by a friend's death soon after childbirth. "How fearfully she was changed by disease and death!" Laura wrote. Young women kept track of mutual acquaintances, categorizing them as married or deceased. "Have thought much of Death," wrote mother-to-be Carline Brooks Lilly in 1839. "The grave banished other thoughts from my mind & while leaning on my affectionate husbands breast, the inquiry arose where will they bury me?"[4]

In the North, Mary Westcott Papineau's mother had died after giving birth, and Mary, who had moved to Lower Canada, was ailing when she delivered her first child. The birth was so difficult that the attending physician warned that he would have to destroy and remove the infant to save Mary's life—the same procedure once endured by her mother. When the physician finally announced the good news that Mary and her newborn daughter were alive and well, Amédée and Mary's father were too relieved to do anything but weep.

Besides infections, poor, badly fed nursing mothers who became pregnant lost calcium and suffered through the agony of childbirth with pelvises deformed by rickets; this was especially true after the Industrial Revolution sent so many into factories and created new eating habits. Workers with long hours and short breaks relied on cheap, sugary tea-with-bread meals that briefly energized them but lacked essential nutrients and ultimately eroded their health. Obstetrical interventions could also be dangerous or deadly. Caesarian sections, first successfully performed in 1793, saved some bone-deficient women but destroyed others; Sir Richard Croft did not perform one on Princess Charlotte because he believed it would kill her. Childbirth was so risky that many women were given Holy Communion at the onset of labour.

Childbirth was often a public event, as neighbours, midwives or physicians, friends, and relatives crowded around the labouring woman. Husbands were supposed to be nearby and ready to help, but in England, though much less so in North America, their presence at the actual birth was considered unlucky and unseemly. Queen Victoria, on the other hand, seemed to suggest they should witness their wives' suffering: "Oh! If those selfish men—who are the cause of all one's misery, only knew what their poor slaves go through!" she wrote.[5]

Occasionally husbands did assist. In June 1739, William Gossip kept his beloved Anne company as she struggled, helped by Mr. Dawes, a physician, through forty-nine and a half hours of "a most painfull tedious & dangerous Labour" during which Mr. Dawes used his "Instrument [to] tear ye child in pieces & bring it away in [that] manner." It was

> *a tedious & terrible operation in which the surgeon was sooner tired with afflicting her than she with Suffering ... such torments as it is surprising how human Nature could subsist under it He ... broke into the abdomen of ye Child with his Instruments, & thence extracted the bowels & other viscera & broke of part of ye ribs, this evacuation made room in ye Uterus for him to insinuate his hands between the belly of ye child & the sides of the collapsed womb, by which means he got hold of ye feet of ye child ... [and] extracted the remains of his*

mangled Carcass, except the arm ... which had been cut of as soon as
the Childs Death was perceived. Its shattered remains were buried
near ye rest of my Children.[6]

Edmund Peel, a half-pay naval officer stationed in Sherbrooke, Lower Canada, not only attended his wife Lucy's long and agonizing delivery but was for days after, Lucy exclaimed, "[my] father, mother, brother, sister, nurse and husband." Edmund had done what he believed was a husband's duty, and considered it "nothing less than false delicacy which would make a man absent himself at a time when his presence and support are most required, it is a fearful thing to see a woman in her pain."[7]

Happily, childbirth could also be an uneventful or joyous event; new father William Ramsden, for example, reported cheerily that "the Baggage"—his wife, Bessy—"looks sleek and saucy; the Brat fat and healthy."[8]

Postpartum depression took its toll as well. Nineteenth-century Englishwoman Ellen Stock's "great depression of spirits" delayed her recovery from childbirth, and other women struggled for months to regain emotional equilibrium. "Even for seasoned matrons," writes Amanda Vickery, "the aftermath of birth remained hard to predict."[9] In her backwoods cabin in Upper Canada, Susanna Moodie suffered excruciating breast pain and "lay like a crushed snake on my back unable to move or even to be raised forward without the most piteous cries."[10] When a doctor finally arrived, he lanced her breast, and infected matter gushed out. Impacted and infected breasts were among several common postpartum conditions that plagued women until well into the twentieth century.

Until the twentieth century, burying babies was a familiar experience for parents. Though influential historians such as Philippe Ariès, Lloyd deMause, and Lawrence Stone have claimed that parents responded with indifference or muted grief, a new generation of scholars argues that the high infant mortality rate did not blunt parents' grief. American Elizabeth Prentiss was inconsolable after losing both her infant and three-year-old son. "Empty hands, empty hands, a worn-out exhausted body, and unutterable longings to flee from a world that has had for me so many sharp experiences. God help me, my baby, my baby! God help me, my little lost Eddy!"[11] Mary Papineau's first-born son died and, she wrote, the "shock was so terrible so sudden and overwhelming that I cannot yet fully realize it … & my poor heart more & more desolate."[12]

Husbands shared their wives' grief. After his eight-month-old daughter Elizabeth died, Martin Luther wrote that he "was exquisitely sick, my heart rendered soft and weak; never had I thought that a father's heart could be so broken for his children's sake."[13] Over a decade later, when thirteen-year-old Magdalena lay dying, he knelt at her bedside weeping bitterly and praying that God would reprieve her until she died in his arms. But he also found solace in the knowledge that she was going to God, and told his dying child, "Dear daughter, you have another Father in heaven, and to Him you will go."[14] Like millions of other mourning parents who took comfort from sermons counselling resignation at God's unknowable ways, Martin Luther sought to accept Magdalena's death as God's merciful will.

After their sixteen-year-old daughter Agnes's death, William and Elizabeth Wirt, who lost several other children, focused on the hope of reunion in heaven: "to that world she is gone—and thither my affections have followed her. This was Heaven's design—I see and feel it as distinctly as if an Angel had revealed it—as if my Angel daughter had been permitted to reveal it," William wrote to a friend.[15] As photography developed in the nineteenth century, parents also found solace in the ritual display of photographs of their dead children.

CONTRACEPTION AND ABORTION

There were countless reasons to restrict family size. An infant born to an impoverished family could compromise the survival of older children. Too many daughters could crush a family with the financial burden of providing them with dowries. In eras of high infant mortality, parents could not endure another death. Women (and sympathetic husbands) dreaded the possibility of fatal postpartum infection. Many women hated multiple pregnancies. Queen Victoria, privileged and healthy, was

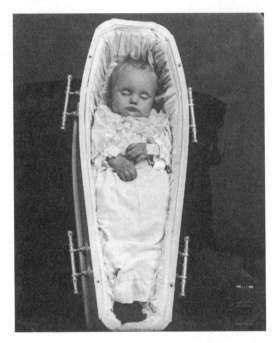

This infant's grieving parents preserved his memory
with this image of their lifeless child in a little coffin.

"furious" that the first two years of her married life had been "utterly
spoilt" by the pregnancies she likened to "being like a cow or a dog."[16]

Unlike the famously prolific queen, the wealthiest classes—or at least
their male members—tended to welcome the arrival of large numbers of
children. The middle and working classes, however, preferred fewer and
tried as best they could to circumvent conception. Certain convenient
customs were not called birth control but effectively controlled births.
Encouraging women to delay their first marriage until about a decade
after menstruation, and simultaneously frowning on premarital sex,
reduced a woman's child-bearing years by a third. A cultural taboo
against sex with a breastfeeding woman helped space out pregnancies.
(Lactation itself had a contraceptive effect for six to twelve months.)

Coitus interruptus, much more effective, was widely practised—
though, as one frustrated seventeenth-century English wife complained,

her husband "did not deal with her in bed as befitted a married man ... what seed should be sowen in the right ground he spent about the outward part of her body and withal threatened if she were with child he would slit the gut out of her belly."[17] Anal sex was so common that it provoked the ire of theologians, who condemned it as sex for pleasure rather than procreation.

Contraceptive devices were used, though most were unreliable and awkward. Grotesque pessaries such as "the root of iris put into the womb or fumigated underneath,"[18] and the sometimes effective vaginal sponge were designed as barriers to conception. (In the 1860s, Northern women had to improvise or find alternative methods of birth control after the Civil War cut off their supply of sponges from Florida.)

Until the nineteenth century, most contraceptive barriers were unreliable, usually associated with prostitution, and intended to prevent venereal disease rather than conception. One of the first was an eighteenth-century English device described by French writer Jean Astruc as "a little bag, made of a thin bladder, which they call a *condum*"—named after its putative inventor, Colonel Cundum.[19] Closed with ribbons, the condom was as expensive as it was uncomfortable. Charles Goodyear and Thomas Hancock invented vulcanized rubber in 1843, but it was only in 1876, at the Philadelphia World Exposition, that rubber condoms were popularized.

The general failure of contraception inspired a wide range of abortifacients that were supposed to terminate unwanted pregnancies. Herbal concoctions in the form of drinks, tablets, suppositories, douches, and amulets prepared from recipes in books or folklore were popular. An English remedy, "A piece of the Pod or husk [of Guinny Pepper], either green or dry ... put into the Mother after delivery," would make her permanently barren.[20] Ergot, known in German as *kindesmord*—infant's death—was used in close to lethal dosages to stimulate the uterus to abort.[21] A Southern abortifacient was cottonroot, supposedly popular with slaves and later with white women, especially after the Civil War. Dilating the cervix—with goosequills or Chamberlain's Utero-Vaginal Syringe—were other, dangerous options. Slower and safer was the "enlarging bougie, a pencil-like cylinder of dried seaweed ... inserted into the cervix and left overnight," gradually swelling and dilating the cervix as it absorbed moisture.[22] Suction devices, an electrically charged "galvanic bougie," and various other electric contraptions were excruciating and used without anaesthesia.

Contemporaries called abortion the bane of seduced or betrayed spinsters or widows who despaired at the prospect of life as unmarried mothers. But analyses of diaries and correspondence reveals that married men and women, who could more easily feign a miscarriage, also resorted to aborting fetuses, with either abortifacients or surgical abortion. Husbands often colluded, telling "fine stories of the diseases of the Wives," and helped to procure from cooperative apothecaries abortifacient concoctions or "female pills" that brought on menstruation. The biographer of seventeenth-century English clergyman Ralph Josselin suspects that Jane Josselin's many "miscarriages" were actually abortions and that Ralph was complicit in them. Another English husband, Edward Stanley, applauded his wife, Henrietta, mother of nine, for inducing a miscarriage by means of "a hot bath, a tremendous walk & a great dose."[23]

Some American husbands were just as obliging. When his twenty-three-year-old wife, Fanny Sheppard, mother of his two young sons, wrote that she was once again pregnant, Confederate General Dorsey Pender invoked "God's will" but also solicited pills from his company's doctor to "relieve" her.[24] (Either the pills didn't work or Fanny refused to take them; Stephen Lee Pender was born several months after his father's death in 1863.) In North America and also in Europe, couples hoping to control conception relied as well on a rhythm method based on the erroneous assumption that ovulation occurs just before or during menstruation, as it does in dogs and other mammals. (This misconception was laid to rest in 1920.) Other strategies supposedly dislodged semen to prevent conception: wives straddled their husbands during intercourse or, post-coitally, sneezed lustily.

Overall, birth control was unreliable, and unwanted pregnancies were common. In any case, most birth control devices—sneezing being an obvious exception—required a husband's cooperation, which many husbands refused. Though Elizabeth Wirt was too often pregnant for her own fragile health and William worried that she might not survive another day, he impregnated her again almost immediately after she gave birth. Elizabeth's opinion that frequent pregnancies were a "curse which alighted upon poor <u>Eve</u> [and terrified] us miserable Females" failed to move William, and he allowed her "no prospect of escape" or any choice in the matter.[25]

A huge industry targeted pregnant women directly through extensive advertising in newspapers and women's magazines. A *British Medical Journal* writer discovered that in Britain, more than half of newspaper ads purporting to relieve temporary female indisposition, regulate menses, or remove impurities and other conditions were really selling abortifacients and abortion services. In North America, such products were hawked relentlessly, often with supposedly French or European provenance, which was presumed to make them superior. Madame Drunette's Lunar Pills, Dr. Peter's French Renovating Pills, Dr. Monroe's French Periodical Pills (advertised as popular among French nobles), Dr. Melveau's Portuguese Female Pills, and Old Doctor Gordon's Pearls of Health (manufactured in Montreal) were all pitched to pregnant women by warning them not to use them—"a blessing to mothers ... pregnant females should not use them, as they invariably produce a miscarriage," one solemnly advised.[26]

Some potions failed to produce miscarriages; others were dangerously effective. Ely van der Warkle, a nineteenth-century American obstetrician, found that products containing savin, a species of juniper, caused, among other symptoms, "violent pain in the abdomen, vomiting, powerful catharsis, tenesmus [agonizing urges to defecate], stranguary [painful, drop by drop urination], heat and burning in the bowels, rectum and anus, intoxication, severe headache, flushed face."[27] Abortifacients were so dangerous that the first American abortion laws were associated with poison control.

The difficulty of inducing miscarriage led to "surgical" abortion, perhaps the principal form of birth control. Abortion was an open secret that evoked raging debate about the point at which a fetus "quickened" into a living being. Doctors and writers inclined toward the moment of conception. Women, however, generally assumed that life took several weeks to take root. Because of health concerns and family and financial issues, writes historian of sexuality Angus McLaren, "abortion played a far more important role in the regulation of fertility than has usually been believed.… Women were not passive in relation to their fertility; they wanted to control it and were willing to go to considerable lengths to do so."[28] Between 1840 and 1870, for example, the rate of abortions among American women rose from one in every thirty live births to one in every five.[29] Dr. Edwin M. Hale of Chicago reported in 1866 that at least 10 percent of married women had aborted a fetus and that abortions terminated as many as a quarter of all pregnancies; many other physicians and medical societies corroborated these statistics in independent studies. Though women risked their health and not infrequently lost their lives, they persevered. One consequence, writes historian Colin Heywood, is that "breeding at levels close to what is biologically possible has been the exception rather than the rule in the West."[30]

Abortionists could be expensive, ranging from 10 to 50 guineas (US$15 to $75) in England, equivalent to at least 5 percent of a lower-middle-class family's annual income. The range was similarly vast in North America. One old male abortionist charged $10, payable in instalments. In Syracuse, van der Warkle reported in 1870, female abortionists using water had "achieved the difficult feat of auto-catheterism of the uterus cavity," and the fees could be so low that "the luxury of an abortionist is now within the reach of the serving girl."[31] In 1854, on the other hand, Ann Caroline Lohman, aka Madame Restell, one of the most successful abortionists, charged a hefty $50.

Lohman was a married English immigrant to the United States who began her career by offering abortifacients and abortions in New York City. She later advertised herself as the French-sounding Madame Restell, "female physician," and in the 1840s opened branches in Boston and Philadelphia.[32] Unlike her rivals, who referred euphemistically to "a medical procedure," her ads presented abortion as a solution for poor men and women "toiling to live, living but to toil," and for destitute widowed mothers of too many children. "Is it desirable, then, is it moral for parents to increase their families, regardless of consequences to themselves, or the wellbeing of their offspring, when a simple, easy, healthy, and certain remedy is within our control?" Restell asked rhetorically. (She also arranged adoptions of unwanted children after unwed mothers boarded with her until they gave birth.)

Women, especially the elite and privileged, flocked to her. She grew wealthy—her worth was at one time estimated at $800,000—and indulged her social aspirations by buying a mansion and fashionable clothes and aping her clients' lifestyle. She was untrained but skilled and intelligent, and if her potions failed, she aborted surgically. She maintained good standards of cleanliness, and no record exists of a client dying at her hands, though some must have; a modern study concludes that "her abortions were probably a little safer than childbirth," at least for the living mother. Restell, often indicted, was charged in 1847 with performing an abortion on Marie Bodine, the mistress of a factory agent. After a sensational trial and conflicting medical testimony, she was convicted of a lesser misdemeanour charge. She served a year in Blackwell's Island prison, where the warden catered to her so generously that he was fired. After her release, she resumed her work and built up her estate.

But though abortion flourished, it had many critics. Some feared that because white, Protestant, middle- and upper-class married women used abortion to delay, space, and limit their child-bearing, America would be swamped by Catholic foreigners and poorer people, "the ignorant, the low lived and the alien," who aborted much less frequently. Others worried that women freed of the consequences of sexual intercourse would become unmanageable and even promiscuous. The newly formed American Medical Association vigorously opposed untrained abortionists performing a medical procedure and, supported by the Roman Catholic and many Protestant churches, began to lobby to declare abortion illegal. Feminists condemned abortion as another assault on women's bodies, whereas the right of refusal to have sex would eliminate most unwanted births. Nonetheless, until the 1870s, Restell was largely untouchable. For one thing, prosecutors dared not risk arresting her and having their own wives and daughters identified as her clients.

Everything changed with the transformation of social values follow-ing the Civil War, when Anthony Comstock, the dour and obsessively puritanical head of the New York Society for the Suppression of Vice, made it his mission to rid the United States of the "filth" of birth control literature, and to prosecute abortionists, in particular Madame Restell. "I have," Comstock boasted, "convicted persons enough to fill a passen-ger train of sixty-one coaches, sixty containing sixty passengers each, and the sixty first almost full."[33] Largely through his efforts, the federal government passed the Comstock Act of 1873, declaring birth control devices obscene.

*This nuanced newspaper portrayal of abortionist Madame Restell's arrest by
Anthony Comstock, head of the New York Society for the Suppression of Vice,
reflects readers' fascination with the subject and, in the weeping woman, predicts
the grief Restell's arrest would cause many would-be clients.*

In 1878, Comstock targeted Restell with a sting operation, buying contraceptives from her, then returning to her house with police and newspaper reporters as witnesses. Restell, lonely and in mourning for her second husband, understood that she was doomed. On April 1, hours before she was to appear in court, she slit her throat.

Restell's suicide marked the end of relatively accessible abortion. (By then, the American Medical Association was defining abortion as "The work of destruction; The wholesale destruction of unborn infants."[34] Afterward, the abortion rate plunged, as Comstock and the anti-abortion movement prosecuted and shut down abortionists and continued proselytizing until public opinion, once tepid about abortion, turned sharply against it. Desperate women still aborted, but they were forced to settle for whatever abortion services they could find; they also tried to scrape, hook, tear, or corrode the fetus on their own, or with the help of friends. Middle-class women who had patronized Madame Restell delivered children they would have preferred to discard.

There was a last-ditch method of dealing with an unwanted infant: infanticide. Widespread well into the nineteenth century, infanticide included abandonment in rural ditches or urban gutters, or "overlaying" (smothering) to death. Infanticide was generally considered a sin rather than a crime, though unwed mothers were sometimes executed for it. In jurisdictions where it became a capital offence, the trend was for courts to avoid convicting the accused because of the harshness of the penalty.

We know what experts and critics said about contraceptive methods and abortion, and from fragments in diaries and personal correspondence, we know how individual men and women approached the issue of controlling birth. But we know little of the way contraception and abortion affected the dynamics of the relationship between husband and wife. We can only guess at the fear and despair unwanted pregnancies generated, the hushed discussions and quarrels, the stealthy planning.

FEEDING BABIES

Though searing or muted grief were common experiences, a majority of babies survived and had to be fed and nurtured, most suckled by their mothers. (A common cause of infant mortality was the traditional belief that colostrum was toxic rather than nourishing.) Guidelines for weaning varied greatly from era to era and between social classes. The primary duty of elite mothers was to nurture their infants, even if this meant neglecting their husbands and other children, and many of these women suckled their children several times a day, and sometimes as often as every two hours, for two or three years. Poorer mothers, on the other hand, often had to deal with severe time constraints. Those who toiled long hours in fields, mills, or factories suckled less frequently, before and after work. To quiet their little ones during the long intervals between feedings, they relied on laudanum and other opiates, and herbal concoctions, though this kind of child care resulted in a very high mortality rate.

But some women were too ill or weakened by childbirth to produce enough milk. Others were repelled by the thought of breastfeeding or had no interest in subjecting their bodies to its demands. Farm women whose families needed their labour and factory women whose families needed their earnings sacrificed extended breastfeeding and weaned early so they could work without interruption. The taboo against sex during lactation also prompted husbands to discourage their wives from suckling, and wives who hoped to prevent sex-deprived husbands from straying welcomed alternatives to mother's milk.

One such alternative was pap—a gruel of crushed breadcrumbs soaked in milk, water, or broth—given in a feeding vessel. Cow's or goat's milk was also used, sucked from a feeding vessel or directly from a cow's or nanny goat's teats. But until well into the eighteenth century, when better pap and feeding vessels were available and artificial feeding became more acceptable, many infants died of bacteria-caused diarrhea. As survival rates improved, more fathers took a keen interest in the feeding process.

Wet nurses—lactating mothers who nursed someone else's child— were much better alternatives, because they offered their client's child the greatest chance for survival. Except for emergency cases, when a friend or neighbour voluntarily nursed a baby whose mother could not, the wet nurse was a hireling whose child had either died or whose needs were sacrificed to those of a paying client's baby. (Wet nurses with wealthy clients hired other wet nurses to suckle their own children.)

Infants were sent to live with their wet nurse for at least six months and usually longer—the infant Jane Austen, for example, was sent to live at the home of Elizabeth Littlewood, who nursed and cared for her for about eighteen months. Unlike Cassandra Austen, some mothers could not bear a child's absence, and in defiance of medical "expertise," started weaning younger than generally recommended, often as early as seven months. Wealthier parents who visited the wet nurse sometimes discovered horrendous conditions. One distraught nineteenth-century mother reported: "when he cried she used to shake him, when she washed him she used to stuff the sponge in his little mouth—push her finger (beast!) into his dear little throat—say she hated the child, wished he were dead—used to let him lie on the floor screaming."[35]

The profession was dogged by stories about abused, underfed, neglected, or even switched babies. Breastfeeding advocates promoted breastfeeding one's own baby as natural and superior to wet-nursing. Yet throughout the eighteenth and into the nineteenth centuries, when more people turned to artificial feeding and more fathers took a keen interest in the weaning process, the practice of wet-nursing persisted.

Wet-nursing was less widespread in North America than in Europe. Puritans, for example, frowned on it; they believed that breast milk was permeated with moral qualities, so that children whose wet nurses had unsuspected character flaws were doomed. About 20 percent of elite American women used wet nurses. Even in the South, with its huge pool of black slaves who could be pressed into suckling duty, the great majority of white mothers nursed their own infants. Perpetually pregnant Elizabeth Wirt, for example, turned to slave nurses only when she was too sick to breastfeed. Otherwise, she endured "very sore nipples, and ... other pains.... And hope to make a good Nurse for our little Babe: who, subsists altogether on my milk."[36]

Slave mothers also nursed, but most were forced to return to work three weeks after giving birth, and for the first eight months were permitted only three daily breastfeedings, afterward reduced to twice daily. On many slaveholdings, the policy was to wean black children as quickly as possible and put them onto pap, though this often led to loss of appetite and malnutrition. Occasionally, when a slave child's life hung in the balance because his mother had died or did not have enough milk, his white mistress suckled him instead.

By the beginning of the nineteenth century, when North Americans were influenced by an idealized vision of motherhood that included nursing on demand for at least one year, wet nurses were employed only in cases of maternal death, illness, or difficulty with lactation, and had to take up residence under their employers' roof. They were usually young, poor, and unmarried, and were forced to send their own infants to foundling hospitals because, in the words of historian Janet Golden, "wet nursing often involved trading the life of a poor baby for that of a rich one."[37] Though wives were primarily responsible for child care and feeding, husbands participated in the decision to hire a wet nurse, and diaries and letters are filled with their observations about their children's wet nurses and associated problems.

In the South, whites embraced the ideal of child-centred families. Many white children were fed on demand before being weaned at the age of two years or older. One mother boasted that her nursing son was "large enough to talk of horse-racing, can make a fire, and feed calves." When, however, white mothers would not or could not breastfeed, the black mother selected as wet nurse had to leave her own infant in the care of an old slave "nurse" who, too decrepit to do other work, was charged with babysitting. "Sometimes you'd hear as many as five or six cryin' on one time. Granny wud give dem some kind uf tea to make dem shut up," one former slave recalled.[38]

By the early twentieth century, pasteurization and refrigeration transformed the bottling industry. Bottled milk, no longer filthy, germ-riddled, and adulterated, eliminated the need for the wet nurse. In the same era, infant "formulas" based on cow's milk were developed and artificial feeding grew in popularity. Promoted by enthusiastic physicians to responsive mothers, formula, with its pseudo-scientific moniker and ease of use, soared in popularity. Formula freed women from the constraints of breastfeeding. It also allowed fathers to feed their infants, though decades passed before cultural attitudes changed enough to encourage this.

RAISING CHILDREN

Scholars agree that child-rearing has always been central to marriage, but they are in profound disagreement about the nature of historical childhood. The controversy revolves around the issue of continuity versus change. Philippe Ariès (*Centuries of Childhood*), Lloyd deMause (*The History of Childhood*), and Lawrence Stone (*The Family, Sex and Marriage in England 1500–1800*) have described historical childhood as abusive, brutal, and loveless; it was, in deMause's words, "a nightmare from which we have only recently begun to awaken. The further back in history one goes, the lower the level of child care, and the more likely children are to be killed, abandoned, beaten, terrorized, and sexually abused."[39] Ariès believed that the Middle Ages had no concept of childhood and that later, children were more harshly disciplined because they were seen as different. He and Stone wrote that even parents who loved their children did not treat them lovingly, as individuals. Mothers lacked a "maternal instinct," were indifferent to infant mortality, and harshly disciplined survivors. Relief came only in the eighteenth century's enlightened notions of childhood, which portrayed little ones as innocent individuals. Only then did parents begin to lavish them with love, and parent–child relations developed to create a happier and more permissive family life.

More recent scholarship challenges this perspective. Linda Pollock (*Forgotten Children: Parent-Child Relations from 1500 to 1900* and *A Lasting Relationship: Parents and Children Over Three Centuries*) and Amanda Vickery (*The Gentleman's Daughter*) are among those who find in contemporary diaries, journals, autobiographies, and other records evidence that parents have always loved their children and treated them with loving care. Consider early-nineteenth-century mother Ellen Weeton Stock's delight in Mary, her toddler: "She has a thousand little engaging actions. Her hair is very light, and curls all over the head like a little mop; and she is all over so fat and so soft. I have many a kiss in the course of the day, and many a laugh at her little droll ways; her father would be quite lost without her, and I am sure, so should I. I wish I had another ... but hush! Don't tell."[40]

"In general, life for infants in the past, at least from the sixteenth century, was relatively pleasant," Pollock writes. "This finding is in direct opposition to the argument of most historians that, prior to the eighteenth century, infants were unwelcome, ignored and neglected by their parents."[41] Vickery adds, "Unsurprisingly ... the story proved at its weakest in the presentation of unremitting misery and severity in the seventeenth-century family—a picture which was laughably easy to disprove using letters, diaries and depositions, which revealed widespread emotional investment in children."[42]

This does not imply that the child born to parents consumed by the demands of earning a living and surviving another day enjoyed the same level of care as a privileged baby. Social class, poverty, financial crises, illegitimacy, ethnicity, disabilities, and myriad other factors shaped children's lives: the dying infant of the desperate wet nurse, the slave child sold away from her enslaved parents, the illegitimate child shunned by society, the child of poor but prolific parents (the latter immortalized in Thomas Hardy's *Jude the Obscure* as Little Father Time, who hanged his two siblings and himself "because we are too menny"). But there was no cultural bias against deep emotional attachment to children, or against affording them as much care as possible.

For centuries, parents swaddled their little ones to keep them warm and safe. Wrapping them in layers of cloth, supporting their heads, and binding their limbs straight down was thought to make their bones strong and their posture straight. The urine and feces that soiled them was not considered unhealthy. Many mothers preferred to dry rather than wash wet diapers to preserve the healing power of urine. Furthermore, swaddled babies could not crawl and wander away. They were protected from domestic and farm animals, especially biting pigs. Their parents were free to concentrate on other tasks.

Until the eighteenth century's barrage of rationalist and medical literature, folk and female lore served as child-rearing guides. Afterward, as physicians pontificated about and medicalized child care, mothers were held to such different and confusing standards that many became guilt-ridden, frustrated, and fearful. As knowledge of the human body increased, they abandoned some traditional kinds of child care, including swaddling.

Fathers as well as mothers were concerned about their children's teething, which usually meant sleepless nights for everyone and could make babies sick. "His Mother and I were in great uneasiness about him," one husband wrote.[43] Sleep-deprived British artist James Cobden-Sanderson temporized: "I thought of the innumerable babies all the world over crying at the same moment, of the babies who up to now had cried, and of the hosts of generations yet destined to do so. And I thought it was indeed absurd to be irritated."[44]

Parents were intensely interested in their children's development, and recorded their toddlers' first steps, first words, inoculations and illnesses—the latter terrifying in an era of high child mortality. "The emotional cost of illness was dear to both parents, the father's panic was as conspicuous as the mother's anguish when the lives of beloved babies hung in the balance," writes Vickery.[45] "Most willingly wou'd I make a pilgrimage barefoot as far as my legs would carry me, to get the poor little Fellow cured," wrote one distraught eighteenth-century father.[46] William Wirt sat up with his sick daughter Laura "for several nights passed."[47]

Playtime also figured in parents' personal records, though a few fathers disapproved of it as a distraction from the more important business of learning. Most described indulgently how their children rambled in the woods, held make-believe weddings, threw snowballs, played sports, fished, staged mock funerals, played house and dolls, boxed, collected shells, and pretended to be soldiers, lamplighters, gardeners, coalmen, organ grinders, and railway engineers.

Education was of far greater concern to both mothers and fathers. Sons and daughters were usually taught different subjects, though both studied religion. Common offerings for girls were embroidery, drawing, sewing, painting, sketching, singing, dancing, geography, history, arithmetic, English, and sometimes French. Good character, meaning obedience and docility, was emphasized; so was good posture. Privileged girls might also be introduced to such skills as reverse painting on glass, wax and shell work, and making artificial flowers. Boys studied the three R's and often progressed to geometry, Latin, and Greek. They might also learn the classics, modern geography and history, philosophy and rhetoric, and even mechanics and fencing.

Before the seventeenth century, most children were schooled at home, often by tutors. By the eighteenth century, some were sent to school; there again girls and boys studied different subjects. Many diarists recorded their frustration at their children's inattentiveness, restlessness, levity, and indifference to the subject matter. A luckier few rejoiced at their precocity and mastery of the material.

Both mothers and fathers disciplined and punished their children. Diaries and autobiographies of adults and children portray a far greater number of lenient parents than strict or harsh disciplinarians. Physical punishment was usually a last resort, after reason, cajoling, and small punishments—no dessert, being sent to bed without supper—had failed. In the mid-eighteenth century, Fanny Glanville Boscawen, a noted bluestocking English intellectual, described how she dealt with her four-year-old Billy's refusal to eat his breakfast: "How perverse and saucy we are, and how much we deal in the words won't, can't, shan't, etc. ... but the rod and I went to breakfast with him, and though we did not come into action, nor anything like it, yet the bottom of the porringer was very fairly revealed."[48]

Some parents tried to break their children's wills, even slapping babies, but they were far outnumbered by those who relied on "humouring and cockering" (indulging) their little ones, in the disapproving words of unmarried, childless philosopher John Locke.[49] Punishments were physically harsher in the first half of the nineteenth century than in the previous two centuries and softened again in the second half.

Husbands and wives argued intensely about child discipline and commiserated with each other over their children's obstinacy and bad behaviour. W. Byrd was "out of humour with my wife for forcing Evie"—their nearly three-year-old daughter—"to eat against her will." Another father was "at times much depressed" at his inability to relate to and empathize with his children.[50] Some despaired of their children's characters and believed they were depraved. Most emphasized the importance of religious instruction and the joys of righteous living. By the nineteenth century, they sought ways to make such teaching agreeable. One boy, for example, aimed to read the entire Bible for his mother's reward of a knife, a wallet, and a coat and his father's of a dollar.

In colonial North America as in Europe, until boys were six or seven they wore dresses, roomy and loose enough for growth and efficient toilet training, and shorter than baby gowns, the ancestor of today's christening gown, designed for babies before they could walk. Until boys wore pants, gender could be so difficult to distinguish that portrait painters included visual clues: leaping dogs, guns, daggers, hats, drums, horse whips, and other items associated with maleness. Boys also tended to have bangs and side-parted hair, and wore darker colours than girls.

Montreal brothers Henry Lawrence and Frederick Gordon Belcher in 1891. Toddler Henry is still in a gown while Frederick has been breeched. His sailor's suit was a typical boy's outfit.

Breeching—dressing a boy in breeches or in trousers—was an important ritual passage; it ended "infancy" and corresponded to the age of reason as most societies understood it. For working-class children not already employed, breeching meant entry into the workplace as domestics, farm helpers, or factory workers.

After breeching, wealthier fathers assumed more control over their sons' education or training, arranging for schools or tutors or personally instructing them. Fathers assigned and reviewed homework. Through encouragement, hectoring, and discipline, they tried to inculcate the value of a proper education. Boys learned Latin, Greek, arithmetic, and the social graces, including dancing, and many proceeded to university or trained for a profession. As photography developed in the nineteenth century, newly breeched boys were often photographed with their fathers.

For girls, puberty was the true rite of passage. As girls matured, both parents expected them to learn womanly skills, notably the future management of a household. Privileged girls began serious training for womanhood, which included handiwork, music, and French; other girls prepared for the work—paid and at home—they were destined for. On special occasions, girls brushed their braids into more formal, upswept hairstyles to signal impending adulthood.

North American Childhood

Through emigrants, literature, and social ideals, European child-rearing strongly influenced North America's. But North Americans adapted the European model to their different circumstances and to their regional needs and perspectives. The Puritans, whose influence still resonates, were disproportionately influential. As elsewhere in the Western world, the Puritan patriarchal structure made fathers responsible for religious teaching and discipline. Both were considered so important that in 1646 the Massachusetts Bay Colony and Connecticut passed laws obliging parents to teach—and their children to learn—Puritan teachings, on pain of death.

Puritan society's severe laws also reflected their concerns about children's misbehaviour. Children over sixteen who struck or cursed either parent faced the death penalty unless they could prove parental neglect in educating them or prove that they had been beaten to the point of mutilation or fear of death. Stubborn or rebellious sons faced the same fate.

In reality, Puritan laws barked but seldom bit, and not even the most egregiously rebellious child was hanged. John Porter, a thirty-one-year-old Salem bachelor, cursed his father as a "liar and a simple Ape, shit-tabed," and his (smelly) mother as "Shithouse" and "Pisshouse," stabbed a servant, threatened to kill his brother, and tried to burn down his parents' house and to slaughter their cattle. But instead of swinging on the gallows, this miscreant was sentenced to stand on them for an hour, with a rope around his neck, wearing a placard inscribed with his crimes.[51]

Puritan parents disciplined their younger children harshly but not brutally. Only one child, eleven-year-old Elizabeth Emerson, laid a charge of parental cruelty under the New England laws, after her father kicked her and beat her with a grain-threshing implement. He was convicted of excessive and cruel beating, and fined. Puritan society tolerated physical punishment of children so long as it broke no bones, drew no blood, or lacerated no flesh. Parents resorted to it more frequently on smaller children, and much more on boys than on girls. (In this era, wives were legally, if not actually, exempted from being beaten; between 1640 and 1680, the Massachusetts Bay and Plymouth colonies were the first in the Western world to pass laws protecting "marryed woemen … from bodilie correction or stripes from her husband.")

While the Puritans established themselves in New England, the French were creating a Roman Catholic patriarchal society in New France. In the eighteenth century, the French Canadians' high birth rate offset their high child mortality rate. Adults often died young as well, so that about half the adolescents in any family lost at least one parent. Widowed husbands and wives remarried, and the blended families they created were a common feature of French-Canadian society.

In that rural society, most children lived on farms and were valued family members who helped with agricultural and domestic chores. If they had any education, it was thanks to Catholic religious orders that provided educational opportunities otherwise unavailable. There was a shortage of teachers for boys, but girls benefited from well-organized female teaching orders and tended to be better educated than their brothers. The nuns taught them religion, reading, writing, sewing, and other skills suited for their futures as wives or—the only other alternative—as nuns.

Unlike girls, some boys undertook a secondary education with Latin, rhetoric, philosophy, and theology. Most boys worked under their father's supervision on the family farm or apprenticed to a tradesman. Poor or orphaned children under twelve, however, were seldom accepted as apprentices. They were put straight to work, often in domestic service, and paid only their room and board.

In the disease-riddled, turbulent, and tobacco-rich Chesapeake colonies of Virginia and Maryland, child-rearing was quite different. Farmers, labourers, and landless younger sons came in high numbers from England, all seduced by propaganda that promised them the chance of fertile land. But the noxious environment of their low-lying tidewater, with its stagnating water contaminated with human waste, fostered mosquitoes and disease. Until the mid-1660s, half of the region's English indentured servants, the majority of the population, died of malaria, typhus, or dysentery within three years of arriving.

This vastly disproportionate male immigration skewed the gender ratio and increased the risk of rape and bridal pregnancy; it also put pressure on teenaged girls to marry, usually to men much older than they were. The consequence of "frequent sickness, early death, and a shortage of women that curtailed marital opportunity for men warped Chesapeake society, making it a parody of the traditional English World the immigrants had left behind," concludes historian Lorena S. Walsh.[52]

The male mortality rate was higher than the female, so that there was an excellent chance that a wife would be widowed. The result was frequent remarriage and an abundance of orphans. In one Virginia county, nearly three-quarters of children up to twenty-one years old had suffered the death of at least one parent, and a third had lost both. Children were equally vulnerable to disease, and unlike in New

England and New France, in an average family only two or three survived to maturity. Second and third marriages that produced large and complex households were exceptional. Deadly disease usually struck so relentlessly that even these families seldom had more than three or four children.

Colonial officials dealt with many of the orphans by arranging apprenticeships for them, which also increased the supply of skilled tradesmen. Another consequence of early parental death was that more young men than in other colonies gained autonomy and matured without the constraints and influence of a patriarch. A substantial minority of these men did not, however, inherit their father's estate until much later. Knowing that they would likely leave younger widows, husbands often specified in their wills that their sons (and sometimes daughters) could touch their inheritance only after the widow no longer needed it to support herself and the family.

Family life on this region's plantations was different still. Isolated from their peers, the sons and daughters of planting families grew very close to each other. But the gender divide was sharp. Older sons inherited the most valuable property, younger sons the less valuable. Daughters often inherited slaves and cash but seldom real estate; they were expected to rely on their future husbands for support. As Thomas Jefferson advised his daughter, Martha, "The happiness of your life now depends on continuing to please a single person."[53] Money or love was seldom a choice for women who had to manipulate the marriage market to obtain a mate who was already prosperous or at least had prospects; men, on the other hand, had more leeway to indulge their personal inclinations.

Much was permitted young white males: drinking, cockfighting, horse racing, and sexual experimentation with black women they owned, employed, or bullied and, despite the myth of white female purity, with the white women they had to marry. (In the mid-eighteenth century in one Virginia county, for example, between one-quarter and one-third of brides were pregnant.) Their upbringing prepared these white males for their adult roles as self-indulgent and authoritarian husbands and fathers.

Enslaved Childhood

Slaves had diametrically different childhoods than their white owners. Their family structure was under constant attack. Few planting families showed any interest in respecting the connection and needs of the black families under their legal control. They actively interfered in their most intimate relationships, forcing a male slave to take two wives to increase fertility, replacing a spouse on another property with a resident one, encouraging a woman with a barren husband to find another man by hiring her out to a far-off employer. A slave owner's wife who called "darkey" marriages "comical, mirthful and hilarious" was likely expressing a typical attitude toward slave unions.[54]

Fully half of slave children were raised in single-parent homes, usually headed by mothers. Owners ended roughly two out of five slave marriages, usually by selling slaves or by giving them away as wedding gifts or as bequests in their wills. A North Carolina study of planters' wills found that only eight out of ninety-two directed their executors to keep slave families intact. Thomas Jefferson justified selling an older slave away from his family, saying that he was "always willing to indulge connections seriously formed by those people" but only where "it could be done reasonably." Planters feeling burdened by too-prolific slave mothers called these excess slave children a "botheration" and gave them away. Mothers and fathers were torn away from their children, and from each other; one of the saddest spirituals slaves sang as they worked was, "Mother, is Master going to sell us tomorrow?/Yes, yes, yes!/O, watch and pray."

To white masters, slave children were quantifiable chattel, either encumbrances or, much more frequently, future assets. In 1858, the *Southern Cultivator* published this article from an unidentified author:

I own a woman who cost me $400 when a girl in 1827. Admit she made me nothing—only worth her victuals and clothing. She now has three children, worth over $3000 and have been field hands say three years in that time making enough to pay their expenses before they were half hands, and then I have the profit of all half hands. She has *only three boys and a girl [surviving] out of a dozen; yet, with all her bad management, she has paid me ten per cent interest, for her work was to be an average good, and I would not this night touch $700 for her. Her oldest boy is worth $1250 cash, and I can get it.*[55]

At every stage in a slave child's life, parental control was sabotaged by whites. In the many cases of "abroad" marriages, when husbands and wives had to live apart on their different owners' properties, mothers were the primary parent, fathers infrequent visitors. But those mothers were at their owners' disposal, and many struggled to snatch time away from work to care for their children. Before long, children were inducted into the world of work. "Work, work, work, was scarcely more the order of the day than of the night," recalled former slave Frederick Douglass. "Us chillen start to work soon's us could toddle," recalled another.[56]

Slave parents, always mindful of the looming presence of whites, often thrashed their children to stamp out behaviour that might enrage white owners. "Learn them to be Smart and Deadent [sic] and allow them to Sauce no person," an absent father instructed his wife.[57] But whites consistently usurped parents' authority and punished black children themselves, and the children quickly learned that their enslaved parents were powerless to help them. Slave Jacob Stroyer tried hard to force his parents to intervene when an overseer repeatedly whipped him. "Father very coolly said to me, 'Go back to your work and be a good boy, for I cannot do anything for you.'" When his mother attempted to intercede, the overseer whipped both her and her son. Then Stroyer experienced the sad epiphany shared by millions of other enslaved children: "The idea first came to me that ... father and mother could not save me from punishment, as they themselves had to submit to the same treatment."[58]

A former slave remembered how his father wept after a beating and sang: "I'm troubled, I'm troubled, I'm troubled in mind./If Jesus don't help me I surely will die./O Jesus my Savior, on thee I'll depend./When trouble are near me, you'll be my true friend."[59]

The mortality rate for infant and adolescent slaves was very high— the 1850 census revealed that slave newborns died at twice the rate of white newborns—the consequence of inadequate supervision, malnutrition (including fetal), convulsions, teething, tetanus, lockjaw, and worms, all linked to too-early weaning; diseases such as tuberculosis, cholera, and influenza; and overwork. The skeletons of slaves reveal unhealed bones broken by beatings and hauling excessive burdens. Their children's fate often embittered the relationship between slave mothers and fathers, and underscored their impotence as mature adults.

Rural and Urban Differences

Throughout rural North America, childhood was far from child's play. In nineteenth-century rural Upper Canada, families averaged five to six children. Until they were five to seven years old, boys were allowed to play and watch their elders. Then they were put to work gathering firewood and water, feeding chickens and collecting eggs and other household tasks that freed their parents for harder, more skilled tasks. Boys assisted with their family's workload or were "put out" as apprentices or farmhands. As their physiques developed, they assumed more adult jobs. By the age of fourteen, most boys were doing the same jobs as adult men.

Young girls had less leisure and, even as toddlers, helped their mothers and learned basic domestic skills. At six, most could spin, knit, sew, and mind younger siblings. A few years later, they swept, washed dishes, mended, cooked, gardened, and cared for domestic animals. Throughout non-slave regions of North America, girls as young as eleven were hired out to other families to learn and practise domestic skills. By sixteen, most girls were doing the work of grown women.

By the latter half of the nineteenth century, middle-class urban parents increasingly considered play an important part of a child's experience. Most other North Americans, however, could not afford the luxury of unemployed children. In *Settlers' Children: Growing Up on the Great Plains*, Elizabeth Hampsten tells the poignant story of rural childhood during the homesteading rush, as recorded in diaries, letters, manuscript collections, and oral histories. These youngsters worked long, hard hours on the farm at the expense of their schooling. Their parents, especially fathers, could be stern disciplinarians. Boys were valued so much more than girls that some women had to apologize for producing daughters.[60]

Yet a stream of visiting Europeans expressed shock at the independence, indiscipline, and insolence of North American children: the pipe-smoking, brandy-swilling French-Canadian boys who disrespected women by keeping their hats on indoors; the young women who dressed up in styles usually reserved for European gentlewomen—in general, "pert, impertinent, disrespectful, arrogant brats."[61]

On both farms and in cities, especially among poorer people, dependence on their children's economic contributions diluted parents' authority. So did (usually paternal) abuse, or overwork at home, on the farm or in waged jobs, all of which inspired children, usually boys, to run away. In his article "Runaway Boys," New York police inspector Thomas Evans singled out adventure and abusive fathers as the main reasons boys ran away. The promise offered by the vastness of the land and the bustle of the cities could fill an unhappy or restless young person with resolve to escape parental authority in favour of independence, no matter how difficult.

MIDDLE-CLASS CHILDHOOD

The springboard for the phenomenon of the developing concept of childhood was the drastic decline in the birth rate that began in the nineteenth century, as North Americans resorted to whatever forms of birth control they could, including abstinence and abortion. Between 1850 and 1900 in the United States, the birth rate plunged from five to three children per family. In Canada, too, fertility declined, with the notable exception of French Canadians, whose birth rate remained high.[62]

By the nineteenth century, urban dwellers who had achieved middle-class economic status presided over the birth of what we now consider modern childhood. "Overall, childhood dependency was prolonged, childrearing became a more intensive and self-conscious activity, and schooling was extended," historian Steven Mintz writes.[63] Mothers were directly responsible for child care, and even wealthy women with nursemaids and domestic help oriented their lives around their children or faced severe criticism for neglecting their duties. Fathers worried, advised, and sometimes assisted their wives, pitching in to calm a crying baby or to nurse a sick one. But they knew that their primary duty was to provide for and protect their family, and that their wife's was to raise their children and to manage the household. Fatherhood added to husbands' marital responsibilities, but motherhood transformed wives. It consumed their time and energy, dictated their priorities, and, in Vickery's words, "all but obliterated their past selves and public profile."[64]

The new ideal of childhood was conceptualized as a series of stages in which devoted parents moulded their child's character because, in William Wordsworth's words, "the child is father of the man." As children stayed longer in school and lived in the family home until their late teens or early twenties rather than leaving for a job elsewhere, their Angel in the House mother protected them from the outside world. These not so young children became an even more important feature of their parents' marriage.

This extended childhood was designed to shape children to be successful, girls as (Angelic) homemakers and mothers, boys as wage-earning husbands and fathers. Mothers were expected to encourage their daughters to nurture girlish qualities, their sons to nurture boyish ones. Girls cuddled, fed, cleaned, dressed, nursed, prayed for, and carried their dolls, often alone; they also helped their mothers cook and clean house and sew and knit. Boys played ball, used little construction tool sets, pulled toy horses, shot marbles, rode wagons, and learned manly skills and qualities—courage, toughness, strength, and dominance—usually as part of a team.

Mothers were responsible for providing their children with suitable toys, like those in the American exhibit at the Universal Exhibition in Vienna during the 1890s that, an expert observer wrote, directed "the mind and habits of the child to home economy and husbandry and mechanical labour."[65] Toys also introduced children to consumerism, the drive to acquire new things, in this case a burgeoning array of items designed to stoke but never satisfy the lust to buy. (One board game, introduced in the 1880s, was The Little Shoppers Game.)

Mothers were responsible as well for identifying and meeting their children's non-toy needs, which during the Victorian era expanded to include fashionable clothing, sporting equipment, special nursery and children's furniture, educational games, and interesting magazines and books, to say nothing of the good food and the new medicines promoted as healthful for children in an era of high child mortality.

The Outdoor Handy Book (1910) explained the goal of such games as marbles: "What we want for a playmate is a fair and square fellow, who will stand by a friend through thick and thin, and, without being quarrelsome, defend his rights and never 'weaken.' ... His manliness will cause him to treat his companion and the girls with courtesy.... He will not cheat."

As consumer items proliferated, gender roles hardened, sharpening how girlhood and boyhood were delineated. Girls were in training to be caring wives and mothers, boys to be benevolently authoritative providers and protectors. Girls (and to a lesser extent boys) had to remain chaste and, if possible, sexually ignorant. Yet before they married, young women often studied and worked. This gave them a taste of freedom from total dependence on their fathers. Often, though, it also fuelled resentment at the knowledge that as soon as they married, they would be expected to revert back into dependence on their husbands.

"In America," mused French visitor Alexis de Tocqueville, "the independence of woman is irrevocably lost in the bonds of matrimony ... an unmarried woman ... makes her father's house an abode of freedom and of pleasure; the [wife] lives in the home of her husband as if it were a cloister.... She has been taught beforehand what is expected of her.... the conjugal tie [is] very strict."[66]

As boys matured into young men, their parents encouraged them to look outside the home and to join clubs, societies, and organizations of all stripes: social, vocational, political, recreational. Middle-class boys gravitated toward Bible and reform organizations that promoted temperance or abolition of slavery. Their working-class counterparts joined volunteer fire and military groups, and urban street gangs.

WORKING-CLASS CHILDHOOD

The new childhood spread from the middle to the working class, at least as an ideal, but the process was slow. While middle-class parents ensured that their youngsters studied and trained for their futures, poorer parents still had to set their children to work so they could contribute to the family's financial survival. The expansion of industry and the market economy, the commercialization of agriculture, and massive immigration served to deepen the chasm between middle-class children and those from the working classes, who manned factories, fields, shops, and houses, and usually had a different kind of relationship with their parents.

Unlike more prosperous women, working-class wives were often pushed by their husbands' low wages and often cyclical employment into the workforce. Factories encouraged this, relentlessly recruiting women and children, whom they paid even less. North America modelled its factory system on England's, where in 1830 in Lancashire alone, 560 cotton mills employed over 110,000 workers, including 35,000 children, some as young as six. In the House of Commons, reformer William Cobbett testified that 300,000 little girls were responsible for England's manufacturing superiority. "It was asserted," he declared, "that if these little girls worked two hours less per day, our manufacturing superiority would depart from us."[67]

In the last quarter of the nineteenth century, women and children formed 42 percent of Montreal's industrial workforce and 33 percent of Toronto's. By the end of the nineteenth century, the overall ratio of men to women and children working in factories throughout North America was about one to four. Some of the consequences were male under- and unemployment, and the transformation of the nature of childhood, marriage, and families.

North American child-labour reforms mimicked England's. In 1832, the New England Association of Farmers, Mechanics, and Other Workingmen resolved: "Children should not be allowed to labor in the factories from morning till night, without any time for healthy recreation and mental culture ... [for that] endangers their ... well-being and health." In 1813, a Connecticut law required working children to have some schooling. In 1836, Massachusetts enacted a law requiring factory workers under the age of fifteen to attend school at least three months a year. By 1899, twenty-eight states had passed laws—inconsistently enforced—regulating child labour. It was only in 1938 that Congress passed the Fair Labor Standards Act that established sixteen as the minimum age for work during school hours, fourteen for certain jobs after school, and eighteen for work considered dangerous.

Canadian child-labour laws paralleled those in the States. In Ontario, school was not compulsory until 1871, when all children between seven and twelve were to attend school at least four months a year. In the early

In a New York tenement, the Romana family sews dresses for the Campbell Kid dolls. Mrs. Romana and her oldest son alternate using the sewing machine. The Campbell Kids, cheery and chubby, were introduced in 1910 and are still made today.

Photographer Lewis Wickes Hine was so struck by the wretched conditions in which poor parents and their children made Campbell Kid dolls that he sought out some of the privileged children who played with and treasured them.

Lincolnton, N.C., mill workers, 1908: John Erwin (left), who worked nights, claimed he was eleven. Dan Biggerstaff (right), ten, had worked three years in the mill but was now attending school.

twentieth century, provincial laws—not always enforceable—required children to stay in school until the age of sixteen.

The dynamics between working children and their parents were very different from the middle-class model, which cast motherhood as a wife's primary vocation. As thousands of photographs and reports testify, children, some as young as three, participated in their family's piecework assignments. Working children seldom played or exercised, and most were deprived of sunlight and fresh air. They often ate poorly and, as investigative commissions throughout North America discovered, were sometimes just too tired to eat. They suffered ill health but, like their parents, had to keep working. When education became mandatory, they were often truant.

Most immigrant children worked, in or outside the home. A 1911 American study of Polish immigrants, for example, found that children of skilled and unskilled workers earned 35 and 46 percent respectively of their families' incomes. As these children became fluent in English

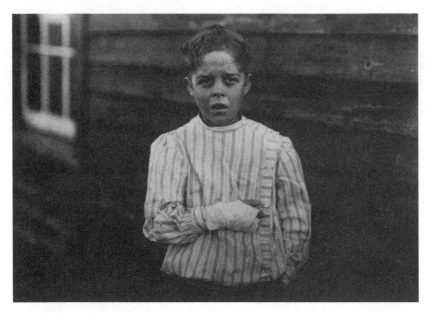

In Bessemer City, N.C., Sanders Spinning Mill worker Edmund Newson, eleven, lost two fingers and had his hand crushed in a spinning machine. His father was fighting for the compensation money Edmund was supposed to receive; his mother was bitter he could no longer work. His aunt told the photograper, "Now he's jes got to where he could be of some help to his ma an' then this happens and he can't never work *no more like he oughter." Edmund's ten-year-old brother continued to work at the mill.*

and acculturated, their relations with their parents reflected cultural chasms, frustration, and resentment. For girls, these tensions were heightened in battles with parents, especially fathers, who tried to impose strict patriarchal values. Some girls used their wages to rebel in various ways, such as to pressure their reluctant fathers to let them get at least some education.

Underprivileged children, understanding their parents' inability to provide for them, were often enterprising. In Toronto, the *World* newspaper's "Police Blotters" described how six little boys "presented themselves at Police Headquarters … asking for three years in the reformatory so they could learn to read and master a trade." Rebuffed because they had committed no crime, they returned with a sleigh they claimed to

Addie Card, twelve, a spinner at North Pownall Cotton Mill, Vermont, in 1910. She started work during the summer vacation and intended to keep her job and not return to school.

John Gannon, fourteen, was too frail and undersized to qualify for an employment certificate. Here, likely wearing his dead father's coat, he beams because he has just been awarded a scholarship. The family was lodging with friends in a New York tenement. Two siblings were in the orphan asylum, and his mother was struggling hard to find cleaning jobs so she could afford her own apartment and reclaim them.

have stolen and pleaded guilty to theft. (The *World* deemed their chances of being sent to the reformatory very slim.)[68]

Some working-class parents, unable to feed their families, surrendered them to orphanages. Unlike desperate European parents who abandoned their children (as happened in the early nineteenth century to about one-fifth of babies born in Paris and to even more in St. Petersburg and Milan), they tried to place them as safely as possible. Between 1860 and 1889, poor or ailing working-class parents placed more than 1,000 girls in Montreal's Saint Alexis orphanage, which provided food and lodging, education, and other training opportunities unavailable to poorer families. In 1895, Montreal's Protestant Infants' Home identified "maternal illness" as the chief cause for leaving children there. When times were better or the children were old enough to work, their parents often reclaimed them. Some stayed only one month; by 1865, the majority stayed less than a year but often returned for another session. Widows and widowers also surrendered their children; widowers, more likely than widows to remarry, usually reclaimed them once they had a new wife to take on the child-rearing. In the 1880s, Saint Alexis demanded small monthly payments, which pushed the poorest families to keep their daughters at home.

CHILD ABUSE

There is a chasm between the way thinkers or public intellectuals and parents have understood the nature of childhood. In seventeenth-century literature, children were often portrayed as depraved, in the eighteenth century as innocent, and in the nineteenth century as a synthesized blend of innocent and depraved. But no matter what their century's philosophical bent, in their correspondence and their memoirs, most parents have spoken of their children as deeply loved individuals with praiseworthy qualities alongside their flaws.

Yet the assumption of endemic child abuse suggested by philosophical writings has influenced historical narratives. Modern scholars reject this interpretation. After reading all *The Times*'s articles for the years 1785 to 1860 that reported child cruelty, historian Linda Pollock found only 385 charges of child neglect or sexual abuse, including 19 for incest. Though many more must have gone unreported, there is little evidence that abuse was rampant. Furthermore, in both tone and content *The Times*'s reports roundly condemned child abuse. In 1810, for example, a woman on trial for "barbarously beating and ill-treating" her four-year-old daughter barely escaped the "fury" of female attendees.[69] At other trials, magistrates, witnesses, and the general public expressed their horror.

This is not to deny that the standards of child discipline were harsher than today's, though memoirs and letters suggest a more nuanced reality: centuries of mild discipline interspersed with whippings (the term used for anything from a perfunctory spanking to a severe beating) and various severe punishments. Persistent reports of widespread parental cruelty among the working classes also had some basis in reality, though it seemed to stem from desperation rather than intent.

Examples of how working-class parents coped with child-rearing illustrate how, to middle-class eyes, desperate measures could seem abusive. There were the working parents who, unable to afford child care, dosed their children with laudanum or alcohol to keep them quiet and unmoving during their long hours alone, or who left them without adult supervision, to be watched—or to watch—other children. This was the case described in the Introduction, when Elizabeth C. Watson, who investigated the conditions of New York tenement buildings, came across four shivering children huddled together in a hallway. Their mother had locked them out while she carried piecework to her boss; otherwise, they might set the apartment on fire, which was worse than being locked out. What else could she do? she demanded of Watson. What indeed?

Parents neglected their children to keep them alive, to keep a roof over their heads, and to put food on the table. The press of time—to say nothing of financial constraints—often meant inferior food. Mothers with outside jobs or piecework assignments bought fast food from pushcarts or delegated the task of cooking to their children. They also stretched their family's food resources by reserving the best food for their husbands, whom they believed needed the nourishment to earn their indispensable wages. In other respects as well, a working husband's health needs were put before children's or women's, with consequences that could be interpreted as abusive.

Working children, even small ones, were harder to control than those entirely dependent on their parents. Boys who worked in the mines alongside their fathers are a case in point. When mine owners saved money by hiring two boys for every man, they created serious intergenerational tensions. In *Boys in the Pits*, his study of the eight-to-fifteen-year-old boys who toiled in Canadian mines, historian Robert McIntosh quotes a nineteenth-century adult miner: "There are no children working in the mine. They may be children when they go in ... but a fortnight or so thoroughly works that out of them. They then become old fashioned boys. They get inured to all sorts of danger and hardship."[70] A father's inability to earn a sufficient living undermined his authority, and some fathers used excessive force to try to control their resentful and rebellious children.

The relations between fathers and mothers and their working children could be strained in ways they were not in middle-class homes, and had not been when children had worked on farms or in home industries under the father's supervision. Many resented being sent into factories, mills, and other workplaces, and, after gruelling and thankless days of toil, balked at having to hand over the small wages they yearned to spend on themselves. They also resented their parents' neediness.

Children were also traumatized by abusive working conditions. Official investigations into the treatment of child workers confirmed that Canadian and American children were beaten, strapped, and locked into their workplaces so they could not escape. Some Canadian cigar factories imprisoned miscreants—for example children who played during working hours—in dungeon-like "black-holes." A Massachusetts glass manufacturer fenced his factory with barbed wire to keep boys younger than twelve, who worked at night carrying loads of hot glass, from escaping.

Employers defended these practices, claiming that they were *in loco parentis* and that parents supported them. Montreal cigar factory foreman Alexander McGregor swore that parents had instructed him to "remove any part of the boy's clothing and chastise them, as I would my own children." A foreman at another cigar factory in Montreal, testifying before the Royal Commission on the Relations of Labour and Capital (1889), declared that "it would not hurt [a misbehaving child] to be hit on the backside with [a metal mould] as much as with the hand." Nor did he see anything indecent in a foreman whacking an eighteen-year-old girl's backside. "When she is very disobedient and there are about fifty or sixty other girls there, I think it is only right that she should be taught a lesson when she deserves it."

Children were physically maimed by dangerous machinery and woefully inadequate training. An Ontario agricultural woodworker, John Davidson, testified about the frequent accidents to boys operating the planer, ripsaw, crosscut saw, and sand-papering machines. "Their fingers are cut off."[71]

Entire generations of working children had to come to terms with the harsh conditions of their employment as well as with their anger at their parents for requiring them to work, for failing to protect them, and for subjecting them to homes that lacked most creature comforts. Some, in adult memoirs, mentioned a mother's lack of tenderness. Others understood that their parents had been helpless to do anything differently or better. A few recalled their parents seeking legal redress against employers who abused them.

Reformer Elizabeth Watson grasped the absurdity, or at least the impossibility, of judging the world of impoverished families by the standards of middle- and upper-class privilege. She asked how the "hallowed" and "beneficent influences of home" applied to "these miserable homework factories with their inmates working ... from early morn to late night in order to earn enough to keep body and soul together." She summed it up with one of the children's "Sorrowful Rhymes": "Jack Sprat had little work,/His wife could get much more./She and the children worked all day/To keep the wolf from the door."[72]

The Empress Josephine's marriage ended because she could give Napoleon no children, while Henrietta Stanley, mother of nine, earned her husband's praise after she "succeeded" in miscarrying a tenth. Ann

Caroline Lohman, aka Madame Restell, earned a fortune as the abortionist to wealthy women, but Princess Charlotte's obstetrician shot himself after she died following childbirth. Poor Montreal parents placed daughters in orphanages that could feed and educate them. An Italian immigrant mother whose husband was away looking for work locked her shivering and whimpering youngsters out of their tenement while she delivered piecework to her boss, earning money to feed them.

The ideals of the nineteenth century's New Childhood model were promoted as universal, but they were rooted in the lifestyles and experiences of the middle and upper classes. Over time, the working and poorer classes absorbed and accepted these values, but because of the very different infrastructure of their lives, they practised a much-modified version. Central to the dichotomy was the need for women and children to work. This chapter's vignettes of the infinitely complicated nature of childhood and of child-rearing allow glimpses of the internal workings of marriage as motherhood transformed wives and profoundly altered the dynamics of their relationships with their husbands.

Chapter 7

When Things Went Wrong

In England in 1805, a wretched wife—let's call her Alice Teush—petitioned Parliament to divorce her nasty and unfaithful husband, who lived openly with his mistress and their children. Mrs. Teush's seemed to be an open-and-shut case, and Lord Eldon, the High Chancellor, declared her the most meritorious woman he had ever heard testify. Nonetheless, Parliament ruled against her. Eldon's colleague, the Bishop of Saint Asaph, explained why: "However hard the rule [governing divorce] might press upon a few individuals, it would on the whole, be better if no bill of this kind were passed."[1] Adultery might be a bad thing, but surely worse was allowing a wife to divorce an adulterous husband.

In 1832, another abandoned and betrayed wife—let's call her Babs Moffatt—walked in Alice Teush's shoes. Though Mr. Moffatt had had his first extramarital fling on their wedding night and subsequently impregnated one of their domestics, Parliament's collective judgment was that Babs should forgive him. At the same time, that august body added, had *she* cheated on *him*, he could not have been expected to forgive her.

A few years later, another unhappy wife took up the cudgels for a woman's right to divorce and to win custody of children. Caroline Norton was the beautiful, brilliant, and battered wife of the Honourable

*Caroline Norton was brilliant, accomplished, industrious, generous, and
luminously beautiful; she was also a battered wife and mother who devoted
much of her life to lobbying to free women from abusive marriages.*

George Norton, a ne'er-do-well, non-practising barrister whose abuse
escalated until Caroline, pregnant with their fourth child, miscarried. In
1836, George banned her from their house and kept all the contents,
including her clothes and personal documents, for himself. He also
denied her the right to visit the children, whom he sent to his (perhaps
kissing) cousin Margaret Vaughan.

George was within his legal rights. Like all married women, Caroline
had no legal identity apart from her husband's. (The first names of Mrs.
Teush and Mrs. Moffatt were so unimportant that their divorce
proceedings failed to mention them.) With Teush, Moffatt, and other
women as precedents, Caroline's lawyers advised her against seeking a
divorce. She could not contest her husband's custody of the children.
She could not refuse to comply with his demand to reveal all her income
and earnings or his subpoena of her servants, publishers, and bankers.
She could not even attend the trial at which George (unsuccessfully)
sued the prime minister for sleeping with her.

Until the passage of the Matrimonial Causes Act of 1857, which set up a special court to hear divorce cases, only wives with the most egregious—and provable—grievances could appeal to the law for marital relief, and between 1801 and 1857, only four women succeeded in their divorce petitions.[2] Even then, the 1857 act that granted husbands the right to divorce adulterous wives still required wives to prove that their adulterous husbands had *also* committed incest, bigamy, cruelty, or desertion. (The enshrined double standard ended only in 1923, when women no longer had to prove their husband's aggravated adultery, just adultery.)

Not all women welcomed this new legislation, and 600,000 petitioned to Queen Victoria against it. Many feared that the act increased their vulnerability to divorce-minded husbands, a dreadful fate. It did not help that the act perpetuated the double standard that granted men and women unequal rights. Other objectors, men as well as women, raged against the introduction of divorce and the loss of the "indissoluble marriage to which we have adhered since England was England."[3] Nonetheless, the act prompted a rush to divorce: fifty times more Englishmen and -women divorced each other than they had before 1857.

Before Christianity conquered and converted Europe, divorce existed as a remedy for failed marriages. Ancient Greece permitted divorce and remarriage. Jewish law gave husbands the right to repudiate their wives. Roman law included divorce and granted *paterfamilias*—male family heads—the right to force their offspring to divorce, to marry, or to remarry. Germanic laws in the declining Roman Empire included a wife's failure to produce a child, female adultery, and male homosexuality as grounds for divorce.

In Christian Europe, the Orthodox Church frowned on divorce but reluctantly allowed it when the "internal symphony" vital to marital unity was destroyed. In Saint John Chrysostom's words, "Better to break the covenant than to lose one's soul." And the church's reading of Matthew 19:9—"I tell you that anyone who divorces his wife, except for marital unfaithfulness, and marries another woman commits adultery"—justified remarriage. (Remarriage was permitted only to a point: a fourth marriage was strictly forbidden.)

The Great Schism of 1054 divided the Greek Orthodox Eastern and Roman Western churches, and by the thirteenth century, the Catholic doctrine that Christian marriages ended only with the death of one of the spouses had become firmly entrenched throughout western Europe. There were exceptions: Christians abandoned by non-Christian spouses could remarry, and spouses in unconsummated marriages could enter a religious order without the other's consent. Under certain circumstances, marriages could be annulled, though this rarely happened. Occasionally church courts granted separations to unhappy spouses who could not be reconciled—as they did in 1442, for example, after John and Margaret Colwell swore "they would prefer death in prison to living together."[4]

In 1563, the Council of Trent made the indissolubility of marriage canon law. The church even frowned on (though it did not forbid) widows' remarrying, though it condoned the marriages of widowers to never-married women. The ban on remarriage after divorce stemmed from theological readings of divorce, adultery, and remarriage, and understood in the context of Judeo-Christian principles, "part of the eternal attempt of Christians to negotiate between the Bible and their culture."[5]

Reforming Marriage

The Protestant Reformation challenged both Catholicism's reverence for celibacy and its ban against divorce. Martin Luther, the former monk happily married to a former nun, accepted sexuality as God-given and natural but also cautioned that, because of Eve's sin in the Garden of Eden, all women deserved their eternal punishment of suffering the agonies of childbirth. Protestant John Calvin argued that the Catholic Church's "unrestrained rhapsodic praises of virginity" had debased the dignity and holiness of marriage.[6]

These reformers did not easily embrace divorce, but their insights into the nature of marital unions convinced them to tolerate it under extreme conditions. Luther, whose doctrines influenced sixteenth-century Scandinavian and German divorce laws, believed that a wife's adultery, refusal to engage in sex, or desertion broke the bonds of marriage, and if forgiveness and reconciliation failed, the marriage should be dissolved and the "innocent" spouse permitted to remarry.

Calvin, whose teachings shaped the divorce legislation in much of the rest of Europe and profoundly influenced North America, despised adultery. "A man may hold the primacy in other things, but in bed he and his wife are equal," he wrote, "for he is not the lord of his body. Therefore if he commits adultery he has defected from marriage and his wife is given freedom."[7] In Calvin's view, an unbeliever's desertion of a Protestant spouse was also grounds for divorce. However, he denied that cruelty, impotence, disease (such as leprosy), or just plain loathing justified ending a marriage, and he responded unsympathetically to a husband miserably married to a "harsh and dreadful wife": "Here are the fruits of original sin and also the corruption that is in [yourself]."[8]

In 1541, officials invited Calvin to implement his doctrine, which he had articulated in *The Institutes of the Christian Religion*, in their newly Protestant French-speaking city of Geneva. Under his leadership, Geneva developed into Europe's most vital Protestant centre; Scottish Protestant reformer John Knox described it as "the most perfect school of Christ."

In *Adultery and Divorce in Calvin's Geneva*, historian Robert M. Kingdon examines specific divorce cases. One was brought by the well-connected Pierre Ameaux against his wife, Benoite, the wealthy widow he had likely married because of her large estate. Benoite held the blasphemous view that because all Christians were members of the single body of Christ, she had the right to sleep with any Christian man—but she denied that she had done so. Convicted and jailed for this heresy, Benoite recanted and begged to be pardoned. Her wish was granted on condition that she apologize publicly to God and the court. She and Pierre were ordered to "live honestly in the holy estate of marriage."

Reluctantly, Pierre took Benoite back under his roof, but he made her life so hellish that she fled to her brother's house. Pierre launched a second divorce suit that resulted in another forced reconciliation. Months later, he succeeded in a third attempt at divorcing her as an adulteress. Benoite's punishment was lifetime imprisonment, in iron chains—unless she repented. With Benoite shackled away, Pierre got his divorce and, several months later, requested and received permission "to remarry with another woman, seeing that his wife was a fornicator and held false opinions and was condemned to perpetual prison." A month later, Benoite's family secured her release after promising to confine her to her bedroom "so as not to give scandal to others." Pierre, now remarried, continued to manage Benoite's children's property.[9]

Calvin was directly involved in his younger brother Antoine's attempt to divorce his wife, Anne Le Fert, for infidelity. Despite Calvin's powerful testimony against Anne, the case ended in a forced reconciliation that endured for years. After Calvin's beloved wife, Idelette de Bure, died in 1549, Anne managed the brothers' joint household, bore Antoine two more children, and helped care for Idelette's two children from her first marriage, whom Calvin had pledged to raise. But the bitterness remained, and in 1557, both brothers filed formal complaints that Anne had taken a lover, a hunchbacked former employee. Anne denied the charges; witnesses vacillated. The Calvins produced more evidence, and Anne was repeatedly interrogated, at least twice under torture.

The stakes were high: capital punishment if she was found guilty. Under torture—the first time, iron grilles fastened to the hands and wrists were painfully manipulated; the second torture session repeated or intensified this procedure—Anne steadfastly denied committing adultery. Finally, the court granted Antoine his divorce with permission to remarry, banished Anne from Geneva, and gave Antoine her dowry as child support. Both Antoine and Anne remarried, he to the widow of a Calvinist minister, she to a young patrician who went into exile with her.

These divorces offer glimpses into how Reformation authorities dealt with severe marriage breakdown. Courts scrutinized the most intimate details of private life, often hearing eyewitness accounts from resident domestic servants. They incorporated torture into their interrogations, and often forced warring spouses to reconcile. They punished adultery with banishment and whipping or, in outlying villages, nine days' imprisonment on bread and water and payment of a fine. Sometimes convicted adulteresses were publicly drowned and adulterers decapitated, though it was only in 1566, two years after John Calvin's death, that Geneva passed a law making adultery a capital offence—except when a husband cheated with an unmarried woman.

Under Calvin, Geneva permitted divorce, usually for adultery or wilful desertion, with the right to remarry. But it was so difficult to obtain that, during his ministry (1541 to 1564), only twenty-six divorces were granted on the grounds of adultery and a few more on other grounds. In other Protestant jurisdictions, divorce was similarly infrequent and granted only as a last resort.

The Anglican Church was the ironic exception to the rule that divorce was possible. England had broken with the Roman Catholic Church over Henry VIII's desire to annul his marriage to Catherine of Aragon. The children's refrain "Divorced, Beheaded, Died, Divorced, Beheaded, Survived" handily summarizes Henry's marriage-ending strategies as he divested himself of wives Catherine, Anne Boleyn, Jane Seymour, Anne of Cleves, and Catherine Howard. (Fortunately for his last wife, Catherine Parr, he died.) But the church established because Henry wanted his marriage annulled remained so hostile to divorce that, until the Matrimonial Causes Act of 1857, England was all but

Catherine Hayes could not divorce and so, with accomplices, disposed of her husband by cutting off his head.

divorce-free. Between 1670 and 1857, only 325 divorces were granted, almost all initiated by husbands. Divorce laws were so skewed against wives that few attempted to obtain them.

Caroline Norton was the best-known casualty of England's anti-divorce stance, rooted as it was in a patriarchal double standard and laws that deprived married women of their property and even their own wages. Caroline Sheridan, grand-daughter of dramatist Richard Brinsley Sheridan, was nineteen when she married the incompetent, lazy, and physically abusive George Norton. To earn household money for her growing family, Caroline wrote articles and books. "Out of our stormy quarrels I rose undiscouraged, and worked again to help him and forward the interests of my children," she recalled. "I have sat up all night,—even at times when I have had a young infant to nurse,—to finish tasks for some publisher. I made in one year a sum of 1,400 £ by my pen; and … provided, without grudging, money that was to be spent on his pleasures."[10]

Denied access to her home and her children, and publicly humiliated by George's accusation that her friend and political associate Lord Melbourne, the prime minister of England, had had "criminal conversation" (the euphemism for adulterous sex) with her, Caroline devoted herself to campaigning for the right of mothers to appeal for custody of children under seven. Thanks to her efforts, the Infant Custody Bill of 1839 became law. Ironically, it did not help her. George Norton simply spirited their children away to Scotland, where the English law did not apply. He relented and allowed her to see the children only after one of their sons died in a riding accident.

With characteristic wit, passion, and clarity, Caroline also lobbied hard on behalf of English wives. In a letter to the new young queen, Victoria, she outlined her argument.

I am, as regards my husband, in a worse position than if I had been divorced. In that case, Englishmen are so generous, that some chivalrous-hearted man might perhaps have married and trusted me, in spite of the unjust cloud on my name. I am not divorced, and I cannot divorce my husband; yet I can establish no legal claim upon him, nor upon any

living human being! My reputation, my property, my happiness, are
irrevocably in the power of this slanderer on false grounds; this rapa-
cious defender of his right to evade written bonds. I cannot release
myself. I exist and I suffer; but the law denies my existence.[11]

The law denied her existence because of *couverture*, the legal notion
that a wife's being was merged with her husband's. Without her own
identity, a woman had no right to her own property, wages, or body, and
the notion of marital rape was inconceivable. Divorce did more than
terminate failed marriages or free spouses to remarry. It freed wives from
couverture. Without a divorce, an abandoned or separated woman like
Caroline had no legal existence. Her comment "I do not consider this
as MY cause, though ... (unfortunately for me) I am an illustration. It
is the cause of all the women" was a sad statement of fact. When the
Matrimonial Causes Act finally passed in 1857, several sections reflected
Caroline's personal experiences.[12]

NORTH AMERICA

Colonial Canada, like the other colonies in Britain's empire, was
supposed to conform to divorce laws in the mother country, and only
the Atlantic colonies, economically linked to the more liberal northern
American colonies, passed divorce laws: Nova Scotia (1761), with adultery and cruelty as grounds, New Brunswick (1791) and Prince Edward
Island (1837), with adultery. Elsewhere, the only legislative recourse
open to bitterly married or deserted colonists was to seek divorce
through private members' bills, which required royal assent.
Overwhelmingly Catholic Lower Canada dissolved marriages by
statute, thereby avoiding the legalization of divorce. (A wife who
proved her husband's extreme mismanagement of her property could
be granted judicial relief in the form of separation of goods; if she could
prove extreme abuse, she could request separation of bed and board.)
Upper Canada withdrew an 1833 bill to legalize divorce on the basis of
official advice that England would disallow such legislation, making its
passage futile.

Upper Canada's first divorce ended John Stuart's marriage to Elizabeth Van Rensselaer Powell, with whom he had children, after she became Lieutenant John Grogan's lover. Stuart sued Grogan for damages and won more than £600 plus costs. (Grogan paid him by selling his military commission.) Then, having legally established Elizabeth's adultery, Stuart initiated divorce proceedings. In February 1840, just before she gave birth to Grogan's child, the Upper Canadian legislature passed the divorce. As soon as royal assent was granted in 1841, Elizabeth and Grogan married and tried to reintegrate into Kingston's disapproving high society.

Some of the colonies to the south felt rather differently about divorce. In the United States as in France, "where revolution was the handmaid of divorce," writes historian Norma Basch in *Framing American Divorce*, "the transformations of family and polity were closely connected. These connections inflected thinking about divorce for years to come."[13] The rationale for breaking the bonds of empire seemed equally applicable to the bonds of bad marriages.

Even before the Revolution, divorce existed. The northeastern colonies had the most liberal divorce laws: Connecticut's were unrestricted enough to process almost one thousand divorces between 1670 and 1799. New York was the exception, with adultery the only grounds for divorce; even then, few divorces were granted. In 1813, however, battered women could obtain legal separations. In 1824, husbands, too, could separate.

After the Revolution, most Southern states made provisions for divorce by legislative statute. Maryland led the way in 1790, and by 1860 all the Confederate states recognized adultery, desertion, cruelty, and other grounds for divorce. Arkansas detailed abusive behaviour, which included rudeness, vulgarity, contempt, incivility, unkindness, "and every other plain manifestation of settled hate, alienation and estrangement, both of word and action."[14] Only South Carolina lagged behind its Confederate neighbours, legalizing divorce in 1872, repealing it in 1878, and legalizing it again only in 1949–50.

The newer states, less constrained by tradition, enacted more liberal divorce laws almost as soon as they achieved statehood. By 1852 Ohio specified ten grounds for divorce. Indiana, even more generous, included the catch-all of "any other cause for which the court shall deem it proper that the divorce shall be granted."[15] Other western states crafted similar legislation with omnibus clauses that freed them from refining divorce provisions.

One of the most significant aspects of these divorce laws was the residency requirement, which ranged from one year to, in Utah, the mere desire to become a resident. Elsewhere, easy residency requirements seemed to circumvent the intention of other states—and countries—which had more stringent divorce laws.

A notorious example was the miserably married globe-trotting, vastly wealthy European entrepreneur-turned-archaeologist Heinrich Schliemann, whose Russian wife, Ekaterina, refused to join him in the United States. "I could sooner die than live with you in a foreign country," she wrote in 1869. Schliemann returned to the United States where, in Indiana, he bought a house, invested in a business, and acquired witnesses to testify that he intended to settle there. Then, as a state "resident," he divorced Ekatarina.

Schliemann's ploy prompted a public outcry. Frustrated opponents of divorce, or at least of "easy" divorce, attacked states such as Indiana for contributing to degeneracy, immorality, and social destruction. Horace Greeley, editor of the *New York Tribune*, charged that lax divorce laws doomed these states to fall as Rome had, "rotted away and perished,— blasted by the mildew of unchaste mothers and dissolute homes."[16] "Marriage indissoluble may be an imperfect test of honorable and pure affection," Greeley argued, "as all things human are imperfect,—but it is the best the State can devise; and its overthrow would result in a general profligacy and corruption such as this country has never known and few of our people can adequately imagine. We are inflexibly opposed, therefore, to any extension of the privileges of divorce now accorded by our laws."[17]

POLITICAL IDEOLOGY OF DIVORCE

Many people saw divorce, like marriage, as a bellwether of society. In antebellum America, "divorce served as a lightning rod for deep-seated tensions over the positive and negative implications of freedom," Basch writes.[18] In the slaveholding South, with the lowest divorce rate of any region, the state was rooted in the patriarchal household whose white male head held authority over all women, children, and slaves within it. Power relations in the South devolved from its racial, gender, and economic systems, all grounded in white supremacy and what American historian Jacquelyn Dowd Hall calls "the web of connections among racism, attitudes toward women, and sexual ideologies."[19]

Specifically, the infrastructure of Southern slavery was rooted in the subordination of both slaves and women, so that the liberation of one implied the liberation of the other. The (il)logic of slavery also elevated the white family to such heights that divorce became a destructive social force rather than a legal mechanism for separating unhappy spouses. South Carolina, for example, forbade divorce on any grounds. At the same time, a few Southern states were sensitive to the plight of individual women and passed laws known as "divorce from bed and board" that, because they included alimony, permitted white women to live apart from their husbands while remaining legally married. Tennessee and North Carolina went further and passed divorce laws, in 1799 and 1814 respectively.

Tellingly, white wives whose husbands effectively supplanted them with black women and also abused them often won divorces. Virginian Jonah Dobyns, for example, battered his teenaged wife Sophia, a colonel's daughter, forcing her to flee back to her parents' on several occasions. When she returned home, Dobyns beat and threatened to kill her. A visitor to the plantation testified hearing Dobyns boast that "in her absence he had taken one of his own Negroe Women into her bed and that he would do it again whenever it Suited him." Sophia's father had recently died, leaving her enough slaves to support herself and her children. Sophia was granted her divorce.

Jonah Dobyns's treatment of his wife was not uncommon, as a perusal of divorce petitions attests. The wretched Virginian Evelina Gregory Roane, whose husband forced her to trade roles with his slave mistress, won not just a divorce but also the right to remarry. Seven months after the birth of their first child, several witnesses testified, Newman Roane beat the again-pregnant Evelina so savagely that she miscarried. Besides battering her, denying her access to her family and church, and threatening to kill her, he established Biney, his mistress, as the head of the household, and had forced Evelina to work as a slave under her.

On the other hand, the white male petitioner, to win his divorce, usually had only to prove that his wife had had sexual relations with a black lover—and that he had not condoned her behaviour. Petition after petition describes the errant wife's delivery of a mulatto child, supposedly incontrovertible proof of her dual transgressions: adultery and crossing racial boundaries. (Much worse would have been to ascribe African blood to one of the spouses.) The "darkness" and "unusual appearance" of Peggy Jones's daughter betrayed her black paternity, which neighbours helpfully corroborated, and Richard Jones got his divorce. To Dabney Pettus's "great astonishment & inexpressible mortification," his wife, Elizabeth Morris, was "deliver'd of a Mulatto Child … begotten by a negro man slave in the Neighborhood." In 1803, Pettus was granted his divorce. Ayres Tatham's wife, Tabitha, produced a mulatto child, and he was granted a divorce; so was Daniel Rose, whose wife, Henrietta White, bore a mulatto child after eight months of marriage, and blamed Bob, one of her grandfather's slaves, for coercing her into it with the threat that if she refused, he would, in unspecified ways, upset or ruin her marriage.

These divorces stemmed from a collective horror of how supplanting white women with black violated white integrity, and how women who sullied their whiteness and their marriage beds flouted their society's core values, both by giving their bodies to black males and by producing mulattoes. (Meanwhile, white men could impregnate black women and create mixed-race children with impunity.) The rigour required of petitioners even in these cases proved that even the notion of divorce struck terror into many prominent Southerners. "The integers out of which the State is constituted are not individuals, but families represented in their parental heads," warned theologian Robert Lewis Dabney.[20] In other words, divorce weakened patriarchy patriarch by patriarch, and threatened the very fabric of Southern society.

"The indissolubility of the marriage tie, the permanence of the family bond, the domestic order that the sentiment of its indissoluble character created, are fast leaving us," warned the *Southern Quarterly Review* in 1854. A few years later, *De Bow's Review* warned: "The danger to the South *in the Union* from the force of Northern example ... is imminent and cannot be exaggerated. Already, the South ... have adopted to a fearful extent, Northern ideas on the subjects of divorce and the independency of married women, through separate estates and exclusive revenues."[21]

Northerners criticized divorce for different reasons. In 1816, Yale University president Timothy Dwight warned that "the progress of divorce, though different in different countries, will in all be dreadful beyond conception.... a virtuous man, if such an one be found, will search in vain to find a virtuous wife. Wherever he wanders, nothing will meet his eye, but stalking, bare-faced pollution. The realm around him has become one vast Brothel; one great province in the world of Perdition."[22] Strong words, widely shared.

But for the battered wife or abandoned husband, for the wife whose children starved because her "breadwinner" husband owed his wages to the tavern keeper or the card shark, for the husband whose wife flaunted lovers and neglected the children, marriage was pollution and divorce salvation. Loveless, indifferent, or hating couples judged their relationships according to the ideals of loving, companionate marriage and yearned to escape. (At one extreme, the revolutionary writer Tom Paine, separated from his wife, believed that almost no marriage was loving and happy, and that divorce was the only way to end the misery.) But in most states, the primacy of monogamy outweighed the exigencies of lovelessness.

Divorce and Drunkenness

A large part of the divorce question concerned defining the grounds for it. A wife's adultery was universally accepted as sufficient to put asunder those whom God had joined together. Often, so were a husband's adultery or desertion, especially if the latter was long-term and unambiguous. Other sorts of bad behaviour, notably habitual drunkenness, cruelty, and insanity, were more contentious and evoked issues of class, ethnicity, and gender. Although law, custom, and religion granted husbands authority over their wives, who had little recourse against submitting, even to corporal "correction," legislators, most of them members of the privileged classes, agreed that upper-class women should usually not be expected to endure physical abuse. They did not, however, see fit to extend this same protection to all women and, instead, discouraged lower-class women from seeking divorces because their husbands abused them.

This was largely because they associated abuse with drunkenness, which they considered a primarily lower-class or immigrant trait ruinous to the families whose men frequented the dens of iniquity known as taverns. The better solution was temperance rather than divorce. By offering protection to women and children, and by reforming family life, temperance would drastically reduce the number of abusive marriages, and hence the need for divorce.

This societal interpretation of intemperance and its direct impact on individuals was in keeping with reformist platforms that focused on the nature of marriage and the family. The anti-slavery abolitionist plea for the ideal of the moral and upright family as an instrument of reform is a notable example. "The right of chastity in the woman, the unblemished household love, the right of parents in their children—on these three elements stands the whole weight of society," preached influential Congregationalist pastor Henry Ward Beecher, Harriet and Catherine's brother.

The equally fervent (and mostly middle-class Protestant) temperance movement aimed at restoring wholesome marriage by stamping out alcohol abuse, usually the husband's. By 1830 in liquor-guzzling North

America, where beer was a dietary staple and whiskey and other spirits traditionally accompanied meals, consumption exceeded seven gallons of alcohol per adult per year, and addiction to readily available opium and cocaine was triple today's rate. Countless drunken husbands (and some wives) spent their wages on liquor instead of on their family's rent and food, often in taverns where gambling and prostitution were other lures. Afterward, temperance literature reported, they staggered home to beat their wives, children, and dogs.

Some critics of divorce questioned whether alcoholism was permanent and irrevocable. Furthermore, as a popular Methodist publication put it, didn't wives have a moral and family duty to reform or at least tolerate their alcoholic husbands? Shouldn't a good woman "love on and hope on, to the end, [so that] when God puts his seal on their foreheads, we know what heroism their lives contained."[23] The solution was not to divorce drunk husbands but to endure or, better yet, convert them from their evil ways. There was, however, general sympathy for men wishing to divorce alcoholic wives, denounced as slatterns who shamed their husbands, neglected their children, and were likely responsible for serious birth defects.

Furthermore, a growing misogynistic subtext in tracts and moralistic fiction blamed the wives of drunkards for their predicament. These women cared for fashion more than civil duty, served wine in their homes, forced liquor on determinedly abstinent men, and tempted them with brandied peaches. Like the "fretful, moody, unhappy" Margaret Nichols in T.S. Arthur's *A Story for Wives*, they drove men to drink. By the mid-nineteenth century, women's role in their husbands' alcoholism had become an urgent theme. If a wife was not patient and forbearing, and her home a cheery refuge, what else could she expect? Certainly not the relief of divorce.

Sometimes women whose drunken husbands were dangerously violent yet still able to earn money were granted legal separation and alimony. A South Carolina judge estimated that between 1814 and 1829, two-thirds of his alimony cases "may be fairly attributed to Intemperance."[24] Quite often these drunkards had to be jailed to safeguard their wives and children, who might otherwise be killed.

Temperance literature, in which homicidal husbands bludgeoned, stabbed, axed, decapitated, and dismembered their wives, highlighted these fears.

By the late nineteenth century, family violence smashed its way into public attention and, in the United States, prompted philanthropists to found 494 child-protection and anti-cruelty societies. The association of violent husbands with alcohol was so strong that several states passed laws granting wives the right to sue tavern keepers for damages if their husbands injured them while under the influence. In Maryland, Delaware, and Oregon, husbands who beat their wives could be whipped at the whipping post.

Yet despite this new sensibility, a great number of those who supported divorce as a final remedy for unstoppable alcoholic brutality still expected the aggrieved wife to endure almost unendurable suffering before calling it quits. Had she responded with sweet understanding to his rages? Had she provided a nice home? Was she the sort of woman a man would *want* to go home to? If the answer was no, she must look within to remedy her own failings rather than seeking to escape her marriage.

DIVORCE AND GENDER

Not everyone recommended such sacrifice and the divorce issue divided the women's rights movement. Amelia Bloomer, Elizabeth Cady Stanton, Susan B. Anthony, and other leaders believed that the knowledge that his (good, virtuous) wife could leave and divorce him, exercise property rights, and obtain alimony was the most effective way to sober a man up, and they argued for easier access to divorce and child custody on the grounds of drunkenness or abuse. "It is a sin against nature, the family, the state for man or woman to live together in the marriage relation in continual antagonism, indifference, disgust,"[25] Stanton argued. She viewed divorce as a vehicle to strengthen marriages, as the threat of it encouraged husbands and wives to live up to ideals, and she challenged the cultural values that made divorce shameful for women.

Like drunkenness, divorce was a gender-weighty issue that elicited strong responses. The fundamental inequality between husband and wife, and the ubiquitous double standard, made it difficult to evaluate its benefits or drawbacks. Apart from issues of fault and blame, divorce involved property and custody rights, and the status of women vis-à-vis males in general and their husbands in particular. Based on these realities, American feminists Antoinette Brown and Elizabeth Oakes Smith opposed divorce in favour of controlling husbands by strengthening marriage. Most compellingly of all, Elizabeth Packard argued against divorce as a remedy to marital strife because, she said, divorce stripped women of marriage's prestige and respectability. "What we want," wrote the grievously wronged Packard, "is protection in the union, not ... a divorce from it."[26]

Elizabeth and Theophilus Packard, fifteen years her senior, had a pleasant but passionless marriage that had lasted twenty-one years and produced six children. "In our mental states we simply grew apart, instead of together," Elizabeth recalled. "He was dwindling, dying—I was living, growing, expanding." Elizabeth was handsome, well educated, energetic, and passionate. When Theophilus invited her to spice up his lacklustre six-man Bible class, she accepted eagerly. Influenced by the ideas and energy of the women's movement, she spoke out in class, her joy in her own spiritual grace giving her the certainty that her voice mattered and should be heard. Specifically, Elizabeth proclaimed the falseness of the doctrine of original sin and the inferiority of women. Before long, her stirring sentiments and provocative comments attracted forty more students to the class.

Theophilus responded to his wife's public challenges with dismay and anger, which Elizabeth interpreted as a "morbid feeling of jealousy [provoked by] this natural development of intellectual power in me ... lest I outshine him." The power struggle between them began after she refused to give up the Bible-class discussions.

"You shall go into an asylum," Theophilus warned. In a "confidential" letter to relatives and close friends he spelled it out: "I have sad reason to fear my wife's mind is getting out of order; she is becoming insane on the subject of woman's rights." He told Elizabeth that putting her into an insane asylum would convince people that she was insane and not worth listening to. "I must protect the cause of Christ!" he declared.

Illinois law was on Theophilus's side; it gave husbands the right to commit their wives if the superintendent of the state hospital for the insane judged them "insane or distracted ... without the evidence of insanity required in other cases." In the early hours of June 18, 1860, as Elizabeth got dressed, a sheriff and two physicians from Theophilus's congregation barged into her bedroom and pronounced her insane because her pulse was racing. Elizabeth declared that she would not enter the asylum voluntarily, without a trial. Theophilus set her straight about her "rights." "You are not a citizen, while a married woman, you are a legal nonentity, without even a soul in law. In short, you are dead as to any legal existence, while a married woman, and therefore have no legal protection as a married woman." He added, "It is for your good I am doing this; I want to save your soul! You don't believe in total depravity [original sin], and I want to make you right."

Elizabeth recalled years later, "Thus I learned my first lesson in that chapter of common law, which denies to married women a legal right to

This famous illustration from Elizabeth Packard's Modern Persecution *(1873) is captioned with quotations from the book: "Is there no man in this crowd to protect this woman!" and "I will get my dear Mamma out of prison! My Mamma shan't be locked up in a prison!"*

her own identity or individuality." Incarceration in an asylum also deprived her of her six children, aged two to eighteen, who continued to live with Theophilus. From then on, Elizabeth Packard had a mission that echoed the earlier one of Caroline Norton: to change women's legal status, and to grant women the right to child custody in a system that almost universally granted it to fathers.

After years of enduring such practices as choking inmates until "their faces were black and their tongues hung out of their mouths," and immobilizing them in straitjackets before beating them, Elizabeth convinced the asylum's trustees that she was sane. In 1863, with the Civil War raging, she was released and fled to her sister's house. After four months of yearning for her children, she returned home.

Theophilus was unforgiving. He locked her into the children's nursery and nailed shut the windows, imprisoning her while he made arrangements to commit her to another asylum. To save herself, Elizabeth tossed a note through a slit in the window to a passerby, who delivered it into the hands of Judge Charles Starr. After witnesses testified that Theophilus "cruelly abuses and misuses said wife," even depriving her of winter clothing, Starr issued a writ of habeas corpus and ordered a trial to determine whether or not Elizabeth was sane.

Packard v. Packard was short and sensational. Stephen Moore, one of Elizabeth's attorneys, described his charismatic and good-looking client as "an original, vigorous, masculine thinker, and were it not for her superior judgment, combined with native modesty, she would rank as a 'strong-minded woman.' As it is, her conduct comports strictly with the sphere usually occupied by woman." Theophilus, on the other hand, was "cold, selfish, and illiberal in his views, possessed of but little talent, and a physiognomy innocent of expression. He has large self-will, and his stubbornness is only exceeded by his bigotry." The jury deliberated for just seven minutes before reaching their verdict: Elizabeth Packard was sane.

But she was also a woman separated from her husband, and he had custody of their children. Elizabeth's plans for her new, solitary future did not include divorce, likely because she believed that adultery alone was legitimate grounds and, whatever else he had done, Theophilus had not committed adultery. She borrowed ten dollars from friends and went to Chicago, where she earned a living writing books and pamphlets. But, like Caroline Norton, she reminded readers that her husband could at any time lay legal claim to her house and all her earnings.

To save herself and other women from this injustice, she devoted herself to lobbying for the passage of her bill "To equalize the rights and responsibilities of the husband and wife," which focused on improving women's property and child-custody rights. On March 24, 1869, a modified version passed into law, entitling a married woman "to receive, use and possess her own earnings, and sue for the same in her own name, free from the interference of her husband." Elizabeth rejoiced: "I, in common with other married women in Illinois, am now protected by law in my rights to my home, bought with my own earnings."

Elizabeth also advocated for women to gain custody of children in a system that almost universally granted that right to fathers. (Her children were now aged eleven to twenty-seven, and the three eldest already lived with her in Chicago.) When she sued for custody of her three minor children, her witnesses included her two oldest sons. When the youngest, Arthur, said that he would prefer to live with the father who had raised him since he was two, Elizabeth acquiesced. But she rejoiced when the two others chose to join her and the older children in Chicago.

In 1871, her son Samuel, by then a practising lawyer, helped her draft the "Bill to equalize the rights and responsibilities of husband and wife" that also, in modified form, passed in the Illinois legislature. Afterward there was a wave of resistance and mourning for men's lost rights, and lawmakers responded to judicial interpretations, changing ideology, and public opinion to enact more nuanced marriage laws. But the 1869 and 1871 acts were steps along the path to women's equality in marriage, and they made Elizabeth Packard and her sisters much safer.

Elizabeth's prolific writings influenced the passage of legislation still known as the Packard Laws, which prohibit a husband from institutionalizing his wife without a jury trial and a court order, as Theophilus had done. Elizabeth also developed a new vision of marriage, a co-partnership in which husband and wife would each exercise their God-given roles, she as homemaker, mother, and nurturer, he as protector and provider.

But they would consult with and listen to each other, and neither would force his or her will on the other. The power dynamic of this arrangement was interdependency, with equal rights to property, earnings (should the wife need to work), and child custody and guardianship. Yet the wife remained a junior partner who could not vote, while the bread-winning husband was a senior manager who could. Elizabeth's proposed union was fundamentally unequal, her way of reconciling her tradition-alist convictions with her progressive ones.

CELEBRITY DIVORCES

Like Caroline Norton in England, Elizabeth Packard fuelled the nineteenth-century phenomenon of the celebrity divorce or failed marriage. The public appetite for the (often salacious, always intimate) details was voracious. Magazines and other print media happily satis-fied it, framing divorce as a spectacle, a voyeuristic journey through someone else's travails. ("I looked through the keyhole, and saw her lying on the sofa—her clothes above her knees. He was doing some-thing to his pants—I can't say what," a domestic servant testified.)[27] Divorce was for cause, and hungry readers wanted to wallow in the guilty party's guilt.

Newspaper reports of divorce cases usually portrayed women sympa-thetically. The *New York Times*, for example, described plaintiff Mary Bennet, who accused her physician husband, George, of trying to force her to have an abortion and overdosing one of their children with laudanum, as "very pretty … small in stature, lively in expression … [with] a silvery voice, brilliant dark eyes, very dark hair, delicate hands, and regular features." George, on the other hand, was "a little man, with jet black hair standing up all over his head, a heavy black beard and a moustache, a restless small black eye." He spoke as if he had "a sponge in his throat."[28]

But courts and public opinion vilified women suspected of adultery, as happened to Abby Sage, an actor/writer who had recently divorced her drunken and abusive husband, the fifty-year-old lawyer Daniel McFarland, in Indiana, where divorce was easier than in rigid New York.

In December 1869, McFarland ambushed his ex-wife Abby's lover, thirty-six-year-old Albert Dean Richardson, a seasoned *Tribune* reporter who had covered the Civil War, and shot him in the stomach. Shortly thereafter, Abby's friend the Reverend Henry Ward Beecher presided over her wedding to the dying man. The wedding—and the attack that precipitated it—dominated New York's newspapers. Sixty hours after he married her, Richardson died in Abby's arms, and McFarland was indicted for murder.

The trial was sensational. Two and a half years earlier, McFarland had shot and slightly wounded Richardson as he accompanied Abby home from the theatre. Nonetheless, his lawyers defended him as "a man overtaken by sorrow and calamity brought on by the unholy, reckless, and lawless passion of a bold, bad libertine, a wife-seducer and child-robber." In their version, McFarland did not murder Richardson, he "sent [him] into eternity." The lawyers also arranged for McFarland's ten-year-old son to run up to his father in the courtroom and sit at his side during the trial. The twelve-man jury, all husbands and fathers, deliberated for just short of two hours before declaring McFarland not guilty.

Divorce, American-style

Elizabeth Cady Stanton called McFarland's acquittal an indictment of American womanhood. Others considered it an indictment of divorce, and Reverend Beecher was severely attacked in the press for having married the divorced Abby Sage to her dying beau. Beecher's vilification, writes Norma Basch, "suggests first that the shock waves of divorce reached far beyond the doctrinal concerns of institutionalized Christianity to grip the attention of the public at large; second, that the growing recognition of the gendered dimensions of each and every divorce suit"—Abby had initiated divorce proceedings—"raised the debate to an entirely new register; and third, that … a quasi-fundamentalist Christianity animated the opposition to divorce."[29]

This was especially true as the fractured American nation recuperated from its Civil War in which hundreds of thousands had died to stave off political divorce. Elizabeth Packard had been clear about this: divorce was rooted in a "secession principle … [that] saps the very foundation of our social and civil obligations."[30]

Another strong argument against divorce was that it permitted remarriage, which even many feminists abhorred as the embodiment of sexual impurity and therefore the violation of lifelong monogamy. Many in the women's movement rejected divorce and focused instead on winning the vote as a way of ensuring family stability. Some women opposed even this and, like Catherine Beecher, worried that women's suffrage would strip away "all the sacred protection of religion, all the generous promptings of chivalry, all the poetry of romantic gallantry" that were defenceless women's main weapons against their subordinate status.[31] But whatever their views on divorce, most women supported the need to separate warring spouses. Celibate separation, with adequate provision for property division, support, and child custody, was a generally acceptable solution.

In practice, the financial disposition of property in divorces was seldom equitable. "I remain aghast at the paucity of support provisions in nineteenth-century divorces," Norma Basch notes.[32] (She uses this to warn contemporary feminists against making common cause with conservatives to roll back no-fault divorce.) Enforcing support payments was also very difficult. Women with independent fortunes large or small, or with their own trades, businesses, or property, tended to fare better. In some states, such as New York, so did women who obtained separations rather than divorces.

In the post–Civil War South, divorce laws perpetuated the double standard, exemplified by a North Carolina high court's pronouncement that there was "a difference between adultery committed by a husband and adultery committed by a wife—the difference being in favor of the husband." A husband who ignored his wife's adultery would be "disgraced," but a wife who ignored her husband's would only be "pitied."[33]

Manifested as paternalist chivalry, that same double standard persuaded Southern legislators to guarantee married women's property rights. Republican J.H. Allen, a South Carolina lawmaker originally from the North, captured the tone perfectly: "I appeal to you who have lived here all your lives, and seen women suffering from the hands of fortune hunters; the plausible villains, who, after securing the property of their wives, have squandered it in gambling and drinking; a class of men who are still going about the country boasting that they intend to marry a plantation, and take the woman as an incumbrance."[34]

The growing conviction that women were morally superior to men and naturally loving and tender resulted in a change in custody rights, with judges increasingly disposed to grant divorcing or separating wives custody of children, especially girls or the young—the "tender years" doctrine. The perception that losing custody should be a punishment for the bad behaviour that had caused the marriage breakup also aided women, who were the overwhelming initiators of divorce proceedings. An Alabama Supreme Court justice explained: "The law, equally with nature, clothes the husband with the highest and most ample authority to protect the wife.... But when the husband's love no longer exists, then the wife's protection becomes uncertain. When ... the wife is evidently imperiled and made unhappy to such a degree as to effect her health, and interfere with the discharge of her duties as mother, then the courts will interpose for her protection."[35]

That protection did not, however, extend to guaranteeing wives adequate financial support. For one thing, in the difficult years of Reconstruction, Southern states were mindful of the need to minimize public spending. The mothers most likely to gain custody were those able to show they could support their children.

Although anti-divorce sentiment intensified after the Civil War, so did divorce. Nationally, from 1861 to 1865, there was an annual average of 6,510 divorces, separations, and annulments. This increased 60 percent in the two years after the conflict. Yale University president Theodore Woolsey, like his predecessor Timothy Dwight, publicly deplored the moral decay he saw running rampant in postbellum society. Official studies were ordered to determine why the Republic was succumbing to the fate of ancient Rome and other decadent societies.

But this was the wrong question to ask, because, as historians now recognize, marriage breakdown is a common consequence of war. As men joined military units and left wives and families at home, often for extended periods, their relationships changed. As soldiers, they were changed by the horrors, banalities, and brief joys—camaraderie, self-worth—of war. Back at home, their wives shouldered new burdens and, except for the wealthiest, seldom or never saw their warrior husbands. Their marriages, rooted in another way of life, foundered in the loneliness that could feel like abandonment, along with financial pressure, sexual tensions, and uncertainty about the future.

Many soldiers were wounded. "If you was ... [here] & See the number of Sick & Disabled Soldiers it would make your Heart Ache. they are Dieing Every Day," a Union soldier wrote to the young woman he later married.[36] A list of successful claims by Union army soldiers for war-related disabilities shows a total of 406,702 between 1862 and 1888. Of these, gunshot and shell wounds accounted for 117,947; chronic diarrhea 55,125; incised and contused wounds and other

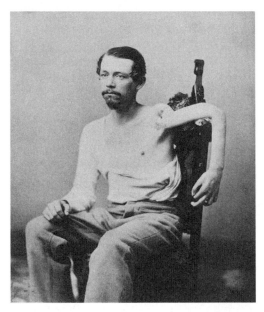

*When Union soldier John F. Claghorn was wounded in the Civil War,
a military doctor removed his severely damaged humerus. Claghorn's empty
arm was then sewed up and dangled like that of a rag doll. His injury no doubt
changed his marriage prospects or, if he was already married, changed the
dynamics of his marriage.*

injuries 41,049; rheumatism 40,790; heart disease, 25,994; lung disease 23,471; rectal disease 22,517; amputations 9,159; partial deafness 8,267; and total deafness 1,420.[37] Army adjudicators, often amputees, rejected at a much higher rate claimants with "invisible" conditions—for example the post-traumatic stress syndrome that was accepted as a legitimate mental disorder only after the Vietnam War.

Alcoholism and opiate addiction were other war-acquired afflictions that wreaked havoc on marriages. "We have lost more valuable lives at the hands of whiskey sellers than by the balls of our enemies," lamented Confederate General Braxton Bragg. Though its purchase was prohibited, soldiers bought or manufactured liquor—Union soldiers concocted a brew of bark juice, tar-water, turpentine, brown sugar, lamp oil, and alcohol—and consumed it immoderately.

So many soldiers in both camps used drugs—morphine, opium, or cocaine—that drug addiction was referred to as "the soldier's disease" or "the army disease." As horrendous injuries decimated the troops, army doctors relieved their pain with injections of morphine. Addiction, easy to fuel in an era of unrestricted availability, often followed. Worse, well-intentioned attempts to cure morphine addiction by substituting cocaine created a new dependency. At war's end, countless veterans returned home alcoholic, drug addicted, or both.

Hundreds of thousands of soldiers, unattached bachelors but also unfaithful husbands, contracted venereal disease, the scourge of the nineteenth century, from the camp-following prostitutes known as "horizontal refreshments," or from brothels in nearby towns and cities. By 1862, for example, both Washington, D.C., and Richmond, Virginia, boasted 7,500 full-time prostitutes. Charles Haydon of the 2nd Michigan Infantry noted in his diary that several fellow soldiers were "injured ... [while] storming a masked battery"—meaning female genitals. If only they would hunt down "rebels as eagerly as they pursue the whores."[38] In the Union army, 73,382 soldiers were treated for syphilis, 109,397 with gonorrhea.[39] (The number of men diseased but untreated would likely double these figures.) Confederates, with less money and hence less opportunity, had fewer infections but still so many that in March 1864, a new hospital opened in Kingston, Georgia, to treat them.

Venereal diseases were chronic and incurable until the advent of penicillin decades later. The symptoms included swollen, throbbing testicles and glans, suppurating genital sores, painful and difficult urination, and debilitating fever. Symptoms were soothed with genital baths of chlorate of potash or zinc or with mercury vapour. Hourly injections through the urethra for twelve hours were excruciating, as were other standard treatments. Worse, they failed to cure, and so infected veterans returned home and infected their women, who developed inflammatory diseases of the pelvis that led to infertility or tubal pregnancies.

Over time, symptoms intensified to include incontinence, bone and joint degeneration, sexual impotence, loss of reflexes, blisters, rashes and tumours, paralysis, insanity, and finally "a lingering and revolting death.... No one knows how many Union and Confederate wives and widows went to their graves, rotted and ravaged by the pox that their men brought home, or how many veterans' children were blinded by gonorrhea or stunted by syphilis," writes Civil War medical historian Thomas Lowry.[40]

Demobilized men often returned to a much different home life from the one they had left. Many had grown closer to their wives or the girlfriends they expected to marry through letters in which they described their experiences, including their fears, hopes, and emotional responses. "If Permitted to live then I exspect to Return Home & See the People & Eat Peaches" was Iowa Infantryman Newton Scott's modest dream.[41]

But many others had difficulty reconnecting with spouses alienated by years of separation and hardship. ("While you all was Haveing Such good times ... on the 4th, we was Shooting Rebels," Newton Scott wrote.[42] In a letter found on a battlefield, one young woman filled three pages describing her new bonnet and comparing it to her rival's.[43]) Some women had had extramarital sex. Others, expecting their husbands to die in combat, entered new relationships. Some sold themselves to survive: "I am not astonished to hear of General Sherman saying he could buy the chastity of any Southern woman for a few pounds of coffee," a Mississippi woman commented in a letter to her husband.[44] At war's end, many returning soldier-husbands and their waiting wives found the strains of life together intolerable. Reunited, they made each other miserable until they finally sought relief in separation or divorce.

But the sharp increase in divorce was not uniform across the nation. Densely populated cities had higher rates than smaller towns and rural areas. Regionally, the West had the highest rates, the North more moderate, and the South the lowest. Southern whites were devastated by their military defeat and the destruction of their personal property, their "burned towns, deserted plantations, [and] sacked villages."[45] Collectively outraged and bitter that their slaves had been freed and that the despised, victorious North was imposing a new order on the old, Southern whites strongly resisted divorcing each other.

Yet the old order had already begun to disintegrate. For one thing, the war had transformed Southern women, who had survived by assuming their absentee husbands' and fathers' manly roles and by summoning up unsuspected reserves of internal strength. But to the men coming home from fighting, many with diseased or shattered bodies, missing limbs, punctured organs, and crushed spirits, the spectre of newly confident and assertive women would have been a mortal blow.

Understanding this, their women welcomed back these broken and dispirited men as if they were still the powerful patriarchs they had once been. Wives, sisters, and daughters tamped down their newfound independence in the common cause of restoring confidence and rebuilding their lives, often in poverty and always in disarray. Once-wealthy plantation women like Mary Boykin Chesnut scrounged to feed their families; Chesnut noted sardonically that the arrival of Lent was "quite convenient, for we have nothing to eat. So we fast and pray."[46] She and her *consoeurs* also tended gardens, raised chickens, taught school, pawned family heirlooms and household goods, and earned money however they could.

Just as crucial as assuaging their men's collective humiliation was the need to maintain racial solidarity; in the common struggle against black freedom, race trumped gender, giving white women yet another reason to restrain themselves in order to maintain racial unity with white men. In the context of shoring up damaged psyches and suffering families, personal divorce seemed even less justified, and the divorce rate remained lower than elsewhere in the recovering nation.

Throughout the United States, the anti-divorce crusaders fought hard. Yale's Woolsey was a movement leader and in 1881 co-founded the New England Divorce Reform League, which fought against easier divorce. (In 1885, it was reconstituted as the National Divorce Reform League.) As part of their proselytizing, league members targeted sexuality, women's rights, venereal disease, prostitution, alcoholism, and drug abuse as contributing to the disease of divorce.

And the disease was rising: the Department of Labor reported that from 1867 to 1886, divorce increased 150 percent, though the population had only grown by one-third. Other reports were just as ominous: between 1880 and 1890, divorce jumped by 70 percent and in the next decade by another 67 percent. Divorce rates rose everywhere in the Western world, but in the United States they skyrocketed. In 1910, for example, there were 83,045 American divorces in a population of 92 million, while England, Scotland, France, Belgium, Holland, Switzerland, Norway, Denmark, and Sweden, with a combined population of 108 million, had only 20,329 divorces.

DIVORCE, CANADIAN-STYLE

Canadians, the northern neighbours who hardly divorced at all, were horrified at the phenomenon of American divorce. They had closely watched the progress of the Civil War, officially neutral but personally engaged. Most abhorred slavery, but many sympathized or had connections with Southern business interests; others descended from or had strong links to the Northern states. After the War of 1812 and the Rebellions of 1837–38, Canadians generally preferred political and constitutional solutions over violence and war. Instead of arms, they took up pen and paper and crafted the paper-strewn path to their Confederation. And instead of divorce, they lived together in misery or simply separated.

Canadians associated American-style divorce with what they perceived as the United States' questionable morals and disintegrating social fabric. Divorce became an important question in the quest to define the character of the new nation, created on July 1, 1867, and to distinguish Canada from its powerful and often domineering American neighbours. Canadians believed that their minuscule divorce rate reflected their moral superiority over Americans. (When they really wanted to divorce, however, they travelled south and obtained American divorces.)

In 1857, England's Matrimonial Causes Act changed the nature of divorce in most of the British Empire by creating a divorce court to replace the cumbrous system of divorcing through a private act of Parliament. The secretary of state for the colonies urged the colonies to adopt a similar system, and many did, beginning with Australia. Thanks in large part to its desire to distinguish itself from the United States, Canada alone in the British Empire did not allow judicial divorce.

Canadian resistance was only partially rooted in moral concerns. It also stemmed from a desire to spare the provinces the jurisdictional quagmire caused by the different divorce laws in each American state. Inter-jurisdictional recognition was a serious issue, both nationally and internationally, and included divorces granted to Canadians in the United States. In 1867, the British North America Act assigned marriage and divorce to federal jurisdiction but granted the related matters of property and civil rights to the provinces, thus dividing the legislative responsibility for family law. The problem of recognizing divorces from the United States and from other parts of the empire remained.

Custody of children was a tremendously important aspect of the divorce question. By granting women custody of their children, the 1857 Matrimonial Causes Act had triggered fears that hordes of unhappy wives would flee their marriages. At the same time, there was deep concern that men could use the right to custody as a weapon, forcing their wives to endure abuse out of fear of losing their children. The solution was to grant custody to the wronged or "innocent" party in the divorce.

In practice, divorce reforms had little practical effect until laws also reformed women's property rights. Before the first such reform, the Married Women's Property Act of 1870, wives were financially and legally dependent on their husbands and, as Caroline Norton so forcefully pointed out, had no right even to their own earnings. Most women without relatives to support them had no choice but to stay married. Working-class women continued to suffer, and even after the 1878 Matrimonial Causes Act, which allowed magistrates to grant women custody and require their husbands to support them, the tendency was to force reconciliation. In 1886, the Guardianship of Children Act was the first to consider the needs of children as well as their parents' marital behaviour or misbehaviour.

Canada's reluctance to tolerate divorce was reflected in its tiny divorce rate: between 1867 and 1907, the American divorce rate (even allowing for the different populations) was 230 times greater than the Canadian—Canada had a mere 431 divorces compared to nearly 1.3 million in the States. "We are free from many of the social cancers which are empoisoning the national life of our neighbours," boasted the *Canadian Methodist Magazine*. In 1910, McGill University's chancellor attributed the high American divorce rate in large part to the raw recklessness of the American psyche, "the same spirit which, carried to the extreme length, is manifested in lynchings and murders and finds a milder expression in the intolerance of control in the family."[47] But although Canada boasted one of the lowest divorce rates in the Western world, so many Ontario residents were appearing in upper New York state divorce courts that a disapproving judge there commented on it.

DIVORCE AT THE DAWN OF THE TWENTIETH CENTURY

Until World War I, Canada remained hostile to divorce. Only Nova Scotia, New Brunswick, and British Columbia had the divorce courts recommended by England, and they almost never granted divorces for any reason other than adultery. In the period between the world wars, Alberta, Saskatchewan, and Ontario established divorce courts. People from other provinces still had to seek divorce through Parliament, an exercise that was expensive, complicated, and public, and one that could be so humiliating, especially to women, that many chose instead to live as fake spinsters, or "grass widows." Instead of divorcing, many unhappy couples simply separated, legally or informally. Some moved away and remarried, hoping their bigamy would remain undetected. Others settled for American divorces, which, though not legally binding in Canada, seemed as close to real divorce as possible.

The question of "migratory" divorces remained corrosive, as ersatz residents who divorced and then resumed residence in their home state or province were, in effect, importing forbidden divorces they then tried to get validated. This was true of both Americans and Canadians.

As they had in other wars, divorce rates escalated after World Wars I and II. Before the wars, divorce laws throughout the Western world were being liberalized, and divorce was a divisive and hotly debated social issue. In England, the average annual number of divorces rose from 701 between 1907 and 1913, to 2,740 in the years 1918 to 1921. In the United States, there was an average annual increase of 40 percent from 1914 to 1921. Canada continued to maintain a low divorce rate, largely because divorce was so difficult to obtain. Women won the right to sue for divorce on terms of equality with men only in 1925. Ontario, the largest province, established divorce courts only in 1930.

The divorce rates associated with the world wars rose for the usual reasons: a frenzied milieu that speeded up notions of life and death and pushed many people to marry on the spur of the romantic, patriotic moment; enforced separation; and widespread wartime adultery by both soldiers and their wives. But spouses waited to reunite at war's end before they divorced, so wartime divorce rates declined. With peace, however, came divorce, and the more people divorced, the less unacceptable divorce became.

The abdication crisis of 1936 reinforced Canada's reluctance to relax its divorce laws. King Edward VIII had fallen in love with a twice-divorced American, Wallis Simpson, and in seeking a constitutional way to marry her, he requested the approval of the British Parliament and all the dominions. But the British public and the Church of England strongly disapproved, and so did Canadians. "Canada is the most puritanical part of the Empire," an official British report declared. "Canadian pride has been deeply wounded by the tattle in the American press, which she feels an intolerable impertinence."[48]

The press gossip was fierce. Wallis Simpson might not even be really divorced from husband #1, at least in England, where the Church of England did not recognize the American grounds of emotional incompatibility. If so, then she was a bigamist with two living ex-husbands and could not contract another marriage. Rumours flew about her busy sex life, much of it not with the king. Joseph Kennedy, the American ambassador to England—and no puritan in his own personal life—denounced her as a "tart." Mrs. Kennedy would not dine with her. The FBI reported that Mrs. Simpson both slept with and spied for the German Reich's ambassador, von Ribbentrop. Edward was told he could not marry her and so, sad, shaken, but determinedly in love, he abdicated. The British Empire was (temporarily) safe from the spectacle of a king marrying a divorcée.

Though Britain liberalized its divorce laws in 1937, Canada's continued to reflect a traditional, deep-rooted conservatism. The abdication crisis did not influence the United States. There, the staggering discrepancy between hard-line states like New York, which divorced only sworn (and famously collusive) adulterers, and Nevada, which had flimsy residency laws and the nation's highest divorce rate, fuelled the problem of migratory divorces. Even New York's governor, Nelson Rockefeller, divorced in Nevada.

The cleansing and reforming 1960s halted the continued tinkering with divorce laws by crafting new grounds. What now made sense was no-fault divorce, which, by the 1980s, most of the Western world had accepted. (Revolutionary France had briefly introduced a similar concept.) Neither church nor state was required to interpret marital breakdown; divorcing spouses were their own authorities. All they had to do was separate and live apart for a specified amount of time, and they had grounds for divorce. England, influenced by the Church of England, reformed its divorce laws in 1969. By 1980, most states, including New York and California, had embraced no-fault divorce or had specified irretrievable marriage breakdown, living apart, legal sepa-

As divorce laws were slowly relaxed and divorce became more common, it was often the subject of humour. In this 1889 image, a man embraces a woman, likely the wife of the sleeping man. Another woman, probably a maid, hides behind the door observing their adulterous behaviour, ground for divorce.

ration, incompatibility, even mutual consent as grounds. The two decades from the 1960s to the 1980s "constituted a third generation of divorce legislation in Western society," writes Roderick Phillips, "following the first generation of the Protestant Reformation, and the second of the nineteenth century. Unlike the first two phases, however, the third abandoned moralistic and fault-based precepts."[49]

Even Canada finally liberalized divorce. The Divorce Act of 1968 introduced the concept of permanent marriage breakdown, though it retained the fault-based grounds of adultery, rape, homosexual acts, bigamy, cruelty, or desertion, equally available to husbands and wives. Other grounds were two years of imprisonment, alcohol or drug addiction, and non-consummation of the marriage. A divorce judge heard the case and adjudicated. Collusion, common if not ubiquitous, invalidated the process. So did a spouse's earlier forgiveness of infidelity, abuse, or any other grounds cited in the divorce procedure, or the judge's perception that reconciliation was possible. (Cohabitation of more than three months in attempts to reconcile annulled a previous separation. A new separation was necessary to qualify as a grounds for divorce.) The first stage of a successful divorce action was a decree nisi, which became absolute in three months, after which the divorced spouses could remarry.

In 1985, no-fault grounds were expanded, making divorce a cheaper, less formidable, and more transparent process. This move was largely the result of the 1976 Law Reform Commission of Canada's *Report on Family Law*, which underscored how the adversarial nature of divorce poisoned issues of child custody and support. Though the report recommended marriage breakdown as the sole grounds for divorce, the act of 1985 still specified hostile grounds for establishing that breakdown: adultery or physical or mental cruelty. (By then, the battered women's shelter movement had emerged, safeguarding some women and their children from their abusers.) The Unified Family Courts it recommended, with exclusive jurisdiction over family law issues, were set up in some jurisdictions.

The 1985 act described bars to divorce, most reiterations of the previous act: collusion, condoning cruelty then citing it as grounds, and failure to make reasonable arrangements for child support. It facilitated uncontested divorces, which constituted an estimated 85 percent. It emphasized the importance of attempting reconciliation through negotiation and mediation, believed to ease the settling of marriage issues faster and more effectively than litigation. It also simplified divorce by removing the two-stage procedures of decrees nisi and absolute.

In the mid-nineteenth century, Caroline Norton and Elizabeth Packard converted their private pain and public humiliation into fuel that powered their campaigns to improve women's rights within marriage, including the rights to divorce and to obtain child custody. Since then there has been steady progress in how Western society deals with unhappy marriages. Today, divorce laws and family laws anticipate and evaluate marital problems and allow for resolution, usually by separation or divorce.

Divorce still has critics who reiterate the arguments of past centuries: that divorce equals failure rather than solution, that high divorce rates reflect moral catastrophe, that easier divorce laws encourage if not actually cause divorce and go hand in hand with the secularization of marriage. Some blame women's improved rights and changing roles for marital dissolution, or at least suspect that there is a strong connection.

But today's divorce laws strongly reflect egalitarian ideals and also the rights of affected children (except the right to an intact family). Forced reconciliation is a thing of the past. So is prohibiting adulterers from marrying their illicit lovers. Increasingly, negotiation and mediation are legal tools to deal with marital conflict, and the concept of fault that was once the bedrock of divorce law has been replaced by its benign antithesis: no fault.

Marriage in the Present and Future

The Way We Think We Were and the Way We Think We Are

The Montrealers' wedding march is more of a waddle because the glowing bride's pregnancy bulges under the simple dress she bought the day before. Her back is aching and her feet hurt. But the ceremony cannot be rushed because it is a complicated blend of her Jewish and his Muslim faiths. A month later their daughter will be born in ecumenical wedlock, in the pleasant house her parents have lovingly prepared for her arrival.

In a medieval walled town in modern Germany, a kindly Lutheran pastor blesses the couple he has just wed, then urges their guests to partake of the wedding cake that, in alternating layers of chocolate and vanilla, symbolize the brown skin of the Indian groom and the white skin of his German bride. Two days later, the newlyweds and their wedding party travel to India, where the blond bride dons a red and gold sari and bangles for her Hindu marriage ceremony.

In San Francisco, two exhilarated couples arrive at City Hall to tie the marital knot. The men are in tuxedoes, the women in elegant gowns. In simple but eloquent ceremonies that leave few guests dry-eyed, Jonathan and Diego pledge themselves to each other. In another room, so do Christine and Ling-Ling.

How times have changed from the old days that we too often cloak in the golden glow of nostalgia! The very nature of marriage is changing.

Racial, religious, and ethnic intermarriages, once forbidden, are commonplace, and in some jurisdictions, same-sex marriages and civil unions, once unthinkable, are legal. Many people cohabit, but they tend to break up more frequently than those who marry. Single people find their lifestyle so attractive that family types have been redefined to include the solitaire. And who of us hasn't heard warnings that even when people do marry, one out of two of those marriages will end in divorce?

Yet this much-quoted warning that fuels our widespread horror of divorce is based on faulty premises and is one of the ways in which we are not quite like the way we think (and fear) we are. The one-in-two divorce rate misrepresents the reality. The devil is truly in the details, and in the case of divorce, statistics are too often analyzed simplistically, and misinterpretation is the result.

In her paper "Divorce: Facts, Causes and Consequences," sociologist Anne-Marie Ambert explains how this happens. "The *number* of divorces in a year is calculated over the *number of marriages* that have taken place during this same year," she writes. "If the number of marriages goes down, as it has in the past decade, it only makes sense that, even if the *number* of divorces remains the same, the *proportion* of divorces will increase." This is, Ambert points out, "a very misleading way of calculating divorce." It is similarly misleading to compare the rate of divorce in one year with the rate of marriage in that same year, for example 1994, in which Canada had 2.7 divorces and 5.4 marriages per 1,000 population. "Thus, the divorce rate (which becomes a ratio) is 50% that of marriages—a false 'fact' ... [often] erroneously used to predict that 50% of people marrying in a year will end up divorced."

The people marrying in any one year are rarely the same ones divorcing in that year. "The fact is," Ambert concludes, "we can know what proportion of marriages end in divorce only after the death of one of the spouses." Rather than the "false fact" that one in two marriages will end in divorce, Canadians and Americans marrying for the first time risk about a 30 percent chance of divorcing. (The much higher U.S. divorce rate reflects many more remarriages that end in divorce; American first marriages are not much more likely than Canadian ones to end in divorce.)[1]

But thanks to false facts and our propensity to believe them, divorce is so entrenched in popular culture that, in response to queries about their marital status, bachelors quip, "I haven't yet met my future ex-wife." Singers sing about divorce: Alicia Keys in "Every Little Bit Hurts," Tammy Wynette in "D-I-V-O-R-C-E," Cher in "You Better Sit Down Kids." Writers write about it in articles and books for both adult and child readers: *I Don't Want to Talk About It, Two Homes,* and *It's Not Your Fault, Koko Bear.* Scholars study it, and there is the scholarly *Journal of Divorce and Remarriage.* Self-help divorce books, support groups, and specialized divorce counsellors address the needs of people contemplating or in the process of divorcing.

And divorce is real even if not as frequent as we suppose. One consequence is that children who live with their married biological parents are now in a minority. Another is that even for them, accustomed to the changing home circumstances of friends, neighbours, and family, divorce is a lurking anxiety, the "dark doppelganger of marriage."[2]

Yet millions of North Americans shuck off society's collective anxiety about the state of marriage and, driven by conviction, parental or community pressure, or the evident satisfaction that some friends and family derive from their marriages—they opt to marry. For them, marriage may be a religious commitment, a bulwark against a threatening world, or a safe place that offers warmth, security, and, if they are inclined to parenthood, the best chance of raising happy, healthy children.

As they begin to plan their joint futures, these marriage-minded folks are wooed, seduced, and often sucked into the vortex of the wedding industry's machine. There is, in fact, a gaping disconnect between laments about the state of marriage and North America's current cultural obsession with weddings. Magazines, newspapers, blogs, and television salivate over celebrity weddings, lavishing as much attention on serial spouses such as Tom Cruise and Liza Minnelli as on first-timers. Photos of Princess Di's 1981 wedding retain their media magic. Barbie bride dolls encourage little girls to plan weddings and to participate in pretend ones with a My Size Bride Barbie, a three-foot-tall doll whose "Wear & Share" gown also fits girls from four to ten years of age. A glossy and didactic bridal media instructs readers about what is required to stage the wondrous spectacle their wedding must be.[3]

For those who cannot get enough of weddings, (unreal) reality TV blasts them right into our homes. *Rich Bride Poor Bride* shows the minute details of planning a wedding, with the plotline centred on finances and the denouement an examination of whether the actual wedding was over or under budget. *Bridezillas*, featuring such episodes as "Life's a Bitch and Then You Marry One," focuses on engaged women as they prepare for their perfect day. Fox promoted the show as stories about "sugary sweethearts who mutate into matrimonial monsters [and] stars of their own horror movie." A Bridezilla, it explained, is "a poisonous green-faced wedding-dress-adorned expletive-spewing fist-waving bride out of control."[4]

Weddings fascinate viewers. Women's Entertainment channel programs hours of daily wedding-related shows, including *Puppy Weddings,* featuring pooches in tuxedoes and tulle. Slice television offers *Bulging Brides*, in which personal trainers known as the Dream Team put brides too pudgy for their wedding through a personal boot camp of diet and exercise. *Hitched or Ditched* follows dysfunctional couples to see if they make it to their wedding day. The list goes on and on, even without such big productions as *The Bachelor* and *The Bachelorette* about the (few) couples who make it to the wedding-planning stage.

Despite the televised ubiquity of lavish, fantastical weddings, some first-time and many second-time real-life couples choose simpler alternatives: civil services, plain religious services, outdoor or other theme-style ceremonies, foreign "destination" weddings with or without a travelling wedding party, and entertain the wedding guests in restaurants, community halls, church basements, or private homes.

But the wedding as extravaganza is much more common. Weddings have become a multibillion-dollar industrial complex of related businesses: bridal boutiques, wedding-garb designers and retailers, tuxedo and wedding paraphernalia rental companies, banquet halls, caterers,

bakers, florists, jewellers, photographers, musicians, DJs, wedding plan-
ners, and trinket, favour, and accessory suppliers. The wedding industry, writes Rebecca Mead in *One Perfect Day: The Selling of the American
Wedding*, depends "for its economic health upon the perpetual spiraling
upward of wedding-day expectations…. the experience of the bride is
only a particularly acute crystallization of the larger experience of all
Americans, which is that of being immersed in a culture whose impera-
tives are derived more and more from the marketplace."[5]

Weddings have become such a self-referential industry that they seem
disconnected from the marriages they celebrate; "marriage is the after-
thought, the residue," writes Anne Kingston in *The Meaning of Wife*;
"the perfect wedding [provides] the necessary structural underpinning
for the perfect marriage. Miss a step, forget the embossed matchbooks
or forgo the butterfly release, and your marriage is imperiled."[6]

Eighty percent of so-called traditional weddings are staged in
churches, synagogues, temples, or mosques. For the unreligious, their
ambiance imparts grandeur and gravitas to the proceedings. For believers, for whom marriage is a sacrament, they radiate spirituality.

The wedding gown, however, is the ultimate symbol of wedding
madness, a fusion of fantasy and extravagance with stark consumerism.
It transforms the fiancée into a bride, a being suspended in time and
released from reality before she transmogrifies, after or even during the
honeymoon, into a wife. The gown's whiteness lends her an ersatz
purity, its yardage the illusion of opulence. Its veil is an anachronistic
prop that suggests coyness and is often topped by a glittering tiara, her
crown for the day.[7] After a childhood of dressing her Barbie dolls in
wedding gowns ranging from frilly polyester to black-accented Vera
Wang, the bride is finally dressing herself.

For many a bride, the gown is a personal challenge. If she does not
have a perfect figure, as svelte as a model or as curvy as Barbie (who, if
she were five foot six rather than eleven and a half inches, would
measure 39–21–33), she may use her engagement period for rigorous
diet and exercise. The wedding day is her target date, and fitting into
her chosen wedding dress is the goal. Bridal magazines and websites
urge her on. Lose ten or twenty pounds before your Big Day! Walk

down that aisle as the woman you've always wanted to be (and not the woman he proposed to or who proposed to him). Brides can even attend Bridal BootCamp where, a Canadian site warns, they must "expect complete and total exhaustion ... the toughest workout you have ever done and expect KILLER results."

A boot camp regimen may not be enough. The bride's nose, lips, ears, chin, or smile may also need adjusting, the breast augmented, the belly nipped, or the vagina tightened. Dental surgery, implants, braces, or whitening strips will take care of imperfect teeth. Increasingly, brides (and a few grooms) are adding cosmetic surgery and other treatments— liposuction, injections, laser, chemical peels—to their "to do" lists.[8]

Weddings do more than sustain a vast industrial complex. They assuage our fears about the state of marriage by seeming to offer a way to perpetuate traditions that are at the core of society and that represent its stability and prosperity. At the same time, weddings symbolize a clash of values between the past we think we had and collectively long for, a time of stable and straightforward family relations, and a past we regret, a patriarchal society pocked by inequities, rigidity, and heartbreak.

Weddings also force us to confront the reality of remarriage, which is so common that it has spawned new protocol: What to wear the third time round? Where to seat a benign ex-spouse, the parent of the bride, or the groom's children? How to integrate often reluctant and mutually hostile offspring at their parents' wedding? Where to seat warring former in-laws (now out-laws)? What to give the bride this time? These thorny issues, couched in etiquette, hint at the minefields on which many modern marriages are celebrated if not constructed.

Our collective failure to remain married—or to marry in the first place—has become the subject of religious sermonizing, scholarly study, and politicized commentary. We justify our right to personal satisfaction but also plead guilty to rushing to divorce. We rejoice in our individuality but castigate ourselves for being selfish, shallow, self-serving, and materialistic, unlike (we believe) our ever-married forebears. We beat our breasts and hurl recriminations at the usual suspects: The ease of divorce! Working women and feminism! Abortion and the pill! Artificial insemination, which allows lesbians and single women to do without men altogether! Godlessness! Greed! Laziness! Hedonism!

At the same time, religious and political leaders, journalists and scholars study and predict the consequences of marriage's perceived institutional failure and suggest how to reverse the tide. Evangelical and other Christian churches urge people to marry (heterosexually) and to stay married. A few promote gay marriage as the alternative to Sodom and Gomorrah depravity. Policy-makers draft regulations and laws to encourage marriage through tax and child-care incentives. Scholars track the fate of the children of the divorced, the remarried, and the still single, of adoptees, and of gay parents, and their reports fuel the fire of the debate about marriage and divorce.

In North America, this debate is too often rooted in historical, static, and romanticized assumptions about historic marriage, which is painted without the real-life backdrops that were described in part 1: the soaring rate of alcoholism and drug addiction, triple that of today; bans against interracial marriage; the dearth of effective birth control and, toward the end of the century, its criminalization; high infant and child mortality rates; the high adult mortality rate that made remarriage an urgent and common occurrence among young widows and widowers unable to cope alone; the grief of child survivors mourning siblings and parents, then coexisting with step-siblings and step-parents, all the while suffering the trauma of loss on a scale unimaginable today.

Whatever would Martha Coffin Wright or Jane Austen have made of our version of their worlds?

But this "Victorian fantasy" has been slow to die. Just before the women's movement exploded into public consciousness with the 1963 appearance of Betty Friedan's *The Feminine Mystique*, the new medium of television offered the popular series *Leave It to Beaver* and *Father Knows Best*. *Beaver*'s iconic parents, perky stay-at-home mother June Cleaver and her kindly husband, Ward, raised their two sons and lived happily in suburbia; *Father Knows Best*'s Jim and Margaret Anderson did much the same with their son, Bud, and daughters Princess (Betty) and Kitten (Kathy). *Father Knows Best* leapt from radio to television in 1954, and 203 episodes aired until 1962; Beaver's 234 episodes ran from 1957 to 1963 and, as reruns, into perpetuity.

French and English Canada's television series *La Famille Plouffe* and *The Plouffe Family* (1953–1959) offered novelist Roger Lemelin's rollicking saga about a working-class family in Quebec City's Lower Town. The Plouffe world was one of streetcar conductors, newspaper typesetters, interfering priests, and prying neighbours in the World War II milieu of conscription, censorship, and trade union militancy. Good women were stay-at-home mothers and their men were good providers and patriarchs. Life was rawer than in American shows, though in the English version, the profanities and sexual references were deleted. Nonetheless (or perhaps because of this), anglophone Canadians preferred to watch the sanitized worlds of *Leave It to Beaver* and *Father Knows Best.*

The Cleavers and Andersons personify a modernized fantasy of the Victorian marriage and family life and, as historian Stephanie Coontz observes, "presented an idealized mixture of values that never coexisted in any real family and that were in many cases quite contradictory.... The hybrid modern expectation that a woman can have an intense, close relationship with her children while simultaneously maintaining youthful sexual excitement with her husband is highly unrealistic, and this has introduced enormous stresses into many women's lives."[9]

Ironically, Billy Gray, the actor who played Bud, became the show's most urgent critic. "I wish there was some way I could tell kids not to believe it—the dialogue, the situations, the characters—they were all totally false," he said in 1983. "The girls were always trained to use their feminine wiles, to pretend to be helpless to attract men. The show contributed to a lot of the problems between men and women that we see today.... I think we were all well motivated, but what we did was run a hoax."[10]

That hoax included the portrait of a marriage, the staging of a cozy interior, and the ease with which a prettily aproned and perfectly groomed June Cleaver cleaned, cooked, and ran her little fiefdom, all with deep personal satisfaction. Yet this hoax, this ahistorical model, continues to influence our historical understanding. Too often, false notions like this one—and like the crazed world of televised weddings—frame our discussions about marriage past and present, and lead us to condemn ourselves as sadly wanting. Yet the more we pine for a past that never was, the more we blind ourselves to today's possibilities. As William Faulkner so wisely observed, "The past is not dead and gone; it isn't even past."

Chapter 8

Unmarried and Often Single

"We Are the Dead"

Early on a May Sunday morning in 1915, Lieutenants Owen Hague of the Canadian Field Artillery's 2nd Brigade and Alexis Helmer of the 1st ventured out to inspect a Canadian battery on the bank of the Yser Canal in the French–Belgian border in an area known as Flanders. German gunners sighted them, and before the two men could travel more than a few yards, a cannon shell exploded. It smashed Hague's left leg, nearly severing it at the thigh, and fractured his right leg. It also blasted him thirty feet away, and that night he died in a French field hospital. Helmer died instantly, his body shattered into fragments.

Hague, a twenty-six-year-old Montrealer, had enlisted in 1914, directly after graduating from McGill University with his master's degree in science, and had won several commendations from his military superiors. Helmer, one month short of twenty-three, had also signed up right after graduating with a McGill science degree. Helmer was engaged to be married to a girl whose photograph he carried with him.

Helmer and Hague had just endured some of the fiercest fighting of the Great War, seventeen days of relentless shelling that included German chlorine gas attacks. Dr. John McCrae, the brigade surgeon, described the battle of Ypres to his mother as "the most bitter of fights. For seventeen days and seventeen nights none of us have had our clothes

John McCrae in 1912. He re-enlisted in the army in 1914 "because I think every bachelor, especially if he has experience of war, ought to go."

off, nor our boots even … In all that time while I was awake, gunfire and rifle fire never ceased for sixty seconds … And behind it all was the constant background of the sights of the dead, the wounded, the maimed, and a terrible anxiety lest the line should give way."[1]

McCrae was Helmer's friend. They had met in Montreal, where McCrae was an assistant pathologist at the Montreal General Hospital, a McGill University lecturer, and a published poet. He had served in the Boer War and was forty-one when he re-enlisted in 1914. "I am going," he explained, "because I think every bachelor, especially if he has experience of war, ought to go. I am really rather afraid, but more afraid to stay at home with my conscience." When Helmer died, McCrae waited for a lull in the merciless bombardment, then instructed his men to collect the pieces of Helmer's broken body and place them in burlap bags. These he fashioned into the shape of a body, covered with a blanket, and fastened with pins.

"Lieutenant Helmer was killed at the guns—a very nice boy," McCrae wrote. "His girl's picture had a hole right through it and we buried it with him. I said the Committal Service over him, as well as I could from memory." The next day, as he sat on the back of an ambulance glancing back and forth between the windblown poppies and Helmer's simple grave, McCrae mourned his friend in quickly scribbled verses now acclaimed as "In Flanders Fields."

Soon after, McCrae's health began to deteriorate, and it is widely believed that he was tormented by memories of Helmer's terrible death. McCrae often sought solitude and took long lonely rides on Bonfire, the horse he had shipped from Canada, with only his spaniel Bonneau, a stray rescued from the battlefield, as a companion. On January 28, 1918, he died, victim of chronic asthma, bronchitis, perhaps the chlorine gas at Ypres, and despair at the horrors he had seen in war.

Besides plunging their families and friends into mourning, the deaths of these soldiers significantly reduced the numbers of men available to marry. Hague's military records left blank his marital status. McCrae, a distinguished physician, was likely a confirmed bachelor. But Helmer had been engaged, and, back home, a woman learned that she would never marry him. More than 62,000 Canadian soldiers died in the Great War, drastically changing the ratio of potential husbands to wives. As McCrae's famous poem lamented,

> *We are the Dead. Short days ago*
> *We lived, felt dawn, saw sunset glow,*
> *Loved and were loved, and now we lie*
> *In Flanders fields.*

A dearth of men, the predictable consequence of war, was one of several reasons women remained single. Others were the lack of a decent dowry, social connections, good looks, charisma, or just plain luck. Women afflicted by one of more of these insufficiencies could take their chances by marrying "down"—if they could find a willing mate. Another alternative was singleness, very often accompanied by celibacy, and in fact large numbers of women did not marry. In the eighteenth century, about 25 percent of English and 30 percent of Scottish aristocratic women remained single, most because of insufficiently large dowries but some by choice. Like Jane Austen (and her sister, Cassandra, and their widowed mother), most of these single women lived with relatives. Some were welcomed as much-loved aunties. Others were belittled and bullied by kinfolk and in-laws who never tired of reminding them that they were burdens.

North America, too, had large contingents of women who, through happenstance or choice, never married. Except for the right to vote, colonial spinsters had the same legal rights as men (English common law was the basis of North American colonial laws) and many exercised them to carve out productive lives as innkeepers, merchants, craftswomen, nurses, teachers, landowners, writers, printers, shipbuilders, tailors, shoemakers, bakers, brewers, painters, gilders, and wallpaper hangers, among other occupations.[2]

Many privileged women with good educations and financial resources also chose to live independently. In bustling Savannah and Charleston, many spinsters led rich lives dedicated to community service and family relationships: they were respected, and were sustained by emotional and social ties with other women, married and single. As "the communicators, caretakers, surrogate mothers, family servants, and benevolent women extending feminine virtues to individuals and organizations," historian Christine Jacobson Carter writes, these women were "the glue [that kept] elite social networks as well as individual families intact" and worked within the framework of patriarchal white authority to further their relatives' social and political power.[3]

Northern and Canadian spinsters, too, dedicated themselves to vocations or, if they had to support themselves, careers; they also threw themselves into the great causes of their day: abolition of slavery, women's suffrage, and temperance among them, often in leadership roles.

Catharine Beecher, Harriet's sister, founded several girls' schools, wrote bestselling books on household management and education, and lectured extensively. Unlike Harriet, whose marriage tied her to a penurious life as a mother, housewife, and writer forced to steal time from her domestic duties to write, Catharine was free to indulge her intellectual passions. She had already experienced life as a homemaker and mother after her own mother's death had forced her to leave school at the age of sixteen to raise her brothers and sisters. Tellingly, this doyenne of household management preferred to live itinerantly, a perpetual visitor with no interest in the permanent home she described with such expertise.

As a single woman with some financial resources, Beecher was committed to the plight of single women who needed to earn a living. Her vision, promulgated through her voluminous publications and lectures, was that they should train to become teachers, to serve as a model for responsible citizenship and to guide children's moral and intellectual development.

Harriet Beecher Stowe in 1853, as she was first gaining fame as the author of Uncle Tom's Cabin.

Canadian Margaret Marshall Saunders, author of *Beautiful Joe*, the first Canadian novel to sell over a million copies, was another never-married woman who parlayed her literary talent and compassion for victims of social injustices into a satisfying and rewarding vocation. *Beautiful Joe*, her story about an abused Airedale, was simple, heart-wrenching, and substantially true, except for being told in the first person. It was translated into eighteen languages including Esperanto and Braille and catapulted her into literary prominence. Saunders wrote another twenty-three books championing social issues such as the aboli-tion of child labour, slum clearance, and the need to recognize women's contributions to society. Childless, she wrote children's books that wove together the reality of slums, overcrowding, and alcoholism with a fantasy world of talking animals with moral agendas.

Yet at the same time that contingents of spinsters were enjoying satis-fying and fulfilled lives, the cult of domesticity's new sentimentality about wives increasingly recast spinsters as socially inadequate losers. The term *spinster*, first recorded in fourteenth-century England to describe someone who spun wool and by the seventeenth century the official term for an unmarried woman, became a pejorative. The spin-ster was never to forget—nor to be forgiven for—the fact that she was not a wife.

Unmarried men, on the other hand, were seldom vilified, because the double standard that judged spinsters so harshly exempted bachelors—except those suspected of "inversion," the term for homosexual inclina-tions. Even then, there was considerable leeway, because until the twentieth century, intense and sustained male relationships were accepted as unremarkable. Stories about Abraham Lincoln and Calvin Stowe illustrate just how greatly customs—and perceptions of them—have changed. Recent speculation that Lincoln was gay or bisexual is based on the fact that during his impecunious years as a fledgling lawyer, he economized by sharing a bed with another young man, Joshua Speed, who became his lifelong friend and to whom, in later years, Lincoln signed his letters "Yours Forever." But if Lincoln was gay, none of this is evidence of it. In an era where notions of privacy were still practised largely in the breach, it was customary for friends—even strangers—to save money or make do with limited space by sharing beds. As for "Yours Forever," it was Lincoln's habitual signature, including to his law partner and a congressman.

The normalcy of sleeping together is epitomized by an anecdote Harriet Beecher Stowe's husband, Calvin, wrote her during her long sojourn in a health spa. Calvin told her that a Mr. Farber, a young man of his acquaintance, had been forced by eye disease to postpone his engagement and subsequently took it "into his little black-curly pate to fall desperately in love with me, and he kisses and kisses upon my rough old face, as if I were a most beautiful young lady instead of a musty old man. . . . The Lord sent him here to be my comfort. He will have me here to sleep with him once in a while, and he says, *that is almost as good as being married*—the dear little innocent ignorant soul."4

Unlike Mr. Farber, who dulled his frustration at having to postpone his wedding by kissing musty old Calvin Stowe, other men who were keen to marry (and enjoy marital sex) languished instead in enforced singleness. Many were engaged but had to wait to wed until they were deemed to have established themselves financially. In 1857 in England, a much-quoted letter from "Theophrastus" to *The Times* deplored the social "laws" imposed by the tyranny of the nation's richest ten thousand; they forced millions in the middle class to postpone marrying until they could afford a fancy house, a footman, and a carriage. Even young couples willing to begin married life "on little more than the proverbial bread and cheese" dared not risk shaming their family by doing so. Apart from "the sad but familiar sight of two young lovers wearing out their best years with hearts sickened with hope long deferred," there was the fact that affianced men were notorious for consorting with courtesans and streetwalkers, thereby contributing to widespread prostitution and venereal disease.

Sometimes professions or vocations kept people single. Most Christian religious orders, both male and female, had to pledge celibate singleness. Female (but seldom male) schoolteachers could work only if they remained unmarried and chaste, and their private lives were monitored to ensure that this was the case. Domestic servants often worked in conditions that effectively forced them to remain single; if they managed to mate or marry, they risked losing their jobs. The eroding tradition of apprenticeship made similar demands, until the apprentice achieved master status. Most professional and clerical jobs did not explicitly require celibate singleness, but the usual practice was for women to resign as soon as they married. Many, however, simply concealed their marital status and daily removed their wedding rings.

By the end of the nineteenth century, as career opportunities for women increased, so did women's options—and confusion—regarding marriage. Nothing illustrates this as well as Chicago's six Eleanor Clubs, which from 1898 to 1930 housed thousands of single white middle-class businesswomen, including stenographers, clerks, bookkeepers, secretaries, students, and teachers in low-cost, safe, and respectable residences, way stations "between the security of family, home, and traditional values, and a changing new world." A former resident recalled, "I looked around at the quiet restfulness of the parlour, the cleanliness of the rooms, and almost wept at the luck that brought me to such a lovely home."[5]

The Eleanors understood that they straddled the chasm between past and present. They set out to their offices in smart clothes and bobbed hair, guided by their "Business Woman's Creed" that lauded "honest work … done by honest women by means of honest methods," and declared their belief in "working, not weeping; in boosting, not knocking, and in the joy and satisfaction of labor well done."[6] But at home in the residence, where a curfew and strict supervision ensured no one had a man in her room, the Eleanors articulated and acted out the fundamental contradictions of their lives.

At Kid Parties, these otherwise urbane businesswomen dressed as infants and toddlers, male as well as female, and flung themselves into child's play. "The years fell away from us and we leaped back into childhood with leapfrog," one resident recalled. They also held Old Maids' Clubs and Spinsters' Conventions at which they wore old-fashioned leg-of-mutton sleeves, wasp waistlines, and feathered hats and acted out their version of Victorian womanhood. At one Spinsters' Convention they debated the topic of women's sphere: was it limited to the home or did it extend to the working world? At another, "Susan B. Anthony" appeared with a giant carving knife to cut the cake. In 1922, at a musical farce called the Old Maids Association, the women responded to a roll-call with quotations such as, "Of all the saddest words that ever was writ, the saddest is these—I'm single yit." They also agreed that "women's highest duty is to adorn a home."

Yet the Eleanors commemorated two real wedding announcements with a mock funeral that included Chopin's Funeral March. As the "lawyer" read a will bequeathing girlish trinkets and love letters to fellow residents, the Eleanors "wailed ... over the loss of the two from our midst." Cupid was a kidnapper, and one future husband was a "bold brigand" whose fiancée was "his plunder." The Eleanors displayed strong ambivalence toward marriage. They equated it with love, companionship, social acceptance, and greater financial security, and considered it a better choice than "blessed singleness." But they also feared it as a sacrifice of both independence and success in the business world.

Eleanor Girls, including Edna Greaves, fourth from right, pose with their housekeeper. After Edna's father died, her mother sent Edna and her sister Lois to the Eleanor Club in Chicago to work and study. Edna later ran a successful travel business in Chicago and Lois became a schoolteacher. Edna married and had one son; Lois married late and remained childless. Both sisters outlived their spouses and lived independently into old age.

The Eleanor women were ideally placed to ponder the choice between living singly or married. Their residences offered security, friendship with compatible women, creature comforts, stimulating activities, and encouragement in their careers. If anyone were well placed to enjoy singleness, it was the Eleanor residents, and they were quick to mock the stereotype of unmarried women as pitiful old maids desperate for a man. Yet despite their confidence and gainful employment, the Eleanors epitomized the confusion and conflict felt by accomplished and thoughtful women who were well placed to choose either marriage or singleness and feared the consequences of either: marriage was desirable, yet they celebrated it with mock funerals.

UNMARRIED IN NORTH AMERICA

Today the meaning of singleness—and therefore its consequences—is drastically different. Singleness no longer implies a solitary existence (even within a communal living arrangement). *Singleness* can claim *autonomous* or *independent* as synonyms; it has become a way of life rich in possibilities and is losing its former sad and negative connotations. And being single can no longer be defined as the opposite of being married.

Even being unmarried is not exactly the opposite of being married, or at least in the traditional sense. Today, millions of men and women are persuaded to live outside of marriage, to the extent that in North America, married couples have become a minority of households. The 2005 U.S. census, for example, reveals that 51 percent of American women, and 47 percent of men, now live without a spouse. (In Canada, the figures are even higher.) "On average," says marriage scholar Stephanie Coontz, "Americans now spend half their adult lives outside marriage."[7]

(Parsed by ethnicity, the statistics translate into 70 percent of black women, 51 percent of Hispanic women, 45 percent of non-Hispanic white women, and less than 40 percent of Asian women living without husbands. In Canada, 41 percent of black Canadians marry, fewer than any other ethnic group, and more divorce. There are more single-parent families among black Canadians than any other group, 27 percent compared with a national average of 15.6 percent.)

Yet many of these husbandless women and wifeless men are not living alone. Instead of marrying, they simply cohabit. Cohabitation, defined as living together as spouses, increasingly rivals marriage as a way of life and as one of two principal alternatives to it (singleness is the other). In Canada and many other jurisdictions, cohabitation has the legal status of common-law union or is registered as a recognized relationship. At least 12 percent of Canadians cohabit; in Quebec the figure rises to 22 percent; 8.1 percent of U.S. households consist of unmarried men and women. (In Europe, by comparison, this figure rises to 21 percent in Finland and 17.5 percent in France.)

Cohabitation often precedes marriage. Three in four Canadians who have cohabited did so before marriage, one out of four after a marriage ended, and a small number both before and after. In this context, marriages preceded by cohabitation break up at greater rates than those that are not, except when an engagement precedes cohabitation.

Increasingly, cohabitation is replacing marriage. (This also explains why the divorce rate is now stabilizing and even declining: there are fewer marriages to end.) Quebec, for instance, now vies with Sweden for the highest percentage of people cohabiting, and 45 percent of cohabiting Quebecers do not intend to marry. The Quebec phenomenon may stem from a fierce commitment to gender equality, with cohabitation seen as a more equitable relationship than marriage. As well, rejecting marriage is part of a collective reaction against the powerful Roman Catholic Church that shaped Quebec's history but that, since the 1960s and the Quiet Revolution, has been bitterly challenged and stripped of much of its influence. Outside Quebec, cohabitation may also reflect a protest against marriage's religious associations.

Many North American critics worry that cohabitation is a greater threat to marriage than divorce because it offers so many of the same features as marriage, yet at the same time ignores or flouts religious and moral conventions. The culture of cohabitation, for example, seems to encourage the classic double standard that winked at a husband's but not a wife's infidelities. In a Canadian study, 41 percent of cohabiting men, but only 21 percent of women, declared that cohabitation does not imply the same degree of sexual loyalty or commitment as marriage.[8] Cohabitation accommodates men and women reluctant to commit to marriage. In this respect it also raises doubts about the fundamental capacity of humans to enter into monogamous unions, and raises the question: does modern longevity preclude the notion of lifelong unions?

Cohabitation is also easier and cheaper to embrace—and to leave—than marriage. As society grows more tolerant of different lifestyle choices and no longer pressures individuals to marry, the popularity of cohabitation has been accompanied by increasing social acceptance. Cohabiters are no longer treated as sinners, and some jurisdictions and institutions such as universities extend spousal benefits to them. Though some American states require cohabiting taxpayers to pay taxes on a partner's benefits and do not permit joint filing, and others forbid unmarried couples to claim one another as dependents, Canadian tax law no longer discriminates (and sometimes does not even distinguish) between married and common-law or cohabiting couples. This desire to avoid discrimination has even created a tax structure that favours unmarried parents, who can each claim a child "as if" that child were a dependent, an important deduction for two-income unmarried parents.

Another change is that the law no longer bastardizes the children of cohabiting parents. And the number of these children is growing. In the United States, for example, as marriage declines and cohabitation increases, at some point about 40 percent of the nation's children will live in a cohabiting household. (At any given time, however, only 3.5 percent do so.)[9] But these children do not fare as well as their peers with married parents, likely because in North America (but not Europe or Quebec), cohabiting parents are more likely to have less education and lower incomes than their married counterparts, and are more likely to split up.[10] But even this finding is complicated by the fact that cohabitation and marriage are so often intertwined unions; a majority of those who marry and remarry first cohabit, and about half of these previously married men and women who later cohabit bring children to these unions, as do about one-third of those who were previously unmarried.

SINGLES AND THE SINGLE LIFE

For all cohabitation's lure, marriage's true rival is singledom. Cohabitation, especially as it is enhanced by new social standards and law, has such a close resemblance to marriage that it looks increasingly like its fraternal twin. The single life, on the other hand, is quite different, although, like marriage, it can last forever or be cut short to embrace—literally—new circumstances.

There is growing interest in and respect for singleness, so long disdained and often dreaded as an incomplete existence synonymous with a sepia-tinted, cobwebby world of frustrated or frigid Miss Havishams, failed spinsters in a wife-filled world. There is also an intensifying scholarly focus on singleness—such as the Scholars of Single Women Network—and a steady flow of books that describe and document its history.

And these scholars of singleness are exposing a deep secret. You'd never know it from most history books but in prior centuries singletons were ubiquitous, and in some eras and places accounted for as many as one-quarter to one-third of the population.[11] As we have seen in previous chapters, economic conditions and financial constraints kept large segments of the adult population single. In times of high mortality, widows and widowers were often very young, and some were merry because they did *not* remarry rather than because they did.

In *The Economics of Emancipation: Jamaica and Barbados 1823–1843*, for example, Kathleen Mary Butler describes the economic role played by single and widowed white women after the abolition of slavery. Unlike married women, they had the same property rights as men and they exercised them vigorously. White women owned 5 percent of Jamaica's sugar estates and some were great landowners, with over a thousand acres. In post-emancipation Barbados, they collected compensation money, bought and sold estates, lent money to other planters, rid themselves of indebted estates, and exercised a disproportionate economic influence in the sugar colony's transition from slavery to new forms of production. Other historical studies of widows show that many used inheritances to maintain themselves in independence. In general, the wealthier they were, the less inclined they were to remarry.

By the early decades of the nineteenth century in North America, industrialization and factory work gave women more personal choice about their futures. At the same time, having few illusions about the realities of married life, some decided to remain single unless a man they truly cared for proposed to them, and engaged women often suffered what historian Nancy Cott calls "marriage trauma," long periods of depression and emotional paralysis at the prospect ahead of them.[12]

Sisters Laura and Frances Snowball pose with women's bicycles in Fredericton, N.B., about 1900, at the height of the North American and European bicycle craze. The girls publicly engaged in bicycling, which epitomized women's independence and provoked bitter controversy. Doctors warned that it caused infertility. Social critics denounced it as wanton and unfeminine. The Snowball sisters compromised by wearing long skirts rather than more suitable bloomers or trousers.

In the ensuing decades, women's horizons expanded and an incipient women's movement percolated. An important theme was "the cult of single blessedness," the notion that single women could also do godly work and service. In her witty two-volume *Married or Single?* (1857), Catharine Maria Sedgwick made it clear that a single life was far preferable to a bitter marriage. Elizabeth Barrett Browning's *Aurora Leigh*, the epic poem that narrated a woman's struggle to fulfill herself in poetry, included this verse:

> *And I breathe large at home. I drop my cloak,*
> *Unclasp my girdle, loose the band that ties*
> *My hair ... now could I but unloose my soul!*
> *We are sepulchred alive in this close world,*
> *And want more room.*

Other writers, too, argued that a woman's fulfillment was not necessarily bound up in a husband and family. Never-married Louisa May Alcott, for example, referred to "all the busy, useful independent spinsters" of her acquaintance and, in her fictionalized essay "Happy Women," observed that "liberty is a better husband than love to many of us."

In times of war, many women had no choice about marrying, as staggering military death rates kept them single or widowed. The American Civil War was one of the most destructive, and at least 618,000 Americans died of battle wounds, disease, accidents, executions, drowning, and a host of other causes. The death toll among Native and African-American Union soldiers was even higher: nearly a third of Indians died, nearly a quarter of blacks. Back home, as official death notices began to arrive, single women realized that many of them would never find husbands. By no means all of them grieved at their fate.

World War I killed at least 62,000 Canadian and 126,000 American soldiers. In England, which counted over 700,000 soldiers dead, newspapers began to publish stories with such headlines as "Problem of Surplus Women—Two Million Women Who Can Never Become Wives." World War II killed another 44,093 Canadians and 405,399

Americans, overwhelmingly male. Tens of thousands of others were wounded in body or soul and often rendered unmarriageable.

Whether because of war, vocation, profession, economics, or personal choice, significant minorities of men and even more women have lived as singles, and theirs is a hitherto hidden history of human relations and marriage. Exploring their lives and circumstances and discovering how they felt about their experiences is enlightening; it also helps as we contemplate our own personal paths today to have the solidity of that history behind us. It isn't new, but it's new to us. We can only imagine how this knowledge might have altered the perceptions of last century's Eleanor residents as those accomplished and thoughtful women dealt with the confusion and conflict their oh-so-comfortable but oh-so-temporary singleness imposed on them.

To put this into clearer context: today's ever growing number of singletons has been described, time and again, as one of the greatest social phenomena of Western society. We now know that this isn't true. Singles—and the single life—are just this century's version of previous centuries' realities.

The new scholarship sheds light on a plethora of issues, beginning with the raw data about singles: their numbers, sex, and geographical location; how many never married; how their society perceived and treated them; official policies and laws governing them; literary and cultural representations of them; their housing arrangements and choices; their roles in their families; their relationships with their siblings, parents, other relatives, and family friends; how the ever looming institution of marriage dominated their lives; and how single women in particular fared during, between, and after the world wars, when anti-spinster rhetoric raged like a modern witch hunt.

The sexuality and sexual expression of singles captures particular attention. What, if any, sexual activity was available or acceptable? How prevalent was homosexuality among singles? In case of pregnancy, what happened? What role did children play in singles' lives? How did they care for, foster, and adopt children? In *The Shadow of Marriage: Singleness in England, 1914–60*, historian Katherine Holden introduces the concept of "family standbys" as the crucial role played by singles, many of whom were deeply engaged in their relatives' child care and support. Yet though their families valued them and their contributions, these "standbys" often felt that their relationships with children lacked permanence.

Virginia Nicholson, who interviewed hundreds of women for her book *Singled Out: How Two Million Women Survived without Men After the First World War*, observes, "The thing that surprised me about the 'surplus' women in the 1920s, whose chances of marrying and having children had been shattered by the loss of so many potential husbands in the trenches, was that they did not resign themselves to loneliness. Some had affairs. Some made careers—their need to earn money for themselves led to a new breed of career girl, affectionately parodied in the musical *Thoroughly Modern Millie.* Some found love with other women—but they lived lives as fulfilled as if they had married in the conventional way."[13]

Single women had to counter bouts of frenzied anti-spinsterism, but they also had resources. In North America, the best known was *Vogue* magazine assistant editor Marjorie Hillis's still in print 1936 bestseller for "bachelor ladies" and "live aloners," *Live Alone and Like It: A Guide for the Extra Woman*, which set a drastically different tone from the Old Maid literature of the nineteenth century with its sympathy, humour, and resignation about the possibilities of being single.[14] Hillis, forty-six when she wrote this book and forty-nine when she married, visualized singles as stylish and glamorous women who needed four bed jackets, seven kinds of liquor, and the right cold cream. They could entertain at home and be entertained in bars. "You will soon find that independence, more truthfully than virtue, is its own reward," she wrote.

In chapters such as "A Lady and Her Liquor," "Pleasures of a Single Bed," and "Solitary Refinement," she urged single women to nurture two passions, "at least one that keeps you busy at home and another that takes you out. Just dabbling in them isn't enough, either. They will not be really efficacious until you're the kind of enthusiast who will stay home to follow the first type in spite of a grand invitation, or go out and follow the second in spite of wind, sleet, or rain."

Hillis's follow-up *Corned Beef and Caviar* (1937) assumed that her readers had part-time maids and little free time, and provided recipes that used canned food. For a summer evening meal after a tiring day at work: iced (canned) bouillon, (canned) seafood Newburg, endive salad, Tricot wafers, and cantaloupe with sherry. Slap together the meal, change into a cool tea dress, and dine on it, alone. In the chapter "Getting the Man with the Meal," Hillis has suggestions for all manner of man: dieter (consommé), teetotaller (creamy things and sweets), on the wagon (candies), heavy drinker (anything, save your money), gourmet (something simple and superlatively prepared), digestive issues (chicken broth, carrot sticks, prune whip, bran muffins). The perfect gentleman, however, should himself contribute a dish or two to the meal.

Three-quarters of a century later, single women are still "singled out," writes Bella DePaulo, author of *Singled Out: How Singles Are Stereotyped, Stigmatized, and Ignored, and Still Live Happily Ever After*, and "Living Single" blogger for *Psychology Today*. Social attitudes, pseudoscience in the form of "matrimania," mockery, discriminatory tax laws and insurance rates, singles' surcharges in hotels, and snide suggestions of frigidity or lesbianism are just some of what single women confront. For their part, single men are suspected of mama's boy infantilism, an inability to commit, or homosexuality.

But the times are a-changing, especially for women. Egalitarianism as a legal and educational standard has propelled an ever increasing number of women into higher education, the professions, and the workplace. They obtain more loans, including for launching businesses, and mortgages—in the United States, for example, women buy 20 percent of residential real estate. (Married couples buy 61 percent.) They can have or adopt children and raise them as single parents; they are no longer in thrall to their biological clocks. They can stay single for a lifetime, in transition from divorce or the death of a partner, or temporarily, until they decide circumstances are ripe to pair off. The choices and possibilities are now so entrenched in North American society that singleness has become both a satisfying choice and a profound threat to the institution of marriage.

Yet the idea of singleness still evokes anxiety in many men and women, and the living proof of successful singles—from the never married to the contentedly divorced or comfortably widowed—is only slowly assuaging it. Single men still find that Jane Austen's "truth universally acknowledged, that a single man in possession of a good fortune must be in want of a wife," is as valid today as it was two centuries ago, and that the same vision extends to fortuneless men as well. Single men may resist attempts to mate them, drawing on a cultural dread or apprehension. Others are single, from defiance or default, or for reasons (to be elaborated in chapter 14) rooted in a current malaise among young men. Still others see singleness as independence and living alone as freedom.

For women and many men, children are the most pressing issue of all. Adopting is increasingly appealing, and in the last few decades, adoption agencies, especially those that arrange foreign adoptions, have accepted single women and lately single men. Like their married counterparts, single women applicants often resort to adoption after failing to conceive with intrauterine insemination by donated sperm or egg. "The common element in that [adoption seminar] room was grief," recalls single adoptive mother Tess Kalinowski about the married couples she met there.[15]

Counterintuitively, because single parents have fewer resources than couples, they are much more likely to be matched with special-needs children; although singles constitute less than 5 percent of all adopters, they adopt an estimated 25 percent of these children.[16] Though prejudice against them is eroding, singles are still penalized for their singleness by being required to carry a bigger burden than married couples.

In *Adopting Alyosha: A Single Man Finds a Son in Russia*, American biology professor Robert Klose describes his convoluted attempts to adopt a son. His single state haunted the process, compelling him to observe, "There ain't no more, folks. I'm it."[17] Some foreign countries ban single parents; Klose notes that Thailand, for example, had cheaper fees but would not consider single applicants, male or female.

Klose also had to justify his single status—"The director wanted me to ask you why you never married," his caseworker, Carl, reported.

Klose gave the right answer: "'It's not as if I've shut the door to the possibility,'" he said. "I am a very independent man who is attracted to very independent women. It is not a recipe for success. In the struggle to preserve our individual goals and habits, we eventually part to salvage a friendship, which, oddly enough, invariably persists."

When Carl arrived for a home inspection, Klose was on his hands and knees scrubbing the kitchen baseboards with a Q-tip. Upstairs, he had already decorated his longed-for son's room, built all the furniture, covered the bed with a superheroes comforter, and hung dinosaur curtains. In the story's happy but distant ending, the thirty-nine-year-old Klose adopted seven-year-old Alyosha from Russia. He also realized that until then, he had not entirely grown up.

Yale professor Doug Hood was "forty-six years old [and] decidedly single" when he made up his mind to adopt, but with trepidation. "If churchgoing couples in their thirties with perfect credit ratings who had spent five years going through the rites of an infertility clinic had to walk on hot coals just to adopt, then what chance did I have?" He was not, after all, "a childless couple holding hands, nor a single woman tricked out of motherhood wringing hers. I was a single man. My motives would be up for questioning. I couldn't just make the same heartfelt claim as a woman: 'I want to be a mother.' ... As a single guy over forty, I had to convince this agency of my intentions—I just wanted a child, pure and simple, and I was willing to be its mother, all the dirty work included."[18] (Hood adopted Suki, a four-year-old girl from China; in 2009 she graduated from high school.)

Toronto Star journalist Tess Kalinowski also adopted a daughter from China. "Not being married seldom bothered me," she recalls. "To say my biological clock was ticking wouldn't be correct. I felt no physical imperative to give birth and my notions of children don't include the creation of a replica of myself or a partner.... [But] the sound of time marching forward started to resonate when I was about thirty-three. By thirty-five, it was deafening."[19] Eighteen months later, that deafening noise was replaced by the cries and laughter of a baby daughter.

For some women, the issue remains the conviction that marriage is the best framework for child-rearing. "One of the most complicated, painful, and pervasive dilemmas many single women are forced to grapple with nowadays: Is it better to be alone, or to settle?" writes Lori Gottlieb in a much-cited article. "My advice is this: Settle! That's right. Don't worry about passion or intense connection.... Overlook his halitosis or abysmal sense of aesthetics. Because if you want to have the infrastructure in place to have a family, settling is the way to go."[20]

Kay Trimberger's book, *The New Single Woman*, "a radical and engaging exploration of how single women over thirty-five are creating fulfilling lives," is striking partly because it needed to be written in the first place. But it did, because North America cherishes a mythical soulmate culture. "The Good News from Planet Singleton is that despite overwhelming cultural messages to the contrary, it's possible for women to live happily ever after alone," *Publishers Weekly* observes in its review. "Women have been in bondage to the dream of the 'soulmate' for far too long," Barbara Ehrenreich declares.

Unlike cohabitation, with its strong resemblance to marriage, singleness represents a very different way of life, one that challenges rather than echoes marriage, especially as singles mobilize, articulate their needs, and lobby politically. But singles should not be condemned as saboteurs of marriage. Changing standards promote changing ways of life, and as singles transform the experience of marriage, they also dignify singleness with new respectability and the promise of personal fulfillment.

Chapter 9

A Gay Focus on the Nature of Marriage

Hidden Unions

Both blond brides wore Zac Posen white wedding garb, exchanged Neil Lane rings, and glowed with the radiance of true love and the joy that finally they could marry their soulmates. On August 16, 2008, after California's Supreme Court ruled that the state's ban on same-sex marriage was unconstitutional, Ellen DeGeneres wed her long-time lover, Portia de Rossi, in the home they share in Los Angeles. "I was already planning on spending the rest of my life with her. But until you're married, you just don't know. It feels wonderful," DeGeneres exclaimed.[1]

De Rossi and DeGeneres were among eighteen thousand couples who raced to take advantage of the Supreme Court decision. But on November 4, Proposition 8, a California ballot proposition, changed the state's constitution, adding the words: "Only marriage between a man and a woman is valid or recognized in California." Less than three months after her wedding, de Rossi wept. Later, posing in front of her wedding portrait, she mocked critics of gay marriage: "When I got married, all I was thinking about was my own joy at committing to my partner for the rest of my life. I didn't think about all the people I was hurting by getting married. That was selfish."

*Ellen DeGeneres and Portia de Rossi pose for photos as they celebrate their
marriage in their Beverly Hills backyard in 2008.*

Though DeGeneres wisecracked that, by becoming her legal wife, de
Rossi was "now officially off the [marriage] market. No one else gets her.
And now she'll cook and clean for me," their marriage has no obvious
historical parallel. Yet in eras when homoeroticism was viewed more
matter-of-factly, as in ancient Egypt, various Greek city states, and the
Roman Empire, there is evidence of same-sex unions, and perhaps
marriage. The Sifra, a third-century commentary on Leviticus often
cited by the Talmud, forbids the Israelites from copying what they
believed to be Egyptian practices:

And what would they do?
A man would marry a man and a woman would marry a woman; a
man would marry a woman and her daughter; a woman would be
married to two men.
That is why it is said, "nor shall you follow their laws."

In ancient Greece, fathers could consent to quasi-marital unions
between their sons and the men who desired them. Similarly, in China's
Fujian province in the Ming dynasty (1368–1644), women ceremoni-
ously bound themselves into intimate unions with girls, and men did
the same with boys. These relationships ended years later, and the adult
spouses then helped their young partners find and marry opposite-sex
spouses.

By the time of the early Roman Empire, there were some references
to same-sex marriages. The Roman historian and biographer Suetonius
reported that the emperor Nero attempted to transform the youthful
Sporus into a woman by castrating him. Then he married the maimed
boy in traditional rites, and afterward treated him as his wife. (Nero had
previously assumed the role of bride and took his wine steward, the
freedman Pythagoras, as his husband.) The satiric—and probably bisexual—poet and social commentator Martial described how "Bearded
Callistratus married the rugged Afer in the usual form in which a virgin
marries a husband. The torches shone in front, the wedding veil covered
his face.… Even the dowry was declared. Are you still not satisfied,
Rome? Are you waiting for him to give birth?"

In 117 AD, the satiric poet Juvenal castigated the aristocrat Gracchus
for having married a male cornet player.

Gracchus gave a dowry of 400,000 sesterces to a cornet player—or
perhaps he'd performed on a straight horn. Marriage documents were
signed, felicitations offered, they sat down to a great banquet, and the
new bride lay in her husband's lap.… This very man who now dons
flounces and a dress and a bridal veil, he bore the sacred implements
swaying on their mystic thong, and he sweated beneath the shields of
Mars.

Father of Rome, how came such sacrilege to your Latian shepherds? How is it, Mars, that such an itch possessed your descendants? Just look at it: a man of high birth and estate is given in marriage to a man, yet you do not shake your helmet, nor strike the earth with your spear, nor complain to your father....

"Tomorrow at dawn I've an obligation to perform in the Quirinal valley." What's the occasion? "No need to ask, a male friend takes a husband and invites a few guests." If we live long enough, this will happen, and happen openly; they will even want it reported in the city gazette.[2]

Contemporary literature also describes lesbian relationships but few marriages, likely because women lacked the influence and power to bring them about. Though same-sex unions were mostly indulged in by men powerful enough to withstand their wider society's disapproval or disgust, they have ancient, albeit fragile—some scholars say suspect—historical lineages.[3]

In the past, many homosexuals did not identify with or even fully understand what homosexuality was, or their relationship to it. What is certain is that most lesbians and gay men either married opposite-gender spouses and tried as best they could to fit into the heterosexual mould their society expected, or remained single and lived chastely, indulged in clandestine liaisons with other homosexuals, or, especially in the case of self-aware gay men, consorted publicly with women whose presences were reassuringly heterosexual.

At least some of these marriages were, in the words of the American broadcaster Keith Olbermann, "sham marriages, or marriages of convenience, or just marriages of not knowing, centuries of men and women who have lived their lives in shame and unhappiness, and who have, through a lie to themselves and others, broken countless other lives, or spouses and children, all because we said a man couldn't marry another man, or a woman couldn't marry another woman."[4]

Until very recently, the reality was that far from having rights—the Mattachine Society, the United States' first national gay rights organization, was founded only in 1950—homosexuals "caught" being homosexual were also criminals.[5] For example, President Dwight Eisenhower's Executive Order 10450, of April 27, 1953, required all civil and military federal employees guilty of "sexual perversion" to be fired, and thousands were. The Senate Appropriations Committee applauded these firings because "one homosexual can pollute an entire government office ... [and] to pussyfoot or take half measures will allow some known perverts to remain in government."[6]

Canada was no gay paradise either. In 1965 in the Northwest Territories, mechanic Everett Klippert, aged thirty-nine, was arrested, charged, convicted, and imprisoned for gross indecency after admitting that he had had consensual sexual intercourse with four men. Five years earlier he had been convicted for eighteen similar offences. Two court-ordered psychiatrists testified that, worse than homosexual, Klippert was "incurably" so. They believed that "the appellant was likely to commit further sexual offences of the same kind with other consenting adult males, [though] he had never caused injury, pain or other evil to any person and was not likely to do so in the future."[7]

The Canadian justice system knew what to do. It declared Klippert a dangerous sexual offender and sentenced him to indefinite "preventive detention." The Supreme Court of Canada upheld this ruling in 1967, with two of its five judges dissenting. Klippert was thrown into the clink.

So many Canadians were outraged by the Supreme Court decision that within six weeks, Prime Minister Pierre Elliot Trudeau introduced what he described as "the most extensive revision of the Criminal Code since the 1950s ... it has knocked down a lot of totems and over-ridden a lot of taboos and ... it's bringing the laws of the land up to contemporary society, I think. Take this thing on homosexuality. I think the view we take here is that there's no place for the state in the bedrooms of the nation. I think that what's done in private between adults doesn't concern the Criminal Code."[8] By 1969, homosexuals were no longer criminals in Canada. Klippert was finally released in 1971.

South of the border as well, great change was afoot. In the wee hours of June 28, 1969, in New York City's Greenwich Village, an international gay rights movement was born after plainclothes police officers stormed the gay-frequented (and Mafia-owned) bar of the Stonewall Inn, arrested employees for selling liquor without a licence, beat up clients, and arrested several transvestites for transgressing a state criminal statute that required citizens to wear at least three articles of gender-appropriate clothing. Suddenly, recalls riot veteran Craig Rodwell, "there was just … a flash of group, of mass anger," and the gay community fought back. Four hundred hastily summoned gay Villagers jeered, jostled, and assailed the police with coins, bottles, and rubbish. The police retreated and called for reinforcements, and so did their opponents. The Stonewall riots lasted for five days and became the catalyst for the emer-

June 28, 1969: An unidentified group celebrates on a stoop near the boarded-up Stonewall Inn the day after the Stonewall riots that led to the modern gay rights movement in the United States.

gent gay-liberation movement that sprang up throughout North America and the Western world.

Afterward, in the freedom-fighting decades of the twentieth century, gay marriage began to seem possible. In 1970, Jack Baker and James McConnell failed to obtain a marriage licence in Hennepin County, Minnesota. They appealed right up to the U.S. Supreme Court, which in 1972 refused to hear their case. But the genie was out of the bottle, and gay marriage had become a cause to fight for.

For want of compelling historical models, the spirited, often bitter debates inspired by the advent of same-sex marriage have centred on determining the nature of marriage: Is procreation and child-rearing its primary goal? Or is love now so central to marriage that loving and being loved outweigh all else? Are children as well served by two mothers or two fathers as by one of each? Can gay-positive jurisdictions such as Ontario or California foist their liberal worldview on their neighbours, who are effectively faced with a *fait accompli* in the form of gays legally married elsewhere? With North America's population heavily reinforced by immigrants, many from less inclusive or overtly homophobic cultures, will Christian fundamentalists find allies to renew legal and social challenges to gay marriage?

ARGUMENTS FOR AND AGAINST GAY MARRIAGE

Supporters of gay marriage argue that marrying a beloved partner is a civil and human right and, for believers, a sacred commitment. Gay marriage signals an end to institutionalized homophobia and welcomes spouses into an accepting society. It makes same-sex partners or spouses eligible for workplace benefits (insurance, pension, death) now limited to opposite-sex partners. It acknowledges the legitimacy of a gay union based on traditional values including monogamy. It provides a legal and social framework for adoptions by married gays. "The Constitution guarantees the right to marry to murderers, to prisoners, to people with a history of neglecting their children, to people who have remarried 10 times, to O.J. Simpson, to Elizabeth Taylor," argues gay writer

Andrew Sullivan. "If all these people have a fundamental civil right to marry, as I think they do, we do too."[9]

Opponents of gay marriage present a cornucopia of counterarguments that range from raw homophobia (Fred Phelps's "God Hates Fags" protests) and scriptural condemnation of homosexuality ("If a man also lie with mankind, as he lieth with a woman, both of them have committed an abomination: they shall surely be put to death; their blood shall be upon them"; Leviticus 20:13)[10] to gays' and lesbians' own rejection of marriage as an institution rooted in patriarchy that defines and controls relationships that should be private.

More mainstream is the Roman Catholic Church's condemnation of gay marriage. A 2003 document entitled "Considerations Regarding Proposals to Give Legal Recognition to Unions Between Homosexual Persons" presented non-doctrinal arguments against gay marriage that its author, Cardinal Joseph Ratzinger (now Pope Benedict XVI), described as based on "the natural moral law" and directed to "all persons committed to promoting and defending the common good of society" as well as to Catholic politicians needing direction about how to legislate.[11] "No ideology can erase from the human spirit the certainty that marriage exists solely between a man and a woman, who … mutually perfect each other, in order to cooperate with God in the procreation and upbringing of new human lives." Furthermore, "there are absolutely no grounds for considering homosexual unions to be in any way similar or even remotely analogous to God's plan for marriage and family. Marriage is holy, while homosexual acts go against the natural moral law…. Under no circumstances can [homosexual acts] be approved."

Other opponents of same-sex marriage distinguish between religious and civil unions, with many favouring homosexual civil unions with all their associated rights but withholding religious sanction. Though devoutly Roman Catholic, Canadian ethicist Margaret Somerville based her reasoned case against gay marriage on neither moral nor religious grounds. Altering the definition of marriage to include same-sex spouses would, she wrote, "weaken the definition and respect for the institution of marriage. It would further weaken the traditional family values essential to our society."

Specifically, "the inherently procreative relationship institutionalized in marriage is fundamental to society and requires recognition as such.... Marriage makes present in the present, the deep collective human memory concerning the norms and values surrounding reproduction." Children and child-centredness are at the core of Somerville's argument against gay marriage and are rooted in the "presumption that, if at all possible, children have a valid claim to be raised by their own biological parents." Gay marriage can at best offer one biological parent and often neither. The discrimination inherent in excluding gays from marrying is therefore justified because children's rights trump adults'.[12]

Somerville contends that marriage is "an inextricably intermingled societal and religious institution" and not mere ceremony or ritual that can be fundamentally altered. Children's rights require that the traditional family remain a societal norm. Rather than gay civil marriage, Somerville suggests in their place gay "civil partnerships."[13]

Other arguments against gay marriage describe traditional marriage as a vehicle for bonding men and women for the good of their children and the common good. Without marriage, they contend, men would not be inclined to immerse themselves in family life. Moreover, marriage encourages a "healthy masculine identity based on a distinctive, necessary, and publicly valued contribution to society—fatherhood."[14] In this view, heterosexual bonding should be publicly supported or promoted and gay marriage should be rejected.

The debate is intensified by a proliferation of studies that explore the meaning of marriage and, now that gay marriage is becoming more entrenched, document how it works. Growing numbers of people reveal how it affects them personally. Among them are millions of once-closeted gays and their wives and ex-wives; bisexual men who have had same-gender sexual relations (estimated at between 1.7 and 3.4 million in the United States) and their wives and ex-wives, and lesbians—about 30 percent of the total—who have married men, and their husbands and ex-husbands.[15]

Navigating Cultural Attitudes toward Gayness

As centuries of historical experience show, gayness is not clear-cut, and its ambiguities complicate gay marriage. For one thing, gay marriage is an alternative only for people who self-identify as gay. But now as in the past, countless married bisexual or straight-identifying men have covert and anonymous sex with other men in places like public washrooms, parks, and adult cinemas while "passing" as straight and being accepted by straight society. Being caught engaging in these activities has revealed the secret and often unacknowledged sexuality of many a husband, and often cost them their reputations, their jobs, and their marriages.

The decriminalization of homosexuality and its inclusion in today's rainbow-hued cultural ambiance is designed to protect people who identify as gay but who, in other times and places, would have declined to do so. But there remains a chasm between official policy and the realities of personal and social life: parental rejection, social ostracism or mockery, and physical danger that includes being bashed as a "fag." Coming out can still be perilous, and many gay men, young and old, prefer the safety of being closeted.

The complexities of gayness are heightened as expatriate gays who once lived clandestinely in their homelands, or the gay children of expatriates, seek to make sense of North American inclusiveness. Some embrace its greater openness, while others find different ways of adjusting. Ruth Vanita, a gender scholar, analyzed the personal ads in twenty issues, from 1998 to 2003, of San Francisco's *Trikone*, a magazine for lesbian, gay, bisexual, and transgendered South Asians. She found that about 12 percent of the ads were placed by gays seeking marriages of convenience with gays of the opposite sex. She also discovered websites devoted to such marriages for gay South Asians. "Decent, very good looking, 29 years, professional doctor, Pakistani citizen in the U.S., need to get married to a lesbian female due to intense family pressure," read one. "My parents are wondering why I don't have a girlfriend and I am being pressured to get married," another explained. "I would like to meet a girl (gay) or one who has no problem marrying a gay guy. I am very str8 acting, I can be a great boyfriend/husband. I just have other needs that I would like to fulfil."[16] These spouse-seekers often expect and desire children, and are prepared to have sex for procreation.

Other gay or bisexual men, coerced or influenced by family, religious precepts, and social values, marry women from whom they conceal their sexual identity and have extramarital sexual relations with other men, a practice known today as the down low. The down low is a modern version of ancient and secretive ways of dealing with bisexuality or homosexuality, the love that until recently dared not speak its name. Lately, the down low has exploded into public awareness as people speak out about how it affects their communities, especially the African-American and African-Canadian, Hispanic, and others that demonize homosexuality as an abomination and a sin primarily associated with effeminate white "faggots."

The reasons for opting for the down low are as complex as the race and social relations that spawned them. In this world view, gayness is seen as so repulsive and unmanly that coming out as gay is too dreadful to contemplate, even in one's heart of hearts. This is especially true of men raised in the shadow of hip hop culture, where thugs rule and make minced meat of sissies, and in pop culture, where gays are white, as Queer as Folk, and the victims of contemptuous straight white men who bash them, and where a black pastor in Chicago thundered from his pulpit, "If the KKK opposes gay marriage, I would ride with them."[17] To admit you are gay, a young black man explains, is "like you've let down the whole black community, black women, black history, black pride," personally besmirching a race that is always under attack.[18]

In Canada as in the United States, many black men who sleep with other men recoil from thinking of themselves as gay, which they see as a white perversion. "In the black community, we black men have to be masculine and in control. Guys who have sex with other men aren't viewed as being real men," explains a man on the down low.[19] Down-low men also accuse the gay (hence white) community of racism, which makes it easy for them to choose to identify with the black community instead.

These charges of racism are well founded. According to sociologist Chong-suk Han, the consequent dearth of gay people of colour in gay bars and clubs and in advocacy groups, the primary vehicles through which "queer visibility" is recognized, reinforce gayness as a "white phenomenon." So do popular media, which promote the gay community as "overwhelmingly upper-middle class—if not simply rich—and white ... and a few white women. If we are a footnote in the gay community," Han continues, "we are an endnote in communities of color ... [where] 'being gay' is a white 'problem.' We are told, early in life, that we must avoid such stigma at all costs. When we try to interject issues of sexuality, we are told that there is precious little time to waste on 'trivial' needs while we pursue racial justice."[20]

At a time when homophobia is officially banned and legal civil unions and marriage are becoming available to gays, an entire segment of the population, one that includes white men, opts for heterosexual mating coupled with sex with other men. One consequence is that mainstream gays who have battled homophobia and cheered the advent of gay marriage complain bitterly that the down low is itself a form of self-inflicted homophobia. Down-low males, on the other hand, define themselves more by race than by sexuality, and in the world as they understand it, men are heterosexual fathers.[21] For them, the down low is an empowering and proudly non-white phenomenon that, unlike gay marriage, permits them to remain full-fledged and accepted members of their communities. "Labeling yourself as [down low] is a way to disassociate from everything white and upper class," says George Ayala, the director of education for AIDS Project Los Angeles.[22] J.L. King, author of *On the Down Low: A Journey into the Lives of 'Straight' Black Men Who Sleep with Men,* told Oprah Winfrey, "If I was a gay man, I may want to be in a relationship with another man and play house. But when you're on the 'down low' all you want to do is have sex."

Changing the attitudes that lead to the down low has already begun. One of the key principles of the Black AIDS Institute, founded in 1999 as a think tank focused exclusively on black people, is to empower women by fostering a culture that values them more. Another is to promote new concepts of black masculinity, introducing a wider range of role models and encouraging academic achievement. The most important principle, however, is to accept that collective survival depends on accepting gay, lesbian, transgendered, and HIV-positive people as an integral part of the community; in turn, they must refuse to live in shame and secrecy.

The institute and many other interest groups are working to confront and eradicate homophobia. But there seems to be little momentum to extrapolate from these premises to advocate for gay marriage. The consequence of such entrenched and widespread reluctance to accept gay marriage is to put its future in question, and this seems true as well of other North American ethnic groups. Until gay marriage becomes culturally and socially accepted, it will remain a curiosity—or worse—in these communities.

As long as racism corrodes society, as long as non-mainstream subcultures link gayness with whiteness and link their collective survival to racial identification, they vilify gayness and ensure that few of their men (or women) will choose gay marriage. The transformation will come by acknowledging that blaming and shaming gayness is a murderous strategy that kills people, erodes families, and poisons male–female relations. Then will come the acceptance of gayness and, afterward, of gay marriage, which will encourage men to reject the down low for an honest life with a male partner and, often, fatherhood and parenting.

GAY PARENTING

In North American culture generally, gay parents and gay parenting are the most contentious consequences of gay marriage, and increasingly they dominate the discussion. The cultural buffering and legal eradication of homophobia have enabled gays to apply to adopt children, though many also arrange to father biological children with willing surrogates, as most lesbian mothers do. The classic questions about gay parenting—How does their parents' gayness affect children? Do gay parents "create" homosexuality in their children?—are adapted to the new circumstance of married gay parents.

The new questions include: Is it better to have two parents rather than one, even if both are fathers or mothers? Are gay parents likelier than heterosexuals to abuse their children? Will their children suffer more bullying or ostracism? What happens in case of divorce—which mother or father gets custody, and under what sort of arrangement? Because the nature of gay marriage means that only one—and often neither—spouse is the child's biological parent, custody disputes are inherently more challenging.

More complicating still can be impregnation by sperm donors whose role the law, if not all the individuals involved, may interpret as fatherhood. A *New York Times* article, "Gay Donor or Gay Dad?" examines such a case in all its Byzantine (or perhaps postmodern) ramifications. A lesbian couple, black and white, used a gay white man's sperm to impregnate the black woman, producing a mixed-race child that reflected both their mothers' backgrounds. The white mother next bore twins fathered by a black sperm donor. Later, the mothers split up and established new relationships, the white woman with a man she had a child with, the black woman with another woman. There are now four related children, two mothers, one stepmother and one stepfather, and a sperm donor intent on being involved as a parent. In the words of the sperm donor, "They're quite a little petri dish of a family, as you can imagine. I'd say they're like divorce kids. They've got a family that split up; they go back and forth."[23]

The children handily navigate their relationships, but defining them within the context of social and legal norms, and without apparent precedent, is challenging. Unlike so many orphaned medieval children raised by widowed step-parents with no blood ties, these children have parents—albeit two mothers—to love and be loved by, and they have bonds with their quasi siblings. But their situation conjures up scenarios relating to gay marriage, including its breakdown, that society must make sense of and the law must pronounce on even though most children of gay parents do not wrestle with such complicated relationships.

There is one thing it's difficult to dispute: the children of gay parents are not victims. Almost all studies, even those whose authors do not couch their premises in gay-friendly terms, conclude that gay parenting is pretty well comparable to its heterosexual equivalent. A quartet of Brigham Young University scholars, for example, conclude that "adolescents raised by gay and lesbian parents typically behave more like youth in two parent biological families, providing little support for gendered-deficit theories."[24] Charlotte Patterson's comprehensive 2005 study for the American Psychological Association interpreted three decades of research comparing lesbian and gay parents to heterosexual parents and concluded: "The results ... are quite clear ... Not a single study has found children of lesbian or gay parents to be disadvantaged in any significant respect relative to children of heterosexual parents.... Lesbian mothers' and gay fathers' parenting skills may be superior to those of matched heterosexual couples ... This was attributed to greater parenting awareness among lesbian nonbiological mothers than among heterosexual fathers.... In contrast to ... the majority of American parents, very few lesbian and gay parents reported any use of physical punishment (such as spanking) as a disciplinary technique."[25]

Good, stable lesbian mothers provide good, stable parenting, and lesbians are happier raising children than gay men or straight couples. Their children seem to establish closer relationships with their non-biological or second mother than stepchildren do with stepmothers in straight marriages. Few are deeply wounded if other children query them about their sexual orientation or tease them for having gay parents. Their parents' homosexuality does not make them homosexual. Very few are molested.

Molestation is a recurrent theme in critiques of gay parenting, and it does happen. But the research shows that most pedophiles—adults who sexually abuse children—are male, and that such behaviour in women is extremely rare. Furthermore, girls are overwhelmingly the victims of male sexual abuse, and gay men are no more likely than heterosexual men to commit it. There is, after all, no association between homosexuality and pedophilia. One study concluded that "a child's risk of being molested by his or her relative's heterosexual partner is over 100 times greater than by someone who might be identifiable as being homosexual, lesbian, or bisexual."[26]

Gay marriage as the locus of child-rearing and adoption is an important focus of activism, and eventually legislation will reflect this. Custody issues are sensitive, as many family courts operate from gay-negative attitudes and assumptions (and scarce legal precedents). Until recently, divorces involving one gay spouse usually meant custody for the heterosexual parent.

A spectacularly egregious example is the 1996 Florida case in which Circuit Judge Joseph Tarbuck removed eleven-year-old Cassie from her lesbian mother Mary Frank's custody and awarded it to her father, John Ward, solely because Mary was living with a female partner and another lesbian couple, and had allegedly watched X-rated videos in Cassie's presence. John, by then married to his fourth wife, had mowed down a previous wife by shooting her with twelve bullets at close range in a Pensacola parking lot. The subject of their deadly argument? Custody of their daughter, Michelle. After John's release from prison eight years later, Michelle lived with him briefly, then ran away because he had molested her.

Ward was a convicted murderer but, he testified, he had sound values: "I'm not gay, and I'm opposed to being gay." Judge Tarbuck was easily convinced. "I believe this child [Cassie] should be given the opportunity and the option to live in a nonlesbian world," he wrote in his judgment. "I don't condemn the mother of this child for living the way she does. But I don't think that this child ought be led into … this lifestyle just by virtue of the fact of her living accommodations."[27]

Sharon Bottoms's mother won custody of her grandson in Virginia on the grounds that Sharon was lesbian, which the judge agreed was dreadful. In a decision upheld by the Virginia Supreme Court, he declared, "I will tell you first that the [current custodial] mother's conduct is illegal. It is a Class 6 felony in the Commonwealth of Virginia. I will tell you that it is the opinion of this Court that her conduct is immoral. And it is the opinion of this Court that the conduct of Sharon Bottoms renders her an unfit parent."[28]

In 2002, Chief Justice Roy Stewart Moore of the Alabama Supreme Court issued an identical opinion about a lower court decision to deny custody to a lesbian mother even though her ex-husband was abusive.

Homosexuality was an "inherent evil and an act so heinous that it defies one's ability to describe it," Moore wrote, adding: "Any person who engages in such conduct is presumptively unfit to have custody of minor children under the established laws of this State."[29] (A year later, the Alabama Court of the Judiciary removed Moore from his judgeship for refusing a federal order to remove a monument of the Ten Commandments he had installed in the rotunda of the state courthouse.)

Moore's unswerving homophobia is exceptional in its transparency, but, as one judge in the Southwest confided, "Homosexuality is probably a factor for judges, but they don't state it." A Boston lawyer concurred, explaining that although the law is supposed to be neutral about homosexuality, which becomes a relevant factor only if it adversely affects the children, hidden human factors also play a powerful role. "Put a sixty-four-year-old male judge on the bench whose wife stayed home raising the kids and say, 'My lesbian lover and I want to raise my ex-husband's child.' What's a judge going to think?"[30]

Judges are also much less likely to award custody to gay fathers with heterosexual ex-wives, writes Denise Whitehead in "Policies Affecting Gay Fathers." Because they are forewarned that "mother-bias is further exacerbated by the presence of a gay ex-spouse seeking full or joint custody," few of these fathers attempt to do so.[31] The literature on gay marriage resonates with such warnings.[32] And now, courts are beginning to adjudicate the cases of gays divorcing gays.

Just as the "gayby" boom is growing in tandem with gay marriage, so is adoption. Canada permits gay or lesbian couples to adopt, as do the U.K., Spain, Germany, Belgium, the Netherlands, Denmark, Iceland, Norway, and Sweden. In the United States, about 60 percent of adoption agencies accept applications from homosexuals. As gay marriage develops and grows, resistance to gay adoption and parenting in general declines. Policies are being and will continue to be rewritten that no longer discriminate or even distinguish between kinds of parents, gay, bi, or heterosexual.

The new culture of gay parenting is proliferating, and with it the happy corollary that these parents develop greater self-esteem and are less conflicted about their sexuality. More physical and online resource centres are available (Children of Lesbians and Gays Everywhere, Family Pride Coalition, Gay Dads). Magazines such as *Gay Parent* and online support communities such as the LGBTQ Parenting Connection, continue to mushroom.

The shift from socially established, legally enforced homophobia to gay civil unions and gay marriage, and thence to gay parenting and gay parental rights, has been extraordinarily fast. In the past, such revolutionary changes took much longer to implement and accept. The focus on gay parenting, though rooted in a growing interest in and commitment to children's welfare and rights, is an acknowledgment of gay marriage and an attempt to cast it in ways acceptable to North America's evolving society.

Despite initially negative or incredulous reactions to gay marriage and its consequences, many commentators now support it. Conservative David Brooks's reasoned approach may induce opponents to rethink and reverse their opinions. In "The Power of Marriage," his widely disseminated op-ed essay in the *New York Times*, Brooks laments the state of marriage today and a general disregard for its sanctity and the sexual fidelity at its core. "Marriage makes us better than we deserve to be.... Married people who remain committed to each other find that they reorganize and deepen each other's lives. They may eventually come to the point when they can say to each other: 'Love you? I am you.'"

But then Brooks veers into different territory. "Gays and lesbians," he notes, "are banned from marriage and forbidden to enter into this powerful and ennobling institution [and] ... the path of fidelity." Rather than forbidding gay marriage, he writes, conservatives "should insist on gay marriage.... We should regard it as scandalous that two people could claim to love each other and not want to sanctify their love with marriage and fidelity." Gays should be part of the movement to salvage monogamous marriage, fidelity through thick and thin, love that deepens and, ultimately, melds the spouses together into one entity.[33]

Increasingly, advocates of gay marriage respond strongly to critics who charge that it corrodes and devalues marriage; they also dismiss as homophobic and unscientific the argument that gay marriage encourages

Tori (left) *and Kate Kendall, who already shared the same last name, hold their five-month-old baby, Zadie, during their wedding on June 17, 2008, in West Hollywood, California.*

An unconventional and very happy family.

gayness by offering an alternative to straight marriage that might otherwise "cure" gayness, or that it offers a vehicle for gay resistance to straight marriage. They argue instead that gay marriage shores up the institution, widely perceived as flailing or even failing. They note that gay marriage welcomes gays into the culture of mainstream society and, in steering them away from multiple partners, reduces their risk of contracting HIV. Lastly, they say that gay marriage ensures that those who raise children may do so in a legally recognized union that augurs well for child-rearing. Not least, gay marriage provides a pool of adoptive parents for children who might otherwise languish in state or institutional care.

GAY DIVORCE

Gay divorce is already a fact of life. The first—and much reported—gay divorce, in Massachusetts, ended a seven-month marriage and granted sole custody of the couple's three cats to one man who had to provide photographs and updates about the cats to his former spouse. Canada's first lesbian marriage ended after fifteen months. The two women had hoped marriage would strengthen their crumbling relationship. It didn't, and divorce lawyer Martha McCarthy reported "a lot of sadness."

In gay divorces, custody issues are the most contentious, and are complicated by the non-biological relationship of at least one parent to his or her children. Unlike in a straight marriage, non-biological gay parents are not step-parents who have married into an existing family and can be ejected from it. They are primary parents who, until things went wrong, were as much the child's father or mother as the one related by sperm or ovum.

During breakups of marriage in which neither spouse is biologically related to the children, custody disputes are more easily resolved, with the best interests of those children paramount. Legal rights are also key, and the growing literature of lesbigay divorce always stresses the importance of establishing them, usually through adoption, in case the marriage fails or one partner dies. In other cases the claims of biology often surge, driven by vengeful anger and pain. Since lesbian unions and the right to motherhood and adoption were recognized, some bitter biomothers have denied their ex-partner's involvement in parenthood, for example by claiming that she **was merely** a babysitter.

In a precedent-setting case in the State Supreme Court of New York in 2008, Beth R. sued for divorce from her wife, Donna M. She wanted to prove the legitimacy of their Canadian marriage so that her relationship with their two daughters, borne by Donna through artificial insemination, would continue. Donna objected on the grounds that because New York did not offer gay marriage, she and Beth were not really married and therefore could not be divorced. In any case, theirs had been a "shotgun type" union that she regarded as mere symbolic commitment, and she had entered into it under pressure from Beth and from her own loudly ticking biological clock.

In 2002, Beth and Donna had moved in together. In 2003, Donna became pregnant by artificial insemination, and they went to Toronto and obtained a marriage licence. They planned then postponed a September wedding because Donna's father died the weekend before. In the obituary she wrote about him, Donna referred to Beth as his "daughter-in-law."

In October, Donna gave birth to a daughter, J. Beth was her delivery room coach and cut the umbilical cord. For J's first four months, the mothers took consecutive maternity leaves and, on Valentine's Day 2004, returned to Toronto and married in the presence of invited friends, family, and their infant daughter, who was carried down the aisle.

In July 2005, Donna was again impregnated by artificial insemination, which Beth paid for. When daughter S. was born, Beth again coached and again cut the umbilical cord. The mothers' birth announcements read: "We joyfully announce the birth of S.R.... Delighted parents and big sister, Donna, Beth and J.R., the R. Family."

Donna did not allow Beth to adopt either J. or S., but she used Beth's surname, and both children carried it on their birth certificates. Donna made a will naming Beth the children's guardian. J. called Beth "Mom" and Donna "Mommy," while Donna's mother and siblings were "nana" and "aunt" and "uncle." Together, Donna and Beth cared for and supported their daughters, selected a pediatrician and a nanny, chose a preschool and camp for J. Both attended parent-teacher meetings and the girls' school events.

In September 2006, Donna told Beth that she wanted to end their marriage. Beth began to sleep in the infant S.'s bedroom. In April 2007, Donna served Beth with an eviction notice. A week later, Beth filed for divorce. While waiting for legal resolution, the women agreed that Beth would move out of the apartment and have visiting rights to the children on alternate weekends as well as Tuesday evening dinners.

Despite Donna's argument that she and Beth were not legally married, Justice Laura E. Drager ruled that they were because New York honours marriages performed out of state unless they are specifically prohibited by law or are "abhorrent to public policy," and gay marriage was neither. Custody arrangements, therefore, were to be determined in light of "the best interests of the children." Drager specified emotional, financial, and legal issues. "A child by the age of three clearly identifies with parental figures. The abrupt exclusion of a parental figure may be damaging to the emotional well being of that child. Although only an infant, it is conceivable that S.R. might suffer emotional consequences as well and [because the artificial insemination that produced her happened during Beth and Donna's marriage] she may well be considered the legitimate child of both parents.... Certainly both children might suffer financial consequences due to the loss of support that would be available to them from [Beth]."[34]

Drager's decision sets an important precedent for divorcing same-sex couples. It will likely forestall such legal ploys as Donna M.'s. It will also require courts to deal with custody of gay-parented children on the same basis as in heterosexual divorces, with the best interests of those children prevailing.

Gay divorces and the marriages they terminate, whether children are involved or not, are scrutinized for proof of frivolity and an inability to commit. "Many people, including judges, think of gay parents as exclusively sexual beings, while heterosexual parents are perceived as people who, along with many other activities in their lives, occasionally engage in sex," writes lesbian stepmother Claudia McCreary.[35] Homosexual men (but not lesbians) are widely regarded as promiscuous, and whether that's the case or not, the presumption is that divorce statistics will reflect their failure at monogamous commitment. Gay and lesbian couples are portrayed as representatives of the gay community and feel shame if their marriage fails. "There's a sense of pressure and visibility," says Rich Domenico, a Boston therapist who counsels gay couples. At the same time, gay couples may also have more difficulty than heterosexuals finding marriage counsellors, mediators, and other resources.

Gay marriage is under the microscope, minutely examined by opponents and advocates alike. Researchers continue to study its causes, and policy-makers recommend legal consequences and consider jurisdictional issues as American states without gay marriage determine how to deal with married gay couples who move there and apply for divorce.

Gay divorce is already seen as a measure of the stability and durability of gay marriages. The first wave of gay divorces reflects an ill-considered rush to marry *because* at long last it was legally possible, and also the fact that some gay couples in failing unions married in order to secure spousal tax, insurance, and benefit rights. But decades must elapse before any authoritative conclusions are possible.

For the first time in history, young people are growing up in the presence of legally sanctioned gay marriage (and divorce), an experience that will influence how they shape their lives in a world that is marching away from homophobia and allowing gays and lesbians to unite in marriage, to raise their children, and to expect to receive the same rights and to be subject to the same obligations as heterosexual spouses. As more gay men and women decide to marry, they will shore up the very institution whose decline the wider society mourns.

Chapter 10

Children and Parenting in Modern Marriages

THE SPOCK GENERATION

By 1998, when he died, Dr. Benjamin Spock's *Baby and Child Care*, the classic parenting manual, had been translated into thirty-nine languages and had sold more than 50 million copies, second only to the Bible. There's good reason for its spectacular sales and longevity. Parenting is the most complicated and difficult, consequential and rewarding of any relationship or job, or so it seems to parents. And, throughout history, procreation and parenting have been primary purposes of marriage.

"Trust yourself. You know more than you think you do," Dr. Spock reassured parents in books and in columns he wrote for thirty years in the *Ladies' Home Journal* and *Redbook*. Millions of North Americans have been raised under the influence of his kindly advice—Don't worry too much! Let your little ones help you and feel special! Hug and kiss them! Don't blame yourself! Children are not all the same!

Like all transcendent authorities, Spock was frequently misinterpreted, in his case accused of promoting child-rearing anarchy—Let the kid do whatever she wants! Raise unruly, undisciplined, and selfish laggards! Spare, spoil, and to hell with the world they're ruining! He was labelled "the father of permissiveness," and vilified as the culprit responsible for the "Spock-marked generation" of hippies. He is still pilloried for supposedly advising stay-at-home mothers to shower attention on

*Dr. Benjamin Spock listens intently as Susannah, his first granddaughter,
whispers—or yawns—in his ear in 1967.*

their husbands at the expense of their forlornly weeping little ones.
Spock, these critics believe, insisted on the primacy of marriage and
marital intimacy over the demands and needs of children.

As a very old man, Spock denied these accusations. "I wanted to be
supportive of parents rather than to scold them," he said. "The book set
out very deliberately to counteract some of the rigidities of pediatric
tradition, particularly in infant feeding." Babies should be fed when
hungry, he taught, rather than by rigid schedule. "It emphasized the
importance of great differences between individual babies, of the need
for flexibility and of the lack of necessity to worry constantly about
spoiling."[1]

Spock had considerable personal experience of marriages, his parents'
and two of his own. He was the eldest of six strictly raised children
whose well-off parents held them to high standards, were emotionally
undemonstrative, and approached sexuality as something "full of
mystery and shame and embarrassment," Spock recalled.

Spock's first wife, Jane Davenport Cheney, was a high-spirited intellectual who introduced him to Freudian theories and radical politics; she was also an unbalanced alcoholic subject to breakdowns, and, after two sons and forty-eight years together, he divorced her. Jane spent her remaining years advocating for older divorced women. After several years of learning first-hand about divorce, Spock married Mary Morgan, four decades his junior, and added remarriage and step-parenting to his repertoire of expertise.

In his later books, which dealt with the realities of divorce and step-parenting, Spock also tackled the contentious issue of whether mothers should return to work, and if they did, when and how. His approach, moderate and child centred, was based on the assumption that some mothers are well prepared to work while others are forced to, and that the issue in either case was how to provide the best possible child care while these mothers were away at work.

"A few professionals in the child development field believe that only a mother or father can give a baby or small child ideal care, because of the intimacy of that relationship and its permanence," Spock wrote. "But a majority feel, as I do, that a well-trained teacher in a high-quality day-care center, or a woman providing excellent day care in her home, or a compatible grandparent, aunt, or uncle, or a full-time sitter can do a satisfactory job during the parents' workday."[2] He added that the government should subsidize the cost of such child care for mothers unable to pay for it.

Spock also discussed the destructive role of television in children's lives, the drug and other problems confronting many parents, and what he decried as pop culture's glorification of casual sex and marital infidelity. To Spock, sexuality had spiritual and emotional dimensions and inspired the kind of empathetic love that led to marriage. Marriage, he stressed, "is not for personal gratification, it is wanting to live the rest of your life with somebody, helping them, and raising fine children."[3] His last book was titled *Rebuilding American Family Values: A Better World for Our Children.*

Nothing is more fraught than child-rearing—on which, every generation of parents is reminded, rests society's future. Dr. Spock's pleas for lifelong marriages rooted in love, respect, and sexual fidelity have been lost in the outraged cries against his alleged responsibility in producing a spoiled-rotten generation of rebellious whiners who defied authority, condemned racial segregation and homophobia, demonstrated for civil rights and gay and women's liberation, and increasingly rose up against the war in Vietnam. Spock's teachings, enemies and critics charged, were destroying all that was good in society.

MOTHERHOOD

Dr. Spock's measured discussion touched a nerve in North America's cultural conversation about marriage and motherhood, and was at odds with the nineteenth-century model of the Good Wife, a child-centred mother devoted to her brood and respected and supported by her Good Husband. That Good Wife model clashes with today's expectations of self-actualization and fulfillment within mutually supportive and satisfying marriage, and so invites the question: what is the *nature* of motherhood? (And, by extension, of fatherhood?) Does motherhood bestow maternal instincts on all—or on some—women, or is motherhood learned? Are mothers truly their children's best caretakers? And, depending on the answer, should they work outside the home and pursue careers while other people care for their children?

The search for answers often leads to the animal world and such noble examples as matriarchal elephant society and fatherhood among emperor penguins. Pulitzer Prize–winning author Natalie Angier, however, warns against romanticizing nature. "Oh, mothers! Dear noble, selfless, tender and ferocious defenders of progeny all across nature's phylogeny," she mocks. "Here is a mother guinea hen, trailed by a dozen cotton-ball chicks. Here a mother panda and a baby panda share a stalk of bamboo ... But wait. That guinea hen is walking awfully fast. In fact, her brood cannot quite keep up with her, and by the end of the day, whoops, only two chicks still straggle behind. And the mama panda, did she not give birth to twins? So why did just one little panda emerge from her den?"

It turns out that many animals give birth to multiple heirs and spares but raise only some of them. "Scientists have accrued abundant evidence that 'bad' mothering is common in nature," Angier writes, "and that it is often a centerpiece of the reproductive game plan. Many species that habitually jettison a portion of their progeny live in harsh or uncertain environments, where young are easily lost and it pays to have a backup."[4] Appeals to noble nature stagger under the weight of too many instances of infanticide, cannibalism, and lethal neglect, and cannot sustain the argument that the animal world is replete with virtuous models for human parents.

The hunt for common denominators in human parenting practices, however, continues to fascinate researchers. Popular theories range from extreme to sensible. Children ruin marriage and their mothers' lives; women are not innately maternal; well-adjusted children need happy (not frustrated, repressed, and oppressed) mothers. Cooperative husbands and good planning will make family life for working mothers satisfying and smooth running; super-womanhood *is* possible. As well, poor mothering is reflected in the lifelong suffering of their offspring's abused Inner Children, and guilt is a Good Guide to warn parents of their parenting deficiencies. Some of these theories are grounded in common sense; others are mired in the all too familiar rhetoric of attack-and-blame, sometimes self-inflicted.

FATHERHOOD

Fatherhood has its own special and urgent issues. Yet Spock's half-century-ago vision of fatherhood could have been written by today's egalitarian idealist. "At its best," he wrote, "parenting occurs in the spirit of equal partnership." Husbands should share child care and housework with their wives, *not* as an act of generosity but because children benefit from "experiencing a variety of styles of leadership and control by both parents—styles that neither exclude nor demean, but enrich and complement the other." Children also see that their father considers child care and housework as "crucial to the welfare of the family, that it calls for judgment and skill, and that it's his responsibility as much as [the mother's] when he is at home. This is what sons and daughters need to see in action if they are to grow up with equal respect for the abilities and roles of men and women."[5]

In an era of male angst, and in keeping with the search for examples in the natural world, some animals are stunning models of solid, often devoted fatherhood. In the convivial and charismatic emperor penguin's ultra-courteous and non-violent society, hens lay their eggs and then go off to sea to forage for months on end while their mates stay home, fasting in the inhospitable rookery, carefully balancing their egg on their feet.

During arctic blasts, these penguin fathers huddle together in dense packs that continually shift to permit each bird his turn in the warm centre. For three freezing months, they keep the eggs safe on their shuffling feet. Penguins fall down precipices, trip, or slide on ice without ever relinquishing their precious cargo. When the female returns from her voyage, the male gently transfers the egg or chick to her. Then he, too, waddles off to find food.

Perhaps the most celebrated father is the seahorse, the only male in the world to become pregnant. During a gracefully swaying dance, his mate deposits eggs into his brood pouch. He seals it shut, then for weeks nurtures the eggs with his bodily substances. After birth, he establishes a nursery where he feeds his tiny children.

Bullfrogs are equally solicitous fathers. They fend off snakes and other foes, and even dig channels to permit their thousands of tadpoles access to deeper water. The sungrebe waterfowl father's chicks fly everywhere with him in two built-in saddlebags. Prairie dog dads defend, kiss, play with, and even sleep with their kits. Beaver fathers share parenting with their lifelong mate, and feed, groom, romp with, and sleep with their kits, and repair the family lodge. Wolf fathers hunt for their cubs, lick them clean, guard their den, and instruct them in wolfly ways.[6]

In Canada, eight- or nine-month sharable parental leaves encourage fathers to follow these examples, and some do. But business culture remains mired in Good Wife/Breadwinner assumptions, and, explains Andrea Doucet, a scholar of fatherhood, "dads still say that work culture is a big issue."[7] In the United States, where maternity leave is still not a right, fathers can hope at best for unpaid leave.

Having Children

It's hard to parent, and criticism is as rife as support is sparse. British poet Philip Larkin's 1971 "This Be the Verse" catches the tone of pervasive parent-blaming and its logical conclusion: don't become a parent.

Larkin's uneasy childhood with a jazz-loving, Hitler-admiring father, and his adult epiphany that he disliked children, forged his determination to avoid marriage and family. Other people also dislike children— or love them too much to subject them to an apocalyptic future—and marry with every intention of remaining childless. But the majority marry expecting and planning for or hoping for at least one child.

In 1955, after millennia of often fatal and frequently futile strategies to control childbirth, the pill—what other name did it need?—gave women the means to do so. In that year, scientists attending the Laurentian Conference on Endocrinology, in Quebec, learned the astounding results of medical trials on women in Puerto Rico, Haiti, and Mexico. Specifically, women taking a pill containing estrogen and progesterone did not ovulate, and, despite side effects, the pill— Enovid—promised 100 percent protection against pregnancy. The news spread far and wide. In 1959, after Enovid was authorized for use in treating severe menstrual disorders, hordes of women complained of menstrual suffering and asked their doctors to prescribe it.

In 1960, the pill was authorized for contraceptive use and touted as a cure for population explosion and strained marriages. Despite bitter opposition from many fronts—the Vatican, social conservatives terrified about the possibilities for radical changes in sexual relationships, people worried about encouraging immoral sexual behaviour, and African-American accusations of a hidden agenda of racial genocide—the pill gained widespread acceptance. In 1968 it was even featured in a Hollywood film, *Prudence and the Pill,* in which David Niven's character substituted aspirin for his wife Deborah Kerr's birth control pills, hoping she would become pregnant with her lover and thereby free him to devote himself to his mistress. In real life, millions of women, married and single, relied on the pill, which enabled them to plan or prevent conception and to enter and remain in the workforce.

Eventually, the majority of couples procreate, most by choice. The great difference between the past and present is that today's contraceptives are reliable and generally safe, and most spouses welcome this ability to plan their families. In Europe, the consequence has been a sharp decline in the birth rate, and this decline correlates with public policy that fails to accommodate working women, as in Italy, Spain, Germany, Austria, Switzerland, Greece, and Portugal, among others. (In these, in 1995, the fertility rate was less than 1.5, much less than the 2.1 needed to at least keep the population from declining.) Elsewhere in Europe, fertility has decreased without plummeting, and some studies suggest that the better the public policies—maternity leave, job security, flextime, daycare, tax relief—the more appealing and feasible child-raising becomes.

This pattern is not true in North America, however. Canada offers more services and benefits for mothers and children than does the United States, but Canada's fertility rate is now 2.5 percent lower. (In 1945, though, Canadians had 3 children versus the Americans' 2.5.) Canadians also wait longer to conceive—Canadian women in their twenties wait about three years longer—and Canadian teenagers have 1.5 fewer babies than American ones. Researchers continue to try to identify the reasons for this substantial difference. Could it be home-ownership rates? Job security? Education level? Government policies? Tax benefits? Social security? Welfare policies? Access to abortion? Religious conviction? Belief in the view that men should be head of the household? The answers will eventually shape public policy to encourage—or discourage, should perspectives change—higher fertility rates.

One common perspective is that "women want it all"—careers, marriage, *and* parenthood. They want, in fact, what men want. In terms of parenting, they urgently wish that fatherhood were much more like motherhood than it now is. Yet opponents of women's pursuit of a higher education and professional training warn that the price will be eternal manlessness; this despite convincing evidence that educated women *do* eventually marry and have children, and in greater proportion than their less-educated sisters.

At the other end of the fertility spectrum, about 10 percent of would-be parents fail to conceive even when they resort to fertility treatments or artificial insemination. Grief over the trauma of infertility, in some historical societies grounds for divorce, is hard to assuage. Blame and guilt take unknowable tolls. Men and women are about equally afflicted by infertility. Diseases and environmental and occupational hazards affect both genders.[8] An estimated 2 percent of infertile North American couples succeed in procreating thanks to assisted reproductive technology, or ART—induced ovulation, artificial insemination, in vitro fertilization, and other techniques to create embryos. A small number of infertile people turn to surrogate mothers.

NUMBER OF CHILDREN

Marriages in which spouses choose to have few or no children are increasingly common. The shrinking size of North American families continues to change the experience of parenthood and hence of marriage. The likelihood of maternal illness, debility, or death is drastically reduced. So is the financial burden of housing, feeding, clothing, caring for, and educating multiple children. Parents with fewer children can either invest more in each child or else stretch their limited means further because their housing, clothing, food, child care, education, and health care cost less.

With fewer children, each one looms larger in the parents' world; their successes and failures carry heavier consequences. This is magnified in the case of single children, who are increasingly common. Today, parents with decent incomes can more successfully manage to work and parent within the marriage framework, and to a much greater extent than their nineteenth- and early-twentieth-century counterparts manage to engage together as companionate spouses. On the flip side, in their later life the state may be expected to assume the role of many aging parents' caretakers, once the role of children.

But large families are not unknown. Certain groups, usually religious, continue to promote them. Quiverful, a Christian movement dating from the mid-1990s, "trusts the Lord for family size [and answers] the questions of those seeking truth in this critical area of marriage." Quiverful celebrates giving one's womb to God to use as He sees fit, as per Psalm 127:3–5: "Lo, children are an heritage of the LORD: and the fruit of the womb is his reward. As arrows are in the hand of a mighty man; so are children of the youth. Happy is the man that hath his quiver full of them: they shall not be ashamed, but they shall speak with the enemies in the gate." Quiverful families do not use birth control and accept each pregnancy as God's wish for them.

Americans Jerry and Heather Milburn had already had two children before they "truly knew God," and it was only then, Heather writes, that she and Jerry became quiverful. After their five children were diagnosed with excruciatingly painful and degenerative mitochondrial disease, Heather writes that a public outcry pressured her and Jerry "to stop producing 'broken children' (insert huge eye roll here). [But] we kept on believing … that HE knew best and so we would keep my womb at His feet until He said otherwise. Well, though we least expected it, He said otherwise.… Right now Jerry and I … are no longer led to be quiverful and are seeking the Lord in how we are supposed to not be quiverful, as this is a new concept to us." At the same time, "I feel our quiver is full regardless of what happens next. But," Heather adds, "there's always room for more."[9]

Even the quiverful do not always conceive, which occasionally (and counterintuitively) leads to even larger families when parents using ART do not abort one or more of the multiple fetuses (and there are good medical reasons to do so). Two recent and very public examples are Jon and Kate Gosselin, whose reality television show, *Jon & Kate Plus 8*, followed the daily lives of their twins and their sextuplets, all conceived by ART. Their marriage has not survived, and its demise prompted an immediate plunge in viewership. The public responded with repelled fascination to news of the so-called Octomom, single mother Nadya Suleman, whose ART-conceived octuplets joined their six ART-conceived siblings in her parents' small house. Because Suleman is a single mother who relied on her retired parents to support and care for her first six children, and whose now bankrupted mother publicly denounced as unconscionable her decision to have any more, much less eight, there is outrage at the likelihood that public funds will be required to care for Suleman's huge brood.

Except for the very rich (or, like Suleman, the very publicity-seeking), the financial burden of having many children is heavy, and sleep deprivation and drastic changes in the parents' lifestyle reshape and strain their unions.

In *Fourteen: Growing Up Alone in a Crowd*, American Stephen Zanichkowsky described, with cathartic pain, his upbringing as one of the fourteen children of devout Catholic parents. "The first kids were already on their way out the door before the last ones were brought home from the delivery room." Between 1942 and 1961, his once-

Ontario's Dionne quintuplets, pictured here in 1934, were the first quints known to survive infancy. The Ontario government had the parents declared unfit and made the girls wards of the state—and a world-famous tourist attraction. The public paid to watch them study and play. In 1943, their parents won back custody. The girls earned millions in advertising fees, starred in Hollywood movies, and made public appearances. At eighteen they left home and had little contact with their parents; in 1995, the three surviving quints accused their father of sexually abusing them.

vampish and vivacious mother was almost always pregnant, and after the fifth child she became so heavy that she ruined her back, her body "taxed to its limits long before she could have derived much pleasure from its use." For thirty-odd years, "housewifery and motherhood got on top of her completely. Like a black hole, her children became the gravity sink around which she collapsed."

Canadian superstar singer Céline Dion, on the other hand, the youngest of fourteen children, was nurtured and encouraged by her musical parents and pampered by her older siblings. In rural French Canada, where the huge families of the past had shrivelled to the lowest levels in North America, the Dions persevered against poverty to perform *en famille* and helped Céline launch her meteoric career. If

Photographed during World War I, this family consisted of father Rev. William Rashleigh, a widower remarried to widow Katharine Maria Theodosia, his second cousin, and thirteen children, including an adopted cousin. Ruth Portia, six, with doll, is the mother of retired Canadian physician Michael Burslem, who was named after the family mutt (pictured) and praises his mother's large family for learning to appreciate each other's needs. On the eve of his children's weddings, Rev. Rashleigh gave each this excellent advice: "Children will behave as little animals until taught not to."

there were resentments, rivalries, or neglect, the Dions do not mention them. Her siblings, Céline declares, work hard, mean well, and "none of us are cuckoo, or stupid."

Growing up in her poor family meant a "foundation of love—of being able to count on brothers and sisters and parents—you know you have someone there to support you." Céline was always close to her mother. "She's a god to me, my idol, the person that I look up to the most.... She had nothing. At the same time, everything we needed, she gave to us. She gave her life to us."[10] Like the Zanichkowskys' marriage, the elder Dions' endured until death parted them.

KINDS OF MARRIAGE

Historical families were often the product of death, as widows and widowers remarried and raised their own children along with their half-siblings, stepchildren, and often orphans from previous marriages. Today, with divorce replacing death as a leading reason for an ended marriage, remarriages and marriages are distinguished as primary, blended, or reconstituted. In primary marriages, children are the biological or adopted offspring of both spouses. In blended marriages, at least one child is their joint offspring. In reconstituted families, the children are biologically or, for adoptees, legally related to only one spouse.

In the case of primary marriage, the biggest issue remains how the mother mothers: does she remain at home or does she work, part-time or full-time, inside or outside the house? As studies delve and arguments rage, most mothers work, and delinquency, school dropout rates, crime, and alcohol and drug abuse are parsed for clues about how much these working mothers contribute to them.

Meanwhile, mothers continue to deal with child-rearing concerns: Should they use cloth diapers or disposable, or should they be greener and train bare-bottomed little ones to potty by catching them in the act? Should they breastfeed and give their child the nourishment of mother's milk, or should they bottle-feed and share the joy of feeding with their husbands? At work, should they retire to an inconspicuous part of the workplace or should they remain in view of co-workers as they pump out and store their breast milk? Should they wean the child after a few months or continue for at least a year? Should they prepare all their baby's food or should they rely on or supplement with commercial products?

These real and important choices often mask another one: should women stay at home to raise children or should they exercise their hard-earned right to study, train, apprentice, and work. Discussions tend to provoke guilt in women for being imperfect mothers, not only failing their children but missing opportunities to gain an education, hone their talents, and develop superior skills. There are armies of warring subtexts: the documented benefits of breastfeeding on demand and joyous, relaxed mothering pitted against painful or insufficient lactation, the resentment and frustration of homebound women, and financial exigencies. Depending on their perspective and personal circumstances, wives and their husbands respond with decisions that shape their marriages.

STEP-PARENTING AND MARRIAGE

About one-third of divorces involve custody of children, and many parents remarry and become step-parents. These remarriages, as well as single-parent first-time marriages, mean that the step or blended family is almost as typical as the childless first-time marriage. One-quarter of North American children will grow up in stepfamilies, and at any one time, about 10 percent are living in them. Even when formed with the best of intentions, these families are delicate structures often riddled with mistrust, resentment, and conflicting loyalties that may challenge the marriages at their core.

Today's remarriage rate mirrors that of the eighteenth century and earlier centuries. But remarriages now look quite different, because today only 18 percent of stepmothers live with their stepchildren. When Elizabeth Packard, Caroline Norton, and thousands of other women broke away from their wretched marriages, their husbands were automatically granted custody of their children. Now the reverse is true, and wives customarily win it. When these women remarry, their new husbands become resident stepfathers. As a result, resident stepfathers are far more numerous than before, and they are redrawing the face of their blended unions.

The dynamics of step-parenting are complex and mysterious, rooted not just in the heart and in the vagaries of human emotion but also in inheritance laws. Yet the relationship between step-parent and stepchild is crucial to the happiness and success of the marriage. All too often, research into this all-important phenomenon serves as ammunition against divorce. Many studies conclude that women who leave their children's father and remarry (or cohabit with a man) put their offspring at greater risk of abuse than children raised by their biological fathers.[11] The evil stepmother's cloak now covers the evil stepfather as well.

Millennia ago, Saint Jerome already knew this. By remarrying, he advised a widowed mother who was contemplating it, "a mother sets over a child not a step-father but an enemy; not a parent but a tyrant … You will not be allowed to love your own children, or to look kindly on those whom you gave birth…. If he, for his part, has issue by a former wife, when he brings you into his house, then even though you have a heart of gold you will be the cruel stepmother."[12]

It is true that more stepfathers than biological fathers are abusive. The Cinderella effect—the theory that children are at far greater risk of physical and sexual abuse and even murder at the hands of resident step-parents, usually stepfathers—has been tested and documented by scores of social scientists.[13] They do not all agree with the Darwinian interpretation that, like lions, dolphins, langurs, or crows, stepfathers are driven to eliminate rivals in favour of their own genetic offspring. Some researchers suggest that the violence may be rooted in the circumstances of the remarriage, for example that poorer, less educated women remarry (or cohabit) sooner than their better-off sisters and bring the stresses of financial struggle to the relationship. Remarriers also court more briefly than couples entering first marriages and they often cohabit before marriage. Most do not make a point of emphasizing step-parenting issues, perhaps to forestall sabotaging the union before it begins, perhaps because they hope to nip any problems in the bud. Remarriers may also bring suffering, angry, and resentful children to their new union, although many other children are relieved to be rid of the tension (or worse) in their parents' broken relationship. As well, the children of remarrying widows or widowers are especially prone to grief, confusion, and betrayal.

Another complication is that step-parents discover that their stepchildren's other biological parent is a presence in the new marriage. Co-parenting arrangements, increasingly common, mean constant contact, communication, and negotiating with former spouses. They require cooperation and assume a courtesy, even geniality, that is often forced or absent. They demand shared values and, to some extent, finances. They also involve additional grandparents and relatives. To avoid breaking down, the marriage must be elastic enough to encompass all these additional players and their stakes in the children.

When remarried spouses have children of their own, making their step- and biological children half-siblings, more complications and divided loyalties arise. This is the case for the nearly half of all women, who in the first two years after remarrying will give birth. Unless the newborn is her and her husband's first child, the dynamics of step-parenting invade the marriage.

Thanks to the prevalence of divorce in North America, a steady stream of studies about step-parenting finds eager audiences. But the fact that so many of today's scholars and journalists know or are stepmothers tends to forestall skewed portrayals. Instead, they acknowledge the challenges stepmothers face, and consider what prompts some to act negatively toward their stepchildren. They wonder why so many feel overwhelmed and helpless, resentful at their husbands' failure to help and support them, hurt at their exclusion from the father–child relationship, exhausted and frustrated because they continue to perform the bulk of the household's child care and housework. A host of support groups has also sprung up: Childless Stepmoms (the most likely to have failed marriages) "trying to adjust to life in a stepfamily"; Life in a Blender, for biomoms and stepmoms focused on children; Second Wives Café and Second Wives Club, online communities that support second wives; Stepmom Retreat; Stepmoms Penpal Network, for mentoring; and Stepmom Station.

Resident stepfathers, far more numerous than resident stepmothers, contend with fewer negative stereotypes. But step-fathering is complicated by the fact that many of these men are divorced fathers whose ex-wives have custody of their own children, and now they live instead with their new wife's children. Others are childless men now expected to co-parent. Often, they will later father children with their stepchildren's mother.

The majority of stepfathers are kind and responsible, steady influences in their stepchildren's lives, though suspicion persists about their fairness, patience, harshness, commitment, and, vis-à-vis stepdaughters, their sexual righteousness. But the studies that document abuse are reinforced by other reports, including memoirs by abused stepchildren or their remorseful mothers. Studies that focus on risk factors are urgently needed to develop better family policies that safeguard children. What sort of marriage is likely to develop interpersonally abusive dynamics? What resources can flailing stepfathers turn to?

RACIALLY DIVERSE PARENTS AND CHILDREN

In increasingly multicultural North America, parents must teach their children how to negotiate their world and to make sense of their racial and cultural identities, a process that is complex and often fraught and, when children are mixed-race, confusing and often alienating. Immigrant families must inculcate values that are workable in North America, addressing matters that range from dating and dress codes to after-school jobs and homework. In addition, parents must anticipate, and advise on how to cope with, prejudice and tension in relations with the larger community.

Anthropologist Elizabeth Chin provides a lens onto these huge issues in "Ethnically Correct Dolls: Toying with the Race Industry," her 1999 study of how African-American girls in a poor, working-class neighbourhood of New Haven, Connecticut, relate to their dolls. Mattel had already introduced (in 1991) Shani, Asha, and Nichelle, African-Americanized Barbies designed to rectify the "assumption of whiteness" inherent in Barbie. But Mattel and other toy makers said they were not responsible for making the new ones available to economically disadvantaged children, and so the poor girls in Chin's study played with their old white Barbies, transforming them by braiding and beading their hair into African-American styles. They "recognize in multiple ways the socially constructed nature of race, the ambiguity of a racialized existence, and the flexibility of racialized experience," Chin concluded.[14]

The parents of mixed-race children have a special mission to guide them as they struggle to come to terms with what often seem ambiguous identities. The process is often accompanied by confusion and anguish. In the United States, for example, it was only in 1999 that federal forms were changed to allow people to self-identify as mixed-race rather than as only one race or another. The multiracial Tiger Woods was born officially "black" or "Asian"; now he can describe himself as Cablnasian—Caucasian, black, Native, and Asian.

Parents must do more than try to keep their mixed-race children safe. They must also help them accept that their parents' marriage, the trigger for—though not the cause of—trying to live in a racialized, conflicted world, is both a safe haven from the world and a living challenge to that world's values. The complex and urgent needs of mixed-race children are an additional and burdensome responsibility for parents. Meeting them strains (but can also strengthen) marriages.

In the past two decades, families with foreign or national adopted children of a different race are increasingly common in North America, and face unique challenges. This development parallels growing multiculturalist and colour-blind (or oblivious) social attitudes and government policies, and reflects the dawn of a striving for racial harmony. Before World War II, adoption of a child not of the parent's (shared) race was almost unheard of. In 1944, in the United States, Operation Brown Baby attempted to adopt Asian, Native, and African-American children into good homes of any race. The civil rights era saw a dramatic rise in such adoptions: in the United States, from 733 cases in 1968 to 2,574 in 1971.

Pearl S. Buck, winner of the Pulitzer and Nobel Prizes for Literature and so acculturated to her Chinese birthplace that the Chinese honour her as a Chinese writer, was so heartsick at the hopeless condition of orphaned or abandoned biracial children that she established foundations that adopted out thousands. She and her husband also adopted seven. "If our American way of life fails the child, it fails us all," Buck explained.

In "I Am the Better Woman for Having My Two Black Children," Buck described adopting the first of these daughters, born in Germany to a German woman and an unfindable African-American soldier. "The ceremony was a double one. I asked the judge to ask her, too, to adopt us. She was then old enough to understand. It was a beautiful and sacred little ceremony, just the four of us in his private chambers. It sealed our love."[15]

In the 1960s, Joe and Jan Rigert of Minnesota, devout liberal Roman Catholics, adopted seven multiracial children—"Japanese, East Indian, Mexican, Black, American Indian, everything"—and Joe, an investigative journalist, often wrote about his multi-hued family. Unlike his wife, who came from a small family, Joe was one of thirteen children—"a terrible thing for my mother"—and was content with their one biological child. But through Catholic social action programs involving adoptions across racial lines, he said, "my wife and I got into the adoption thing.... One child led to another. My wife was pushing, pushing to do more of this and I was going along with it ultimately."

The Rigerts lived first in a small, almost semi-rural parish with a very liberal Irish priest, and later in open-minded Minneapolis. "It's a neat family," Rigert says, with "all kinds of wonderful diversity.... They just do all kinds of things and I think that's great ... for me and my wife, too. Just the excitement of all of the change and differences ... it's really been a great experience for us."[16]

That era's thinking about interracial adoption changed drastically when, in 1972, the National Association of Black Social Workers took "a vehement stand against the placement of black children in white homes for any reason." Ethnicity, they declared, "is a way of life in these United States, and the world at large; a viable, sensitive, meaningful and legitimate societal construct. This is no less true nor legitimate for black people than for other ethnic groups."[17] Adoptions of black children into non-black homes plummeted to almost zero.

Two decades later, attitudes shifted again. Adoption placements no longer used strict same-race guidelines.[18] Inter-race marriage, with its resultant mixed-race babies, rocketed. The new tolerance for out-of-wedlock births encouraged unmarried women to keep and raise their babies. A dearth of adoptable children sent would-be adopters else-where, to the far ends of the earth for little ones to love and cherish and complete their lives.

Thousands of them are Chinese girls, abandoned and unwanted by parents subject to the one-child-per-family rule in an authoritarian nation with a son-loving culture. "Chinese females are so unwanted, so unloved, that they are … left under bridges, in hospital waiting rooms, near police stations. If they survive, they end up in orphanages," writes journalist Jan Wong.[19] This background alleviates the guilt adoptive parents might feel about removing children from their continent, country, and culture. (And in fact 91 percent of Chinese adoptees are girls.)

But China and most other nations that permit foreign adoptions do not make adoption easy, and impose increasingly rigorous standards for would-be parents. In 2007, China stipulated that adopters must be married; like the obese, the facially deformed, and those who have taken antidepressants in the past two years, singles are now ineligible.[20] China believes that children are best raised by healthy, financially sound, educated men and women in a strong marriage, and foreigners must comply.

Whether their children are Chinese or another ethnicity, adoptive parents have responsibilities over and above those of birth parents. They must acquaint themselves with their child's culture of origin, introduce others of that same culture into her life, and make related activities part of their routine. They must be aware of any medical issues associated with that origin, such as sickle-cell anemia or thalassemia. They must learn how to enhance their child's appearance, dress their black child's soft, fragile curls. They must also address the visible differences between family members—skin colour, eye shape, hair texture, the plethora of physical characteristics that define racial origin.

Most of all, adoptive parents must confront racism, the casual slur, the ethnic joke, the racist stab, the unspoken assumption. They need to exercise constant vigilance but also master sensitivity, tolerance, and the healing power of laughter. Nor must ethnicity overshadow daily life and the loving family. Children and their different experiences and perceptions are good guides. "People ask me whether or not I'm embarrassed about having white parents," writes Jasmine Bent, adopted from China, "and truthfully, I'm just embarrassed having *my* parents. I'm glad that my parents are not traditional Chinese parents, who often seem to put a lot of pressure on their children to be perfect at everything academic and who seem to think that leisure activities are not important.... With that being said, life when I was younger would have been easier if I looked like my parents." Lia Calderone, adopted from China by Italian parents, responds to the often asked question about the identity of her "real parents": "The parents I live with are my real parents.... I've never really wondered about my biological parents." Lia's little sister Alissa, however, is more curious and wants to find her biological Chinese parents.[21]

Burgeoning interracial and foreign adoptions are a new dimension of North American child-rearing. In the context of marriage, such adoption alleviates the despair of infertility or enriches the lives of families eager to share their advantages with children who lack them. It substitutes for the nine-month uterine pregnancy a two- or three-year paper-trail pregnancy, and ushers parents into new and supportive adoptive-parent communities. It encourages (and in some cases forces) cohabiters to marry so that they conform to the standards of China or other countries. Its very high fees and demands limit most such adoptions to high-earners, so that adopters are almost always upper-middle-class men and women, and usually white. It is a new but much-studied movement, which in the coming years will yield up its secrets about these marriages and the children raised in them.

Pegi Dover and Phil Jessup with their eleven-year-old daughter, Beth, adopted in infancy from China. The family has made several trips to China and as much as possible reinforces Beth's knowledge of her birthland.

TOMORROW'S CHILD-RELATED POLICIES

Governments and public officials, including religious, have always conceived and designed public policies about marriage, families, and children. Until the advent of cyberspace, if they consulted the public, they held formal hearings, townhalls, and community meetings and corresponded with experts and legislators. But cyberspace enables citizens to find like-minded individuals and groups and, easily and independently, to create brainstorming collectives, to hash out common interests, to define priorities, and to attract supporters to join them. Empowered by ease of communication, and clear in their needs and purposes, these new groups then lobby governments with a power once restricted to well-financed and well-connected lobbyists.

In the United States, such a group is the formidable MomsRising, hundreds of thousands strong and aiming for millions "working to build a massive grassroots online resource to move motherhood and family issues to the forefront of the country's awareness." Because child care and families are integral to marriage, the policies that MomsRising advocates could profoundly influence how Americans raise their children. With their logo of a transformed Rosie the Riveter holding aloft a baby, MomsRising is a formidable force that clearly articulates the need for sensible public policies to help mothers—and fathers—raise their children better.

MomsRising seeks as well to change the cultural mores that keep the old ways in place and that make the United States the West's most backward nation when it comes to parental leave—worldwide, the only other nations without any form of paid maternal leave are Lesotho, Swaziland, and Papua New Guinea. "We are stuck in a 1950's mentality which assumed that there was a full-time wife at home taking care of the children (although this was not often possible for lower income women)," MomsRising declares. "It is time for our legislative policies and workplaces to match the dynamics of the modern American family…. Countries with family-friendly policies in place—such as paid family leave, accessible health care, flexible work policies and subsidized child care—do not have the same wage gap for mothers as we do here. This begins to explain why there are so many American women and children living in poverty, and why there are so few women in leadership."

MomsRising cites statistics that clarify the crisis arising in many marriages. Even before the 2008 recession, a quarter of U.S. families with children less than six years old lived in poverty. Nine million children lack health-care coverage or are under-insured. Fourteen million children, including forty thousand in kindergarten, are unsupervised after school due to a lack of affordable after-school programs. Working married mothers earn 73 cents to a man's dollar, single mothers about 60 cents. Yet three-quarters of American mothers, married or unmarried, are in the labour force.

What is needed, MomsRising argues, are maternity and paternity leaves, laws permitting open and flexible work hours, universal child health care, excellent child care and accessible after-school programs, and, most radical of all, realistic and fair wages. MomsRising's recommendations aim to improve child welfare, which would in turn strengthen the structure and stability of the marriages or relationships those children are raised in.

Canadian policy much more closely resembles Europe's.[22] In 2000, Canada expanded parental leave from ten to thirty-five weeks, added to fifteen weeks' maternity leave, with maximum benefits up to $413 a week assumed by Employment Insurance. Those fifty weeks can be shared between mothers and fathers. Because of Canada's universal health care, the medical expenses of childbirth, if any, are negligible.

But as in the United States, Canada's child-care situation is deeply unsatisfactory, and a great many parents struggle to find competent and affordable daycare or babysitters. In 2002–2003, about 54 percent of Canadian children aged six months to five years were cared for by someone other than their parents, up from 42 percent eight years earlier. As the number of caregivers rose, so did the proportion of those licensed and trained. But there are never enough and, except in the province of Quebec, the strain of locating decent child care is a constant refrain of the wealthy, middle, and working classes alike.[23]

In Canada, child care is a provincial responsibility, and so the situation differs from province to province. But Quebec's official policy includes the right to reliable and affordable child care as a strategy to fight poverty, provide equal opportunities, develop the social market economy, ease the transition from welfare to the workforce, and increase support to working parents to "reinforce the most important values of our society: sense of family and love of children," in the words of Pauline Marois, minister of education. Marois added that the growing number of single parents, blended families, and working women had forced the government to adapt its policies to their children's changing needs by ensuring their development and success in school through early childhood intervention and child care.

Quebec remains the exception—even though a 2003 poll found that 86 percent of Canadians agreed that a publicly funded child-care system should make quality child care available to all Canadian children. Canadian government statistics confirm the legitimacy of parents' laments about the scarcity of good child care. Though a Quebec family with two children and an income of $75,000 pays only $1,207 per child in daycare, in Saskatchewan, the next cheapest province, the cost soars to $6,974. The Canadian average (excluding Quebec) is $7,145.

As the principle that children deserve excellent care, whether or not their parents have the means to pay for it, gains ground, so will state-subsidized child care. The effect on marriages (and on other parenting arrangements) will be strong and positive despite critics who denounce the "nanny state" and repeat their warnings that mothers should be staying home. But like most women, wives will continue to work, and accessible child care will improve their lives and their ability to cope with their family responsibilities, including their marriages.

A changing world and the pill helped usher out the ideal of the nineteenth century's self-abnegating, all-giving Good Wife. Dr. Spock, gentle and sensible, was the spokesman for the new wave of motherhood—children planned and wanted by women who sought self-actualization in their lives and in other important ways wanted what men wanted. Spock also guided generations of parents as they reared their children and sought to make sense of their lives. Nevertheless, North American child-care policies lag far behind society's ideas and standards about children, even while the nature of the family structure has significantly shifted.

Chapter 11

For Richer or Poorer: Marriage and Money

WHEN THE MATH OF MARRIAGE EXACTS A HIGH PRICE

In 2006, for a single wretched month, *Globe and Mail* reporter Jan Wong assumed the identity of a single mother forced by domestic problems to return to work. Her assignment? To experience life working forty hours a week at the minimum wage.

Wong soon discovered that, in the past thirty years, inflation has eroded the minimum wage's buying power by 13 percent in real terms, all while the national standard of living soared. The result was that a fully employed minimum-wage earner would not even bring in half of what Statistics Canada identified as the low-income cut-off line (considered the unofficial poverty line) of $31,126 for an urban family of three. Even a $10 hourly wage was woefully inadequate. The reality is that one in six Canadians, a majority of them female, works full-time for wages officially deemed too low to maintain a decent standard of living. (In Toronto, where Wong lives and works, one-quarter of food-bank users are married, and 17 percent of these have children.)

Wong became a maid for a cleaning company and earned $300 a week, working eleven days every two weeks. She tallied her income and expenses like a modern-day Henry Thoreau, but the apartment she rented for her experiment was no Walden. The Hovel, as she and her two sons called it, was an illegally converted basement unit with

Working people who never imagined they would need help to feed their families are increasingly turning to soup kitchens. When the choice is rent or food, many opt to keep a roof over their heads. The strain on their marriages, and on their relations with their children, is often intense.

windows and no cockroaches. It cost $750 a month including utilities, internet, and access to the landlord's washer and dryer. It had two bedrooms (but no living room), fulfilling the social-services standard of separate quarters for children, and left her with $22.06 per day. Had this been the real deal, she would have received a low-income tax refund, a monthly Child Tax Benefit of $204.67, and a National Child Benefit Supplement of $268.66, bringing her a mere $7,631.08 below the low-income baseline.

The (usually) well-off Wongs learned to economize and eat within their budget. Wong provides a sample of a day's menu:

Breakfast:
  1 English muffin $0.18
  4 hot dogs $1.10
  1 oz. cheddar cheese $0.38
  3 boiled eggs $0.62

Butter, jam, peanut butter $0.50
Milk $1.20
Tea $0.20

Packed lunch:
 6 slices luncheon meat $1
 6 slices bread $0.60
 3 Granny Smith apples $1.08
 Dried nuts and dates $0.75

Supper:
 Indian butter-chicken sauce $3
 2 thighs $2.34
 Basmati rice $0.75
 Broccoli $1
 Milk $1.20
 3 bananas $0.50

Total: $16.40

Wong, already slender, lost six pounds in ten days. Her sons grew lethargic and neglected their homework. "Of all the humiliations inherent in poverty, there's no failure more resounding than being unable to feed your kids," Wong reflected. She knew how badly they were eating, and that stir-fries, rice, and beans would have been much healthier. But her job was so physically taxing that, at home, she resorted to more easily prepared bargain food items.

Jan Wong was attempting to replicate the experiences of a single working mother. What changes would there have been if she had had a working husband? If he had been a full-time worker earning slightly over $10 an hour, and if she worked full-time as well, they would barely earn enough to claw themselves over the low-income threshold.

These same spouses would likely also work more hours to earn proportionately less than they would have thirty years earlier. The poor in both Canada and the United States have become poorer, and with a recessionary interconnected global economy, their plight is worsening.

For richer or poorer, marriage and money go hand in glove. In the twenty-first as in previous centuries, marriage feels quite different in the comfort zone than on nickels and dimes. Having to pay for the essentials of daily life, from rent or mortgage and food to transportation, clothes, and entertainment, shapes the marriage experience.

In the global recession that began in 2008, risky financial vehicles that fuelled the subprime mortgage industry—essentially permitting people unable to afford mortgages to get them anyway—contributed mightily to the near collapse of the world's banking and financial system. It also drove millions of Americans out of their homes, engorging the ranks of working, underemployed, and unemployed homeless (or inadequately housed) spouses and their children.

The economic crisis has also killed jobs, decimated industries, and devastated communities dependent on mono-manufacturing such as automobiles and auto parts. And it has struck hard at marriages, crushing hopes and dreams in the bitter reality of impoverishment and hopelessness, despair and rage sometimes articulated in spousal, child, or pet abuse, all three a crescendo of pain in a world gone awry. Marriage counsellors and divorce lawyers report more clients desperate to escape or remedy their failing situations. When the cost of moving out is prohibitive, the solution may be a marital "separation" effected by hanging a curtain down the middle of a room.

Even in "normal" times, finances powerfully affect marriages. Almost half of all Canadian families—3.8 million—are raising children under the age of eighteen. (This includes single-parent and two-parent cohabiting and married families.) Among these, the rich (with a household income $131,000 or more annually) grew richer, earning 82 times more than the poorest, who raised their children on $9,400 or less annually. The huge swath of people in-between worked an average of nearly 200 more hours to maintain their standard of living. The same situation prevails in the United States, where 7.8 million people, about equally divided between men and women, held two or more jobs.

There was trouble even before the recession. Minimum wages failed to keep up with inflation. In Canada in 2009, the provincially set minimum wage ranged from $7.25 in New Brunswick to $8.50 in

Nunavut; it was $8 in all the largest provinces, Alberta, British Columbia, Manitoba, Ontario, and Quebec. In the United States, the federal minimum hourly wage is $7.25. State wage laws range from a high of $8.55 in Washington to a low of $5.15 in Wyoming. The Southern states of Alabama, Louisiana, Mississippi, South Carolina, and Tennessee have no minimum wage at all.

The well-paid manufacturing jobs were disappearing, and the new service-sector jobs paid much less. As a result of these bleak realities, union workplaces have declined in number. Contract and temporary employment is increasing. Federal government policies—for example the monthly tax-free Canada Child Tax Benefit—blunt but cannot reverse the consequences of declining incomes. Canada has one of the world's highest proportions (21 percent) of low-paid workers, defined as earning wages less than two-thirds of the national median annual earnings.[1]

How does this translate into quotidian life? "Families are doing everything they're told to succeed," writes Canadian economist Armine Yalnizyan. "They get a better education. They delay family formation. They work harder than ever before. They should be better off than their parents' generation. But 80 per cent of families cannot say that."[2]

Another consequence of the global recession is that across North America, household debt has skyrocketed; in Canada, the savings rate has plunged from 20 percent in 1982 to 1.8 in 2005 and by August 2009 had risen to 4.7; in the United States, it has reached 6.9 percent. With virtually no savings, large numbers of Canadians are a payday away from the abyss. "Economic hardship, the feeling that you can never make ends meet, and you have this long-term burden, can result in anxiety, depression, anger [and] failed relationships," said University of Toronto sociologist Scott Schieman.[3] In the United States, where the crisis is more aggravated, shelters are receiving record numbers of homeless families, many headed by married parents. Depression, self-doubt, and mutual recrimination haunt many married homeless, eroding the chances that their marriages will survive as healthy unions.

As we saw in part 1, finances and property have always played a vital role in arranging and establishing marriages, and their role did not diminish after the wedding. Money and standard of living are essential ingredients in marriage and shape daily life and family and personal priorities. To examine marriage outside of its economic context is a meaningless exercise. This is especially true when spouses are mired in poverty or struggling to avoid it.

"Every problem magnifies the impact of the others," David Shipler muses in *The Working Poor*, "and all are so tightly interlocked that one reversal can produce a chain reaction with results far distant from the original cause. A run-down apartment can exacerbate a child's asthma, which leads to a call for an ambulance, which generates a medical bill that cannot be paid, which ruins a credit record, which hikes the interest rate on an auto loan, which forces the purchase of an unreliable used car, which jeopardizes a mother's punctuality at work, which limits her promotions and earning capacity, which confines her to poor housing."[4]

In *Nickel and Dimed: On (Not) Getting By in America*, in which Barbara Ehrenreich describes her year-long experience as a working woman/undercover researcher "serving in Florida, scrubbing in Maine and selling in Minnesota," she emphasizes that "no secret economies … nourish the poor; on the contrary, there are a host of special costs."[5] The price of lacking first and last month's rent for an apartment is almost always much worse accommodation payable weekly. Without proper kitchens to prepare economical and nutritious meals, people resort to fast food or microwaveable or prepared food. Without enough money to get through until the next pay period, they pay ruinous (but legal) rates of interest for "payday" loans. Helpless to take that stitch in time that will save nine, they scramble to prevent their lives from unravelling.

Rent is ineluctably linked to salary and cash flow and credit checks, and much of North America is in the grips of a critical shortage of affordable housing. In Canada in 2007, the average rent for a two-bedroom apartment ranged from a low of $472 in Saguenay, Quebec, to $1,061 in Toronto. At low wages ($10 an hour or under), these apartments are unaffordable.

In 2003, one in five Canadian and American households was forced to spend 30 percent or more of their pre-tax income on housing.[6] The lower the income, the greater the percentage of it that went to housing. At the same time, vacancy rates in the lowest price range were much lower than in the higher price range. In the United States, with foreclo-sures in the millions, the impact on individual marriages is brutal.

An associated cost in the math of marriage is that children often work for wages, not to help their parents as in previous centuries but to purchase their own consumer goods: cell phones, iPods, clothing, music downloads, concerts, movies, fast food, bling. This, too, can affect the marriage of low-wage parents, either easing the financial strain or poisoning family dynamics if money empowers children to disrespect parents. In this instance, the relationship dynamic that's affected is the North American parental role of raising children to be the consumers that keep the economy perpetually expanding. When children assume this important role, they may undermine their parents' role and their self-respect, which in turn erodes the financially flailing marriage.

When the Math of Marriage Equals High Returns

Finances also influence the marriages of North America's prosperous classes, encouraging them to demand larger houses and to shower their children with services—lessons, classes, tutoring—as well as goods. Between 1945 and 1991, the average Canadian house size grew from 800 to 1,500 square feet, and from then to 2007 it increased another 27 percent, to 1,900 square feet. In the United States, new homes average 2,459 square feet. At the same time, the size of the families moving into these McMansions decreased from four members to fewer than three.

Inside these homes, children usually have their own rooms and often their own bathrooms. These suites—which is really what they are—tend to be self-sufficient, with televisions, computers, and electronic equip-ment as well as desks and telephones, enabling children to live at a phys-ical remove from their parents. Their marriage may still be child-centred, but the dynamics are necessarily different from the marriages of more closely confined spouses. The closest historical paral-lel is nineteenth-century Europe's privileged way of life, which in England was characterized by children's quarters, nannies and governesses, even special meals: tea was a child-sized supper taken before the parents ate their own evening meal.

These privileged parents had high expectations for their children but spent less time in their physical presence than poorer parents did. Today's privileged parents have equally high expectations that their children excel or at least perform adequately in music, sports, dance, and art, maintain top grades, and integrate socially with the right sort of other children who attend the same classes and schools and after-school groups. Mothers especially often double as chauffeurs who transport their children from one improving activity to another, in addition to their duties managing the large establishment that is their home, and very often having outside employment as well.

The price of spacious houses as well as of more modest houses and condominiums has escalated in tandem with the financial culture of easy mortgages that pushed the world's economy into recession. Housing prices and unsustainable mortgages have had grievous effects on marriages, as millions of spouses struggle to stave off financial ruin. Canada has not fallen victim to irresponsible mortgages, but between 1999 and 2005, skyrocketing house prices have driven up individual debt by 43 percent. The nation's household debt totalled $760 billion, three-quarters of it for mortgages.

Husbands Missing-in-Action: Men Behind Bars

Throughout history, poverty, military obligations, and other factors have prevented people from marrying. These and other impediments still exist. North America's deepening poverty effectively eliminates large segments of the population from the marriage market. Wartime duties, injuries, and traumas thrust others out of it, though the prospect of imminent service prompts others to marry. Some want to formalize relationships before possible deployment. Others are motivated by the promise of base housing (or rental allowances for off-base housing) and health insurance and other benefits for military spouses. But a new barrier to marriage—prison—now keeps millions of men from becoming husbands.

The United States has the world's highest documented incarceration rate. In 2008, more than 1 percent of the adult population was behind bars. Millions of others were under judicial control either on probation or parole. Nationwide, 737 people per 100,000 are incarcerated. Over 90 percent are males, less than half convicted of non-violent crimes.[7] Nearly 55 percent of federal and 21 percent of state prisoners are incarcerated for drug offences. Eleven percent have committed public-disorder offences: drunken driving, parole violations, contempt of court. The correctional system has become so gigantic that it employs more Americans than General Motors, Ford, and Wal-Mart combined.

These statistics also reveal a stunning racial discrepancy. About 10.4 percent of black men aged twenty-five to twenty-nine are in jail, compared with 2.4 percent of Hispanic and 1.2 percent of white men. Overall, 41 percent of all male prisoners are African American; most are poor, and about half were unemployed when they were arrested. So many young blacks are jailed that one in three in their mid-thirties has a prison record. A black child born today has a 29 percent chance of doing time, and the rate rises substantially if that infant is born into poverty. In 2000, one in ten African-American children under ten years of age had a father in prison or jail.

As a consequence of stricter sentencing implemented in the mid 1970s, prisoners serve longer sentences. More than one-third of all state and federal prisoners are between the ages of thirty-five and fifty-four; another third are between twenty-five and thirty-four; and a fifth are between eighteen and twenty-four. Most will be in jail for an average of two years for property crimes (such as theft and fraud) and four years for violent crimes.

The prison experience is seldom reformatory. Rape and coerced sexual activity are pervasive. Inmates remain in or are inducted into violent gangs and often become more hardened criminals than they were. They have health problems; hepatitis C afflicts between 20 and 40 percent. They work for a pittance. Federal prisoners, for example, who work for Unicor Federal Prison Industries earn 23 cents to a maximum of $1.15 hourly (5 percent of Unicor's expenses), usually in manufacturing or assembling for the prison-industrial complex. They make a wide range of military equipment including all its helmets, office furniture, prescription glasses for federal eye care recipients, paints and paintbrushes, stove assemblies, home appliances, airline parts, restaurant equipment, and much more. Unicor has trade shows and conventions, sales catalogues and representatives, architectural and construction companies. It has investment interests, and it lobbies hard and successfully to maintain and expand the prison-industrial complex's functions.

Though Unicor strives to enlist as many inmates as possible, so far it "employs" only 18 percent. At least half of their earnings go to court-ordered fines, child support, and/or restitution. Inmates also send money to their families. Unicor argues that they learn the value of work, responsibility, self-worth, and respect for others as well as actual work skills that they can use to reintegrate into society. It cites studies showing lower recidivism among inmate workers.

Critics charge that Unicor is a form of scab labour that undermines private industry and competes with law-abiding citizens' ability to earn decent wages. As well, some of the industries inmates learn skills for, for example the clothing industry, are disappearing from the United States and can no longer absorb newly released inmates. Instead, critics argue, inmates should be trained for thriving industries that will not be hurt by Unicor's presence and that will employ former convicts. (Oregon Prison Industries has developed a more successful product line: Prison Blues denims. "Your prison blues are made to do hard time," their online ad reads.)

Let's reframe this imprisonment of millions of American males in terms of marriage. Well over two million mostly poor men, the great majority in their prime, the age when most other men marry, are incarcerated. Some inmates are married but will divorce or lose their families before their release. Those who return to their families are least likely to reoffend. The majority, however, are not married, though they may be fathers, and, imprisoned, they have none of the life experiences that prepare men for marriage, including holding steady jobs.

This has a hugely disproportionate impact on the (heavily African-American) communities these men come from and will return to. High unemployment rates, eroding and crime-ridden urban cores, rampant drug abuse or addiction, idleness and gangster culture honed by their personal pasts and, perhaps, predilections will push two-thirds of them back to prison within a few years. The American penal system, explains sociologist Bruce Western, has become a way to solve social problems. "Instead of drawing people at the margins of society back into the mainstream, the penal system walls them off from mainstream society.... The prison system is restricting citizenship rather than repairing it."[8]

Upon their release into the same communities and culture that spawned them, ex-prisoners confront high unemployment and reduced rights, including the right to vote. The least slip—missing a meeting with a parole officer, for example—risks a return to jail. Their jobs will pay an average of 10 percent less than jobs they had before they were jailed, and they will work on average at least one-third fewer hours. Convicted drug offenders who attempt to better their prospects with a college education find they are ineligible for student loans. Former inmates battle personal demons, including prison rape. Their family relations and resources are strained. Their chances of divorce, separation, or bachelorhood are higher. Yet they still have sexual relationships and father babies—who, at birth, already have two strikes against them.

The key marriage-related questions that emerge are: Does incarceration in itself cause these low marriage rates? Or are people who commit crimes less marriageable to begin with? What consequences of incarceration contribute to the low marriage rates? To domestic violence? What do these low marriage rates mean for the women who remain unmarried? What about the affected communities? What about the children born to these fathers?

A wealth of research suggests likely answers. On the one hand, black men with college degrees marry at much higher rates, hold decent jobs, and are seldom incarcerated. But the approximately 25 percent who just graduated or dropped out from high school face limited job opportunities or joblessness, which in turn contribute to the lure of criminal pursuits. Marriageable women assess these men's potential and many decide not to risk permanent ties with them. They worry that their live-in boyfriend might stash drugs or weapons in their home, attracting police or social workers who might take away their children. They have clear-sighted concerns about the likelihood of such a man earning a decent living and they consider prison records "even more repellent than chronic unemployment."9

One of several consequences of high male incarceration is that poor black women have a lopsided marriage market. In Washington, D.C., for example, there are only 62 males for every 100 females, reducing the likelihood of women marrying and increasing the likelihood of single motherhood. The huge increase in jailing men for non-violent, usually drug-related crimes reduced black women's marriage rate by 19 percent. Between 1970 and 2000, their marriage rates plunged to 30 percent from around 60 percent, while those of white women declined much less, to over 60 percent from over 80. As well, less educated black women's rate of single parenthood rose to over fifty percent from about one-third.

If they do marry and if their husbands are jailed, these women have to shoulder the burden of raising any children. They must decide if they wish to visit their spouse, half the time jailed more than a hundred miles away. Continued contact means accepting collect phone calls and writing and receiving letters that correctional authorities examine. Visits involve arranging transportation, submitting to searches, surrendering identification, and passing through metal detectors, the non-criminal subjected to the regimen of the criminal. After her husband's release, the once independent and self-sufficient wife must adjust to his reappearance and the almost inevitable consequences of his incarceration, notably the prison record that will haunt and hobble him. If she has not been faithful, if she has formed a new romantic attachment, or if he is a violent man now free to resume his abuse, the reunion can be more bitter than sweet.

The fragility of marriage in the poor black neighbourhoods that spawn inmates was exacerbated but not created by drastic War on Drugs initiatives and harsh sentencing guidelines in the 1970s and 1980s. The approximately 25 percent of blacks who lived in poverty are mired in conditions scarily similar to those observed by African-American sociologist W.E.B. Du Bois in 1896 through 1898. Just three decades after the Civil War, the traditions of "the slave regime still show themselves in a large amount of cohabitation without marriage," Du Bois wrote, the memory of "almost unbelievable" poverty still lingered, employment opportunities were limited, and rents for decrepit housing were egregiously high. Only substance abuse was noticeably absent: "the intemperate liquor is not one of the Negro's special offences," Du Bois noted.[10]

For young men in such communities, the personal and financial strains meant, as urban anthropologist and ethnographer Elliot Liebow lamented in 1966, that "marriage is an occasion of failure. To stay married is to live with your failure, to be confronted by it day in and day out. It is to live in a world whose standards of manliness are forever beyond one's reach, where one is continuously tested and challenged and continually found wanting."[11]

Juxtaposed against the American situation, Canada jails 620 percent fewer of its citizens; of those, 97 percent are men. Nearly half of males in federal prisons are between the ages of twenty-five and thirty-four; in provincial and territorial jails, about a quarter are between twenty and twenty-four. Nearly three-quarters of federal prisoners are white, and more than 20 percent are aboriginal, a heavy overrepresentation given that they make up only 3.8 percent of the general population. An aboriginal is three times more likely to be jailed than an African American. African Canadians, at 1.9 percent of the population, are also overrepresented in prisons, where they account for 5.4 percent.

Half of all Canadian prisoners have committed violent crimes; less than one-tenth committed drug offences. The majority of inmates in provincial and territorial jails have committed property crimes. Two-thirds will serve one year or less, most of the rest one to two years. Half of federal prisoners are serving two- to six-year sentences; one-tenth are serving life sentences, and they are eligible for parole after one-third or two-thirds of their sentence. Since Bill C-41 in 1996, some convicts serve instead "conditional sentences" in community service. The Canadian recidivism rate is 40 percent, versus 65 percent in the United States.

As in the United States, the majority of all Canadian male inmates are single. The contrast with men in the general population is striking: 12 percent of prisoners are married, compared with 43 percent of non-offenders, whereas roughly 33 percent of prisoners have common-law unions, compared with 12 percent of non-offenders. Prisoners were also more likely to be separated from their partners: 6.4 percent versus 2.6 percent for non-offenders.

In both the United States and Canada, promoting higher education should be part of a concentrated effort to improve the lot of millions of citizens trapped in communities with inferior infrastructures and inadequate services. This is an obvious solution to end the plight of the poorly trained and unskilled. It will increase the chances of decent employment and decrease the draw of criminality. But this is far from all. Entire communities need infrastructural overhauling. Housing is an urgent problem. So are the needs of children without proper medical care and a host of other deprivations, including the absence of a stable, safe, and comfortable home.

Welfare and Marriage

Debates about welfare and its role in ushering out marriage as a way of life will continue to rage as the economy falters and people become increasingly desperate. Does welfare act as a deterrent to marriage and a catalyst for its breakdown? Does a sizeable percentage of the poorer classes view welfare as an alternative to marriage?

Research (and common sense) continues to show that low-waged earners approach welfare as an option, calculating its benefits and drawbacks relative to working for a small salary or combining households and expenses by marrying or cohabiting. Welfare income may even determine whether or not they divorce or have children. The closer welfare payments parallel wages, the likelier it is that welfare will encourage—or permit—women to divorce or to give birth to and keep children without marrying. This is partly because there is often little difference in living standard for those on welfare and those with full-time, low-waged employment.

Welfare rescues people from the consequences of financial disaster, but in terms of marriage, it has a negative effect. In tandem with an economy with great gaps between high- and low-wage earners, welfare does not give its recipients much incentive to return to ungratifying work that pays little more. As well, a plunge in marriage rate is heavily associated with those who are less well educated and poorly paid. Whether their poverty stems from surviving on welfare or on low wages, they are less likely to marry or to stay married.

Higher education, on the other hand, usually leads to satisfactory employment and, later, more stable marriage. Well-educated women will continue to marry and have children; their sustained education has not, despite the direst predictions, kept them single and childless. But men are no longer pursuing their education at the same rates as they did even two decades ago. If statistical models are correct, many immigrants and young men between eighteen and thirty-four seem destined for low-paying and insecure jobs, making them less obvious candidates for the marriage market.

Marriages rooted in financial struggle operate under strains that affect all aspects of the relationship, including child-rearing. Comfortable circumstances, on the other hand, offer much more satisfaction and, ultimately, stability. Yet today's unsettling demographic trends do not bode well for many of those who lack the training and education to secure good jobs. The current trend of more women but fewer men seeking higher education is troubling because of the strong relationship between education—and its concomitant financial rewards—and marriage. Also worrying is the high percentage of young men imprisoned in the United States and, to a lesser extent, in Canada. The man who cannot earn enough to support himself and contribute to a family has little to offer a prospective spouse. Educational deficits lead to unskilled jobs, underemployment, or unemployment, if not to crime, and to a serious reduction in the marriage market. North Americans must understand the relationship of all these factors as they map out policies designed to remedy them and to encourage people to marry and to raise their children in stable homes.

Chapter 12

Marriage and Race

In June 1958, two childhood sweethearts left their home state of Virginia and travelled to Washington, D.C., where they married. Mildred Jerer was eighteen, pregnant, and deeply in love with Richard Loving, her neighbour and friend since she was eleven. Richard knew what Mildred did not: that because of Virginia's Racial Integrity Act of 1924, they had to marry out of state. Mildred was a mixed-race African and Native American, and Richard was white. "We loved each other and got married," Mildred said. "We [were] not marrying the state. The law should allow a person to marry anyone he wants."[1]

In Virginia, however, the law allowed no such thing. Article 5 of the Act to Preserve Racial Integrity spelled it out: "It shall hereafter be unlawful for any white person in this State to marry any save a white person, or a person with no other admixture of blood than white and … one-sixteenth or less of the blood of the American Indian and have no other non-Caucasic blood." According to that law, Mildred and Richard had committed the crime of miscegenation.

After the Lovings returned home to Virginia, the local sheriff and his deputies strode into their bedroom one night and arrested them for violating the miscegenation law. They were pleaded guilty to cohabiting as man and wife and were sentenced to a year's imprisonment, suspended for twenty-five years if they moved out of the state. To avoid

*Mildred and Richard Loving. "He used to take care of me,"
Mildred recalled. "He was my support, he was my rock."*

prison, they moved back to D.C. and settled into married life and parenthood. But the couple missed visiting with their families, who had been their neighbours in Virginia. Mildred made a written complaint to Attorney General Robert Kennedy, and set in motion the legal marathon that would end in the U.S. Supreme Court. Before then, however, Virginia Supreme Court Justice Harry L. Carrico upheld the constitutionality of the 1924 law and the Lovings' criminal convictions under it.

"Almighty God created the races white, black, yellow, malay and red, and he placed them on separate continents," Carrico wrote in his judgment. "And but for the interference with his arrangement there would be no cause for such marriages. The fact that he separated the races shows that he did not intend for the races to mix." The Lovings appealed, and in 1967, the Supreme Court struck down centuries of miscegenation laws, arguing that racial distinctions were "designed to maintain White Supremacy" and were, therefore, "odious to a free people whose institutions are founded upon the doctrine of equality." Consequently Virginia's (and by extension all) miscegenation laws were "unsupportable" and unconstitutional.[2] A century after the Civil War ended slavery, marriage laws could no longer be wielded as weapons to segregate and subjugate black citizens.

White Supremacy across State Lines

The Lovings' home state of Virginia was a hotbed of white supremacist ideology with its associated terror of race mixing. Dr. Walter A. Plecker, a militant advocate of eugenics, was convinced that because of miscegenation, most Indians in Virginia were really mixed-race blacks trying to pass as white. "Like rats when you're not watching, [they] have been sneaking in their birth certificates through their own midwives, giving either Indian or white racial classification," he wrote.

As head of the Virginia Bureau of Vital Statistics, Plecker made it his life's vocation to enforce whatever draconian measures he considered necessary to halt the mongrelization of the white race. This included making sure that every child born in Virginia was registered, and that the "one drop" rule was rigorously enforced, especially by African-American midwives, who might "slip up" and register as white an infant contaminated with a drop of non-white blood.

Plecker's policies resulted in a "bureaucratic genocide" that classified Indian children as black on their birth certificates. He also "guessed" at non-white bloodlines and recorded his suspicions as documented fact. "This is to inform you that this is a mulatto child and you cannot pass it off as white," he informed one new mother. "You will have to ... see that this child is not allowed to mix with white children. It cannot go to white schools and can never marry a white person in Virginia." He told a Pennsylvania woman to forbid her daughter to marry her Virginian fiancé, whom he suspected of having black blood.[3] Another feature of his policy was the enforced sterilization of hundreds of mixed-race, Indian, and black women.

In 1932, Plecker gave a keynote address at the Third International Conference on Eugenics, in New York. One admirer was Germany's Ernst Rudin, a Nazi official researching strategies used by white supremacists elsewhere to exterminate racial impurity and who soon after helped draft Hitler's eugenics law. Plecker reciprocated the admiration. In 1935, on official letterhead, he wrote to Walter Gross at Germany's Bureau of Human Betterment and Eugenics, detailing Virginia's racial-purity laws and requesting that his name be included on the mailing list for bulletins. He also complimented Gross on the sterilization of six hundred children born in Algeria to German women and black men. "I hope this work is complete and not one has been missed," he wrote. "I sometimes regret that we have not the authority to put some measures in practice in Virginia."[4]

It is impossible to overstate the ferocity of white supremacist thinking and its profound influence on legislation. The Loving case is a striking example of how marriage, the organizing principle of society, has evolved as the product of official policy-making. In antiquity, as we saw in chapter 3, marriage developed as a contractual arrangement that ranged from the quasi purchase of a wife through a bride price to a verbal contract.

As Christianity rooted and matured, marriage became one of its seven sacraments, and the only one in which the consent of the two parties was essential, though priestly participation or religious invocation were not. As church—in the form of the Roman Catholic and, later, other Christian denominations—and state battled for control over it, the institution of marriage developed differently in different jurisdictions. Most notably, Reformation theologians denied that marriage was a sacrament, and the various Reformed rites developed their own characterizations. Lutherans, for example, deemed marriage a "social estate" and a secular matter,[5] Calvinists deemed it a "covenant" and Anglicans a "little commonwealth." By the eighteenth century, most Protestant churches revered it as the spiritual union of companions fulfilling their (gendered) Christian vocations.

In North America, the classic example of the influence of contemporary attitudes, values, and beliefs on policy-makers is how antebellum Southern states regulated slave marriage. Thanks to the racism that anchored slavery and white supremacy, whites in those states were expected to embrace Christian marriage but slaves were not allowed to. Acknowledging the legality of slave unions would—or at least could—have implied that a married slave was eligible for citizenship. That would, in turn, force masters to keep spouses and their children together rather than selling them off at will, and to admit that spouses on different properties had the right to visit each other. It would prevent lustful white males from sexually violating slave women. It would stop slave owners from undermining slave unions by depriving male slaves of the power to protect their wives, and those newly empowered black husbands would displace white owners who had usurped their role as the head of slave families.

Under the South's Black Codes, the state and local laws that restricted or denied the civil rights of African Americans, even slaves who married with their owner's permission had no legal recourse if, for instance, that

In 1917, the author's mother posed with her favourite toy, a black rag doll.
Black rag dolls were often white children's only exposure to another race.
In the South, black children forbidden to have white dolls played with
two-headed topsy-turvy rag dolls. When an overseer appeared, they flipped
the doll's long skirt over the white head, transforming her into a black doll.

owner's finances or attitude changed, or if he died and his heirs decided to sell off slave families in separate lots. A Freedmen's Bureau analysis of slave records showed that slave owners in Mississippi, Tennessee, and Louisiana, for example, destroyed 32 percent of 2,888 documented slave marriages by selling one or both spouses. The policy of depriving slaves of legal marriage was "one of the things that made them 'racially' different," writes historian Nancy Cott.[6]

After the Civil War, new laws reversed slave-era policies by recognizing the marriages of former slaves and legitimizing the children born to them. The Freedmen's Bureau went even further and urged unmarried ex-slaves to unite in monogamous Christian marriages, the moral influence of which would civilize them.

But in the postbellum frenzy, the push to coerce slaves into marrying had little to do with either religion or morality. Instead, it was part of a new policy designed to enable white men to recover much of the power they had lost in the Civil War, by establishing social and economic controls over freed blacks. Though freedmen celebrated their newly acquired right to marry, and many did so, new husbands often found themselves "aggressively" prosecuted and punished for violating marriage laws, including sexual infidelity. "Marriage laws were expressly deployed by the larger culture to discipline African Americans who failed 'to act like citizens,'" concludes historian Katherine Franke.[7]

Soul Wounds and Marriage

Once upon a time, North America's Natives lived and married on their own terms. Even after European settlers occupied their lands, they retained a degree of cultural autonomy. By the era of Reconstruction, however, white supremacist convictions also inspired an agenda of policies that, in both the United States and Canada, sought to eradicate Native culture, custom, religion, and language—killing the Indian soul in order to "civilize" the Indian people.[8]

This policy was inspired by Canada's 1857 Gradual Civilization Act, designed to assimilate Natives, and in the United States, by President Ulysses Grant's 1869 Peace Policy, which had the same objectives. But how to achieve this aggressive assimilation of so many people? The answer was to target Native children, removing them from their parents and raising them in church- or state-run residential or day schools where they would be taught to hate and forget all things Native and, at the same time, be indoctrinated in the colonial society's language, mores, and religion.[9]

U.S. Indian Affairs commissioner Thomas Jefferson Morgan put it more bluntly: "We must either fight Indians, feed them, or else educate them. To fight them is cruel, to feed them is wasteful, while to educate them is humane, economic, and Christian."[10] The schools established to accomplish this, operated by an alliance of government and religious establishments—in Canada, the Roman Catholic, Anglican, Methodist (later United), and Presbyterian churches—would not merely educate, acculturate, and Christianize Native children. They would also, declared Canadian Nicholas Flood Davin in his influential *Report on Industrial Schools for Indians and Half-Breeds* (1879), provide the "care of a mother."[11]

Native boys at St. Cyprian's Residential School, Brocket, Alberta, ca. 1920.

Some mother! Children as young as five were forced into church-run boarding schools or day schools where they endured a litany of abuses: overwork, hunger, "unmonitored and unchecked physical and sexual aggression." Lakota survivor Mary Crow Dog lamented: "It is almost impossible to explain to a sympathetic white person what a typical old Indian boarding school was like; how it affected the Indian child suddenly dumped into it like a small creature from another world, help-less, defenseless, bewildered, trying desperately and instinctively to survive it all."[12]

Sick, alienated, abandoned, and mistreated, the children died in droves. Duncan Campbell Scott, a senior official in Canada's Indian Affairs Department, estimated that, system-wide, "fifty per cent of the children who passed through these schools did not live to benefit from

The campaign to "kill the Indian spirit" used photography to compare Natives before and after they were forced to assimilate into white culture. In the early 1900s, Cheyenne Woxie Haury was photographed in Native and Western wedding dresses. On the right, in a boned bodice, she stands next to her husband.

the education which they had received therein." *Saturday Night* magazine lamented that "even war seldom shows as large a percent of fatalities as the education system we have imposed upon our Indian wards."[13]

In 2001, Canada's Truth Commission into Genocide documented more than 50,000 deaths among an estimated 150,000 Native children in the residential school system, killed by starvation, beating, poisoning, electric shock, prolonged exposure to sub-zero cold while naked, and medical experimentation that included surgical organ removal. Native girls were sterilized, sometimes en masse. Their infants, born after priests or staff raped them, were murdered. Runaways were common, and countless died trying to reach home. Some committed suicide or tried to; as late as June 1981, a group of little girls tried to hang themselves with socks and towels tied together.

By 1920, these schools were compulsory, and priests, Indian agents, and police officers worked in tandem to snatch children from families who refused to surrender them or who tried to hide their little ones. By 1931, Canada had eighty residential schools, the United States nearly five hundred, most church-run. Some children thrived in the schools and assimilated to white culture, but most survivors returned to their parents as strangers, communicating with difficulty in forgotten mother tongues, traumatized by sexual assault or relentless punishment, depressed, despairing, damaged.

Survivors were haunted by feelings of worthlessness and of abandonment because their parents had failed to protect them. "I always hated my mother," recalled Margaret Supernault. "Until her dying day I asked her 'Why did you do this to me?' and she could never answer me because she was also brought up in a mission." Mothers and fathers, in turn, welcomed the returnees back to broken homes where, bereft, crushed, and bitter, they had increasingly resorted to the solace of alcohol and drugs. The children were foreigners, raised in loveless hostility and taught to hate everything Native. Their Native parents had lost their experience of parenting, and could not communicate with their estranged offspring.

In "killing the Indian in the child," the residential school policy succeeded in its goal, "severing the artery of culture that ran between generations and was the profound connection between parent and child sustaining family and community," the 1996 Royal Commission on Aboriginal People concluded.

Cultural anomie is not the only cancer. The toxic effects of endemic sexual abuse of both boys and girls continue to reverberate. The Aboriginal Healing Foundation describes the consequences: "The unresolved trauma of Aboriginal people who experienced or witnessed physical or sexual abuse in the resident school system is passed on from generation to generation. The ongoing cycle of intergenerational abuse in Aboriginal communities is the legacy of physical and sexual abuse in residential schools."[14]

Martha Joseph and her little sister endured twelve years of abuse, including rape, at British Columbia's Alberni Indian residential school. After six years at Alberni, Martha returned home, alienated and angry with her parents. "I didn't know them and I didn't care," she said. "All the feeling I had for my mum was taken away." Willie Blackwater, raped by dormitory supervisor Arthur Henry Plint, suffered "the worst pain I ever felt in my life." Wounded, hating, Blackwater blamed his father as well as Plint. "I hated my dad. I blamed him for allowing me to go to residential school. I blamed him for letting me be raped and everything," he said. "And it wasn't until later, in the last five years of his life, that I found out he had no choice in the matter."[15] Survivor Bill Seward's poignant observation—"How does a man who was raped every day when he was seven make anything out of his life? The residential schools were set up to destroy our lives, and they succeeded"[16]—is a succinct and profoundly sad summation.

The intergenerational impact of the children's years in residential schools was fully felt when, in their late teens, they returned home for good, minimally trained to hold a job, psychologically disturbed, emotionally shut down, and devoid of parenting skills. Many were unable to receive or to give love. But the schools had sexualized them, and they married and had children.

"Not surprisingly," writes psychiatrist Charles Brasfield, who treats survivors, "they had difficulty parenting those children. They tended to parent as they had been parented in the [residential schools]. That is, they punished their own children physically for misbehaving, and in many cases, treated them as sexual objects.... This whole pattern was repeated for generations."[17]

Aboriginal leaders speak out as well. In 1992, Grand Chief Edward John of the First Nations task force group said in a statement to Justice Minister Kim Campbell: "We are hurt, devastated and outraged. The effect of the Indian residential school system is like a disease ripping through our communities." Other Natives refer to it as their unhealed "soul wound."

In 2008, Canadian prime minister Stephen Harper formally apologized for the residential school system and its hellish legacies. Harper acknowledged the systemic abuses and said, in part: "We now recognize that, in separating children from their families, we undermined the ability of many to adequately parent their own children and sowed the seeds for generations to follow, and we apologize for having done this.... Not only did you suffer these abuses as children, but as you became parents, you were powerless to protect your own children from suffering the same experience, and for this we are sorry."

There is much to sorrow over. After a century of destructive policies, Native communities are fragile and in need of healing. They are more youthful than others: in both Canada and the United States, over half of Aboriginals are under twenty-five, a strong contingent for marriage. Yet in that same age range, their respective alcohol-related deaths and suicide rates are seventeen and three times higher than the national averages, and they have the highest rate of sexually transmitted infections. Over 60 percent of Indian women have suffered sexual violence, and Status indigenous women between the ages of twenty-five and forty-four have a 500 percent greater chance than all other women of dying violently.[18] Aboriginal educational results are improving too slowly: in Canada, 43 percent have not completed high school; in the United States it's over 30 percent. Nearly half of Natives in urban areas live in one-parent homes, and a majority of all Natives live in poverty.

The litany of sad statistics quantify what Prime Minister Harper described as "the burden of this [residential school] experience" that continues to victimize Native communities and relations between men, women, and their children. It is the cause of that people's failed family life, once notable for its respect for women's "separate but equal" status and their presence in governance, ceremonial life, and trade, as well as indulgent child-rearing and the absence of domestic violence. The policy that conceived residential schools was indeed a soul wound and, until it is cauterized and healed, it will continue to fester and make entire communities strangers to the intimacy, love, and caring that are at the foundation of solid relationships and parenting.

NATIVE MARRIAGE AND STATUS

The residential schools policy was not the only one designed to assimilate Natives. In 1876, Canada's amended Indian Act of 1868 drastically changed the nature of Native marriage by linking it with status. The criterion was patrilineality, which was consistent with *couverture*, the legal concept that a wife's legal existence was merged with her breadwinner husband's.

Translated into the realm of Native marriage, this new policy meant that the Status woman, for example the Cree who married a Status Mohawk, became Mohawk as well, but if she then divorced, not only would she lose her Mohawk status but she would not be reinstated as Cree unless she remarried a Cree. The Native woman who married a non-Native man lost her tribal status, including the right to live on her reserve or own property there. She could no longer participate in her band's government, services, and programs, and her legally non-Native children were also excluded. If she fell ill, separated or divorced, or was widowed, she had no right to return to the reserve. When she died, she could not be buried there with her ancestors. The non-Native woman who married a Native man, on the other hand, gained all those same rights, and so did her legally Native children.

In 1951, the Indian Act was again amended to establish a centralized registry. In the spirit of the previous policy, and despite decades of protests, this registry embraced non-Native women married to Native men, and also their children; at the same time, it continued to exclude Native women married to non-Native men. They had to suffer the grief of banishment from their family home and community, a personal heartache and a heavy weight on any marriage. Even if that marriage failed or ended, the ban was implacable.

In the energized and reform-minded 1970s, Native women and their allies launched a series of legal challenges. Jeannette Vivian Corbiere was a Nishnawbe woman from the Wikwemiking Reserve on Manitoulin Island in Ontario and a founding member of the Ontario Native Women's Association. In 1970, soon after she married David Lavell, a non-Native, the Department of Indian Affairs and Northern Development notified her that, in accordance with section 12(1)(b) of the Indian Act, she was no longer considered an Indian. Jeannette appealed the decision, but York County Court Judge Ben Grossberg upheld it, ruling that by marrying out, she had gained more than she lost, having gained equal rights with Canadian women even though she lost Native status. Jeanette appealed again and, in 1971, the Federal Court of Appeal ruled in her favour on the grounds that the Indian Act contravened the Bill of Rights by granting different rights, rather than equality, to men and women.

Thanks to pressure from the federal government and also such Native organizations as the National Indian Brotherhood, which claimed that reserve chiefs and band councils and not Canadian courts had the right to decide Indian status, Lavell's victory was short-lived. Her case—and that of Yvonne Bedard, an Iroquois who married out, lost her status, then was evicted by her band council after she separated from her husband and moved back to her own home on the reserve—was appealed to the Supreme Court. On August 27, 1973, that court ruled, in a split decision with four of nine judges dissenting, that the Bill of Rights did not apply to that particular section of the Indian Act.

The issues at the heart of the Lavell and Bedard cases polarized Native communities, with gender defining the fault lines. Because the protesting women were appealing to the Bill of Rights, Native men accused them of complicity with Canada's racist and assimilationist policies, of undermining Native rights to self-government, and of being not just non-Indian but anti-Indian. They also damned Lavell and Bedard for being "women's libbers" out to force bands into compliance with an ideology they demonized as based on "selfish individualism and personal entitlement." Concludes Native scholar Joanne Barker: "Indian women's experiences, perspectives, and political agendas for reform were perceived as not only irrelevant but dangerous to Indian sovereignty movements."[19]

In a twisted turn of events, the National Indian Brotherhood and band councils found more common ground with federal government Indian policy than with Indian women. As scholar and chief of the Indian Association of Alberta Harold Cardinal explained: "We do not want the Indian Act retained because it is a good piece of legislation It isn't. It is discriminatory from start to finish. But it is a lever in our hands and an embarrassment to the government, as it should be.... We would rather continue to live in bondage under the inequitable Indian Act than surrender our sacred rights. Any time the government wants to honour its obligations to us we are more than ready to help devise new Indian legislation."[20]

Sandra Lovelace, a Maliseet woman, was one victim of the amended Indian Act. In 1979, after her marriage to a non-Native failed, Lovelace returned to New Brunswick's Tobique Reserve. After she and her children were denied the housing, education, and health care the Indian Act made available to Status Indians, Lovelace appealed to the United Nations Human Rights Commission. The commission proceeded slowly, even reluctantly, in the case of *Lovelace v. Canada*, and rendered its decision in 1981: because Lovelace had lost her Indian status and was denied the rights and privileges of membership in her band, Canada was in breach of Article 27, the International Covenant on Civil and Political Rights: "In those States in which ethnic, religious or linguistic minorities exist, persons belonging to such minorities shall not be denied the right, in community with the other members of their group, to enjoy their own culture, to profess and practice their own religion, or to use their own language."

Canada's Department of Indian Affairs respected the U.N. ruling by granting exemption from discriminatory clauses in the Indian Act to bands that requested it. Then, in 1985, against the opposition of many male-dominated band councils, Parliament revised the Indian Act so that Native women who married non-Native men would not lose their status, nor would their children.

But Bill C-31 was cautiously drafted. By retaining the full status of Indian men and their wives and children, but reinstating Indian women to a diminished status, it allows these women to pass on their status to their children but not to their grandchildren. Only claimants who can prove they have two parents entitled to Indian status (and this includes non-Native wives married to Status husbands before 1985) are registered under Section 6(1) of the Indian Act and can pass their status on to their children; those with only one Status parent are registered under Section 6(2) and can pass on their status only if they marry a Status Indian.

When British Columbia law student Sharon McIvor, whose ex-husband was a non-Indian, requested Status registration for herself and her children, she but not her children received it. McIvor asked for a review of this decision. In 1989, nearly two years later, the decision was upheld, and McIvor launched a legal challenge to the Indian Act.

McIvor's story was an ironic illustration of the complex and discriminatory nature of the Indian Act. Her grandmother, Mary Thom, was a Status Indian who married out, so that her daughter, Susan Blankenship (Sharon's mother), lived and died without status but was reinstated posthumously, after the Bill C-31 amendment of 1985. Because Sharon's father was a Non-Status Indian, she, too, had no right to status until 1985.

In her quest for birthright, Sharon McIvor became the torchbearer for an estimated 300,000 Native women, and in the seventeen years before her case was heard, mobilized a wellspring of support. Just before the case went to the B.C. Supreme Court in 2006, the federal government agreed to restore status to one of her sons. But it relegated another son to 6(2) status, unable to pass status on to his children unless he marries another Status Indian.

McIvor testified in court about her family's "hurt and stigmatization" because they lacked status cards. They had to harvest berries and roots and hunt or fish clandestinely, though these were traditional activities. When her children attended the annual aboriginal Christmas party, "there were no presents under the community tree for them because they were Non-status Indians.... When my children graduated [from high school], there were no recognition ceremonies for them because they are Non-status Indians." Yet though one of McIvor's brothers also married out, the amended Indian Act granted his children full status that they can pass on to their children.

Madam Justice Carol Ross agreed with McIvor's arguments. "I have concluded that the registration provisions embodied in [Section 6] of the 1985 Indian Act continue the very discrimination that the amendments were intended to eliminate," she wrote. "The evidence of the plaintiffs is that the inability to be registered with full 6(1)(a) status because of the sex of one's parents or grandparents is insulting and hurtful and implies that one's female ancestors are deficient or less Indian than their male contemporaries.... The implication for an Indian woman is that she is inferior, less worthy of recognition." Judge Ross added, "It seems to me that it is one of our most basic expectations that we will acquire the cultural identity of our parents; and that as parents, we will transmit our cultural identity to our children."[21]

The federal government appealed and lost. In April 2009, in a unanimous ruling, the B.C. Court of Appeal gave the government one year to amend the two sections of the Indian Act that violate equality provisions of the Charter of Rights. Sharon McIvor and her supporters were finally vindicated. This decision will affect hundreds of thousands.

Two crucial issues dominate the case. The first is that because at least half of Canadian Natives marry non-Natives, many more Native women will be able to pass on their status to their children. The second is that this compulsory striking down of the gender discrimination at the heart of the Indian Act will allow Native communities to recreate a more authentic culture that respects women's roles in band councils, trade, and celebrations and as wives in "separate but equal" marriages, traditions that crumbled under the assault of conquest and the assimilationist policies that gave birth to residential schools and the Indian Act. Children, once seen as "gifts from the spirit world ... [who] have to be treated very gently lest they become disillusioned with this world and return to a more congenial place," will resume their "special place" in their society, renewing "the strength of the family, clan and village and mak[ing] the elders young again with their joyful presence."[22]

Despite the racism that demeaned Natives and deprived them of opportunities except on the reserves, federal government policy "elevated and empowered" Native men at the expense of Native women. The consequence was that the marriage relationship took on the same gender inequalities and imbalances.

COME ONE, NOT ALL

Immigration policy was an often used vehicle to manipulate and control the marriages—hence the lives—of immigrants of colour. In the early twentieth century, the North American West was open for economic and agricultural development, and developers looked to East Asia for a cheap, reliable labour pool. The first immigrant workers were Chinese, who worked as cheaply and reliably as expected. But, to ensure that whites retained their demographic primacy in stocking the American nation, government policies permitted very few Chinese women to enter the country. Before long, lonely Chinese workers were portrayed in the popular press as lascivious drug users who lusted after white women. The few Chinese women immigrants were depicted as harlots intent on corrupting white men.

The hostility to Chinese immigrants grew so strong that it created a racial panic. This in turn produced the United States' 1882 Chinese Exclusion Act, featuring a ten-year exclusion of "skilled and unskilled laborers and Chinese employed in mining," and other rigid restrictions, with prison and deportation the penalty for violations. One consequence was that Chinese males resident in the United States could neither send for their wives nor establish new families with Chinese women.

Canada's official policy was nearly identical. Although the nation-building Canadian Pacific Railway depended largely on imported Chinese labourers—seventeen thousand between 1880 and 1885—anti-Chinese prejudice was rampant. The Chinese were paid half-wages, and after they were no longer needed, the government imposed a head tax of $50—increased in 1900 to $100, then to $500 in 1903—to discourage them from immigrating to Canada. This policy raked $23 million into the federal government's coffers until the next labour shortage occurred, whereupon both Chinese and Japanese workers were again invited to Canada. Then, on July 1, 1923, Dominion Day for Canadians but "humiliation day" for the Chinese, Canada passed its own Chinese Exclusion Act. This act applied to all ethnic Chinese and remained in force until 1947; it was so effective that Canada accepted only 12 Chinese immigrants in that period, while 61,213 registered to return to China.[23]

As in the United States, Canada's exclusionary policies effectively prevented the mainly male Chinese community from marrying. The prohibitive head tax meant that husbands intending to send for their wives could never save enough money to do so, and few bachelors could find wives in communities with a ratio of one woman to ten men. Thomas MacInnes, a proponent of an apartheid-like segregation of Canada's Asians, justified the government's exclusionary policies in his 1927 book, *Oriental Occupation of British Columbia*:

> *It may be very right indeed to separate a man by law from his wife and family if he belongs to a race whose increase in the country would be disastrous to those already in occupation of it; especially if such intruding race be very prolific and very difficult to assimilate; and by reason of a more meagre standard of living capable of undoing the masses of those to whom such a country belongs. But aside from all that, the Chinese cannot rightly be said to be separated by any Canadian law from their wives and children in China. They are free to go back to their wives and children any time, and God speed them!*[24]

The next wave of Asian immigration was from Japan. The Japanese, too, were denigrated as debauched, but immigration regulations permitted Japanese women to join their men. The official rationale behind this revised policy was that the availability of Japanese women would keep Japanese men away from white women, and together they would establish families and provide a cheap labour pool for the exuberantly expanding West. Married men sent for their wives, and some bachelors invested in a trip back to Japan to find one. But the cost of the voyages was prohibitive, and men remaining in Japan for more than thirty days risked conscription into the army. The safest, most sensible solution was to find a "picture bride."

Between 1910 and 1920, about half the Japanese brides who immigrated into the United States were picture brides whose families had responded to the expatriate Japanese requests for wives. Traditional matchmakers used the new technology of photography to match up couples continents apart. Heads of households did the selecting, looking at daguerreotypes and photographs but also weighing the more important criteria of family genealogy and fortune, education and health, and the men's lives and prospects in the United States or elsewhere. Matchmakers facilitated discussions between the families, who agreed on the marriages without meeting the absent groom. The couple then became engaged and, despite the husband's absence from his own wedding, married. These weddings were legal as long as the groom's family entered his bride's name in the family registry.

Most picture brides went to the West Coast, where they spent their first days in California's Angel Island Immigration Station undergoing physical exams and treatment for endemic hookworm. They also experienced their first taste of racial discrimination as officials disparaged their Shinto religion and proselytized for Christianity and American-style marriages.

After meeting their husbands, many picture brides were distressed to discover that their families had been given flattering, out-of-date photographs and false information. Their new mates were all too often struggling labourers who, because of anti-Japanese legislation, were legally forbidden to buy land. Failed marriages were common as the brides realized they could support themselves or find better men. The runaway picture bride became a media fixture, and newspapers gleefully reported the details of how picture brides were murdered by jealous husbands.

Most picture brides went to the West Coast, where they spent their first days in California's Angel Island Immigration Station.

Anti-Japanese spokesmen also alleged that picture brides produced five times the children that white women did. In 1919, Senator James Phelan testified to the House Committee on Immigration that, as part of a "plot" to saturate the United States with Japanese, every picture bride delivered a child within a year of landing. In this tense atmosphere of official and cultural prejudice, and often married to unsatisfactory husbands, Japanese picture brides struggled to build tolerable lives in their difficult new world.

Marriage American-style was both a metaphor for citizenship and a tool used to shape residents and immigrants into American citizens. White supremacist notions and a collective fear or hatred of Asians shaped policies that affected every aspect of their lives, including whom, how, and whether they married.

For centuries, racism and white supremacist ideologies permeated North America's official policies pertaining to people of colour: the imported Africans and their descendants, the Natives who had been colonized, the Asians invited to come as cheap labourers. In both Canada and the United States, those policies closely resembled each other, to the degree that some laws—for example, the Chinese Exclusion Act—had identical titles. As well, they were all used as vehicles to manipulate and control the marriages, and thereby the lives, of slaves, citizens, Natives, and immigrants of colour.

Chapter 13

Marriage Policies

Battered Brides

On March 9, 1977, in Michigan, Francine Hughes rushed her four young children outside to the car and told them to stay there. Next she went to the garage, got a gas can, and took it into the ground-floor bedroom of the house where her husband, Mickey, lay in a drunken stupor. Francine poured gasoline on and around the bed, set it on fire, then raced back to her children. As the house burned to the ground, killing Mickey, she drove to the sheriff's office and confessed.

In 1963, when she'd met James "Mickey" Hughes at a school dance, Francine was fifteen; they fell in love, and married a few months later, after she turned sixteen. Almost from the first, and whether or not he was drunk, Mickey slapped, kicked, beat, choked, and burned his young wife, even during her four pregnancies. He also taunted, humiliated, and threatened her, kicked one of the babies, and tormented the pets she and the children loved so much. When Lady, the family dog, was struggling to give birth, Mickey refused to allow them to help and locked the animal outside in the freezing weather, where she froze to death. He also wrenched a cat from his youngest daughter's arms and wrung its neck, killing it.

Francine often left him, once for six months, during which he stalked and threatened her. In 1971 she divorced him, but, after he was severely injured in a suicidal car accident, she returned to him, moving in next

*James Gillray's 1782 sketch mocks harsh judge Francis Buller, carrying bundles of
rods and saying, "Who wants a cure for a rusty Wife? Here's your nice Family
Amusement for Winter Evenings! Who buys here?" while a woman screams,
"Help! Murder for God's sake, Murder!" as a man with a rod gets ready to strike
her and shouts: "Murder, Hey? It's Law you Bitch! It's not bigger than my
thumb." Gillray implies that Buller agrees that the law permitted a husband to
thrash his wife if the stick was no bigger than his thumb.*

door so she could help his mother care for him. Mickey's accident had
left him unfit to work but well enough to spend his days in a bar, drinking and brooding. On his last day of life, Francine returned from a class
at the business college where she was studying in preparation for leaving
him for good, and served him a TV dinner. Furious at such poor fare,
Mickey flung it onto the ground, ordered her to clean it up, then
rubbed the sticky mess into her face and hair. After slapping and kicking

her, he forced her to burn her school notes and textbooks and instructed her to quit school. When she argued, he beat her again, and their twelve-year-old daughter called the police.

Even after the police arrived, Mickey threatened to kill Francine, but, as had happened so often before, they decided against arresting him. After the officers left after declining to help her, Francine torched Mickey's bed and killed him. In a trial that had enormous repercussions, she was acquitted of first-degree murder on the grounds that she had dispatched Mickey Hughes while temporarily insane.

PUBLIC POLICY ABOUT SPOUSAL ABUSE

Just as white supremacist and other racialist visions have suffused public policies about marriage, so have contemporary standards and values—and prejudices and obsessions—about a vast array of other issues, including the right not to be battered.

In *Public Vows: A History of Marriage and the Nation*, historian Nancy Cott describes how, in the era of the Revolution and its aftermath, marriage was a living metaphor for the republic, constructed on voluntary consent with mutually accepted gender roles in which the husband's rationality complemented the wife's passions. In British North America, where English common law also prevailed, this gendered arrangement was seen as the way marriages should operate. One consequence was the husband's right, even responsibility, for "correcting" his wife, including with physical force.

(A brief exception was the pre-Revolutionary Puritan colonies, where civil authorities mediated domestic disputes and undertook any corrections, and specifically prohibited husbands from whipping or inflicting "stripes" on their wives. After the Revolution, however, "American reversion to a Common Law standard ... put the stick back in the husband's hand so that each man might keep his own house in order," notes Ann Jones in *Women Who Kill.*[1])

The right to "correct" was spelled out in the law. In 1824, for example, the Mississippi Supreme Court decreed that a husband had the right to chastise his wife moderately "without subjecting himself to vexatious prosecutions for assault and battery, resulting in the discredit and shame of all parties concerned." In the mid-nineteenth century, a North Carolina court went further: the state must not "invade the domestic forum or go behind the curtain" but instead "leave the parties to themselves, as the best mode of inducing them to make the matter up and live together as man and wife should." The court also confirmed a husband's right to chastise without any state intervention unless "some permanent injury be inflicted or there be an excess of violence."[2]

But despite euphemistic references to husbandly "corrections," and lofty political metaphors, the reality was that wife battering was a real though unacknowledged problem. At the end of the nineteenth century, official policies denounced the changing attitudes toward the "revolting precedent" that had formerly allowed the husband "to teach the wife her duty and subjection.... to beat her with a stick, to pull her hair, choke her, spit in her face or kick her about the floor, or to inflict upon her other like indignities."[3]

Concern in the last third of the nineteenth century about this now disowned "domestic tyranny" also led to the establishment of 494 child-protection and anti-cruelty societies to care for abused women and children. The widespread belief that alcohol was linked to spousal abuse prompted several states to enact laws allowing wives to sue saloon keepers for abuses inflicted by a drunken husband.

But in the twentieth century, reformers who lobbied for more effective legislation to deal with spousal abuse encountered a number of obstacles: Freudian-influenced interpretations of violent behaviour that blamed victims as much as perpetrators, the ideal of keeping families intact, and fears that interventions largely targeted the poor. From the mid-1950s onward, as civil rights and anti-war sentiments challenged the status quo, this began to change. Perceptions altered, so that wife murder, for example, was seen as domestic violence rather than the criminal act of one berserk individual.

But hidebound attitudes changed only slowly and fitfully. On the one hand, Betty Friedan's apocalyptic *The Feminine Mystique* (1963) was the articulation of a generation of house-bound middle-class women's *cri de cœur* about their profound dissatisfaction. On the other

The "Holy War" was the nineteenth-century crusade for temperance and prohibition. Here, armour-clad women shatter barrels of spirits—the "Enemy's Works." The leg of a fleeing man is just visible at lower right. In the background are two banners: "In the Name of God and Humanity" and "Temperance League."

hand, three physicians involved in diagnosing thirty-seven men charged with assaulting their wives in Framingham, Massachusetts, set out to write a book about wife batterers but instead wrote "The Wifebeater's Wife" (1964), the victims easier and more cooperative subjects than their violent and uncommunicative husbands. Published in the *Archives of General Psychiatry*, "The Wifebeater's Wife" reported that battered wives often sought outside help at an adolescent child's request, and thereby disturbed "marital equilibrium which had been working more or less satisfactorily."[4] Battered wives, these medical experts concluded, "have a masochistic need that the husbands' aggression fulfils."[5]

No wonder, then, that even changed laws did not mean enforced laws, if experts implied that wife beating was not really criminal assault but merely an overly strong expression of frustration and anger. Why not just summon experts to talk and mediate things out? Surely angry husbands, even violent ones, shouldn't be arrested like common criminals. True, domestic squabbles sometimes escalate rather scarily, but how much nicer to psychoanalyze and resolve the issue at home than to arrest the wife beater.

A debate along these lines kept real reform at bay until the battered women's movement began to publicize the issue and made battering a public problem, "reframing the violence as an act of injustice perpetrated by men against their wives and girlfriends," writes sociologist Gretchen Arnold. "It is the complicity of our institutions in this behavior that condones and reinforces it. While individual wife beaters are responsible for choosing their behavior ... society shares responsibility for stopping it [by] ... changing state laws and training law enforcement officers at all levels."[6]

People began to absorb these new ideas, and women had to learn to identify themselves as battered. But that was not easy to do when 1975's Nobel Peace Prize went to Eisaku Sato, former prime minister of Japan, whose wife noted, "Yes, he's a good husband, he only beats me once a week." In the same year, *Vogue* magazine's December issue featured a pummelled model grimacing in pain, wearing a jumpsuit that could "really take the heat." And on wildly popular sitcoms, *I Love Lucy*'s Ricky Ricardo turned his wife over his knee and spanked her, while on almost every episode of *The Honeymooners*, Ralph Kramden balled his huge fist at his wife, shouting, "To the moon, Alice, to the moon!" or "One of these days, Alice, one of these days. Pow! Right in the kisser!"

Strong institutional responses supported changed policies that had begun in the 1970s. Shelters offered emergency care for battered women and their children: Los Angeles's Haven House was North America's first, in 1964. In 1974, Toronto's Interval House and Vancouver's Transition House were Canada's. New laws allowed battered wives to bring criminal actions against their husbands. The United States' first legal centre for battered women, in Chicago, provided legal assistance.

In the mid-twentieth century, Chase & Sanborn promoted its coffee with this ad. Until recently, spanking was a common advertising device, though most ads featured irate mothers spanking their sons.

Battered women in California could claim compensation for their injuries. Slowly, the notion of marital rape gained credence and was written into laws as an assault. Literature by and about battered wives flooded shelters and bookstores, and popular women's magazines carried articles about domestic violence. Del Martin's 1976 *Battered Wives*, a powerful and popular book, argued forcefully that sexism was at the root of violence against women. The term "battered women" entered the public consciousness. "Battered spouse" and "battered woman" also gained scientific credibility and were added as categories to the World Health Organization's International Classification of Diseases. Battered women's syndrome became a legal defence for abused women who killed their abuser.

But Francine Hughes's 1977 trial, which became a *cause célèbre* for battered women, did not test it. Instead, her attorney chose the time-tested and safe defence of temporary insanity and successfully argued that Mickey's battering, rather than any female predisposition, caused Francine to go to pieces. Afterward, the judge expressed regret that the trial had not focused on the real issue—that "we have thousands of people who have had no recourse under the law. Where are we when these people are crying out for help? Self-defense is a real issue, but it was never really covered in the trial."[7]

Because Francine's lawyer had avoided the controversial issue of self-defence, her victory held out little promise of great change. At the same time, her acquittal led to gruesome predictions about killing sprees as vengeful women dispatched their men. There was a ferocious backlash. An especially egregious example came from the Chattanooga, Tennessee, trial of Lillian Quarles, who had killed her husband as he smashed her with a chair. Quarles pleaded self-defence and also gave evidence that for the past fifteen years he had beaten her so savagely that he broke her vertebrae and ribs, triggered premature childbirth, and caused her to lose her sight in one eye. The judge agreed that Lillian had been battered but decided, with zero evidence, that her husband had been battered as well. He warned the accommodating jury that acquitting Lillian would set a "dangerous precedent" and, as he sentenced her to ten years in prison for second-degree murder, declared, "This battered wife syndrome is just another cause, just a new word for your old fighting couple."[8]

In 1978, a like-minded Indiana prosecutor, James Kizer, charged a wife killer with manslaughter rather than murder even though a witness had seen the accused beating and kicking and raping her as she lay dying. "He didn't mean to kill her," Kizer said. "He just meant to give her a good thumping."[9]

Feminists and legal scholars thought they had a test case for battered women in the case of Roxanne Gay, who slit her husband Blenda's throat with an eight-inch kitchen knife as he lay sleeping. Roxanne was a five-foot-one, 106-pound mother of an infant daughter, Blenda a six-five, 225-pound defensive lineman for the Philadelphia Eagles.

Neighbours testified that whenever the Eagles lost a game, Blenda would pound his tiny wife against the walls of their house. During their three-and-a-half-year marriage, she had been hospitalized once, signed then dropped a complaint against him, and called the police at least twenty times pleading for help after being beaten.

But despite a defence committee with such prominent supporters as Gloria Steinem, Roxanne's claim that she was battered dissolved as four male psychiatrists engaged by Blenda's family testified that she "suffered from delusions that her husband, her family and police were plotting to kill her." She was subjected to a sanity hearing and diagnosed as a paranoid schizophrenic. Murder charges were dropped, and Roxanne Gay was incarcerated in a New Jersey state hospital for the insane.

For all the legal caution and fear, for all the editorial panic about the imminent demise of battering men, battered women found some strong supporters. A growing body of research dispelled many of the myths about them: they were not masochists, and many managed to consult lawyers and afterward decided to divorce. Surprisingly, like Francine Hughes, 80 percent of battered women had already divorced. In the popular press, these women found another strong supporter in the advice queen Ann Landers. To a man arguing that suicidal battered husbands needed shelters, Landers gave a no-nonsense response: "I'm sure more men beat up their wives than the other way around, but if you think there is a need for a Shelter for Battered Husbands, gather together those of like mind and get one going. I'm working the other side of the street, Mister."[10]

The other side of the street finally had a legal triumph in the Washington Supreme Court's 1977 retrial of Yvonne Wanrow's 1974 conviction for second-degree murder and first-degree assault with a deadly weapon. Wanrow was represented by feminist attorneys Elizabeth Schneider of New York's Center for Constitutional Rights, Susan B. Jordan of San Francisco, and Mary Alice Theiler from Seattle. The case ended with a landmark ruling: Wanrow had the right to have a jury use gender-neutral language and to consider her actions "in the light of her perceptions of the situation, including those perceptions which were the product of our nation's long and unfortunate history of sex discrimination. Until such time as the effects of that history are erad-icated, care must be taken to assure that our self-defense instructions afford women the right to have their conduct judged in light of the indi-vidual physical handicaps which are the product of sex discrimination. To fail to do so is to deny the right of the individual woman involved to trial by the same rules which are applicable to male defendants."

Wanrow was five-four and on crutches; the victim, William Wesler, was a drunken six-foot-two man known as a mentally unbalanced pedophile who had just dragged her seven-year-old son off his bicycle and into a house (the boy escaped and ran to tell his mother). Wanrow's perception of the danger Wesler posed to her son was crucial to her defence; her lawyers from the Center for Constitutional Rights argued successfully that "failure to apply such individualized standard was prej-udicial to all women claiming self-defense." The court also noted: "In our society women suffer from a conspicuous lack of access to training in and the means of developing those skills necessary to effectively repel a male assailant without resorting to the use of deadly weapons."[11] (Wanrow pleaded guilty to reduced charges of manslaughter and second-degree assault. She was sentenced to five years' probation.)

The Wanrow decision was the first time a U.S. court recognized the unique legal problems of women who defend themselves or their chil-dren from male attackers, and it justified their resort to self-defence when, from their perspective, they were in danger. The concept of women's equality, including when it is separate but equal, as in Wanrow's case, was changing the face of marital relationships by intro-ducing new standards of behaviour and legal rights. For the first time, the perspective of gender was introduced into legal standards for self-defence. Historically, self-defence evoked images of a male soldier or a man defending his home, his family, his woman. As attorneys Elizabeth Schneider and Susan Jordan explained, "The body of law, made by men, for men, and amassed down through history on their behalf, codifies masculine bias and systematically discriminates against women by ignoring the woman's point of view."[12]

In 1990, in the *R. v. Lavallee*, Madam Justice Bertha Wilson of Canada's Supreme Court also cited *State v. Wanrow* as a "helpful" precedent "in illustrating how the factor of gender can be germane to the assessment of what is reasonable," specifically "the reasonableness of the female appellant's use of a gun against an unarmed intruder."[13] ("God made men and women equal and Smith and Wesson makes damn sure it stays that way," a Smith and Wesson ad declares. A U.S. bumper sticker dissents: "God didn't create men and women equal. Samuel Colt did.") After Manitoban Angélique Lyn Lavallee shot her abusive common-law husband in the back of the head, the Manitoba Court of Appeal ruled that at her original acquittal, psychiatric evidence should not have been admitted. Justice Wilson, writing for the Supreme Court, disagreed. "We need help to understand [the so-called 'battered wife syndrome'] and help is available from trained professionals," she explained.[14] That help included debunking the common assumption that battered women either exaggerate their injuries or else stay with their abusers because they are masochistic and enjoy the beatings.

Justice Wilson saw the Lavallee appeal as an excellent chance to review "aspects of the law that needed to be rethought from a gender perspective and ... to begin doing it by looking at the defence of self-defence and how it was essentially male oriented." Wilson understood that "violence against women in the home is an expression and manifestation of power and is perpetuated by the fact that men do and women do not have power in our society. The economic, political and social inequality of women both fuels and justifies violence against women in a society which values power over all else."[15] In their majority judgment that allowed juries to hear evidence pertinent to battered women's syndrome in cases where battered victims were charged with killing their batterers in self-defence, Wilson and her colleagues changed the nature of how the law regarded spousal abuse.

In addition to these substantial legal changes, the publication of scholarly research on specific issues and lobbying by women's groups inspired the development of an institutional apparatus to deal with spousal abuse. Amendments to the Criminal Code have clarified and strengthened laws related to spousal abuse, including matters of arrest, prosecution, and conviction. The United States' Violence Against Women Act, signed in 1994 and reauthorized in 2006, enhanced investigation and prosecution of abusers. It also lengthened the period of pretrial detention, imposed automatic and mandatory restitution (the defendant must pay to the victim the full amount of losses determined by the court), and permitted victims to pursue civil recourse in cases that prosecutors chose not to prosecute.

Increasingly, North American police are trained to treat wife beating as an assault rather than as a "domestic matter" or solely a manifestation of a poor marriage. "A wife beating is foremost an assault—a crime that must be investigated," the International Association of Chiefs of Police reminded its members in 1976.[16] Mandatory charging and no-drop (or evidence-based) prosecution policies mean that the police assume the responsibility of laying charges against abusive men, freeing these men's victims from doing so. (In rare cases the abusers are women and the accusers men; occasionally, with gay spouses, they are same sex.)

Other protective tools are peace bonds and restraining orders, though these are often ineffective because the estranged spouses or partners they target are often the most dangerous. (In the early 1990s, the U.S. Department of Justice estimated that three-quarters of domestic assaults occurred after the couple separated. Canadian statistics from 1994 to 2004 show that of police-reported spousal abuse, 43 percent is committed by separated spouses, 36 percent from current spouses.) Many jurisdictions offer emergency protection or intervention orders outside court hours. The shelter system, a vital resource for abused spouses trying to extricate themselves from abusive homes, has expanded despite a chronic shortages of beds: in Canada in 1999–2000, for example, 448 shelters took in 96,359 women and children.

Public education about spousal abuse is another preventive measure. California and other states include literature about it with applications for marriage licences. The Government of Ontario's website Dealing with Spousal Abuse calls it "a tragedy that affects everyone in our society" and provides practical resource material such as the phone number of the Assaulted Women's Helpline (with interpreters in 154 languages). The site advises, "If this is an emergency and you are afraid for your life, call 911 or your local police service." It also explains how to remove an internet browsing history.[17] No frightened spouse could doubt that the government's official policy is to condemn abuse and to extend a helping hand to its victims.

PUBLIC POLICY AND DIVORCE

Divorce has been one of the thorniest issues that public policy has had to tackle because intolerable marriages have always existed. Throughout history, unhappy spouses have separated (or more rarely divorced), husbands have abandoned their wives and children, and occasionally wives have abandoned their husbands and children. Spouses have been unfaithful, and sometimes they have married again without first divesting themselves of their original spouse. Yet until the last few decades, divorce was widely deplored as an institution that threatened morality and undermined society. It was forbidden by the Roman Catholic Church and, in North America and Europe, was very difficult to obtain.

Chapter 7 described how the Canadian colonies incorporated England's 1857 Matrimonial Causes Act, with its gender-specific divorce grounds. A husband could divorce his adulterous wife quite easily; however, a wife could divorce her adulterous husband only if she could also prove that he was guilty of cruelty, had deserted her, or had committed incestuous adultery, rape, sodomy, bestiality, or bigamy. The Matrimonial Causes Act was later amended to allow wives to base divorce petitions on adultery alone, a policy that was grounded in the ideal of the pure woman, one who might find her husband's extramarital sexual escapades unforgivable. That same ideal held women to high(er) moral standards, and adulterous wives forfeited all rights to alimony. (Men could not claim alimony, a policy grounded in the gaping economic disparities between the sexes.) Heavily Roman Catholic Quebec and Newfoundland had no divorce laws, and so unhappy spouses could seek legal redress only through an act of Parliament presented as a private member's bill.

In the United States, where divorce is under state rather than federal jurisdiction, the laws varied from region to region, often rigid in the East and forgiving in the West. A further complication was that although the Constitution ordered the states to give "full faith and credit" to each other's court judgments, individual states exercised discretion about recognizing divorces obtained elsewhere. This created a divorce marketplace, enabling wealthier citizens to bypass their home state's strict laws by obtaining out-of-state divorces.

As public policy, divorce in the United States echoed the ideology of Revolution, self-government, and political liberty. Writes historian Norma Basch, "No sooner ... did Americans create a rationale for dissolving the bonds of empire than they set about creating rules for dissolving the bonds of matrimony."[18] Founding Father Thomas Jefferson linked divorce to independence and the pursuit of happiness, remarking that divorce "preserves liberty of affection" and "restores to women their natural right of equality."[19]

Eighteenth- and nineteenth-century Americans tended to see marriage as a contract that, like all contracts, could be broken for non-compliance by one or both parties, and public policy reflected this perspective. Divorces were often preceded by abandonment, the easiest way to terminate a marriage. Women filed for most divorces, often after being abandoned but also on the grounds of adultery or sexual incapacity, both of them obstacles to the pursuit of happiness. In the nineteenth century, as states assumed more control over the marriage contract, they expanded the grounds for divorce, including, as was usually the case in Canada as well, imprisonment and deviant or homosexual sex. By 1886, 80 percent of states included mental or physical cruelty.

As more people divorced, some women's rights advocates applauded the liberation of women trapped in bad marriages while others worried that divorce made older wives vulnerable. In the latter decades of the nineteenth century, the belief that divorce was destroying the American family, if not society, generated an anti-divorce movement that lobbied for reform. Public policy incorporated some of these concerns as some state legislatures passed more restrictive divorce laws. Divorce rates, however, did not go down.

New York at the time, for example, permitted divorce only on the grounds of adultery. But instead of the intended result of fewer divorces, the law encouraged divorcing couples to become accomplices in perjury. To satisfy the law's requirements of proving adultery, men and women reluctant to reveal adulterous relationships, or for whom adultery was not an issue, paid people to provide false testimony about their sexual liaisons with one of the divorcing spouses, usually the husband. In 1934, for example, the *New York Mirror* discovered that an unidentified blond legal secretary had given such testimony in more than one hundred divorce cases.

Another alternative was for unhappy spouses to travel to jurisdictions that had slacker divorce laws; Nevada and Idaho, for instance, became divorce havens after enacting laws that permitted divorce after only six weeks' residence. Later, so did Mexico, home of the twenty-four-hour divorce for foreigners.

THE CHANGING TIMES

Throughout North America, the 1960s saw drastic changes in attitudes toward marriage, sex, gender, and civil rights. These were echoed in Canada's 1968 Divorce Act, which removed the adversarial character of divorce and added permanent marriage breakdown as grounds for seeking it. Other grounds included adultery, cruelty, desertion, rape, homosexual activity, and bigamy. The act also ended the double standard that had made it much harder for women to initiate divorce proceedings.

The 1985 Divorce Act further simplified divorce, allowing marriage breakdown, adultery, or physical or mental cruelty as grounds for divorce. (Until the 1980s, when marital rape and battery were criminalized, public policy treated them as "domestic" matters.) The 1985 act also instructed lawyers to discuss with their clients the possibility that they reconcile and, when they could not, facilitated support and custody resolutions, with the best interests of the children an important consideration.

Public concern about non-payment of alimony and child support, and about the effects of divorce on children, have led to further modifications in determining and enforcing child support (and related taxation measures), and refining access and custody arrangements. Some provinces require divorcing parents to develop a parenting plan to protect their children from the emotional and financial hardships that often arise after divorce.

By the late 1970s, most provinces had amended their family-property laws to make property acquired after marriage jointly held, but it took the shocking case of an Alberta farm wife to galvanize public opinion about the inequities of women in divorce cases. In 1968, rancher Alex Murdoch socked his wife, Irene, in the face and shattered her jaw in three places, causing permanent damage. He drove her to the local hospital's emergency department and left her there. Irene returned home with her jaw wired and discovered that Alex had locked her out of the house and blocked her credit at local stores.

In 1973, the Supreme Court of Canada ruled that Irene Murdoch's twenty-five years' of farm work was merely "the work done by any ranch wife" and she had no claim to half the property Alex Murdoch sold for $95,000.[20]

Five years later, in the case of another divorcing farm couple, the court reversed the inequitable principle at the heart of this ruling. It recognized both the wife's direct and indirect contributions to the farm properties and awarded her one half of the couple's real and personal property. Within a year, most provinces had amended their own family-property laws to make property acquired after marriage jointly held, and today Canadian family courts also assign greater value to indirect or non-pecuniary contributions such as the work routinely performed by the farmwife or the housewife.

American divorce laws, too, were modified in response to the changing times. In 1969, California led the way with no-fault divorce and non-judgmental grounds such as incompatibility and irreconcilable differences. The ideological shift went from identifying which spouse was at fault, and how, to acknowledging that the marriage had simply failed and should, therefore, be ended. Other states followed California's lead and amended their laws. As in Canada, the nature of property and support settlements resulted in disastrous post-divorce finances for many women. Slowly, state legislatures redressed these inequities through laws that mandated equitable distribution of property and resources, including income.

Besides equity, the well-being of children is an important consideration in divorce. The children of divorce number in the millions; in the United States in 1990, for example, one million children's parents divorced. The divorce-related economic and social costs are sky-high: an American government study found that between 1970 and 1991, only 9 percent of children under eighteen whose parents were married were identified as poor, as opposed to 46 percent in female-headed and 23 percent in male-headed single-parent families.

In recent years, a "marriage movement" that blames divorce and egalitarianism for much of society's ills has pushed for governments to repeal or at least to reform divorce, urging that it be made more difficult to obtain, that the concept of fault be reintroduced, and that waiting periods be longer and counselling compulsory.

The marriage movement also promotes "covenant marriage," which includes compulsory premarital counselling, a contractual commitment to preserve the marriage, and, in case of marriage failure, a fault-based or extended separation before divorcing. Though few people opt for it, covenant marriage is, in 2009, available in Louisiana, Arkansas, and Arizona, a triumph of ideology translated into state policy.

THE PUBLIC MEANINGS OF MARRIAGE

As the cultural and political meanings of marriage have evolved, public policy has incorporated them into laws and regulations. The changing role of the wife illustrates how public policy also defines and institutionalizes gender relationships. Between the world wars, growing numbers of women worked, most in modestly paid jobs, and men remained their family's primary breadwinners. The Depression, however, changed the economic face of North America—President Roosevelt's lament that "the country was dying by inches" applied equally to Canada—and eroded the wage-earning capacity of men and women alike.

Government initiatives to salvage the situation were heavily influenced by beliefs about gender and were designed to treat men as their families' breadwinners. In the United States, Roosevelt's New Deal excluded women from some programs, including the popular and relatively well-paid Civilian Conservation Corps. (Reflecting the current racial thinking as well, the Corps enrolled only limited numbers of black men.) After 1932, only one family member could hold a federal government job, a measure tantamount to dismissing wives. (Many wives, desperate to keep their jobs, responded by trying to conceal their marital status.) In Canada, where women had been legally deemed persons (as opposed to non-persons) only in 1928, the federal government also considered the plight of unemployed men of paramount importance. Like their American brothers, Canadian men were supposed to support their families, and federal policies were geared to help them do so.

Today, the notion that men should solely support their families has fierce defenders and equally fierce opponents. Recast as a debate about the role and rights of women in society, it usually assumes the form of a statistic-laden battleground of studies and interpretations about the consequences of women working, women's rights, and women's educational achievements.

The discussion is framed in questions about results, consequences, and comparisons. How do children fare in daycare? How do their experiences compare to those of children cared for by stay-at-home mothers? Are they more or less delinquent, unstable, or insecure; do they go on to succeed or fail in school and, later, in personal relationships and marriage? Studies are analyzed, anecdotal evidence presented, and passionate conclusions drawn. Then, depending on the government policy-makers' agenda, daycare facilities are expanded, subsidized, encouraged, regulated, altered—or left unchanged.

During World War II, as war-bound North American men marched out of civilian workplaces, June Cleaver's real-life counterparts flooded into the workforce alongside Rosie the Riveter to replace them. In Canada, more than a million women (out of three million) and in the United States over six million manned factories, foundries, mills, farms, and military services, learned skilled trades, earned their own money, and enjoyed income tax concessions as they facilitated military production and sustained the national economy. (Many had already been working in lower-paid, traditionally female jobs; in the States, half of these wartime workers were either African-American or working class.)

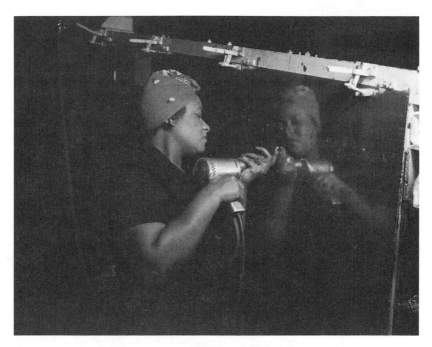

Operating a hand drill at Vultee-Nashville, a woman works on a Vengeance dive bomber, 1943. She protects her clothing with overalls and her hair with a scarf, but keeps her fingernails polished and wears rings.

At first neither government recognized the urgency of recruiting more women, and advised mothers with children under fourteen to remain at home. Soon, however, even women with children under six entered the wartime workforce, prompted by offers of federally funded daycare and by patriotic pleas for their suddenly invaluable services. As the Royal Canadian Air Force advertised, "Women between the ages of 18 and 35, and in good health, are wanted to work in eastern war plants. 'Keep 'em firing' is the motto used.... We take girls absolutely unskilled in war industries and train them right at the plant ... a farmer's daughter, domestic servant, waitress, clerk, stenographer, college graduate or debutante—if she is willing to learn—has the qualities of a good war worker."[21]

The daycare issue, today so fraught with ideological (to say nothing of pedagogical) concerns, had been resolved almost overnight by government policy-makers responding to the urgency of the wartime crisis and labour shortage. "Women are needed as an essential part of the defence program and it is a public responsibility to provide appropriate care for children while mothers are at work," began a 1941 report of the U.S. Department of Labor, *Standards for Day Care of Children of Working Mothers.*[22] Patriotic women worked so their patriotic husbands could fight, and grateful (and pragmatic) governments cared for the little ones. In striking contrast to today, the issues of women's role in the home, society, and industry, and the recognition that they needed access to affordable and reliable daycare when they worked, shaped North America's wartime public policy.

At war's end, when the fighting men returned home, these wartime policies were shot down like Luftwaffe bombers. The Riveting Rosies retired or were pushed from their jobs. The ideological functions of marriage were recast to portray it as a refuge from the uncertainties of the Cold War and the dangers of creeping communism. Marriage was also an economic unit of consumption to fuel the postwar economy, and a model for redefining gender roles and relationships as women were nudged out of wartime jobs and fighting men settled back into civil society.

Free child care and tax concessions ended. So did the applause. Women had helped to win the war but were now needed back in their homes. Now public policy and popular culture transformed nations of Rosies into charming, competitive, and child-centred housewives.[23] Poorer women who had to work returned to the lower-paid jobs they had held before the war.

North America's wistful June Cleaver image was a distortion of more complex realities that included an accelerating divorce rate. Yet, in an overarching personalization of the political, "good" marriage took on even greater significance in foreign relations. "In confrontations with the Soviet Union and its socialist allies," Nancy Cott writes, "American propaganda and Americans themselves often translated their political economy into private aspirations, linking capitalism and representative democracy to personal choices in marrying, having children, buying a home, and gaining access to a cornucopia of consumer goods."[24]

Canada was less aggressive, but essentially asquiesced and embarked on a postwar economic reconstruction that looked quite similar to the American. Canada also enacted similar legislation that recast its wartime working women as housewives. One woman's experience was typical, though its resolution was anything but: in 1954, when teacher Bertha Wilson, the Scottish-born wife of naval chaplain John Wilson, applied to the School of Law at Dalhousie University in 1955, Dean Horace Read scoffed, "Madam, we have no room here for dilettantes. Why don't you just go home and take up crocheting?" Wilson, who was "terrible at cooking and no good at all at sewing,"[25] persisted, and in 1982, after graciously overriding decades of gender discrimination—barred from her law school's common room and tavern hangout, discouraged from accepting a Harvard scholarship, waiting nine instead of five years for a law partnership, banned from doing litigation, rejected by fellow judges—became Canada's first female Supreme Court judge.

Keenly aware of the balance of power in all aspects of society and in the home, Justice Wilson swiftly became one of Canada's most progressive judges. In the Lavallee case described earlier, she wrote the majority judgment that allowed juries to hear evidence pertinent to victims of battered women's syndrome charged with killing their batterer in self-defence. In *R. v. Morgentaler* (1988), she said that in the context of the profound psychological, economic, and social consequences of terminating a pregnancy, prohibiting a woman from doing so violated her liberty and personal autonomy. A woman being so prohibited, she wrote, "is truly being treated as a means—a means to an end which she does not desire but over which she has no control. She is the passive recipient of a decision made by others as to whether her body is to be used to nurture a new life. Can there be anything that comports less with human dignity and self-respect? How can a woman in this position have any sense of security with respect to her person?"[26]

Over six decades later, the majority of women work, and their struggle to find accessible daycare is so severe that it constitutes a public crisis. Yet the debate about daycare is bitter and revisits the question of the role of women as mothers and, by extension, wives. Are working mothers selfish beings who sacrifice their young to ambition or greed, or, at the other end of the spectrum, are they hard-working contributors to their family's financial well-being whose efforts provide their children with otherwise unattainable benefits? Does the availability of daycare encourage women to work rather than stay at home, or, conversely, does it encourage them to marry and raise children when they might otherwise not have? One topic that never surfaces is the recollection of how swiftly and easily North America's wartime governments introduced free daycare as part of their concerted efforts to overcome the enemy.

The debate extends into the training school, universities, and the workplace. As academic institutions admit more women, and in many cases more women than men, women's education has become a point of contention. Does the decision to pursue higher education limit women's marital prospects? Does an educated woman's greater earning potential free her to reject her spouse's infelicities and increase her likelihood of divorce? Should employers be permitted to require women to reveal their marital status and parenthood? Should government policies support or penalize working mothers through taxation schedules and health insurance, daycare and after-school programs, children's allowances, parental leave, flexible hours, and guaranteed days off to care for sick children?

Welfare and Workfare

Welfare programs are a classic example of how public policy can shape marriage. Governments control what they dole out, especially to their neediest citizens. Because of this, even direst poverty does not guarantee eligibility. Applicants must satisfy various conditions and confront a tortuous and multi-stage application process. One northeastern American county, for example, requires six in-person appointments, including a home visit by a fraud investigator, documents such as birth certificates, school records, proof of residence notes from the landlord and a "professional person," wage and bank records, and a note from past employers confirming termination of employment. Sometimes the application also demands car registrations, divorce papers, even—for recent widows or widowers—funeral programs.[27] Often, successful applicants must attend classes, seminars, or other "lifestyle events" designed to change and improve their lives.

To avoid the intense criticism so often generated by welfare programs, notably aimed at cheaters and unmarried mothers, Canadian and American government agencies try to monitor their welfare clients and document successful transitions to gainful employment and mainstream life. The title of President Bill Clinton's 1996 welfare bill, the Personal Responsibility and Work Opportunity Reconciliation Act (PRWORA), conceived as a block grant administered by the states, made good on his promise to "end welfare as we know it." It also suggested the widespread belief that single motherhood was responsible for welfare dependence, and, to nudge welfare mothers out to work, PRWORA limited welfare to five years.

PRWORA had another agenda: marriage. The states were urged to assist needy families to care for their children at home or with relatives; promote job preparation, work, and marriage; reduce out-of-wedlock child-bearing; and to "encourage the formation and maintenance of two-parent families." The act listed three (of ten) "findings" that spelled out the pro-marriage ideology: 1. Marriage is the foundation of a successful society. 2. Marriage is an essential institution of a successful society which promotes the interests of children. 3. Promotion of responsible fatherhood and motherhood is integral to successful child-rearing and the well-being of children.

Although a related bill to support responsible fatherhood passed the House but failed in the Senate, promoting married fatherhood remains an urgent goal. In the United States, at least 30 million children are fatherless. As a former assistant secretary for children and families testified to Congress, "All available evidence suggests that the most effective pathway to involved, committed, and responsible fatherhood is marriage. Research consistently documents that unmarried fathers, whether divorced or unwed, tend over time to become disconnected, financially and psychologically, from their children.... We need a public policy that supports [fathers] as nurturers, disciplinarians, mentors, moral instructors and skill coaches."[28]

President George W. Bush, who had sworn to "give unprecedented support to strengthening marriages," signed the Promoting Safe and Stable Families Amendments, which permitted states to use block-grant money allocated for vulnerable families to promote healthy marriages. Healthy marriage and responsible fatherhood became high-priority public policies.

Supporters of these policies lamented the fate of children in single-parent, divorced, or blended families and cited studies showing that such children are more likely to be delinquent, academically backward, psychologically scarred, and at risk for abuse. They quantified the enormous economic and social costs of marital breakdown and child poverty. They cited studies showing that good fathering skills and connection with children are much more in evidence in married and cohabiting men than in non-resident fathers. Based on all these studies, they proposed measures to implement healthy marriage and responsible fatherhood.

President Barack Obama is a fervent supporter of responsible fatherhood and is committed to policies that foster it. In his 2008 Father's Day address to Chicago's Apostolic Church of God, Obama praised fathers as "teachers and coaches ... mentors and role models ... examples of success and the men who constantly push us toward it." But, he lamented, "what too many fathers also are is missing—missing from too many lives and too many homes. They have abandoned their responsibilities, acting like boys instead of men. And the foundations of our families are weaker because of it."

Despite widespread bipartisan agreement about this issue, detractors of marriage-building policies worry that governments have neither the right nor the knowledge to engage in marriage building. They note that marriage is in decline throughout the Western world, they doubt that anything can reverse the trend, and they challenge the assumption that marriage is better than cohabitation or singleness. They suspect that an anti-women's-rights agenda is marriage promotion's hidden evil twin. They fear that the rush to marriage will push pregnant women into unsafe and violent marriages and keep abused wives from leaving them. They believe that government-sponsored marriage initiatives discriminate against single people and homosexuals. They wonder, in the case of men and women who have had children with multiple partners, what criteria would be used to indicate which of these partners should marry.

A key aspect of marriage promotion as public policy is its use of marriage as a tool to reduce the poverty endemic in one-parent families, in the United States a disproportionate number of them African-American. The issue is fraught with controversy, scholarly disputation, and class and racial uneasiness. The challenge is always the same: to achieve the seeming impossibility of reaching consensus—or at least majority acceptance—about the nature of the problem and the related issues policy-makers are trying to address.

Specifically, does the institution of marriage lessen poverty? Are married couples less poor because they are married, or are they married because they are less poor? What about the many low-income single mothers who value marriage but do not wish to marry their children's undereducated and underemployed fathers because they have seen too many marriages ravaged by poverty and chronic indebtedness, inadequate housing and child care, and the stresses of violent neighbourhoods? Does encouraging poor people to marry rescue them from poverty, or does it result in dangerous marriages and, ultimately, divorce? Because there are no definitive answers, and hence no obvious policy to follow, ideology is a significant force in shaping policy decisions.

Because two people are at least marginally better off economically if they live together, whether in marriage or cohabitation, some states adopt marriage-promotion programs. One pilot program, the Minnesota Family Investment Program (MFIP), tackled the problem of low wages by subsidizing the earnings of employed welfare families. Though the Minnesota program did not specifically promote marriage, the marriage rate of single-parent participants rose, and the divorce rates of married participants declined, as did the overall rates of domestic violence. Minnesota's gamble that increased income would stabilize marriage seemed to have paid off.

Other states prefer to provide non-economic support. In Oklahoma, which has the country's fourth-highest divorce rate, the Governor's Marriage Initiative focuses on improving relationships and parenting skills through free marriage-education classes on the one hand and on toughening divorce laws on the other. Arizona has a similar marriage initiative and offers free courses on marriage and on premarital abstinence. Florida has compulsory marriage and relationship skills training in its high schools.

TAXING MARRIAGE

Throughout history, taxation policies have been written to reward or punish marital status, and to shape or reform the institution of marriage as practised. In sparsely settled seventeenth-century New France, pro-marriage policies resulted in a punitive "bachelor tax" and a decree that banned bachelors from hunting, fishing, or engaging in the fur trade, the colony's economic mainstay, until all the marriageable women shipped over from France for that express purpose had been married off. Three centuries later, and by then worried about a declining birth rate in the motherland, France imposed a tax on its bachelors.

Today, tax schedules factor in marital status, and depending on the taxpayer's income, number of dependants, itemized deductions, and other calculations, levy either a "marriage penalty" or a "marriage bonus." In 1997, for example, the U.S. General Accounting Office listed 1,049 federal laws with marriage-related components; these laws dealt with everything from Social Security and related housing and food stamps programs to federal natural resources and related laws. These laws privileged some married people and penalized others, but all took marital status into account.

Attempts to clarify the effect of such tax laws suggest that over 40 percent of married couples pay a penalty averaging $1,400, while more than 50 percent save even more through federal marriage bonuses, especially when one spouses earns 70 percent or more than the other.[29] However, very low wage earners may pay a disproportionately high marriage tax.[30] Tax expert Eugene Steurle calculates, for example, that a single mother of two children who earns the minimum wage would have an extra $8,060 if she lived with, instead of married, a fully employed partner earning $8 an hour. Steurle called the marriage penalty in this example, which is about 25 percent of household income, "a charge on vows and commitments."[31]

Some specific marriage-rewarding features include not taxing spousal employee benefits and allowing spouses the option of filing jointly, which often saves them money. Single and cohabitating taxpayers, however, pay taxes on a partner's benefits and may not jointly file. In states where cohabitation is a criminal offence under adultery laws, unmarried couples may not claim that one is the other's dependant. The inequalities continue even after death, when spouses may inherit unlimited wealth free of federal tax, but an unmarried beneficiary will pay between 26 and 60 percent in federal estate taxes.

To some extent, taxation usually functions as a government tool to promote and reward marriage and, by the same token, to penalize cohabiting and single people. An unintentional effect of the U.S. tax law structure is also to penalize unmarried, low-waged African Americans, who are also the primary targets of aggressive programs to promote marriage and responsible fatherhood. Their lower-than-average life expectancies and wages result in many of them being cheated of their fair share of Social Security benefits, at the same time effectively subsidizing wealthier, longer-living citizens.[32]

The Canadian tax system, too, has incorporated elements of social engineering into its schedules. Today, however, unlike the United States, Canada's tax law no longer discriminates—and sometimes does not even distinguish—between married and common-law or cohabiting couples. This desire to avoid discrimination has even created a tax structure that favours unmarried parents, who can each claim a child "as if" that child were a dependent spouse. For two-income unmarried parents, this can be a significant deduction. It is also an example of how Canada's public policy reflects contemporary views about the importance, even primacy, of choice in its citizens' personal relationships.

CHALLENGING OFFICIAL VERSIONS OF MARRIAGE

Some North Americans have always challenged official versions of marriage. Before the Civil War, utopian communities reinvented marriage and modified gender roles. Advocates of free love disregarded chastity, in women as well as in men. Mormon mavericks from Utah embraced polygamy as a religious duty and a moral alternative to infidelity and prostitution.

Polygamy was an especially worrisome threat to marriage ideals. In the 1878 case of George Reynolds, a thirty-two-year-old Mormon who had recently married a second wife, the U.S. Supreme Court not only rejected Reynolds's claim that religious freedom guaranteed by the First Amendment required him to practise bigamy, it also effectively criminalized polygamy. In analyzing this ruling, historian Nancy Cott shows how the court associated monogamy with democracy and juxtaposed them against polygamy and despotism.[33]

Apart from outlawing polygamy, the U.S. government zealously promoted monogamous marriage in other ways, most notably through the Comstock Act of 1873. The driving force behind that act was Anthony Comstock, who preached that birth control devices facilitated extramarital sex by removing the fear of pregnancy. The act that bore his name declared birth control devices obscene and banned them. Until then, shops and mail-order businesses sold condoms, pessaries, and douches to a wide range of customers: husbands and wives hoping to limit their family size as well as the cheating spouses and the unmarried singles that were Comstock's worst nightmare. The Comstock Act did not succeed in its objective of forcing people to be monogamous or chaste. It did, however, drive the contraception business underground, leading to a rise in unintended pregnancies, fatal abortions, and unwanted children. Decades would pass before advocates managed to cleanse birth control of its stigma and to promote it as a medical issue and as an alternative to abortion or unplanned parenthood.

In recent decades, the movement in favour of gay marriage has challenged lawmakers to rethink and reformulate public policy vis-à-vis marriage. Gender has become the new arena in which to test the judgment made in the 1967 Loving case, that marriage is "one of the vital personal rights essential to the orderly pursuit of happiness by free men." In 1996, President Bill Clinton responded to Hawaii's impending legalization of gay marriage by signing the Defense of Marriage Act

(DOMA), which defined marriage as, and limited it to, the legal union between one man and one woman as husband and wife.[34] DOMA was designed to ensure that the federal government would not be required to recognize same-sex or polygamous marriages. For the same reason, most states also passed defence of marriage acts of their own, often accompanied by new provisions for equivalent-to-marriage civil unions or domestic partnerships for gay couples, which conferred the same benefits and obligations as marriage.

In Canada in 1999, Parliament reaffirmed (by a vote of 216 to 55) the traditional definition of marriage as the union of one man and one woman to the exclusion of all others. After a few years of strenuous lobbying by gay marriage advocates, and court decisions across the country denying the constitutionality of the traditional definition of marriage, Parliament reversed itself. In 2005, it passed the Civil Marriage Act, which redefined "marriage, for civil purposes," as "the lawful union of two persons to the exclusion of all others."[35] In legalizing same-sex marriage—which by then was already legal in nine of the thirteen provinces and territories—Parliament was belatedly putting its stamp of approval on a deed almost completely done.

As happened in the legal and constitutional battles over interracial marriage, lobbyists and legislators engaged in the war against gay marriage have adopted the strategy of encouraging states that do not permit gay marriage to refuse to recognize the validity of gay marriage legislation in other jurisdictions.[36] In this respect, Canadian legislation has complicated the American situation, as affianced gay Americans rush northward to marry. Now American states have begun to accept gay marriage, adding more jurisdictional challenges to the issue. As well, the passage of California's Proposition 8 is proof that policy can be overturned, making policies about marriage—and other issues—fluid and changeable.

As the cultural and political meanings of marriage evolve, public policy incorporates them into new laws and regulations, affirming, shaping, reforming, sometimes punishing. The laws that allow battered women who kill their abusers to argue self-defence from their own perspective, including their need to use weapons, reflected the growing acceptance of women's right to equality. The defence of marriage laws, on the other hand, attempted to forestall legislative acknowledgment of same-sex marriage.

Today, policy-making about marriage is grounded in romantic, companionate ideals leavened by egalitarian principles that demand respectful gender relations, accept homosexuality, abhor violence, and worry about children. It mirrors contemporary attitudes and values about the right to choice within moderate guidelines: it does not tolerate polygamy, for example. Recent challenges to gay-marriage legislation in both Canada and the United States are cautionary and remind us that, like marriage, public policy is always evolving.

Chapter 14

Issues at the Heart of the Marriage Debate

WOMEN BECOME PERSONS

It is February 1893—or perhaps 1896 or any year in between. It is Winnipeg, or perhaps Toronto. But the stage setting is the same: a theatrical mock Parliament, or women's Parliament, with fifty-two seats entirely inhabited by female legislators.[1] They begin deliberations with a bill seeking "to prevent men from wearing long stockings, knicker-bockers and round-about coats when bicycling." The concern, a woman lawmaker explains, is that if permitted long stockings, men will aspire to "other articles of woman's clothing, as, the divided skirt, the subtle influence of which would create a desire to fill women's positions in the world!" (This bill invokes the then controversial question of reforming women's clothing, especially the new fashions—for example bloomers and split skirts—that were designed for riding bicycles, a new physical activity that freed women and constituted a challenge to their physical and social restrictions.)

Weightier matters follow. Should men who marry be dismissed from their jobs as schoolteachers? (This bill was an exact replica—with the sexes reversed—of the policy of dismissing female schoolteachers who married, and referred as well to the Toronto Public School Board's policy of overseeing, even to the point of spying on, female teachers' private lives, and refusing to hire any woman over thirty or any woman

*The "Women are Persons!" monument, on Parliament Hill, Ottawa,
commemorates the Persons case and the five women involved. Previously, only
dead prime ministers, monarchs, and Fathers of Confederation were so honoured
on the Hill.*

with a husband to support her.) Should men's wages, only half or one-third the sum paid to women for the same work, be increased? (This parodied the reality, but again with the sexes reversed. It also invokes the nineteenth-century notion of the "family wage," justified by the argument that men required a higher salary because they had wives and children to support.)

Finally Parliament addresses the day's most pressing business: a petition from Canada's disenfranchised (hence socially disadvantaged) men, pleading for the right to vote. But women's rights activist Nellie McClung's character, turning traditional arguments on their head, argues, "It's hard enough to keep them at home now ... Politics unsettle men and unsettled men means unsettled bills, broken furniture, broken vows, and divorce ... Man has a higher destiny than politics."[2] McClung adds: "There is no use giving men votes. They wouldn't use them. They would let them spoil and go to waste. Then again, some men would vote too much.... Giving men the vote would unsettle the home.... The modesty of our men, which we reverence, forbids us giving them the vote. Men's place is on the farm.... It may be that I am old-fashioned. I may be wrong. After all, men may be human. Perhaps the time may come when men may vote with the women—but in the meantime, be of good cheer."[3]

EQUITY, LOVE, WORK

Today, an ideal marriage model is a partnership, and many spouses introduce and refer to each other as partners. Equity is a cherished value, hard fought for and long in arriving. Like fog, equity has crept into marriage on little cat's feet, a whisker here, a paw print there. Gender equality is a new invention that began in women's (and a few men's) hearts and has been slowly transcribed into North America's laws and rules, culture and customs. And into individual marriages, most now sealed by vows of love and respect followed by traditional kisses.

Today, few wives pledge to obey their husbands, and as august an authority as the Church of England's Archbishop of Canterbury, Dr. Rowan Williams, agrees with the Archbishops' Council report *Responding to Domestic Abuse* (2006) that promising to obey a husband could be interpreted as allowing domestic violence. Instead, Reverend Williams advises, priests should emphasize that in the eyes of God, men and women are of equal value.

It was not even a century ago that North American women won the right to vote in federal elections: 1918 in Canada and 1920 in the United States. (To Manitoba premier Rodmond Roblin's comment that "nice" women did not want the vote, wife and mother of five Nellie McClung retorted: "By nice women ... you probably mean selfish women who have no more thought for the underprivileged, overworked women than a pussycat in a sunny window for the starving kitten in the street. Now in that sense I am not a nice woman for I do care."[4]) Canada's Supreme Court pondered long and hard before deciding, in 1928, that the nation's women were legally not "persons." On appeal, and unanimously, the Judicial Division of the British Privy Council reversed that decision: excluding women from public office because they were not "persons" was "a relic of days more barbarous than ours."[5]

Gender equity, or at least equilibrium, within marriage continues to be a key issue in the marriage debate. Today, as women strive to achieve in a wide sweep of fields, entering colleges, universities, and professional schools in large numbers—and boardrooms and even spaceships in lesser numbers—their successes and experiences lead them to expect a level of satisfaction in their personal relationships that derives from a sense of fairness and balance in power dynamics.

The centrality of love in marriage is so important, and often crucial to this balance, that it is officially acknowledged. People "take it for granted that they will marry for love and emotional gratification rather than for economic or other instrumental reasons," notes a Canadian parliamentary study.[6] Love can weigh heavily, anchoring the union or, if it fails or founders, burdening it. This raises the same questions today as it did when romantic love began to be accepted as a working element in marriage: If love hurts or dies, should the ensuing lovelessness lead to separation or divorce? Conversely, does love demand expression even if its object is not the spouse? Is love such an imperative that it justifies infidelity?

With egalitarianism unleashing and empowering love, an industry of pop culture feeds—sincerely—on love-related topics, definitions, diagnosis, and, always, advice. Despite the inclination to confine love and lock it up in marriage, love also flourishes independently of marriage. So does its erotic dimension, joyous hedonism unfettered by anxiety about procreation, though in the context of marital infidelity, that can also be guilt-ridden.

In that same context, gender equity and the pill have all but collapsed the double standard into a solo standard that cloaks infidelity with emotional and social implications and no longer exonerates male cheaters while crucifying female ones. In more tolerant North American society, sexual mores have changed not only to accept premarital, non-marital, and same-gender sexual relations but at the same time to condemn sexual harassment, rape, and the sexual violation of children—and to disapprove of infidelity as a betrayal of trust and commitment in what should be a union of equals. Infidelity is a marriage-related problem that also questions the meanings of erotic and romantic love.

The answers are everywhere and nowhere. They resonate in myths that reflect our longings for how marriage should be—a shared vision of rock-solid, lifelong unions based on mutual respect and affection. They are found as well in comforting analyses of the stages of passionate love and its inevitable cooling (but solidification), and its reincarnation as comfortable commitment. They live in spouses' personal histories of loving each other, and in their children's inherited features—her aquiline nose, his broad forehead—which recall and rekindle earlier,

Just-wed Dina and Ivan rejoice as they leave the church as
a married couple for whom mutual love and shared values
are more important than racial and cultural differences.

tenderer feelings. Gender equality has changed the equation. When women are equal to their men, their hearts command more attention because they need no longer pit love against the practicalities and economics of living.

Pervasive and persuasive as egalitarianism is, including for millions of men, others feel threatened and resentful. They accuse feminism of bringing about changes in society that, in expanding women's opportunities and attitudes, have destroyed nurturing nuclear families. They point to males' rising school dropout rates and decreasing enrolment in colleges and universities and wonder if women's increasing educational advancements are having an emasculating effect. They mourn the erosion of male self-esteem, and they fear that the natural balance between the sexes has been irrevocably disturbed.

On the other hand, legions of men and women celebrate women's successes, their educational advancement, their march into professions and executive suites, their higher earning power, and the egalitarian laws that protect their status. They salute the end of the days of unwanted babies, back-street abortions, or unwed mothers bullied into surrendering their bastards for adoption. They deny that women's rights trump men's and do not allow that a daughter succeeds in school at the expense of a brother.

They are right. The decline in young men's educational and vocational pursuits is real, but the culprit is not women's progress: it is the changing nature of work and industry, and the recessions that have savaged North America's skilled and semi-skilled industrial jobs. Not enough of these displaced workers have found employment (and even fewer have found satisfaction) in the new kinds of jobs that have been spawned, including the grim realms of telemarketing and outbound telephone sales, inbound script-driven customer service, and the more challenging telecommunications and computer industries. As this economic trend has continued, increasing numbers of dependent younger men can look forward to futile jobs and bitter prospects, yet they do not seek an escape through higher education.

Resentful at being cheated of their expectations, many undervalued and rudderless males identify women and, to a lesser extent, job-snatching immigrants as the enemy. A virulent and deep-rooted misogyny permeates their thinking. Among young men, masculinity is now defined as "a performance game to be won in the marketplace, not the workplace ... An ornamental culture encourage[s] young men to see surliness, hostility, and violence as expressions of glamour," writes Susan Faludi in *Stiffed: The Betrayal of the American Man*.[7] Feeling betrayed, many males lash out at women and their need for equality.

The Promise Keepers men's movement, a product of this malaise, casts blame instead on godlessness and seeks to nourish inter-male intimacy and males' spiritual leadership over biblically submissive wives and families. In the 1990s men joined in droves, then exited quietly when Promise Keepers failed to deliver. In 1995, in a spectacular campaign of cultural rebirth, the Million Man Marchers, led by African-American Minister Louis Farrakhan of the Nation of Islam, pledged self-improvement in all aspects of life and in family life, never to abuse or otherwise disrespect their wives, and never to call women "bitches." In these and other intensely religious movements, men lacerate themselves for having ceded leadership to women, and vow to once again assume that responsibility and, with love and wisdom, to guide and protect their families.

There is another common, and gender-neutral, response to the current economic crisis: to seek safe haven in home, family, and marriage. In contrast to the frightening world, the home seems safe and predictable, an (imaginary) reflection of the carefree and optimistic postwar world. In addition, technological advances facilitate working at home, and increasing numbers of men and women focus all aspects of their lives there. Intensive cocooning is enhanced by a home life anchored by marriage or at least cohabitation, providing emotional and sexual comforts as well. In these homes, equity may flourish or wither, but it is seldom the defining element in the initial cocooning impulse.

SAME-SEX EQUITY

Gender concerns are not restricted to male–female relations. They are part of the struggle for civil rights, and the egalitarianism at their heart extends as well to gay equality, specifically to the right to marry and to obtain spousal recognition, respectability, and the economic benefits that marriage traditionally conveys. It also provides a legal and social framework for adoptions by married gays, and it allows them to raise those children. The growth of gay weddings modified from heterosexual models testifies to the desire to share mainstream life. That includes honeymoons, mothers-in-law, and, as time is now telling, separation and divorce.

Many supporters of gay marriages also see it "through a black-white prism,"[8] and often remind us that it was as late as 1967 that the U.S. Supreme Court struck down the miscegenation laws and that, in that same year, *Time* magazine called the marriage of U.S. Secretary of State Dean Rusk's white daughter, Peggy, to African-American Guy Smith "A Marriage of Enlightenment." (Peggy's controversial marriage also prompted Rusk to proffer his resignation to President Lyndon Johnson, who refused it.)[9]

Mildred Loving, who knew all about love and marriage through that black-white prism, recently endorsed gay marriage on the grounds that marrying for love is a civil right. "The older generation's fears and prejudices have given way, and today's young people realize that if someone loves someone they have a right to marry.... I believe all Americans, no matter their race, no matter their sex, no matter their sexual orientation, should have that same freedom to marry. Government has no business imposing some people's religious beliefs over others. Especially if it denies people's civil rights.... I support the freedom to marry for all. That's what Loving, and loving, are all about."[10]

Some heterosexuals refuse to marry until gay marriage is legalized. Brad Pitt said of himself and Angelina Jolie, "Angie and I will consider tying the knot when everyone else in the country who wants to be married is legally able." Charlize Theron announced that she will not marry her fiancé, Stuart Townsend, until "the day that gays and lesbians can get married."[11]

Egalitarianism sparks much of the support for gay marriage, but another kind of argument—the cautionary slippery slope—is frequently invoked as well. The right to marry a dog is a particularly popular scenario thrust into anti-gay-marriage rhetoric, while legalizing polygamy heads the list as its "obvious" logical consequence: if same-sex partners can marry, then why not change the rules about numbers in a marriage as well? Meanwhile, even the once-polygamous Church of Jesus Christ of Latter-day Saints excommunicates polygamists and does not acknowledge as Mormon anyone who joins polygamous splinter groups.

THE MATING GAME

A consideration that should (but doesn't) dominate the marriage discussion is how best to find a mate. Marriages are likeliest to succeed when spouses are educated, relatively mature, and intellectually, socially, and sexually compatible. It's clear: proper mating is crucial. Yet there persists a quasi-superstitious belief in serendipity as the preferred way to meet a soulmate. Coincidences and chance meetings are thought to be "romantic" and perhaps supernaturally preordained; shopping for a mate with a checklist of desirable qualities is seen as crass, insensitive, and even mercenary. Chemistry is paramount; it will produce sensations of primal connection, and there can be—should be—no turning back.

The science behind this atavistic concept of mutual attraction may be real. But the notion that random encounters are romantic and predestined is the fluff stuff of pop culture. Certainly there are few advocates for a return to the days of bartered brides and grooms, with familial financial needs and other considerations, including astronomy, paramount. But to think about marriage should also be to think about matchmaking, perhaps the world's second-oldest profession, and how the internet is potentially a superb instrument for finding a mate.

There are, however, many problems that trial, error, and analysis must solve before this happens: the inadequacy of screening methods, the duplicity and naivety of candidates, and the stunning lack of clarity in expectations, standards, and monitoring. Introductions via dating sites may begin with emails, and North America's culture of instant electronic confidences, coupled with effusive and facile expressions of emotion, may conjure up the impression of "falling in love" by email. Subsequent face-to-face meetings in the light of day, even the darkened day of coffee shops or bars, are often rude reminders that what seems too good to be true almost never is.

Yet the ideas and motives behind dating sites remain legitimate, though new approaches are necessary. Dating services should adopt the boutique as opposed to the warehouse approach, relying on individual successes rather than volume, and charging appropriate fees for crucial services rendered. This is already happening with services modelled on old-fashioned matchmaking, which are labour intensive and demand high levels of personal resources, social contacts, and confidentiality.

Some dating services negotiate the quagmire of online dating by targeting specific communities—vegetarians, bowlers, Christians, Jews—on the assumption that people want to meet kindred spirits. Other specialized sites cater to specific wishes: older women seeking younger men who are seeking older women; white men seeking Asian women seeking white men; millionaire men seeking young beauties seeking millionaire men.

An often abused form of matchmaking introduces "mail-order brides"—Filipina and Russian are very popular—to North American men. These mail-order bride websites, modern-day versions of the Japanese and Korean picture brides of the early twentieth century, tend to attract men who reject North American women as too outspoken and independent and who seek out vulnerable women hoping to emigrate to North America. The men claim to believe these women's (often rote) stories of hardship and abuse, and believe, too, that they are saving them. They also accept the women's protestations that they are marrying not for the landed-immigrant status or to secure a green card sponsor but to find "true love," a soulmate to care for until death do them part.

"I search for the true love!!!!!!!!!!!!!!!!!!" declares a petite blond Ukrainian who describes herself as a non-drinking, non-smoking Christian college student. Open-mindedly (and typically), she offers an age range of eighteen to sixty for the man with whom she would like to engage in "friendship, romance, relationship, marriage." With everything to offer except the desired immigration status, she competes with thousands of other (allegedly) excellent candidates by avoiding demands or restrictions. The sardonic caption to a cartoon of a bulging, hawk-nosed old man glued to his computer screen captures perfectly this surreal world of mail-order mating: "Bob searched far and wide for his soul mate. It looked promising, aside from the language barrier and the shipping costs."

Because they deal in immigration matters, mail-order bride marriages are officially tracked, and U.S. Citizenship and Immigration Services reports that for the years for which they have been tracked, at least 80 percent of the four to six thousand mail-order marriages remain intact, a higher percentage than other American marriages. This happy statistic has contradictory explanations. One is that men seeking "traditional" women try to dominate the relationship and terrify their foreign brides into obedience. In *Romance on a Global Stage: Pen Pals, Virtual Ethnography, and 'Mail Order' Marriages,* scholar Nicole Constable recommends that governments develop policies that mitigate any possibility of widespread abuse.

In both Canada and the United States, a tortuous bureaucratic process intended to roust fraudulent relationships (or bad intentions) precedes the bride's or fiancée's entry into the country. There must be evidence of a genuine relationship: vacation, family and wedding photographs, love letters, joint bank accounts, telephone bills showing long conversations. The North American must commit to supporting the spouse for a specified length of time, and in the States, the immigrant's permanent legal status is conditional on maintaining the marriage for a specified time.

Both critics and supporters agree that North American feminism and egalitarianism are at the root of men's attraction to mail-order match-making's foreign brides. These men contrast North American women's (perceived) antipathy to full-time homemaking and catering to men with foreign women's (perceived) aptitude for homemaking and submissiveness, and find the latter more appealing. A large majority of husbands are considerably older than their wives. Many have been married before and want a different experience from their brides: Molly Maids in the house, Marilyn Monroes in the bedroom, and Martha Stewarts in the kitchen.

Mail-order matches should not be models for other spouse seekers. If many of the marriages seem to last, they do so because the women fear deportation if they disobey or complain, even about abuse, or they feel unable to support themselves if they leave. They may not speak the language well. They do not know how to get help or where to flee for safety. "Most women have no clue of the dangers involved," says Elsa Batica, a consultant on the mail-order bride business.[12]

PARENTING

Parenting remains a key focus in any discussion of marriage, and includes such related questions as birth control and the widespread acceptance of joint spousal involvement in parenthood, beginning with planning it. But step-parenting and blended marriages are equally important because divorce and remarriage rates guarantee that at least a quarter of North American children are growing up in stepfamilies, and 10 percent live in them at any one time.

Marriage for step-parents has several dimensions. One is practical, as they deal with the quotidian frustration of building joint lives with disjointed members; many reach out to each other through support groups and websites, sharing experiences, seeking and offering assistance. On the theoretical side, a growing amount of research focuses on the complexities of step- or blended families, especially their effect on children. Those who lament the demise of "traditional" marriage tend to paint a gloomy picture of blended families and their children, claiming much more abuse by step-parents than by biological parents (discussed in chapter 10). Those who accept these families as a postmodern reality tend to more optimistic interpretations.

One given in any discussion is that the wife as stepmother plays a pivotal role in the smooth running of her new family, that she is weighed down by stereotyped prejudice and high expectations, and that as an "intimate outsider," she is likely more depressed and angry about her family relationships than is her husband.[13] The stepmother has often approached her new role by trusting in the power of love, specifically the instant love—the Brady Bunch myth—she will share with her stepchildren. If this fails to materialize, she may sink into a state of guilt tinged with resentment at her unloving or ambivalent stepchildren, hostility to the biological mother whom they do love (and are much more likely to live with), anger at her husband for his divided loyalties, and frustration and fear at the prospect of her marital future. And she is right, because reports show that marriages like hers have a greater chance of ending in divorce than those that begin childless. Most stepmothers are all too aware as well of the assumption that they are to blame. Some capitulate and blame themselves. Many others, however, rage at the injustice.

Yet the blended family is the family of the future, and debate about it has an urgent quality. To borrow from Tolstoy, every blended family is alike in that so much is at stake, the odds are not reassuring, children are the marriage's impediment as well as one of its central purposes, and the stepmother is cast in at least two very different roles: second mother to her husband's children and wife to her husband. When mothers bring children into marriages, stepfathers negotiate other emotional landmines. When both bring children to the marriage, they create new complexities; when they then have children together, as half do, they add to these complexities.

DIVORCE

Another key question in the debate about the state of modern marriage is the relative ease of divorce and its consequences. Changing social attitudes have erased its stigma and led to greater choices and better employment opportunities for divorced people, especially women. States and provinces have modified their divorce laws, often introducing no-fault provisions, equitable division of property, and child-friendly custody arrangements. No-fault divorce means that abused spouses, most of them women, no longer have to document their abuse with medical or physical evidence and witnesses. One consequence has been a decline in the rates of domestic violence. No-fault provisions also discourage the perjury so common in old-style divorce. Yet styling the mechanics and aftermath of divorce "easy" is misleading; "easier," perhaps, but dividing property is at best difficult, and arranging shared responsibility for children is at best painful and often heartbreaking for both parent(s) and children.

Critics of divorce—or of so-called easy divorce—usually link it to selfishness, moral sloth, and an unwillingness to put the necessary effort into making marriages work; they complain that it permits one disgruntled spouse to end a marriage that the other might have worked hard to save. One scholarly study concludes that "the deplorable state of marriage right now … has been caused by hedonistic and irresponsible straight people" who have reduced it to "the proverbial 'piece of paper' at worst and pure sentimentality at best," as evidenced by such popular televisions shows such as *The Bachelor, The Bachelorette*, and *Who Wants to Marry a Multi-Millionaire?*[14] Many people are convinced that if divorces were harder to obtain, the institution of marriage could be salvaged, although they generally concede that ending abusive or dysfunctional marriages is the least bad solution when children are involved. Some critics see such a fine line between polygamy and divorce followed by remarriage that they style the latter "serial polygamy."[15]

Some divorce critics believe that religious worship heals hurt marriages and keeps them intact. "The family that prays together, stays together" is the motto of several Christian groups, among them United Christian Family and Families for Christ. Yet the reality is that Baptists and other conservative Christians have higher divorce rates than agnostics and atheists.[16] Ethnicity is also an important factor in the likelihood of divorce: for example, the chance is that Asians will divorce less and that African Americans will divorce more.

In many ways, and despite serendipity and the mysteries of the human heart and interpersonal dynamics, divorce has a discernible profile. People who divorce are more likely to have married younger, to have first cohabited with either their spouse or someone else, to have less education and money; after they divorce, they may remarry or cohabit, bringing children from their previous relationships into the new ones, which have a greater chance of breaking down. This suggests that rather than less accessible divorce or more religious fervour, the divorce rate could be lowered by raising the age of marriage and encouraging more people to continue their education.

The bitterest issue in divorce is what happens to the children. "I thought how is this possible?" a child of divorce recalled. "Why did it have to happen to me? So I asked my Mom and she said, 'because life isn't fair.'"[17] Most North Americans claim the right to divorce if they feel unsatisfied, unhappy, or unsafe in a marriage, and they assume that children in all but high-conflict divorces will weather the experience quite nicely. But what if this assumption is wrong, as Canada's parliamentary study, *For the Sake of the Children* (1998), suggests, and their parents' divorces cause children long-term problems and dysfunctions?

For the Sake of the Children makes the compelling case that "the impact of divorce on children is significant and potentially harmful," and it urges shared parenting except in cases of abuse because, for a child, the worst thing in the world is "the loss of a parent who's been a constant, living presence in one's life, the loss of a parent who is part of who one is, an integral part of one's identity."[18]

Despite the small percentage of high-conflict cases that garner public attention, divorce is almost always preceded by conflict or sadness. Though most divorce proceedings are consensual, privately, about one-quarter to one-third of couples are mired in anger and bitterness for at least three years after the actual divorce, and the effect on their children can be devastating. Several subjects in particular need immediate attention, beginning with changing the language of divorce.

At present, most divorce laws share the language of imprisonment—custody, access, visiting rights—which reflects, in the words of social work professor Howard Irving, "a bygone era in which women and children were legally chattels in the possession of the head of the household, the father."[19] Instead, a less loaded vocabulary is critical to reducing conflict in divorce—"parental responsibility" as in Australia, or "shared parental responsibility" as in Florida, or "residential placement" and "parenting functions" as in Washington; "visitation" or "parenting time" could replace "access."

Gender bias in the courts is another charged topic. Maternal custody and the "tender years" guideline are not quite the givens that paternal custody once was, but most decisions are heavily weighted in that direction. Yet children's relationships with both parents (and grandparents) should remain as close after as before divorce, with shared parenting the goal. This is already the case in Quebec. Article 600 of the Quebec Civil Code reads, "The father and mother exercise parental authority together. If either parent dies, is deprived of parental authority or is unable to express his or her will, parental authority is exercised by the other parent."

Elsewhere, an emerging fathers' rights movement, inconceivable in previous centuries when husbands got custody of their children as a natural right, usually without maternal visiting rights, is rallying fathers deprived of their children. A Canadian group's bitter invitation is typical of the movement's tone:

- *If you are a divorced or separated father who is not being treated fairly by the courts, lawyers, or other professionals.*
- *If you have been falsely accused or charged by your ex.*
- *If you are not being given a fair chance at custody or shared parenting.*
- *If you have been reduced to being just a visitor to your own child.*
- *If a vindictive mother is interfering with your access to your child.*
- *If you are having your back broken by unfair support.*
- *If your basic civil rights are being violated as a father.*
- *If you are threatened with debtor's prison because you cannot pay crippling child support.*
- *If your driver's licence has been or may be suspended because you are behind on child support.*

YOU ARE NOT ALONE. JOIN THE THOUSANDS OF OTHER FATHERS IN THIS NIGHTMARE AND FIGHT BACK!

The fathers' rights movement is partly a backlash to women's rights and egalitarianism. As well, stepfathers' anguish is often driven by the perception that a stepfather will abuse or exploit the children, or alienate them from their "real" father. The movement's ferocious attacks on child support as "crippling," "punitive," and "unfair" can be juxtaposed against oceans of statistical evidence of divorced mothers' poverty and their struggles to raise children.

Scholars Teresa A. Sullivan, Elizabeth Warren, and Jay Westbrook summarize multitudinous studies of the economic consequences of divorce, much of it centred on the relationship of child support to the economic well-being of children of divorce: "Despite considerable controversy and disagreement, almost all studies agree on two points: divorce leads to a sharp drop in income for women, and women are much worse off financially than men after divorce."[20] Canadian economist Ross Finnie's analysis of longitudinal data confirms the same trend: right after a divorce, women's income decreases by slightly more than 40 percent, then rises somewhat in subsequent years. As well, a substantial percentage of women sink into poverty after divorcing.[21] Though well-off women seldom risk poverty, their incomes decline even more steeply than those of less well-off women.[22]

Some despairing men are indeed unfairly barred from being father to their children. Yet courtroom gender bias is not the principal reason for the widespread estrangement of divorced fathers from their children. The reality is, *For the Sake of the Children* concludes, that fathers become less involved after divorce and often fail to use their visiting or access rights. According to a witness from Legal Aid in Halifax, Nova Scotia, every alleged case of access denied is matched by ten verified cases where parents, almost always fathers, do not show up.

A woman describes a simple scene: "Picture if you will, two young children dressed in their best clothes, packing their little suitcases or knapsacks and waiting for their dad to pick them up. They're excited; looking forward to the visit.... They wait and they wait. The phone rings. It's dad. He can't make it."[23]

The children are disappointed, sad, and angry. They unpack their little suitcases, and their mother comforts them. She may not resist making barbed comments about their father, her errant ex-spouse. And her children are not alone. One of the most pressing concerns about divorce is, as research suggests, that more than half of non-custodial fathers will eventually lose contact with their children. Something must be done to reverse this: shared parenting; careful planning; official and societal encouragement, including mediation and increased and new resources such as, for example, Michigan's unified Family Court and a Circuit Court division called the Friend of the Court that investigates, recommends, and enforces child custody, parenting time, and financial support. These issues are central to the marriage debate. If they are not resolved, generations of children will grow into adulthood at risk of being wounded or stunted, susceptible to depression and social withdrawal.

Bring up the topic of marriage in any group of people and expect a passionate discussion that ranges far and wide; it affects us all, and both shapes and reflects our society and how we live. But some themes dominate today's discussion though they would not have in the past. Egalitarianism, the principle of equity that has changed the modern world, looms largest and casts the longest shadow. Ironically, both

Increasingly typical are marriages such as Jon Bankson and Carol McPhee's, both divorced, who celebrated their wedding in 2007 with their now blended family: Carol's adopted children, Danica Renée and Will, and Jon's daughters Cassidy and Savannah.

romantic love and male angst, its unintended by-products, are crucial elements in the marriage debate. So is gay marriage, rooted in equity and civil rights.

Divorce is another urgent aspect of marriage; it evokes fairness, religion, personal responsibility, and a legion of other concerns. Most importantly, it raises the question of how divorce and its aftermath affect children. The blended family, too, with its complex mix of stepparents with their step- or biological children, or both, is another consequence of divorce and remarriage.

Matchmaking is often downplayed as an essential part of marriage, but there is good reason that it is one of the world's oldest professions. No matter how much we learn about marriage, no matter how much we shape and hone it through policies and social attitude, two individuals remain at the heart of any union. Working to match them up for compatibility should be a key component of thinking about marriage.

Stop Sign

Like biblical love, *A History of Marriage* never ends, and this epilogue-cum-personal reflection is only a stop sign. As I worked on and talked about this book, the subject matter evoked discussions that were passionate, far-ranging, and (usually) rooted in personal experience and concerns. For example, the aftermath of a neighbourly, all-woman focus group was that the next morning a husband confronted me in the dog park and declared, with not entirely feigned anger, "No more focus groups on your marriage book! Now all the neighbours know everything there is to know about me."

He was right. Except for the scholars who did not stray from their areas of expertise, my pre-publication readers have almost always related to the text on the most intimate levels, often in the form of confidences. In that sense, *A History of Marriage* is living proof of the vital connection between the institution's past and its present.

Another constant response to my book, at least from people who have not yet read it, are these questions: the often wistful "Does marriage have a future?" and the more forthright "Are you for marriage or against it?"

I have answers, but they're not easy yes or no ones. The first is embedded in my book's descriptive analysis of how marriage has evolved, shaped and transformed by religion and culture, institutions, circumstances, and the experiences of millions of individuals. Faulkner's witticism bears repeating: "The past isn't dead and gone, it isn't even past."

A History of Marriage is very much a dialogue between past and present, and therein lie the clues to the puzzle of the future of marriage.

The key is to understand marriage's nature as a lived experience with multi-dimensional expectations and demands that range from economic to emotional. Domestic ideals about housework and cooking, for example, have always figured largely in marriages. The new scholarship of the history of housework—the "domestic economy"—weds culture and technology to open a lens on the daily lives of millions of families throughout history. The dreaded chore of laundry, relentless, abrasive, tedious, and exhausting, enervated wives, including those forced by inadequate resources to lower their standards; images of Happy Laundry girls juxtaposed with tenement apartments overhung with laundry underscore its inescapability. Ironically, the detergent industry–sponsored "soap operas" that are central to modern afternoon television programming promise (mostly) female viewers both relief from drudgery and escape into the dramatic, crisis-filled on-air world of (laundryless) marriages, adulteries, and other relationships.

Which brings us—and them—to sex and love, and the roles they have played in historical marriage. Remember the image of the tiny Korean children as they catch their first glimpses of the spouses they are about to marry? What about the despair of the daughter whose father beat her into submissive acceptance of the marriage he had arranged for her for business reasons? Remember and rejoice! because today, egalitarian values that empower women and offer them previously unheard-of opportunities also release them from the trap of coerced marriage and unleash the possibilities of romantic and erotic love and their important role in creating and cementing consensual unions.

What about the memoirs of grieving parents and the image of a tiny, perfect infant in his coffin? Until well into the last century, death was an ever-present fact of marriage and of life; it killed women giving birth, it killed newborns and older children, it killed men, and it ended marriages. Compare childbirth then with now, when death is a remote and unusual tragedy, and nobody in their right mind who wanted two children would give birth to four in the expectation that two would die. Compare life then with life now, when longevity extends lifetimes—and hence marriages—by decades. What does this mean for the future? Answers abound, often conflicting, about child-rearing, about grieving as a constant in marriage, and about "until death do us part" as a workable marital prognosis.

The image of Civil War veteran John F. Claghorn with his ruined dangling arm speaks directly to the devastation of soldiers in today's Iraq, Afghanistan, and elsewhere; there are (unlearned) lessons galore about the profound impact of the human detritus of war on historical marriages.

In a not dissimilar vein, the recently ended policy that consigned millions of Native children to residential schools that destroyed the lives of so many, and altered their experience of marriage and of child-rearing, is also a cautionary tale about the consequences to marriage of abusive treatment.

Then there were the Eleanors, those hopeful and ambitious young women blessed with the rare opportunity to fulfill their potential and achieve their dreams in safety and comfort, in the company of the like-minded. I had the great good luck of communicating with the niece of two Eleanor sisters, and learned that both these women treasured their opportunity to hone their skills and take life by the horns. I rejoice at their strength and internal resources, and how much they made of their lives, as professional women, as wives, one as a mother, and in later life, as widows. The Eleanors strode into adulthood with confidence and determination, and their chances and choices teach so much about the history of marriage and confirm so much about the role that education and choice play in it. The Eleanor experiment also supplies bits of the puzzle that constitute the question: "Does marriage have a future?"

And now to the second question: Am I for marriage or against it? *A History of Marriage* has convinced me that, despite its patriarchal origins, marriage is a flexible institution that can provide a strong framework for raising children, for pooling resources, sharing necessary duties, obtaining security and extended family and social connections, and I am for such marriages. I am also for marriages that, on an individual basis, satisfy, comfort, and provide care for their inhabitants. But I do not believe that marriage is the right way of life for everyone, and

I am against coercive, exploitative, deeply unhappy, and unsatisfying unions.

I believe that children's welfare is paramount. I believe that marriage with children has a different dimension from childless marriage. I believe that individual women must not be expected to surrender the gains collectively won as a condition of staying married. I believe that gays and lesbians who wish to marry should be able to do so with the same rights and responsibilities as other consenting adults. I believe that there is a fundamental causal link between satisfying marriages and men and women's educational and economic statuses. I believe that many public policies—including maternity, paternity, and parental leave; child care; health care; tax laws; judicial, prison, and immigration policies; divorce laws; and egalitarian public standards—profoundly affect marriage. I believe that outside events shape the nature and development of individual marriages: wars and recessions; the collapse of North America's manufacturing base and its associated living wages, benefits, and security; homophobia and racism; popular culture; and human longevity. I believe that marriages in mansions and marriages in shacks feel quite different. I believe that divorce is not necessarily a failure, that it may also be a solution or a release.

This credo brings me to another stop sign, a new direction, and the question: How can we improve the state of North American marriage today? The history of marriage is rich in answers. The first is to acknowledge that marriage is one of several possible living arrangements that include cohabitation and singleness. The second is to recognize that divorce will not fall into disuse but that, if better support and coping mechanisms are provided, spouses will resort to it less. The third is to agree that children, whether their parents are single, separated, divorced, cohabiting, or married, should be our society's top priority. The fourth is to accept same-sex marriage as a human right that will benefit society by validating the institution and, often, by providing a comfortable framework for child-rearing.

To make all this possible, workable programs and policies are needed to address such marriage-related issues as living wages and accessible daycare. Policy-makers should heed studies about the growing gap between rich and poor and the struggles of the latter as they nickel-and-dime their way through life; they should recognize how this affects and erodes individual marriages and gives rise to the notion that marriage is becoming (or has already become) a luxury item for the wealthy. They should draw lessons from the governmental responses to the urgency of accommodating female workers during World War II and make decent child care a national priority. *A History of Marriage* is an ongoing story, and these efforts will all form part of the future narrative.

Notes

≈

CHAPTER 1

1. Jean Talon to Jean-Baptiste Colbert, November 10, 1670, *Manuscrits de Paris*, 1631–1674, Musée de la civilisation, Québec. Loosely translated by Elizabeth Abbott. www.mcq.org/histoire/filles_du_roi/index.html.
2. Quoted in Roscoe, *Changing One*, p. 3.
3. Shaw, "The Age of Roman Girls at Marriage," p. 30.
4. Caldwell, Reddy, and Caldwell, "The Causes of Marriage Change in South India," p. 345.
5. Stoertz, "Young Women in France and England," p. 32.
6. Quoted in Stoertz, "Young Women in France and England," p. 25.
7. Angel Day, *The English Secretorie* (1586), quoted in Macfarlane, *Marriage and Love in England*, p. 134.
8. Gandhi, *An Autobiography*, http://en.wikisource.org/wiki/The_Story_of_My_Experiments_with_Truth/Part_I/Child_Marriage.
9. Quoted in Burton, "From Child Bride to 'Hindoo Lady'," p. 1125.
10. Cartledge, "Spartan Wives," pp. 84–105.
11. Shaw, "The Age of Roman Girls at Marriage," p. 44.
12. One notable exception was Tuscany. See Botticini, "A Loveless Economy? Intergenerational Altruism and the Marriage Market in a Tuscan Town, 1415–1436": "The most striking feature of Tuscan society … is the absence of the so-called European marriage pattern, which has been shown to dominate in modern Western Europe. In late medieval and early Renaissance Tuscany, women married in their late teens while men married much later. Celibacy among women was virtually unknown: 97 percent of Tuscan women were married before the age of 25. Meanwhile, many men, especially those living in towns, delayed getting married, or never married: just 47 percent of Florentine men were married at the time of the *Catasto* of 1427. The age gap between men and women when marrying for the first time was lower in the countryside, where men married a bit earlier than their urban counterparts" (p. 107).
13. Watkins, "Regional Patterns of Nuptiality in Europe, 1870–1960," p. 203.
14. Friedlander, "The British Depression and Nuptiality: 1873–1896," p. 19.
15. Pickles, "Locating Widows in Mid-Nineteenth Century Pictou County, Nova Scotia," p. 74.
16. Haines, "Fertility and Marriage in a Nineteenth-Century Industrial City," pp. 154–55.
17. Roth, "Age at Marriage and the Household," note 13, p. 721.
18. Clark, *Women in Late Antiquity*, p. 41.

19. India's 1992 National Family Health Survey of 3,948 married women, aged 13 to 49, in Tamil Nadu, found that 48 percent had married their relatives, especially in rural areas and among illiterate Hindus of Scheduled Castes and Tribes.

20. All references in this section are taken from Botticini, "A Loveless Economy?"

21. Yves Landry, in "Gender Imbalance," discovered that only 41 percent of the 606 marriage contracts made by *les filles du roi* mention a dowry granted by the king. Fewer than a third in the period from 1663 to 1673 benefited.

22. Ben Jonson, *Epicoene* (1609), quoted in Siggins, *In Her Own Time*, p. 364.

CHAPTER 2

1. Caroline Norton, quoted in Forster, *Significant Sisters*, p. 20.

2. At the same time, menstrual blood has evoked fear and disgust in most societies. The Roman historian Pliny wrote in his *Natural History*, "Contact with it turns new wine sour, crops touched by it become barren, grafts die, seed in gardens are dried up, the fruit of trees falls off, the edge and steel and the gleam of ivory are dulled, hives of bees die, even bronze and iron are at once seized by rust, and a horrible smell fills the air; to taste it drives dogs mad and infects their bites with an incurable poison.... Even that very tiny creature the ant is said to be sensitive to it and throws away grains of corn that taste it and does not touch them again" (quoted in Delaney et al., *The Curse*, p. 9).

3. Harris, *English Aristocratic Women 1450–1550*, p. 28.

4. William Gouge, *Of Domestical Duties* (1622), www.mountzion.org/text/gouge-duties.rtf.

5. Leonardo Fioravanti, quoted in Bell, *How to Do It*, p. 249.

6. Martin Luther, *Table Talk*, WA TR III, no. 2847b, quoted in *Luther on Women*, ed. Karant-Nunn and Wiesner-Hanks, p. 197.

7. Rev. Daniel Wise, *The Young Lady's Counselor, or, The Sphere, the Duties, and the Dangers of Young Women* (1857), p. 232.

8. Dio Lewis, *Our Girls* (1883), p. 191.

9. Popenoe, *Modern Marriage* (1925), p. 85.

10. Harland, *Eve's Daughters* (1882), pp. 416, 407.

11. Rowbotham, *Good Girls Make Good Wives*, p. 17.

12. Mainardi, *Husbands, Wives, and Lovers*, p. 155.

13. Wise, *The Young Lady's Counselor*, p. 232.

14. Otto and Andersen, "The Hope Chest and Dowry: American Custom?" p. 6.

15. Jabour, *Scarlett's Sisters*, p. 116.

16. Laura Wirt, quoted in Jabour, *Scarlett's Sisters*, p. 134.

17. Penelope Skinner Warren, quoted in Jabour, *Scarlett's Sisters*, p. 211.

18. Wirt, quoted in Jabour, *Scarlett's Sisters*, p. 177.

19. Skinner Warren, quoted in Jabour, *Scarlett's Sisters*, p. 224.

20. Wirt, quoted in Jabour, *Scarlett's Sisters*, p. 206.

21. Miles, *Every Girl's Duty*, p. 52.

22. Miles, *Every Girl's Duty*, p. 16.

CHAPTER 3

1. The following interpretations are drawn from: Carroll, "In the Name of God and Profit"; Hall, "The Arnolfini Betrothal"; Koster, "The Arnolfini Double Portrait"; Panofsky, "Jan van Eyck's Arnolfini Portrait"; and Seidel, *Jan van Eyck's Arnolfini Portrait*. Koster's closely reasoned arguments are the most persuasive.

2. After the eleventh century this began to change as the Catholic Church issued regulations making priests more central to what constituted a valid marriage.

3. Coontz, *Marriage, a History*, p. 117.

4. Hanley, "The Jurisprudence of the Arrêts," p. 21.

5. Roper, "Going to Church and Street," p. 84.

6. Roper, "Going to Church and Street," p. 82.

7. Roper, "Going to Church and Street," pp. 66, 67.

8. Moodie, *Roughing It in the Bush* (1852).

9. Reed-Danahay, "Champagne and Chocolate," pp. 750–76.

10. Peters, "Gender, Sacrament and Ritual," p. 88.

11. All the material in this section comes from Ladurie, *The Beggar and the Professor*.

12. Quoted in Cott, *Public Vows*, p. 31.

13. Cott, *Public Vows*, p. 39.

14. Van Kirk, "Many Tender Ties," p. 40.

15. Many white men married to Native women later abandoned them and married white women. See Abbott, " 'Country Wives' in Colonial America," in *A History of Mistresses*, pp. 187–90.

16. John Lawe to Robert Hamilton, quoted in Peterson, "Prelude to Red River," p. 42.

17. See Cott, *Public Vows*, p. 33.

18. Chesnut, *A Diary from Dixie*, p. 225.

19. The origins of jumping the broom are obscure. The only other known instance of this was in an eighteenth-century community in North Wales, which is unlikely to have influenced the slave ritual. An unproven explanation may be the domestic implications of a broom in a doorway.

20. Penny Thompson, quoted in Dunaway, *The African-American Family in Slavery and Emancipation*, p. 119.

21. Lizzie Grant, quoted in Dunaway, *The African-American Family in Slavery and Emancipation*, pp. 119–20.

22. Quoted in Dunaway, *The African-American Family in Slavery and Emancipation*, p. 261.

23. Quoted in Dunaway, *The African-American Family in Slavery and Emancipation*, p. 262.

24. Quoted in Bardaglio, *Reconstructing the Household*, p. 132.

25. Quoted in Dunaway, *The African-American Family in Slavery and Emancipation*, p. 261.

26. Curtiss, "Royal Wedding Gown."

27. Lyttelton, one of Victoria's ladies-in-waiting, quoted in *New York Times*, July 7, 1893.

28. Coontz, *Marriage, a History*, p. 167.

CHAPTER 4

1. Quoted in Le Faye, *Jane Austen*, p. 92.

2. Quoted in Le Faye, *Jane Austen*, p. 92.

3. Le Faye, *Jane Austen,* p. 92.

4. Quoted in Le Faye, *Jane Austen*, p. 144.

5. Quoted in Coontz, *Marriage, a History*, p. 185.

6. Letter dated November 18, 1814, quoted in Le Faye, *Jane Austen's Letters*, p. 280.

7. Jerome, *Against Jovinian*, p. 367, quoted in Abbott, *A History of Celibacy*, p. 54.

8. Shaw, "The Family in Late Antiquity," p. 36.

9. Vickery, *The Gentleman's Daughter*, p. 82.

10. Cott, *Public Vows*, p. 12.

11. Quoted in Hufton, *The Prospect Before Her*, p. 127.

12. This section on Martin Luther and Katharina von Bora is based on Karant-Nunn and Wiesner-Hanks, eds., *Luther on Women*, and Smith, "Katharina von Bora through Five Centuries."

13. Quoted in Smith, "Katharina von Bora," p. 749.

14. Quoted in Smith, "Katharina von Bora," pp. 762, 771.

15. Quoted in Smith, "Katharina von Bora," p. 12.

16. Karant-Nunn and Wiesner-Hanks, eds., *Luther on Women*, p. 197.

17. Coontz, *Marriage, a History*, p. 139.

18. Vickery, *The Gentleman's Daughter*, pp. 72–73.

19. Peter Kalm, "The Ladies in French Canada" (1749), in Hart and Hill, *Camps and Firesides of the Revolution*.

20. Quoted in Landry, "Gender Imbalance, Les Filles du Roi, and Choice of Spouse in New France," p. 28.

21. Dumont-Johnson, *Quebec Women*, p. 44.

22. Landry, "Gender Imbalance, Les Filles du Roi, and Choice of Spouse in New France," p. 33.

23. Quoted in Hufton, *The Prospect Before Her*, p. 122.

24. Quoted in Hufton, *The Prospect Before Her*, p. 148.

25. Quoted in Vickery, *The Gentleman's Daughter*, pp. 52–53.

26. Quoted in Vickery, *The Gentleman's Daughter*, pp. 63, 62.

27. Vickery, *The Gentleman's Daughter*, p. 41.

28. Coontz, *Marriage, a History*, p. 146.

29. Quoted in Harrison, *The Dark Angel*, p. 23.

30. Miles, *Every Girl's Duty*, pp. 43, 106

31. Quoted in Jabour, *Marriage in the Early Republic*, pp. 13, 17.

32. O'Brien Journal, March 6, 1830, quoted in Errington, *Wives and Mothers, Schoolmistresses and Scullery Maids*, p. 39.

33. Quoted in Jabour, *Scarlett's Sisters*, p. 89.

34. Chesnut, *A Diary from Dixie*, p. 193.

35. Cécile Pasteur to Julie Duvernay, Montreal, April 22, 1817, quoted in Noël, *Family Life and Sociability in Upper and Lower Canada*, p. 19.

36. Quoted in Noël, *Family Life and Sociability in Upper and Lower Canada*, p. 20.

37. Quoted in Jabour, *Scarlett's Sisters*, p. 159.

38. Quoted in Noël, *Family Life and Sociability in Upper and Lower Canada*, p. 53.

39. Quoted in Noël, *Family Life and Sociability in Upper and Lower Canada*, p. 55.

40. His father, Louis-Joseph Papineau, was granted amnesty in 1844. In 1845, he returned to his seigneury. He made a fortune from timber concessions and built a grand manor house at Montebello.

41. Mary A. Westcott to Mary E. Westcott, May 18, 1845, quoted in Noël, *Family Life and Sociability in Upper and Lower Canada*, p. 57.

42. Mary Westcott to Amédée Papineau, May 28, 1845, quoted in *I Do: Love and Marriage in 19th Century Canada*, Library and Archives Canada, www.collectionscanada.gc.ca/love-and-marriage/031001-2001-e.html#a.

43. James Westcott to Amédée Papineau, June 20, 1845, quoted in *I Do*, http://data2.collectionscanada.gc.ca/e/e333/e008311222-v8.jpg.

44. Mary Westcott to Amédée Papineau, June 22, 1845, quoted in *I Do*, http://data2.collectionscanada.gc.ca/e/e333/e008311222-v8.jpg.

45. Mary. Papineau to James Westcott, June 4, 1846, quoted in Noël, *Family Life and Sociability in Upper and Lower Canada, 1780–1870*, p. 78.

46. All quotations in this section are from Chesnut, *A Diary from Dixie*.

47. Quoted in Susanna Moodie, "Old Woodruff and His Three Wives: A Canadian Sketch," *The Literary Garland and British North American Magazine*, January 1847, pp. 16–17.

48. Quoted in Errington, *Wives and Mothers, Schoolmistresses and Scullery Maids*, p. 32.

49. Errington, *Wives and Mothers, Schoolmistresses and Scullery Maids*, p. 39.

50. Henry Mackenzie, *Julia de Roubigné* (1777), quoted in Errington, *Wives and Mothers, Schoolmistresses and Scullery Maids*, p. 29.

51. Quoted in Jabour, *Marriage in the Early Republic*, pp. 56, 53.

52. Coontz, *Marriage, a History*, pp. 164, 156.

53. William Wirt to Laura Wirt, quoted in Jabour, *Scarlett's Sisters*, p. 84.

54. Quoted in Coontz, *Marriage, a History*, p. 191.

55. Abraham H. Galloway, quoted in Bardaglio, *Reconstructing the Household*, p. 178.

56. Quoted in D'Emilio and Freedman, *Intimate Matters*, p. 86.

57. Quoted in Jabour, *Scarlett's Sisters*, p. 218.

58. Jane Goodwin to James Goodwin, quoted in Lowry, *The Story the Soldiers Wouldn't Tell*, pp. 37–38.

59. Quoted in Jabour, *Scarlett's Sisters*, p. 221.

60. Quoted in Hedrick, *Harriet Beecher Stowe*, pp. 178–80.

61. Faderman, *Odd Girls and Twilight Lovers*, p. 22.

62. Stopes, *Married Love or Love in Marriage*.

63. O.S. Fowler, *Creative and Sexual Science, or Manhood, Womanhood and their Mutual Interrelations … as Taught by Phrenology and Physiology* (1875), quoted in Jean Stengers and Anne van Neck, *Masturbation: The History of a Great Terror*, trans. Kathryn Hoffmann (New York: Palgrave, 2001), p. 107.

64. Henry Rice Stout, *Our Family Physician: A Thoroughly Reliable Guide to the Detection and Treatment of All Diseases That Can Be Either Checked in Their Career or Treated Entirely by an Intelligent Person, Without the Aid of a Physician; Especially Such as Require Prompt and Energetic Measures, and Those Peculiar to This Country* (1871), p. 334.

65. Thomas Laqueur, *Solitary Sex: A Cultural History of Masturbation* (New York: Zone Books, 2004), quoted in Ontario Consultants on Religious Tolerance, "Masturbation: Medical Beliefs in Past Centuries," www.religioustolerance.org/masturba4.htm.

66. At different times, this nebulous condition was also called suffocation of the mother, uterine congestion, pelvic inflammation, hysterical paroxysm, hysteroneurasthenia, and frigidity.

67. Rachel Maines, *The Technology of Orgasm: 'Hysteria,' the Vibrator, and Women's Sexual Satisfaction* (Johns Hopkins Press, 1999), quoted in Natalie Angier, "In the History of Gynecology, a Surprising Chapter," *New York Times*, February 23, 1999.

68. John Marten, *Gonsologium Novum*, quoted in McLaren, *Impotence*, pp. 78–79, 81.

69. Quoted in McLaren, *Impotence*, p. 101.

70. Andrea Tone, "Contraceptive Consumers: Gender and the Political Economy of Birth Control in the 1930s," *Journal of Social History*, vol. 29, no. 3, p. 1.

71. A.H. Agard, surgeon and pension examiner, quoted in Schmidt, "Private Parts."

72. Mumford, "Lost Manhood Found," p. 48.

73. Cott, *Public Vows*, p. 158.

CHAPTER 5

1. Martha C. Wright, "Hints for Wives," delivered at Seneca Falls and first published in *United States Gazette* (Philadelphia), September 23, 1846, quoted in Livingston and Penney, *A Very Dangerous Woman*, pp. 79–80.

2. Livingston and Penney, *A Very Dangerous Woman*, p. 4.

3. Quoted in Boydston, *Home and Work*, p. 78.

4. Perkins, *Christian Oeconomie* (1609), quoted in Longfellow, "Public, Private, and the Household in Early Seventeenth-Century England," p. 323.

5. Ariès, *Centuries of Childhood*, p. 404.

6. Quoted in Stone, "The Public and the Private in the Stately Homes of England, 1500–1990," p. 234.

7. Langton, *A Gentlewoman in Upper Canada*, p. 146.

8. Foster, *American Houses*, p. 92.

9. Jabour, *Marriage in the Early Republic*, p. 33.

10. Sarah Frances Hicks Williams, quoted in Genovese, *Roll, Jordan, Roll*, p. 336.

11. Mary Boykin Chesnut, quoted in Genovese, *Roll, Jordan, Roll*, p. 426.

12. Dunaway, *The African-American Family in Slavery and Emancipation*, p. 92.

13. Quoted in Clark, "Domestic Architecture as an Index to Social History," p. 50.

14. Michelle Perrot, ed., *A History of Private Life*, vol. 4, quoted in Hareven, "The Home and the Family in Historical Perspective," p. 260.

15. Quoted in Kleinberg, "Gendered Space," p. 147.

16. Quoted in Rourke, *Trumpets of Jubilee*, p. 99.

17. Quoted in Hareven, "The Home and the Family in Historical Perspective," p. 261.

18. Quoted in Jabour, *Scarlett's Sisters*, p. 183.

19. Noël, *Family Life and Sociability in Upper and Lower Canada*, p. 107.

20. Quoted in Rourke, *Trumpets of Jubilee*, p. 111.

21. Boydston, *Home and Work*, p. 132.

22. Quoted in Rourke, *Trumpets of Jubilee*, p. 98.

23. Quoted in Boydston, *Home and Work*, p. 107.

24. Quoted in Boydston, *Home and Work*, p. 113.

25. Riis, *The Making of an American*.

26. Quoted in Mintz, "Housework in Late 19th Century America."

27. Catharine Beecher, *A Treatise on Domestic Economy* (1841), p. 149.

28. Quoted in Mintz, "Housework in Late 19th Century America."

29. Quoted in Boydston, *Home and Work*, pp. 81–82.

30. Boydston, *Home and Work*, p. 85.

31. Beecher, *A Treatise on Domestic Economy*, pp. 144, 143.

32. Beecher, *A Treatise on Domestic Economy*, p. 145.

33. Martha Bute, "Homemakers Male and Female," in Margaret Marsh, ed., *Suburban Lives* (New Brunswick, NJ: Rutgers University Press, 1990), p. 88.

34. Hampsten, *Settlers' Children*, p. 18.

35. Hampsten, *Settlers' Children*, p. 235.

36. Hampsten, *Settlers' Children*, p. 40.

37. Hampsten, *Settlers' Children*, p. 236.

38. Hampsten, *Settlers' Children*, p. 214.

39. Gilman, *The Home*, pp. 183, 272.

40. Gilman, *Women and Economics*, p. 58.
41. Gilman, *Women and Economics*, pp. 116–22 passim.
42. Trollope, "Philadelphia, Pennsylvania, August 1830."
43. Riis, "Genesis of the Tenement," in *How the Other Half Lives.*
44. Riis, "Genesis of the Tenement," in *How the Other Half Lives.*
45. Margaret Frances Byington, *Homestead: The Households of a Mill Town* (1910; Charleston, S.C.: Bibliolife, 2008), p. 145.
46. Quoted in Lubove, *The Progressives and the Slums*, p. 7.
47. Sara R. O'Brien, *English for Foreigners* (1909), quoted in Hareven, "The Home and the Family in Historical Perspective," p. 282.

CHAPTER 6

1. Éléonore was Napoleon's sister Caroline's secretary and, when introduced to Napoleon, she was also Caroline's husband's mistress.
2. Quoted in Ryken, *Worldly Saints*, p. 50.
3. Jabour, *Scarlett's Sisters*, p. 225.
4. Quoted in Jabour, *Scarlett's Sisters*, p. 226.
5. Queen Victoria to Princess Vicky, July 11, 1860, quoted in Palmer, "Queen Victoria's Not So 'Victorian' Writings."
6. William Gossip's Memorandum Book, quoted in Vickery, *The Gentleman's Daughter*, pp. 103–4.
7. Quoted in Noël, *Family Life and Sociability in Upper and Lower Canada*, p. 136.
8. Quoted in Vickery, *The Gentleman's Daughter*, p. 105.
9. Vickery, *The Gentleman's Daughter*, pp. 106, 107.
10. Susannah Moodie to John Moodie, January 11, 1839, Library and Archives Canada, www.lac-bac.gc.ca/moodie-traill/027013-119.01-f.php?rec_id_nbr=20& anchor=027013-1100.3-f.html.
11. Quoted in Heywood, *A History of Childhood*, p. 60.
12. Quoted in Noël, *Family Life and Sociability in Upper and Lower Canada*, p. 146.
13. Quoted in Heywood, *A History of Childhood*, p. 59.
14. Quoted in Karant-Nunn and Wiesner-Hanks, eds., *Luther on Women*, p. 199.
15. William Wirt to Dabney Carr, quoted in Jabour, *Marriage in the Early Republic*, pp. 145–46.
16. Queen Victoria to Princess Vicky, April 21 and June 15, 1858, quoted in Palmer, "Queen Victoria's Not So 'Victorian' Writings."
17. Quoted in McLaren, *Reproductive Rituals*, p. 76.
18. The 1450 edition of the first English gynecological handbook, quoted in McLaren, *Reproductive Rituals*, p. 101.
19. Quoted in McLaren, *Reproductive Rituals*, p. 84.
20. *Blagrave's Supplement or Enlargement to Mr. Nich. Culpepper's English Physitian* (1674), quoted in McLaren, *Reproductive Rituals*, p. 73.

21. Lowry, *The Story the Soldiers Wouldn't Tell*, p. 96.

22. Lowry, *The Story the Soldiers Wouldn't Tell*, p. 97.

23. Quoted in McLaren, *Reproductive Rituals*, pp. 95, 97–98.

24. Gordon, *The Moral Property of Women*, p. 24.

25. Jabour, *Marriage in the Early Republic*, p. 40, 75.

26. Potts and Campbell, "History of Contraception," p. 8.

27. Quoted in Kate Worsley, "Trends in Medical Abortion Provision in the United Kingdom: An Overview," Global Safe Abortion Conference, 2007, www.global-safeabortion.org/Media/Session04/Presentations/Seminar_19_Kate_Worsley.pdf.

28. McLaren, *Reproductive Rituals*, p. 111.

29. Lowry, *The Story the Soldiers Wouldn't Tell*, p. 97.

30. Heywood, *A History of Childhood*, p. 46.

31. Quoted in Potts and Campbell, "History of Contraception," p. 8.

32. The main source for the section on Madame Restell is Lori Kenschaft, "Abortion in the Life and Times of 'The Most Evil Woman in New York,' Madame Restell," Celebration of Our Work conference, Rutgers University Institute for Research on Women, 1990, www.kenschaft.com/restell.htm.

33. Quoted in Potts and Campbell, "History of Contraception," p. 8.

34. "The American Medical Association's Positions on Abortion, 1859–1996," Life Research Institute, www.geocities.com/kekogut.

35. Quoted in Pollock, *Forgotten Children*, p. 218.

36. Elizabeth Wirt to William Wirt, nine days after their daughter's birth, quoted in Jabour, *Marriage in the Early Republic*, p. 77.

37. Golden, *A Social History of Wet Nursing in America*, p. 97.

38. Quoted in Dunaway, *The African-American Family in Slavery and Emancipation*, p. 136.

39. Lloyd deMause, ed., *The History of Childhood*, pp. 1–2.

40. Quoted in Vickery, *The Gentleman's Daughter*, p. 121.

41. Pollock, *Forgotten Children*, p. 235.

42. Vickery, *The Gentleman's Daughter*, p. 91.

43. Quoted in Pollock, *Forgotten Children*, p. 222.

44. Quoted in Pollock, *Forgotten Children*, p. 225.

45. Vickery, *The Gentleman's Daughter*, p. 113.

46. Quoted in Vickery, *The Gentleman's Daughter*, p. 122.

47. Quoted in Jabour, *Marriage in the Early Republic*, p. 41.

48. Quoted in Pollock, *Forgotten Children*, p. 157.

49. In *Some Thoughts Concerning Education* (1692), John Locke prescribed an abstemious regimen for children instead of the coddling he saw all around him. "For when their children are grown up, and these ill habits with them; when they are now too big to be dandled, and their parents can no longer make use of them as play-things, then they complain that the brats are untoward and perverse; then

they are offended to see them wilful, and are troubled with those ill humours which they themselves infus'd and fomented in them ... [yet the child] had the mastery of his parents ever since he could prattle; and why, now he is grown up, is stronger and wiser than he was then, why now of a sudden must he be restrain'd and curb'd? Why must he at seven, fourteen, or twenty years old, lose the privilege, which the parents' indulgence 'till then so largely allow'd him?" (www.fordham.edu/halsall/mod/1692locke-education.html).

50. Quoted in Pollock, *Forgotten Children*, p. 110.

51. Pleck, *Domestic Tyranny*, p. 26.

52. Walsh, "Community Networks in the Early Chesapeake," quoted in Lois Green Carr, Philip D. Morgan, and Jean Burrell Russo, eds., *Colonial Chesapeake Society* (Chapel Hill: University of North Carolina Press, 1991), p. 244.

53. Quoted in Mintz, *Huck's Raft*, p. 41.

54. Quoted in Dunaway, *The African-American Family in Slavery and Emancipation*, pp. 52, 53.

55. Quoted in King, *Stolen Childhood*, p. 2.

56. Frederick Douglass and Jacob Branch, quoted in King, *Stolen Childhood*, pp. 21, 23.

57. Prince Woodfin, quoted in King, *Stolen Childhood*, p. 68.

58. Jacob Stroyer, quoted in Dunaway, *The African-American Family in Slavery and Emancipation*, p. 75.

59. Quoted in King, *Stolen Childhood*, p. 98.

60. Hampsten, *Settlers' Children*, p. 101.

61. Quoted in Mook, "Les Petits Sauvages," p. 43.

62. Before the nineteenth century, fertility levels throughout North America equalled or surpassed those in today's less developed countries.

63. Quoted in Mintz, *Huck's Raft*, p. 77.

64. Vickery, *The Gentleman's Daughter*, p. 122.

65. Kate Douglas Wiggin, children's author, quoted in Heywood, *A History of Childhood*, p. 94.

66. Alexis de Tocqueville, *Democracy in America*, www.marxists.org/reference/archive/de-tocqueville/democracy-america.

67. Quoted in Del Col, "The Life of the Industrial Worker in Nineteenth-Century England," www.victorianweb.org/history/workers2.html.

68. Quoted in Houston, "The 'Waifs and Strays' of a Late Victorian City," p. 129.

69. Pollock, *Forgotten Children*, p. 93.

70. Robert McIntosh, *Boys in the Pits: Child Labour in Coal Mines* (Montreal: McGill-Queen's University Press, 2000), quoted in Ernestine Patterson Leary, *Monthly Labor Review*, March 2001.

71. Stephen J. Cole, "Commissioning Consent: An Investigation of the Royal Commission on the Relations of Labour and Capital, 1886–1889" (PhD diss., Queen's University, Kingston, 2007), pp. 364, 365, 367.

72. Watson, "Home Work in the Tenements."

CHAPTER 7

1. Quoted in Abbott, *A History of Celibacy*, p. 299.

2. Mrs. Battersby was a case in point: she had separated from Mr. Battersby six weeks after marrying because he consorted with prostitutes and had contracted venereal disease, but neither tried to obtain a divorce. Twelve years after they separated he married bigamously, giving Mrs. Battersby the legal grounds, and she obtained her divorce. Mr. Battersby was deported to Australia.

3. See Wolfram, "Divorce in England 1700–1857," p. 178.

4. Quoted in Phillips, *Putting Asunder*, p. 14.

5. Rev. David Reed, email to the author, April 18, 2009.

6. John Calvin, *Institutes of the Christian Religion*, vol. II, p. 1252, quoted in Phillips, *Putting Asunder*, p. 41.

7. John Calvin, *A Harmony of the Gospels Matthew, Mark and Luke*, vol. I, p. 190, quoted in Phillips, *Putting Asunder*, p. 53.

8. Quoted in Phillips, *Untying the Knot*, p. 16.

9. Quoted in Kingdon, *Adultery and Divorce in Calvin's Geneva*, pp. 39, 62, 63.

10. C. Norton, *English Laws for Women in the Nineteenth Century* (1854), http://digital.library.upenn.edu/women/norton/elfw/elfw.html.

11. Caroline Norton, "A Letter to the Queen on Lord Chancellor Cranworth's Marriage and Divorce Bill" (1855), http://digital.library.upenn.edu/women/norton/alttq/alttq.html.

12. Clause 21: A deserted wife's earnings might be protected from her husband's claim on them. Clause 24: The courts could order separate maintenance payments made to a wife or to her trustee. Clause 25: A wife could inherit and bequeath property like a single woman. Clause 26: A wife separated from her husband could make contracts, sue, and be sued in civil proceedings.

13. Norma Basch, *Framing American Divorce*, p. 15.

14. Arkansas Supreme Court, quoted in Phillips, *Untying the Knot*, p. 145.

15. Quoted in Phillips, *Untying the Knot*, p. 147.

16. Quoted in Phillips, *Untying the Knot*, p. 149.

17. Henry James, Sr., Horace Greeley, and Stephen Pearl Andrews, *Love, Marriage, and Divorce* (1853/1889), http://praxeology.net/HJ-HG-SPA-LMD-3.htm.

18. Basch, *Framing American Divorce*, p. 16.

19. Quoted in Bardaglio, *Reconstructing the Household*, p. 38.

20. Quoted in Bardaglio, *Reconstructing the Household*, p. 135.

21. Quoted in Bardaglio, *Reconstructing the Household*, p. 120.

22. Quoted in Phillips, *Putting Asunder*, p. 441.

23. Quoted in Basch, *Framing American Divorce*, p. 78.

24. Quoted in Martin, "A Star That Gathers Lustre from the Gloom of Night," p. 279.

25. Quoted in Basch, *Framing American Divorce*, p. 69.

26. The source for this section on Elizabeth Packard is Levison, "Elizabeth Parsons Ware Packard."

27. Quoted in Basch, *Framing American Divorce*, p. 150.

28. Quoted in Basch, *Framing American Divorce*, p. 166.

29. Basch, *Framing American Divorce*, p. 71.

30. Quoted in Basch, *Framing American Divorce*, p. 75.

31. Catherine Beecher, *Essay on Slavery and Abolition*, quoted in Boydston, *Home and Work*, p. 162.

32. Basch, *Framing American Divorce*, p. 191.

33. Quoted in Bardaglio, *Reconstructing the Household*, p. 134.

34. Quoted in Bardaglio, *Reconstructing the Household*, pp. 134–35.

35. Quoted in Bardaglio, *Reconstructing the Household*, p. 142.

36. Newton Scott to Hannah Cone, October 24, 1862, *Letters Home from an Iowa Soldier in the American Civil War*, www.civilwarletters.com.

37. Peter Blanck, "Civil War Pensions and Disability."

38. Quoted in Lowry, *The Story the Soldiers Wouldn't Tell*, p. 107.

39. Lowry, *The Story the Soldiers Wouldn't Tell*, p. 104.

40. Lowry, *The Story the Soldiers Wouldn't Tell*, p. 108.

41. Newton Scott to Hannah Cone, July 22, 1864, www.civilwarletters.com.

42. Newton Scott to Hannah Cone, July 23, 1863, www.civilwarletters.com.

43. Chesnut, *A Diary from Dixie*, p. 201.

44. Quoted in Lowry, *The Story the Soldiers Wouldn't Tell*, p. 31.

45. Chesnut, *A Diary from Dixie*, p. 382.

46. Quoted in "Unhappiness Abroad: Civil War Refugees," Fort Ward Museum and Historic Site, Alexandria, Virginia, http://oha.alexandriava.gov/fortward/special-sections/refugees.

47. Phillips, *Untying the Knot*, p. 155.

48. Phillips, *Untying the Knot*, p. 194.

49. Phillips, *Untying the Knot*, p. 219.

PART 2 INTRODUCTION

1. Anne-Marie Ambert, "Divorce: Facts, Causes and Consequences," Vanier Institute of the Family, www.vifamily.ca/library/cft/divorce_05.html.

2. Jonathan Ames, "What Is the Future of Marriage?" quoted in "Voice Box," Nerve.com, www.nerve.com/dispatches/voicebox/futureofmarriage/question1.asp.

3. *Brides* magazine, for instance, in 2009 the largest magazine in the United States in terms of ad pages (seven hundred per issue), has a circulation of 405,000 and is published six times a year. Kingston, *The Meaning of Wife*, p. 41, credits Martha Stewart's 1987 book *Weddings* with injecting the notion of tradition as the wedding standard.

4. Rebecca Traister, "Bridezilla Bites Back!" *Salon,* June 18, 2004, http://dir.salon.com/story/mwt/feature/2004/06/18/bridezilla/index.html.

5. Rebecca Mead, *One Perfect Day: The Selling of the American Wedding* (New York: Penguin, 2007), pp. 222, 223.

6. Kingston, *The Meaning of Wife*, p. 34.

7. Céline Dion's tiara weighed a neck-crushing twenty pounds.

8. See, for instance, Marcelle S. Fischler, "A New Nose, Then the 'I Do,'" *New York Times*, January 30, 2005; "Plastic Surgery, Breast Implants Popular at Bridal Fair," *The StarPhoenix* (Saskatoon), January 22, 2007.

9. Coontz, "In Search of a Golden Age," p. 18.

10. Quoted in "Biography for Billy Gray," Internet Movie Database, www.imdb.com/name/nm0336474/bio.

CHAPTER 8

1. All McCrae quotations are from letters to his mother quoted in CBC, "Horror on the Battlefield: In Flanders Fields," episode 12 of *Canada: A People's History*, http://history.cbc.ca/history.

2. Major studies include Frances Manges, "Women Shopkeepers, Tavernkeepers, and Artisans in Colonial Philadelphia" (PhD diss., University of Pennsylvania, 1958); Mary Roberts Parramore, "'For Her Sole and Separate Use': Female Sole Trader Status in Early South Carolina" (master's thesis, University of South Carolina, 1991); Elisabeth Anthony Dexter, *Colonial Women of Affairs: A Study of Women in Business and the Professions in America Before 1776* (New York: Houghton Mifflin, 1924); and Jean Jordan, "Women Merchants in Colonial New York," *New York History* (1977), vol. 58, pp. 412–39.

3. Christine Jacobson Carter, *Southern Single Blessedness: Unmarried Women in the Urban South, 1800–1865* (University of Illinois Press, 2006), p. 7.

4. Quoted in Hedrick, *Harriet Beecher Stowe*, pp. 180–81.

5. All quotes are from Fine, "Between Two Worlds."

6. *Eleanor Record*, May 1915, quoted in Fine, "Between Two Worlds," note 21.

7. Quoted in Roberts, "51% of Women Are Now Living without a Spouse."

8. Bibby, "Cohabitation."

9. Smock, in "Cohabitation in the United States," reviews the literature on cohabitation.

10. Cohabiting men earn about 10 to 40 percent less than married men. Married and cohabiting women earn about the same, but cohabiting women are less likely to benefit from their partners' earnings.

11. There are many reasons for this lacuna. For one thing, evidence is scanty. Until recently, for example, censuses did not include information about female employment. And the stigma often faced by single women, especially poorer ones, could make them invisible in their own societies. But they existed in large numbers, and there are ways of researching their lives, for example through examining police and court ledgers to see if poverty led them into crime and prostitution, and examining where they lived, what part they played in religious organizations, and how they engaged in letter writing, volunteer work and other features of daily living. Insofar as single women were feared by authorities as a threat to the social order, policies put in place to monitor and control them exist to be studied. Even historians of the family have neglected singles, who lived as integral family

members, in other arrangements or alone; they focused entirely on married men and women.

For recent research on single women, see, for example, Froide, *Never Married*; Froide and Bennett, eds., *Singlewomen in the European Past, 1250–1800*; Hill, *Women Alone*; Chambers-Schiller, *Liberty*; Hartman, *The Household and the Making of History*; Froide, *Singlewomen in Early Modern England*; Holden, *The Shadow of Marriage*; and Nicholson, *Singled Out*.

12. Cott, *No Small Courage*, pp. 181–83.
13. Nigel Jones, "A New Type of Woman," *Mail Online*, June 5, 2008, www.dailymail.co.uk/home/books/article-1024405/INTERVIEW-Meet-Virginia-Nicholson-author-Junes-book-Singled-Out.html.
14. See Koppelman, ed., *Old Maids*, which includes thirteen stories written between 1834 and 1891.
15. Kalinowski, "As Traditional as a Child," in Rauhala, ed., *The Lucky Ones*, p. 13.
16. National Adoption Information Clearinghouse, *Single Parent Adoption: What You Need to Know*, www.childbirthsolutions.com/articles/preconception/adoption/singleadopting.php.
17. All quotations are from Klose, "In the Beginning."
18. Hood, "Sometime in the Night."
19. Kalinowski, "As Traditional as a Child," p. 8.
20. Gottlieb, "Marry Him!"

CHAPTER 9

1. All quotes from *People*, August 19, 2008.
2. Juvenal, quoted in Frier, "Roman Same-Sex Weddings from the Legal Perspective."
3. In "Roman Same-Sex Weddings from the Legal Perspective," for example, Bruce W. Frier, argues that Roman marriage had a social dimension and a legal, because "the Roman government … declined to oversee the process of marriage through licensing or even through registration, so that marriage arose as a largely private event outside of government scrutiny." Frier adds that "it may even be fair to posit that these same-sex ceremonies were intended, at least in part, as deliberately subversive of the traditional social institution of marriage."
4. Keith Olbermann, "Gay Marriage Is a Question of Love," msnbc.com, November 10, 2008, www.msnbc.msn.com/id/27650743.
5. The first known American gay rights organization, the Society for Human Rights in Chicago, was founded in 1924. Canada's first gay-positive organization, the Association for Social Knowledge, or ASK, was founded in Vancouver in 1964.
6. Burroway, "Today in History."
7. *Klippert v. The Queen*, [1967] S.C.R. 822, http://csc.lexum.umontreal.ca/en/1967/1967rcs0-822/1967rcs0-822.html.
8. CBC, "Same-sex Rights: Canada Timeline," www.cbc.ca/news/background/samesexrights/timeline_canada.html.

9. Quoted in David Adox, "What's the Difference Between a Homosexual and a Murderer?" Salon, May 2, 1997, www.salon.com/may97/sullivan970502.html.

10. Gay-hating literature and websites also reference Leviticus 18:22, Genesis 19, Romans 1:18–32, I Corinthians 6:9–11, I Timothy 1:10, and Jude 7.

11. This document is seen as undemocratic interference even by some who also oppose gay marriage. Canadian ethicist Margaret Somerville, for instance, criticizes the Vatican document because "whether to legalize such partnerships as a civil institution is a civil decision. Everyone, including religious people, can make their views, including their own moral views, known. But, in a secular, democratic society, the views of religions have no special status in such decisions" ("The Other 'Rights Question' in Same-Sex Marriage," The Institute for the Study of Marriage, Law and Culture, www.marriageinstitute.ca/pages/otheright.htm).

12. Margaret Somerville, "The Case Against 'Same-Sex Marriage,'" brief submitted to the Standing Committee on Justice and Human Rights, 2003, www.marriageinstitute.ca/images/somerville.pdf.

13. Margaret Somerville, "Jean, Paul, and Jean-Pault: Politicians, the Pope, and Same-Sex Marriage Confusion," Institute for the Study of Marriage, Law and Culture, www.marriageinstitute.ca/pages/jpaul.htm.

14. Young and Nathanson, "Marriage-a-la-mode: Answering Advocates of Gay Marriage," paper presented at Emory University, Atlanta, 2003.

15. See Strock, *Married Women who Love Women*, p. 74. These statistics are estimates.

16. Quoted in Vanita, *Love's Rite*, pp. 166–67.

17. Pastor Gregory Daniels, quoted in Boykin, "Whose Dream?"

18. Quoted in Denizet-Lewis, "Double Lives on the Down Low."

19. Quoted in Douglas, "Guy Meets Guy on the Down Low."

20. Han, "A Different Shade of Queer."

21. A scholarly contribution to this issue is Hull, *Same-Sex Marriage*.

22. Quoted in Denizet-Lewis, "Double Lives on the Down Low."

23. Bowe, "Gay Donor or Gay Dad?"

24. Dufur, McKune, Hoffmann, and Bahr, "Adolescent Outcomes in Single Parent, Heterosexual Couple, and Homosexual Couple Families."

25. Patterson, "Lesbian and Gay Parents and Their Children."

26. Jenny Carole et al., "Are Children at Risk for Sexual Abuse by Homosexuals?" quoted in American Civil Liberties Union, "Overview of Lesbian and Gay Parenting, Adoption and Foster Care."

27. American Association for Justice, "Convicted Killer, Not Lesbian Mother, Awarded Custody of Girl," www.thefreelibrary.com/Convicted+killer,+not+lesbian+mother,+awarded+custody+of+girl-a018341036.

28. Quoted in Kendell, "Lesbian and Gay Parents in Child Custody and Visitation Disputes."

29. Quoted in Kendell, "Lesbian and Gay Parents in Child Custody and Visitation Disputes."

30. Quoted in Rosenwald Smith and Abrahms, *What Every Woman Should Know about Divorce and Custody*, p. 72.

31. Whitehead, "Policies Affecting Gay Fathers."

32. See, for example, Hoghughi and Long, *The Handbook of Parenting*, p. 135: "Perhaps because, other things being equal, gay fathers are extremely unlikely to win custody battles over their children after divorce, fewer such cases seem to have reached the courts."

33. Brooks, "The Power of Marriage."

34. *Beth R. v. Donna M.* (2008), http://data.lambdalegal.org/pdf/legal/robinson/beth-r-v-donna-m-decision.pdf.

35. Claudia McCreary, "Custody Battles: Don't Ask, Don't Tell," www.suite101.com/article.cfm/gay_parenting_families/66402.

CHAPTER 10

1. John Mullins, "Dr. Benjamin Spock Dies at 94," Athens Banner-Herald, www.onlineathens.com/1998/031698/0316.a3spock.html.

2. Benjamin Spock, *Dr. Spock on Parenting* (New York: Pocket Books, 2001), p. 10.

3. Verbeek, "Dr. Spock's Last Interview."

4. Angier, "One Thing They Aren't: Maternal."

5. Spock and Needlman, eds., *Dr. Spock's Baby and Child Care*, p. 392.

6. Masson, *The Emperor's Embrace*.

7. Quoted in Christopher Rootham, "Parental Leave in Canada," Canadian Lawyers.ca, www.canadian-lawyers.ca/understand-your-legal-issue/family-law/1036284.

8. In parts of India, childless women are punished and discriminated against, and in Africa, divorced or replaced by new wives. In China and other Confucian cultures, childlessness has religious implications: there will be nobody to care for parents or to honour ancestors.

9. Quoted in http://blessed-quiver.blogspot.com/2009/07/interview-with-quiverful-family.html. For a family without medical complications, see, for example, http://asarrows.tripod.com/quiverful.

10. Veciana-Suarez, "She's Back!"

11. Daly and Wilson, *The Truth about Cinderella*; Ganong and Coleman, *Stepfamily Relationships*.

12. Saint Jerome, ca 400, quoted in Wald, *The Remarried Family*, p. 49.

13. Daly and Wilson, *The Truth about Cinderella*; Ganong and Coleman, *Stepfamily Relationships*.

14. Chin, "Ethnically Correct Dolls," pp. 305, 306, 315.

15. Pearl Buck, "I Am the Better Woman for Having My Two Black Children," *Today's Health*, January 1972, pp. 21–22, 64.

16. Interview with Joe Rigert, University of Minnesota Digital Conservancy, http://conservancy.umn.edu/handle/50110.

17. National Association of Black Social Workers, "Position Statement on Trans-Racial Adoption."

18. In the United States, for example, the 1994 Howard M. Metzenbaum Multiethnic Placement Act prohibited agencies that received federal assistance, and that were involved in foster care and adoptions, from delaying or denying placing a child on the basis of race, colour, or national origin. A 1996 amendment, Interethnic Adoption Provisions, refined this legislation by specifying that the placement could not be delayed or denied *solely* on the basis of race and national origin.

19. Quoted in Rauhala, ed., *The Lucky Ones*, p. 2.

20. Webley, "Why Americans Are Adopting Fewer Kids from China."

21. Jasmine Bent, "Just Known as Me," and Lia Calderone, "A Long Way from Hunan," quoted in Rauhala, *The Lucky Ones*, pp. 174, 178.

22. Sweden, for instance, allows all working parents to take up to eighteen months' paid leave per child; at least three of these months must be used by the "minority" parent, usually the father, which encourages fathering. Norway and Estonia have similarly long parental leaves. The U.K. has a fifty-two-week maternity leave.

23. Tracey Bushnik, "Childcare in Canada," Statistics Canada, Children and Youth Research Paper Series, Catalogue no. 89-599-MIE—No. 003, www.statcan.ca/english/research/89-599-MIE/89-599-MIE2006003.pdf. See also Ingrid Peritz, "Quebec Campaign: Revenge of the Cradle Redux," *Globe and Mail*, November 22, 2008.

CHAPTER 11

1. The United States, the world's richest country, has 26 percent. Europe has a much better ratio, from Finland's 7 percent to Germany's 13 percent.

2. Yalnizyan, "The Rich and the Rest of Us."

3. Quoted in Wong, "House Bidding Wars Stretching Budgets," *Toronto Star*, November 6, 2007. Lefebvre and Merrigan, "Social Assistance and Conjugal Union Dissolution in Canada," note on p. 131 that "economic hardships linked to the husband's economic situation increase conjugal instability."

4. Shipler, *The Working Poor*, p. 11.

5. Barbara Ehrenreich, *Nickel and Dimed: On (Not) Getting By in America* (New York: Owl, 2002), p. 27.

6. In North America, 30 percent of gross income is considered the highest percentage a family should spend on housing, either rent or, in the case of homeowners, mortgage, taxes, insurance, and utilities.

7. The rate of female incarceration in Canada is now 7 percent and growing.

8. Quoted in Elizabeth Henderson, "Locked Out," *The American Prospect* (December 5, 2006), www.prospect.org/cs/articles?articleId=12277.

9. Bruce Western, *Punishment and Inequality in America* (New York: Russell Sage Foundation, 2006), p. 141.

10. W.E.B. Du Bois, *The Philadelphia Negro*, p. 277.

11. Elliot Liebow, *Tally's Corner* (1966), quoted in Bruce Western, "Incarceration, Marriage, and Family Life," Russell Sage Foundation, September 2004, p. 5, www.russellsage.org/publications/workingpapers.

CHAPTER 12

1. "Black History Spotlight: Mildred Loving," May 2008, http://concreteloop.com/2008/05/black-history-spotlight-mildred-loving.

2. Pascoe, "Miscegenation Law, Court Cases and Ideologies of 'Race' in Twentieth-Century America," pp. 479, 480.

3. Quoted in Fiske, "The Black-and-White World of Walter Ashby Plecker."

4. Quoted in Fiske, "The Black-and-White World of Walter Ashby Plecker"; see also Kenny, "Toward a Racial Abyss."

5. Peters, "Gender, Sacrament and Ritual," quotes Martin Luther on marriage: "'As many regions as customs' says the proverb. Thus since wedding and marriage is a secular concern, it is not fitting that we clerics and church officers should regulate anything in this matter, rather we should allow each town and region to keep their own customs. In some places the bride is led to the church twice, both in the morning and in the evening; elsewhere only once; in some places they preach and call the banns two or three weeks before the marriage. All these things and related matters I leave to the leaders and council to devise as they wish, it is not my concern" (*Die evangelischen Kirchenordnungen*, ed. Sehling, i, 23).

6. Cott, *Public Vows*, p. 4.

7. Franke, "Reconstruction Era and African American Marriages," http://academic.udayton.edu/RACE/04needs/family03.htm.

8. Captain Richard H. Pratt, a veteran of the U.S. Indians wars who opened the first federally sanctioned boarding school for Native children, opposed exterminating all Indians in favour of "civilizing" them: "Kill the Indian and save the man," he declared.

9. Nicholas Flood Davin's "Report on Industrial Schools for Indians and Half-Breeds" (1879) recommended that John A. Macdonald's federal government establish residential schools for aboriginal children. Earlier, there had been one small residential school in Upper Canada, the Alnwick School, which operated from 1848 to 1856.

10. "Thomas Morgan as Commissioner of Indian Affairs, 1889–1893," Clarke Historical Library, Central Michigan University, http://clarke.cmich.edu/indian/treatyeducation.htm#tm.

11. Quoted in Royal Commission on Aboriginal Peoples, *Report*, 1996, www.ainc-inac.gc.ca/ap/rrc-eng.asp.

12. Mary Crow Dog, quoted in Ferguson, ed., *Mapping the Social Landscape*, p. 555.

13. Duncan C. Scott and *Saturday Night* (November 23, 1907), quoted in Royal Commission on Aboriginal Peoples, *Report*, vol. 1, chapter 10.

14. Aboriginal Healing Foundation, "Where Are the Children? Healing the Legacy of Residential Schools: Intergenerational Impacts," www.wherearethechildren.ca/en/impacts.html.

15. Quoted in Turning Point: Native Peoples and Newcomers Online, "*Time* Magazine Article on Residential Schools," August 26, 2003, www.turning-point.ca/?q=node/274. In 1997, Plint pleaded guilty to assaulting thirty Native boys. Justice Douglas Hogarth called him a "sexual terrorist" and sentenced him to eleven years in prison. But most teachers and administrators went unpunished.

16. Bill Seward, quoted in "Hidden from History: The Canadian Holocaust," *Nexus Magazine*, vol. 9, no. 2 (February-March 2002).

17. Charles Brasfield, "Indian Residential Schools: The Aftermath," *Visions*, vol. 3, no. 3 (2007), pp. 9–10, www.heretohelp.bc.ca/publications/visions/trauma-victimization/bck5.

18. Amnesty International Canada, "Stolen Sisters: Discrimination and Violence against Indigenous Women in Canada," 2004, www.amnesty.ca/campaigns/sisters_overview.php. See also Ferguson, ed., *Mapping the Social Landscape*, p. 555.

19. Barker, "Gender, Sovereignty, and the Discourse of Rights in Native Women's Activism," p. 137.

20. Quoted in Barker, "Gender, Sovereignty, and the Discourse of Rights in Native Women's Activism," p. 138.

21. *McIvor v. The Registrar, Indian and North Affairs Canada*, 2007 BCSC 827, www.courts.gov.bc.ca/jdb-txt/sc/07/08/2007bcsc0827.htm.

22. Royal Commission on Aboriginal Peoples, *Report*, vol. 3, p. 23.

23. This act exempted only merchants, diplomats, foreign students, and those with "special circumstances."

24. MacInnes, *Oriental Occupation of British Columbia*, pp. 12–13.

CHAPTER 13

1. Jones, *Women Who Kill*, p. 283.

2. Jones, *Women Who Kill*, pp. 283–84.

3. Jones, *Women Who Kill*, p. 284.

4. John E. Snell, Richard J. Rosenwald, and Ames Robey, "The Wifebeater's Wife: A Study of Family Interaction," *Archives of General Psychiatry*, vol. 11, no. 2 (1964), p. 109, quoted in Schechter, *Women and Male Violence*, p. 21.

5. Schechter, *Women and Male Violence*, p. 21.

6. Gretchen Arnold, "Social Movement 'Success': The Battered Women's Movement's Discourse and Institutional Change" (paper presented at the annual meeting of the American Sociological Association, San Francisco, 2004), www.allacademic.com/meta/p109112_index.html.

7. Ray C. Hotchkiss, quoted in Jones, *Women Who Kill*, p. 289.

8. Quoted in Jones, *Women Who Kill*, p. 315.

9. Quoted in Jones, *Women Who Kill*, p. 308.

10. Quoted in Jones, *Women Who Kill*, p. 302.

11. *State v. Wanrow*, 559 P.2d 548 (1977), Center for Constitutional Rights, http://ccrjustice.org/ourcases/past-cases/state-washington-v.-wanrow. For analysis

of the precedent established by this case, see also www.libraryindex.com/pages/ 2082/When-Women-Kill-Their-Partners-LEGAL-ISSUES-SURROUNDING-BATTERED-WOMEN-WHO-KILL.html.

12. Jones, *Women Who Kill,* pp. 310–11.

13. *R. v. Lavallee* [1990] 1 S.C.R. 852, http://csc.lexum.umontreal.ca/en/1990/ 1990rcs1-852/1990rcs1-852.html.

14. Quoted in Anderson, *Judging Bertha Wilson,* p. 220.

15. Quoted in Anderson, *Judging Bertha Wilson,* pp. 219, 222.

16. Quoted in Jones, *Women Who Kill,* p. 303.

17. See www.ontario.ca/en/life_events/abuse/ONT03_020543.

18. Basch, *Framing American Divorce,* p. 21.

19. Quoted in Glenda Riley, *Divorce: An American Tradition* (Lincoln: University of Nebraska Press, 1997), p. 31.

20. Robert Remington, "Celebrating a Reluctant Feminist Heroine," *National Post,* April 6, 2000, www.fact.on.ca/news/news0004/np00040m.htm.

21. Regina *Leader-Post,* December 5, 1942, quoted in Mona Holmlund and Gail Youngberg, eds., *Inspiring Women: A Celebration of Herstory* (Regina: Coteau Books, 2003), p. 152.

22. U.S. Department of Labor, Children's Bureau, *Standards for Day Care of Children of Working Mothers* (1942), http://digitalcollections.smu.edu/cdm4/item_ viewer.php?CISOROOT=/hgp&CISOPTR=437&CISOBOX=1&REC=1.

23. "A widespread reluctance to see mothers as citizens with an equal right to earn wages, as well as a failure to understand that childrearing and domestic duties were work that carried public economic value, constituted key parts of a postwar conservative gender ideology that was an important roadblock to continuing public child care funding" (Stoltzfus, *Citizen, Mother, Worker,* p. 2).

24. Cott, *Public Vows,* p. 197.

25. An unnamed friend, quoted in obituary of Bertha Wilson at her alma mater, University of Aberdeen, http://abdn.ac.uk/alumni/contacts/obituaries.php.

26. Stribopoulos, "The Passing of the Honourable Bertha Wilson."

27. Zuckerman, "Welfare Reform in America."

28. Wade Horn, quoted in Rodriguez, "Do Fathers Make a Difference."

29. Legislative Analyst's Office, "Californians and the Marriage Penalty," December 16, 1999, quoted in Thomas F. Coleman, "The High Cost of Being Single in America, or the Financial Consequences of Marital Status Discrimination," Unmarried America, www.unmarriedamerica.org/cost-discrimination.htm. See also Joint Committee on Taxation, *Report to the House Ways and Means Committee,* June 22, 1999.

30. Daniel R. Feenberg and Harvey S. Rosen, "Recent Developments in the Marriage Tax," National Bureau of Economic Research Working Paper No. W4705, April 1994.

31. Steurle, of the Urban Institute, quoted by Jane Koppelman, "Promoting Marriage as Welfare Policy: Looking at a Public Role in Private Lives," National Health Policy Forum Issue Brief No. 770, February 15, 2002.

32. Coleman, "The High Cost of Being Single in America."

33. Cott, *Public Vows.*

34. Congress passed the Defense of Marriage Act by a vote of 85–14 in the Senate and 342–67 in the House of Representatives.

35. The act specified that "officials of religious groups are free to refuse to perform marriages that are not in accordance with their religious beliefs."

36. In late 2009, thirty states had constitutional bans to gay marriage. In several others, state legislation bans gay marriage. Six states—Massachusetts, Maine, Vermont, Connecticut, Iowa, and (as of 2010) New Hampshire—permit gay marriage through legislation or court rulings, but in Maine, Washington, and Michigan, future votes will decide whether or not to uphold them.

CHAPTER 14

1. Much of this section on the women's Parliament comes from Kym Bird, "Performing Politics: Propaganda, Parody and a Women's Parliament," *Theatre Research in Canada*, vol. 13, nos. 1 & 2 (Spring/Fall 1992). Bird suggests that there may have been nine different plays and at least twelve performances, four in Manitoba, six in Ontario, and two in British Columbia. The first *Women's Parliament* was staged at Winnipeg's Bijou Theatre in February 1893 by the Women's Christian Temperance Union, which also collaborated in most other productions.

2. Quoted in Historica-Dominion Institute, "Nellie McClung," *Historica Minutes,* www.histori.ca/minutes/minute.do?id=10643.

3. Quoted in Saskatoon Women's Calendar Collective, "Suffrage: The Women's Parliament," Herstory: An Exhibition, http://library2.usask.ca/herstory/woparl.html.

4. Quoted in Centre for Canadian Studies, Mount Allison University, "Nellie McClung 1873–1951," www.mta.ca/about_canada/study_guide/famous_women/nellie_mcclung.html.

5. Library and Archives Canada, "The 'Persons' Case, 1927–1929," http://epe.lac-bac.gc.ca/100/206/301/lac-bac/famous_five-ef/www.lac-bac.gc.ca/famous5/053002_e.html.

6. Special Joint Committee on Child Custody and Access, *For the Sake of the Children,* chap. 1, 1998, www2.parl.gc.ca/HousePublications/Publication.aspx?DocId=1031529&Language=E&Mode=1&Parl=36&Ses=1.

7. Faludi, *Stiffed,* p. 37.

8. Liptak, "Gay Marriage through a Black-White Prism."

9. In the United States, 5 percent of marriages are intermarriages. In 2001 in Canada, 217,500 mixed unions (marriages and common-law unions involving a visible

minority person with a non-visible minority person or a person from a different visible minority group) accounted for 3.1 percent of all unions.

10. Loving, "Loving for All."

11. Schaefer, "The Sit-In at the Altar."

12. Nissa Billmyer, "Mail Order Brides Discussed," www.universitychronicle. com/2.12299/mail-order-brides-discussed-1.1708425.

13. The phrase is stepfamily scholar Patricia Papernow's.

14. Young and Nathanson, "Marriage-a-la-mode."

15. Young and Nathanson, "Marriage-a-la-mode."

16. See "U.S. Divorce Rates for Various Faith Groups, Age Groups, and Geographic Areas," www.religioustolerance.org/chr_dira.htm.

17. An unnamed twelve-year-old witness, quoted in *For the Sake of the Children*, chap. 1.

18. Edward Kruk, professor of social work, University of British Columbia, quoted in *For the Sake of the Children*, chap. 1.

19. Howard Irving, University of Toronto, quoted in *For the Sake of the Children*, chap. 1.

20. Sullivan, Warren, and Westbrook, *The Fragile Middle Class*, p. 174.

21. Ross Finnie, "Women, Men, and the Economic Consequences of Divorce."

22. See also Fine and Harvey, eds., *Handbook of Divorce and Relationship Dissolution*; American Board of Family Medicine, "Children of Divorce: Consequences of Divorce," *Journal of the American Board of Family Medicine*, vol. 14, no. 3 (2001), www.medscape.com/viewarticle/405852_4; MacLean and Weitzman, eds., *Calculating the Costs*.

23. Cori Kalinowski, National Action Committee on the Status of Women, *For the Sake of the Children*, chap. 1.

Select Bibliography

BOOKS

Elizabeth Abbott, *A History of Mistresses*. Toronto: Harper Perennial Canada, 2004.

Ellen Anderson, *Judging Bertha Wilson: Law as Large as Life*. Osbodde Society for Canadian Legal History. Toronto: University of Toronto Press, 2001.

Philippe Ariès, *Centuries of Childhood: A Social History of Family Life*. Translated by Robert Baldick. New York: Knopf, 1962.

James Edward Austen-Leigh, *A Memoir of Jane Austen*. London: Richard Bentley and Son, 1871. Project Gutenberg eBook #17797, transcribed by Les Bowler.

Peter Bardaglio, *Reconstructing the Household: Families, Sex, and the Law in the Nineteenth-Century South*. Chapel Hill: University of North Carolina Press, 1995.

Norma Basch, *Framing American Divorce*. Berkeley: University of California Press, 2001.

Catharine Beecher, *An Essay on Slavery and Abolition, with reference to the duty of American females*. 1837. Prepared for the University of Virginia Library Electronic Text Center, 1998. http://etext.lib.virginia.edu/toc/modeng/public/BeeEssa.html.

——*A Treatise on Domestic Economy*. 1841. New York: Schocken Books, 1977.

Rudolph M. Bell, *How to Do It: Guides to Good Living for Renaissance Italians*. Chicago and London: University of Chicago Press, 1999.

Jeanne Boydston, *Home and Work*. New York: Oxford University Press, 1994.

Dave Brown, *Faces of War: A Collection*. Renfrew, Ont.: General Store Publishing House, 1998.

Kathleen Mary Butler, *The Economics of Emancipation: Jamaica and Barbados 1823–1843*. Chapel Hill: University of North Carolina Press, 1995.

Lee Virginia Chambers-Schiller, *Liberty: A Better Husband. Single Women in America: The Generations of 1780–1840*. New Haven: Yale University Press, 1984.

Mary Boykin Chesnut, *A Diary from Dixie, as Written by Mary Boykin Chesnut, Wife of James Chesnut, Jr., United States Senator from South Carolina, 1859–1861, and Afterward an Aide to Jefferson Davis and a Brigadier-General in the Confederate Army*. Edited by Isabella D. Martin and Myrta Lockett Avary. New York: D. Appleton and Company, 1905. http://docsouth.unc.edu/southlit/chesnut/menu.html.

Gillian Clark, *Women in Late Antiquity: Pagan and Christian Life-styles*. Broadbridge Alderley: Clarendon Press, 1994.

Stephanie Coontz, *Marriage, a History: From Obedience to Intimacy, or How Love Conquered Marriage*. New York: Viking, 2005.

——*The Way We Never Were: American Families and the Nostalgia Trap*. New York: Basic Books, 2000.

Nancy Cott, *No Small Courage: A History of Women in the United States*. New York: Oxford University Press, 2004.

——*Public Vows: A History of Marriage and the Nation.* Cambridge, Mass.: Harvard University Press, 2002.

Kyle A. Cuordileone, *Manhood and American Political Culture in the Cold War.* New York, Oxford: Routledge, 2005.

Martin Daly and Margo Wilson, *The Truth about Cinderella: A Darwinian View of Parental Love.* New Haven: Yale University Press, 1999.

Katharine B. Davis, *Factors in the Sex Life of 2200 Women.* 1929. http://trivia-library.com/a/history-of-sex-survey-factors-in-the-sex-life-of-2200-women.htm.

Janice Delaney, Mary Jane Lupton, and Emily Toth, eds., *The Curse: A Cultural History of Menstruation.* Champaign: University of Illinois Press, 1988.

Lloyd deMause, ed., *The History of Childhood: The Untold Story of Child Abuse.* New York: Peter Bedrick Books, 1988.

John D'Emilio and Estelle B. Freedman, *Intimate Matters: A History of Sexuality in America.* University of Chicago Press, 1997.

W.E.B. Du Bois, *The Philadelphia Negro.* 1899. Philadelphia: University of Pennsylvania Press, 1996.

Wilma A. Dunaway, *The African-American Family in Slavery and Emancipation.* Cambridge University Press, 2003.

Jane Errington, *Wives and Mothers, Schoolmistresses and Scullery Maids: Working Women in Upper Canada, 1790–1840.* Montreal, Kingston: McGill-Queen's University Press, 1995.

Lillian Faderman, *Odd Girls and Twilight Lovers: A History of Lesbian Life in Twentieth-Century America.* New York: Penguin, 1992.

Susan Faludi, *Stiffed: The Betrayal of the American Man.* New York: William Morrow, 1999.

Susan J. Ferguson, ed., *Mapping the Social Landscape: Readings in Sociology.* New York: McGraw-Hill, 2007.

Mark A. Fine and John H. Harvey, eds., *Handbook of Divorce and Relationship Dissolution.* London: Routledge, 2005.

Margaret Forster, *Significant Sisters: The Grassroots of Active Feminism 1839–1939.* London: Secker and Warburg, 1984.

Gerald L. Foster, *American Houses: A Field Guide to the Architecture of the Home.* Boston: Houghton, Mifflin, Harcourt, 2004.

Leigh Fought, *Southern Womanhood and Slavery: A Biography of Louisa S. McCord, 1810–1879.* Columbia: University of Missouri Press, 2003.

Amy Froide, *Never Married: Singlewomen in Early Modern England.* Oxford University Press, 2005.

Amy Froide and Judith Bennett, eds., *Singlewomen in the European Past, 1250–1800.* Philadelphia: University of Pennsylvania Press, 1999.

M.K. Gandhi, *My Autobiography, or The Story of My Experiments with Truth.* 1929. Translated by Mahadev Desai. http://en.wikisource.org/wiki/An_Autobiography_or_The_Story_of_my_Experiments_with_Truth.

Lawrence H. Ganong and Marilyn Coleman, *Stepfamily Relationships: Development, Dynamics, and Interventions.* New York: Kluwer Academic/Plenum Publishers, 2004.

Eugene Genovese, *Roll, Jordan, Roll: The World the Slaves Made.* New York: Vintage Books, 1976.

Charlotte Perkins Gilman, *The Home: Its Work and Influence.* 1903. Edited by Michael S. Kimmel. Walnut Creek, Cal.: AltaMira Press, 2002.

—— *Women and Economics.* New York: Source Book Press, 1970.

Janet Golden, *A Social History of Wet Nursing in America.* Columbus: Ohio State University Press, 2001.

Linda Gordon, *The Moral Property of Women: A History of Birth Control Politics in America.* Chicago: University of Illinois Press, 2007.

Amy Laura Hall, *Conceiving Parenthood: American Protestantism and the Spirit of Reproduction.* Grand Rapids, Mich.: Eerdmans, 2007.

Edwin Hall, *The Arnolfini Betrothal: Medieval Marriage and the Enigma of Van Eyck's Double Portrait.* Berkeley: University of California Press, 1994.

Elizabeth Hampsten, *Settlers' Children: Growing Up on the Great Plains.* Norman: University of Oklahoma, 1991.

Marion Harland, *Eve's Daughters; or Common Sense for Maid, Wife, and Mother.* New York: John R. Anderson and Henry S. Allen, 1882.

Barbara Harris, *English Aristocratic Women.* Oxford University Press, 2002.

Fraser Harrison, *Dark Angel: Aspects of Victorian Sexuality.* Glasgow: William Collins, 1979.

Albert Bushnell Hart and Mabel Hill, *Camps and Firesides of the Revolution,* Electronic Text Center, University of Virginia Library.
http://etext.virginia.edu/toc/modeng/public/HarCamp.html.

Mary S. Hartman, *The Household and the Making of History: A Subversive View of the Western Past.* Cambridge University Press, 2004.

Joan D. Hedrick, *Harriet Beecher Stowe: A Life.* Oxford and New York: Oxford University Press, 1995.

Colin Heywood, *A History of Childhood: Children and Childhood in the West from Medieval to Modern Times.* Cambridge: Polity Press, 2001.

Bridget Hill, *Women Alone: Spinsters in England 1660–1850.* New Haven: Yale University Press, 2001

Masud Hoghughi and Nicholas Long, *The Handbook of Parenting.* London, California; Sage Publications, 2004.

Katherine Holden, *The Shadow of Marriage: Singleness in England, 1914–60.* Manchester University Press, 2007.

Susan E. Houston, "The 'Waifs and Strays' of a Late Victorian City: Juvenile Delinquents in Toronto." In *Childhood and Family in Canadian History,* edited by Joy Parr. Toronto: McClelland and Stewart, 1982.

Olwen Hufton, *The Prospect Before Her: A History of Women in Western Europe, 1500–1800.* London: Harper Collins, 1995.

Kathleen E. Hull, *Same-Sex Marriage: The Cultural Politics of Love and Law.* Cambridge University Press, 2006.

Kay Hymowitz, *Marriage and Caste in America.* Chicago: Ivan R. Dee, 2006.

Chrys Ingraham, *White Weddings: Romancing Heterosexuality in Popular Culture.* New York: Routledge, 1999.

Anya Jabour, *Marriage in the Early Republic: Elizabeth and William Wirt and the Companionate Ideal.* Baltimore and London: Johns Hopkins University Press, 1998.

—— *Scarlett's Sisters: Young Women in the Old South.* Chapel Hill: University of North Carolina Press, 2007.

Lisa Jardine, *Reading Shakespeare Historically.* New York: Routledge, 1996.

Ann Jones, *Women Who Kill.* Boston: Beacon Press, 1996.

Tess Kalinowski, "As Traditional as a Child." In Ann Rauhala, ed., *The Lucky Ones: Our Stories of Adopting Children from China.* Toronto: ECW Press, 2008.

Harnett T. Kane, *The Bayous of Louisiana.* New York: Bonanza Books, 1943.

Susan C. Karant-Nunn and Merry E. Wiesner-Hanks, eds., *Luther on Women: A Sourcebook.* New York: Cambridge University Press, 2003.

Wilma King, *Stolen Childhood: Slave Youth in Nineteenth-Century America.* Bloomington: Indiana University Press, 1996.

Robert M. Kingdon, *Adultery and Divorce in Calvin's Geneva.* Cambridge, Mass.: Harvard University Press, 1995.

Anne Kingston, *The Meaning of Wife: A Provocative Look at Women and Marriage in the Twenty-first Century.* New York: Farrar, Straus and Giroux, 2005.

S.J. Kleinberg, "Gendered Space: Housing, Privacy and Domesticity in the Nineteenth-Century United States." In *Domestic Space: Reading the Nineteenth-Century Interior*, edited by Inga Bryden and Janet Floyd. Manchester, New York: Manchester University Press, 1999.

Robert Klose, "In the Beginning." Chap. 1 in *Adopting Alyosha: A Single Man Finds a Son in Russia.* www.nytimes.com/books/first/k/klose-adopting.html.

Susan Koppelman, ed., *Old Maids: Short Stories by Nineteenth Century U.S. Women Writers.* Boston: Pandora Press, 1984.

Emmanuel Le Roy Ladurie, *The Beggar and the Professor.* Translated by Arthur Goldhammer. University of Chicago Press, 1997.

Yves Landry, "Gender Imbalance, Les Filles du Roi, and Choice of Spouse in New France." In *Canadian Family History: Selected Readings*, edited by Bettina Bradbury. Toronto: Copp Clark Pittman, 1992.

Thomas Laqueur, *Solitary Sex: A Cultural History of Masturbation.* New York: Zone Books, 2004.Deirdre Le Faye, *Jane Austen: A Family Record.* Cambridge University Press, 2003.

Deirdre Le Faye, ed., *Jane Austen's Letters.* Philadelphia: Pavilion Press, 2003.

Dio Lewis, *Our Girls.* New York: Clarke Bros., 1883.

James D. Livingston and Sherry H. Penney, *A Very Dangerous Woman: Martha Wright and Women's Rights.* Amherst: University of Massachusetts Press, 2004.

John Locke, *Some Thoughts Concerning Education.* 1692. www.fordham.edu/halsall/mod/1692locke-education.html.

Thomas P. Lowry, *The Story the Soldiers Wouldn't Tell: Sex in the Civil War.* Mechanicsburg, Pa.: Stackpole Books, 1994.

Roy Lubove, *The Progressives and the Slums: Tenement House Reform in New York City, 1890–1917.* Westport, Conn.: Greenwood Press, 1974.

Alan Macfarlane, *Marriage and Love in England: Modes of Reproduction, 1300–1840.* Oxford and New York: Blackwell, 1986.

Thomas MacInnes, *Oriental Occupation of British Columbia.* Vancouver: Sun Publishing, 1927.

Mavis MacLean and Lenore J. Weitzman, eds., *Calculating the Costs: The Economic Consequences of Divorce in International Perspective.* Oxford University Press; 1992.

Lisa McCauley, *Du Crow's Nest par Pascal Fuselier.* Lulu.com, 2008.

Angus McLaren, *Impotence: A Cultural History.* Chicago and London: University of Chicago Press, 2007.

——*Reproductive Rituals: The Perception of Fertility in England from the 16th to the 19th Century.* New York: Routledge and Kegan Paul, 1985.

Sally G. McMillen, *Southern Women: Black and White in the Old South.* 2nd ed. Wheeling, Ill.: Harlan Davidson, 2002.

Patricia Mainardi, *Husbands, Wives, and Lovers: Marriage and Its Discontents in Nineteenth-century France.* New Haven: Yale University Press, 2003.

Alice Catherine Miles, *Every Girl's Duty: The Diary of a Victorian Debutante.* Edited by Maggy Parsons. London: Andre Deutsch, 1992.

Steven Mintz, *Huck's Raft: A History of American Childhood.* Cambridge, Mass.: Harvard University Press, 2004.

Susanna Moodie, *Roughing It in the Bush.* 1852. http://digital.library.upenn.edu/women/moodie/roughing/roughing.html#II-14.

Peter Mook, "Les Petits Sauvages: The Children of Eighteenth-Century New France." In *Childhood and Family in Canadian History*, edited by Joy Parr. Toronto: McClelland and Stewart, 1982.

Caroline Moorehead, *The Lost Treasures of Troy.* London: Weidenfeld and Nicolson, 1994.

Major James A. Moss, *Manual of Military Training.* 2nd rev. ed. 1917. www.vlib.us/medical/manual/manual1.htm.

Jeffrey Moussaieff Masson, *The Emperor's Embrace: Reflections on Animal Families and Fatherhood.* New York: Pocket Books, 1999.

Virginia Nicholson, *Singled Out: How Two Million Women Survived without Men After the First World War.* London: Penguin, 2008.

Françoise Noël, *Family Life and Sociability in Upper and Lower Canada, 1780–1870.* Montreal and Kingston: McGill-Queen's University Press, 2003.

Caroline Norton, *English Laws for Women in the Nineteenth Century.* 1854. http://digital.library.upenn.edu/women/norton/elfw/elfw.html.

——*A Letter to the Queen on Lord Chancellor Cranworth's Marriage and Divorce Bill.* 1855. http://digital.library.upenn.edu/women/norton/alttq/alttq.html.

Joy Parr, ed., *Childhood and Family in Canadian History.* Toronto: McClelland and Stewart, 1982.

William Perkins, *Christian Œconomie.* London: 1609.

Michelle Perrot, ed., *From the Fires of Revolution to the Great War.* Vol. 4 of *A History of Private Life*, edited by Philippe Ariès and Georges Duby, translated by Arthur Goldhammer. Cambridge, Mass.: Harvard University Press, 1994.

Peggy Pascoe, "Miscegenation Law, Court Cases and Ideologies of 'Race' in Twentieth-Century America." In *Sex, Love, Race: Crossing Boundaries in North American History*, edited by Martha Hodes. New York: NYU Press, 1999.

Roderick Phillips, *Putting Asunder: A History of Divorce in Western Society.* Cambridge University Press, 1988.

——*Untying the Knot: A Short History of Divorce.* Cambridge University Press, 1991.

Elizabeth Pleck, *Domestic Tyranny: The Making of a Social Policy Against Family Violence from Colonial Times to the Present.* Champaign: University of Illinois Press, 2004.

Linda Pollock, *Forgotten Children: Parent-Child Relations from 1500 to 1900.* Cambridge University Press, 1984.

Paul Popenoe, *Modern Marriage: A Handbook.* New York: Macmillan, 1925.

Malcolm Potts and Martha Campbell, "History of Contraception." In *Gynecology and Obstetrics*, edited by J.J. Sciarra. Vol. 6, chap. 8. CD-ROM. Lippincott, Williams and Wilkins, 2003.

Donna S. Quick, Patrick C. McKenry, and Barbara M. Newman, "Stepmothers and Their Adolescent Children: Adjustment to New Family Roles." In Kay Pasley and Marilyn Ihinger-Tallman, *Stepparenting: Issues in Theory, Research, and Practice*. Westport, Conn.: Greenwood Publishing Group, 1995.

Ann Rauhala, ed., *The Lucky Ones: Our Stories of Adopting Children from China*. Toronto: ECW Press, 2008.

Jacob A. Riis, *How the Other Half Lives: Studies Among the Tenements of New York*. 1890. http://bartleby.com/208.

—— *The Making of an American*. 1901. http://gutenberg.readingroo.ms/etext04/thmkn10.txt.

Lyndal Roper, *Oedipus and the Devil: Witchcraft, Sexuality, and Religion in Early Modern Europe*. New York: Routledge, 1994.

Will Roscoe, *Changing Ones: Third and Fourth Genders in Native North America*. New York: Palgrave Macmillan, 2000.

Constance Mayfield Rourke, *Trumpets of Jubilee: Henry Ward Beecher, Harriet Beecher Stowe, Lyman Beecher, Horace Greeley, P.T. Barnum*. New York: Harcourt, Brace, 1927.

Judith Rowbotham, *Good Girls Make Good Wives: Guidance for Girls in Victorian Fiction*. Oxford: Blackwell, 1989.

Leland Ryken, *Worldly Saints: The Puritans as They Really Were*. Holmes, Pa.: Zondervan, 1990.

Robert Blair St. George, ed., *Material Life in America, 1600–1860*. Boston: Northeastern University Press, 1988.

Susan Schechter, *Women and Male Violence: The Visions and Struggles of the Battered Women's Movement*. Cambridge, Mass.: South End Press, 1982.

Catharine Maria Sedgwick, *Married or Single?* 1857. Cornell University Historic Monographs. http://digital.library.cornell.edu/cgi/t/text/text-idx?c=cdl;cc=cdl;rgn=main;view=text;idno=cdl353.

Linda Seidel, *Jan van Eyck's Arnolfini Portrait: Stories of an Icon*. Cambridge University Press, 1993.

David Shipler, *The Working Poor*. New York: Knopf, 2004.

Maggie Siggins, *In Her Own Time: A Class Reunion Inspires a Cultural History of Women*. Toronto: HarperCollins, 2000.

Gayle Rosenwald Smith and Sally Abrahms, *What Every Woman Should Know about Divorce and Custody*. New York: Perigee, 1998.

Dr. Benjamin Spock and Robert Needlman, eds., *Dr. Spock's Baby and Child Care*. 8th rev. ed. New York: Pocket Books, 2004.

Emilie Stoltzfus, *Citizen, Mother, Worker: Debating Public Responsibility for Child Care after the Second World War*. Chapel Hill: University of North Carolina Press, 2003.

Marie Stopes, *Married Love or Love in Marriage*. 1918. http://digital.library.upenn.edu/women/stopes/married/1918.html.

Carren Strock, *Married Women Who Love Women*. New York: Alyson Books, 2000.

Teresa A. Sullivan, Elizabeth Warren, and Jay Westbrook, *The Fragile Middle Class: Americans in Debt*. New Haven: Yale University Press, 2001.

Frances Trollope, "Philadelphia, Pennsylvania, August 1830." *Day in the Life of a Philadelphia Matron; Habit of Young Married Couples to Reside in Boarding Houses.* http://xroads.virginia.edu/~hyper/DETOC/FEM/trollope.htm.

Ruth Vanita, *Love's Rite: Same-Sex Marriage in India and the West.* New York: Palgrave-Macmillan; New Delhi: Penguin India, 2005.

Sylvia Van Kirk, *Many Tender Ties: Women in Fur-Trade Society in Western Canada, 1670–1870.* Winnipeg: Watson and Dwyer Publishing, 1980.

Amanda Vickery, *The Gentleman's Daughter: Women's Lives in Georgian England.* Yale University Press, 1999.

Esther Wald, *The Remarried Family: Change and Promise.* New York: Family Service Association of America, 1981.

Barbara Williams, ed., *A Gentlewoman in Upper Canada: The Journals, Letters, and Art of Anne Langton.* University of Toronto Press, 2008.

Walter L. Williams, *The Spirit and the Flesh: Sexual Diversity in American Indian Culture.* Boston: Beacon Press, 1992.

Rev. Daniel Wise, *The Young Lady's Counselor, or, The Sphere, the Duties, and the Dangers of Young Women. Designed to be a Guide to True Happiness in This Life, and to Glory in the Life Which is to Come.* New York: Porter, 1857, 1866.

ARTICLES

David Adox, "What's the Difference Between a Homosexual and a Murderer?" *Salon,* May 2, 1997. www.salon.com/may97/sullivan970502.html.

American Civil Liberties Union, "Overview of Lesbian and Gay Parenting, Adoption and Foster Care," April 6, 1999, www.aclu.org/lgbt/parenting/11824res19990406.html.

Natalie Angier, "One Thing They Aren't: Maternal." *New York Times,* May 9, 2006.

Joanne Barker, "Gender, Sovereignty, and the Discourse of Rights in Native Women's Activism." *Meridians: Feminism, Race, Transnationalism,* vol. 7, no. 1 (2006), pp. 127-61.

Roni Berger, "Stepfamilies in Cultural Context." *Journal of Divorce and Remarriage,* vol. 33, nos. 1 and 2 (2000).

Reginald Bibby, "Cohabitation." The Future Families Project, Vanier Institute of the Family. www.vifamily.ca/library/future/2.html.

Kym Bird, "Performing Politics: Propaganda, Parody and a Women's Parliament." *Theatre Research in Canada,* vol. 13, nos. 1 and 2 (Spring/Fall 1992).

Black AIDS Institute, *AIDS in Blackface: Twenty-five Years of an Epidemic.* 2006. http://pubs.cpha.ca/PDF/P41/24478.pdf.

Peter Blanck, "Civil War Pensions and Disability." *Ohio State Law Journal,* vol. 62, no. 1 (2001), pp. 109–249. http://moritzlaw.osu.edu/lawjournal/issues/volume62/number1/blanck.pdf.

Alan Booth and Judy Dunn, eds., *Stepfamilies: Who Benefits? Who Does Not?* Hillsdale, N.J.: Lawrence Erlbaum Associates, 1994.

Maristella Botticini, "A Loveless Economy? Intergenerational Altruism and the Marriage Market in a Tuscan Town, 1415–1436." *Journal of Economic History,* vol. 59 (1999), pp. 104–21.

John Bowe, "Gay Donor or Gay Dad?" *New York Times Magazine*, November 19, 2006.

Keith Boykin, "Whose Dream?" *The Village Voice*, May 18, 2004.

David Brooks, "The Power of Marriage." *New York Times*, November 22, 2003. www.nytimes.com/2003/11/22/opinion/22BROO.html.

Jim Burroway, "Today in History: Eisenhower Signs Executive Order 10450." *Box Turtle Bulletin*, April 27, 2008. www.boxturtlebulletin.com/2008/04/27/1886.

Michael Burslem, "A Eulogy of Large Families." February 2009. Niagara Anglican Online. www.niagara.anglican.ca/newspaper/article.cfm?article=A%20eulogy%20of%20large%20families.

Antoinette Burton, "From Child Bride to 'Hindoo Lady': Rukhmabai and the Debate on Sexual Respectability in Imperial Britain." *The American Historical Review*, vol. 103 (October 1998), pp. 11–19.

J. C. Caldwell, P. H. Reddy, and Pat Caldwell, "The Causes of Marriage Change in South India." *Population Studies* (November 1983), pp. 343–61.

Margaret D. Carroll, " 'In the Name of God and Profit': Jan van Eyck's Arnolfini Portrait." *Representations*, vol. 4 (Fall 1993).

Paul Cartledge, "Spartan Wives." *Classical Quarterly*, vol. 31 (1981), pp. 84–105.

Elizabeth Chin, "Ethnically Correct Dolls: Toying with the Race Industry." *American Anthropologist*, New Series, vol. 101, no. 2. (June 1999), pp. 305-21.

Clifford Clark, "Domestic Architecture as an Index to Social History: The Romantic Revival and the Cult of Domesticity in America, 1840–1870." *The Journal of Interdisciplinary History*, vol. 7 (1976), pp. 33–56.

Laura Del Col, *The Life of the Industrial Worker in Nineteenth-Century England.* www.victorianweb.org/history/workers2.html.

Stephanie Coontz, "In Search of a Golden Age: A look at Families throughout U.S. History Reveals There Has Never Been an 'Ideal Form.'" *In Context* (Spring 1989). www.context.org/ICLIB/IC21/Coontz.htm.

Judy Curtiss, "Royal Wedding Gown." *The Victorian Society in America Newsletter*, February 21, 2007. www.northstarvsa.com/Newsletters/02–21–07%20Newsletter.pdf.

Robert Darby, "The Masturbation Taboo and the Rise of Routine Male Circumcision: A Review of the Historiography." *Journal of Social History*, vol. 27 (Spring 2003) pp. 737–57. www.cirp.org/library/history/darby4.

Benoit Denizet-Lewis, "Double Lives on the Down Low." *New York Times Magazine*, August 3, 2003.

Orville Lloyd Douglas, "Guy Meets Guy on the Down Low." *Now*, August 16–23, 2001. www.nowtoronto.com/news/story.cfm?content=128701&archive=20,50,2001.

Mikaela Dufur, Benjamin McKune, John Hoffmann, and Stephen Bahr, "Adolescent Outcomes in Single Parent, Heterosexual Couple, and Homosexual Couple Families: Findings from a National Survey." Paper presented at the annual meeting of the American Sociological Association, New York City, 2007. www.allacademic.com/meta/p184075_index.html.

Lisa M. Fine, "Between Two Worlds: Business Women in a Chicago Boarding House 1900–1930." *Journal of Social History*, vol. 19, no. 3 (Spring 1986).

Ross Finnie, "Women, Men, and the Economic Consequences of Divorce: Evidence from Canadian Longitudinal Data." *Canadian Review of Sociology and Anthropology*, vol. 30 (1993).

Warren Fiske, "The Black-and-White World of Walter Ashby Plecker." *The Virginian-Pilot*, August 18, 2004. www.manataka.org/page1275.html.

Katherine M. Franke, "Becoming a Citizen: Reconstruction Era Regulation of African American Marriages," *Yale Journal of Law and the Humanities*, vol. 11 (Summer 1999), pp. 251–309.

Dov Friedlander, "The British Depression and Nuptiality: 1873–1896." *Journal of Interdisciplinary History*, vol. 23, no. 1 (Summer 1992), pp 19–37.

Bruce W. Frier, "Roman Same-Sex Weddings from the Legal Perspective." *Classical Studies Newsletter*, vol. X (Winter 2004). www.umich.edu/~classics/news/newsletter/winter2004/weddings.html.

M.J. George, "Skimmington Revisited." *The Journal of Men's Studies*, vol. 10, no. 2 (2002), pp. 111–27.

Lori Gottlieb, "Marry Him! The Case for Settling for Mr. Good Enough." *The Atlantic*, March 2008. www.theatlantic.com/doc/200803/single-marry.

Michael R. Haines, "Fertility and Marriage in a Nineteenth-Century Industrial City: Philadelphia, 1850–1880." *Journal of Economic History*, vol. 40, no. 1 (March 1980), pp. 151–58.

Chong-suk Han, "A Different Shade of Queer: Race, Sexuality, and Marginalizing by the Marginalized." http://bad.eserver.org/issues/2006/76/gaysofcolor.html.

Sarah Hanley, "'The Jurisprudence of the Arrêts': Marital Union, Civil Society, and State Formation in France, 1550–1650." *Law and History Review* (Spring 2003). www.historycooperative.org/journals/lhr/21.1/hanley.html.

Tamara Hareven, "The Home and the Family in Historical Perspective." *Social Research*, vol. 58, no. 1 (1991), pp. 253–85.

Doug Hood, "Sometime in the Night: A Single Man Becomes a Father." *Adoptive Families* (2000). www.adoptivefamilies.com/articles.php?aid=172.

Stewart Justman, "'The Reeve's Tale' and the Honor of Men." *Studies in Short Fiction* (1995).

Shannon Kari, "Lesbian Couple Gets First Gay Divorce." *The Ottawa Citizen*, September 14, 2004.

Kate Kendell, "Lesbian and Gay Parents in Child Custody and Visitation Disputes." *Human Rights Magazine* (Summer 2003). www.abanet.org/irr/hr/summer03/custody.html.

Michael G. Kenny, "Toward a Racial Abyss: Eugenics, Wickliffe Draper, and the Origins of the Pioneer Fund." *Journal of the History of the Behavioral Sciences*, vol. 38, no. 3 (Summer 2002), pp. 259–83. www.iupui.edu/~histwhs/h699.dir/KennyPioneer.pdf.

Rachel Naomi Klein, "Harriet Beecher Stowe and the Domestication of Free Labor Ideology." *Legacy: A Journal of American Women Writers*, vol. 18, no. 2 (2001): 135–52.

Jack L. Knetsch, "Some Economic Implications of Matrimonial Property Rules." *The University of Toronto Law Journal*, Symposium: Economic Perspectives on Issues in Family Law, vol. 34, no. 3 (Summer 1984), pp. 263–82.

Margaret Koster, "The Arnolfini double portrait: a simple solution." *Apollo*,
   September 2003.
Pierre Lefebvre and Philip Merrigan, "Social Assistance and Conjugal Union
   Dissolution in Canada: A Dynamic Analysis." *The Canadian Journal of Economics*,
   vol. 30, no. 1 (February 1997), pp. 112–34.
Jennifer Rebecca Levison, "Elizabeth Parsons Ware Packard: An Advocate for Cultural,
   Religious, and Legal Change." *Alabama Law Review*, vol. 54, no 3 (2003). pp.
   987–1077.
Adam Liptak, "Gay Marriage through a Black-White Prism." *New York Times*,
   October 29, 2006.
Erica Longfellow, "Public, Private and the Household in Early Seventeenth-century
   England." *Journal of British Studies*, vol. 45, no. 2 (2006), pp. 313–34.
Mildred Loving, "Loving for All." Positive Liberty. 2007.
   www.positiveliberty.com/2007/06/mildred-lovings-statement.html.
Brenda Maddox, "The Grimms Got It Right." *New Statesman*, October 16, 1998.
Scott C. Martin, " 'A Star That Gathers Lustre from the Gloom of Night': Wives,
   Marriage, and Gender in Early Nineteenth-Century American Temperance
   Reform." *Journal of Family History*, vol. 29, no. 3 (2004), pp. 274–92.
Steven Mintz, "Housework in Late 19th Century America."
   www.digitalhistory.uh.edu/historyonline/housework.cfm.
Kevin J. Mumford, "Lost Manhood Found: Male Sexual Impotence and Victorian
   Culture in the United States." *Journal of the History of Sexuality*, vol. 3, no. 1
   (1992), pp. 33–57.
National Association of Black Social Workers, "Position Statement on Trans-Racial
   Adoption," September 1972. The Adoption History Project, University of Oregon.
   http://darkwing.uoregon.edu/~adoption/archive/NabswTRA.htm.
David Newton, "Homosexual Behavior and Child Molestation: A Review of the
   Evidence." *Adolescence*, vol. 13, no. 49 (1978). www.aclu.org/lgbt/parent-
   ing/11824res19990406.html.
Ontario Consultants on Religious Tolerance, "Masturbation: Medical Beliefs in Past
   Centuries." www.religioustolerance.org/masturba4.htm.
Herbert A. Otto and Robert B. Andersen, "The Hope Chest and Dowry: American
   Custom?" The Family Life Coordinator, vol. 16, nos. 1/2 (January–April 1967),
   pp. 15–19.
Heather Palmer, "Queen Victoria's Not So 'Victorian' Writings."
   www.victoriana.com/doors/queenvictoria.htm.
Erwin Panofsky, "Jan van Eyck's Arnolfini Portrait." *The Burlington Magazine for
   Connoisseurs*, vol. 64, no. 372 (March 1934).
Maureen Park, "Dürer's *The Birth of the Virgin*: Art and Midwifery in 16th Century
   Nuremberg." *The Lancet*, vol. 358, no. 9289 (2001), pp. 1265–67.
Charlotte J. Patterson, "Lesbian and Gay Parents and Their Children: Summary of
   Research Findings." American Psychological Association, Lesbian and Gay
   Parenting 2005. www.apa.org/pi/lgbc/publications/lgpsummary.html.
Ingrid Peritz, "Quebec Campaign: Revenge of the Cradle Redux." *Globe and Mail*,
   November 22, 2008.
Christine Peters, "Gender, Sacrament and Ritual: The Making and Meaning of
   Marriage in Late Medieval and Early Modern England." *Past and Present*, no. 169
   (November 2000), pp. 63–96.

Jacqueline Peterson, "Prelude to Red River: A Social Portrait of the Great Lakes Métis." *Ethnohistory*, vol. 25 (Winter 1978).

Katie Pickles, "Locating Widows in Mid-Nineteenth Century Pictou County, Nova Scotia." *Journal of Historical Geography*, vol. 30, no. 1 (January 2004), pp. 70–86.

Deborah Reed-Danahay, "Champagne and Chocolate: 'Taste' and Inversion in a French Wedding Ritual." *American Anthropologist*, New Series, vol. 98, no. 4 (December 1996).

Robert Remington, "Celebrating a Reluctant Feminist Heroine." *National Post*, April 6, 2000.

Sam Roberts, "51% of Women Are Now Living without a Spouse." *New York Times,* January 16, 2007.

James C. Rodriguez, "Do Fathers Make a Difference: Social and Public Policy as a Catalyst for Responsible Fatherhood." Fathers and Families Coalition of America. December 20, 2007. www.azffc.org/show_old_article.php?id=16.

Lyndal Roper, " 'Going to Church and Street': Weddings in Reformation Augsburg." *Past and Present*, vol. 106, no. 1 (1985), pp. 62–101.

Martha T. Roth, "Age at Marriage and the Household: A Study of Neo-Babylonian and Neo-Assyrian Forms." *Comparative Studies in Society and History*, vol. 29, no. 4 (October 1987), pp. 715–47.

Maryam Sanati, "Here Comes the Bill." *Toronto Life*, June 2003.

Kayleen Schaefer, "The Sit-In at the Altar: No 'I Do' Till Gays Can Do it, Too." *New York Times*, December 3, 2006.

James M. Schmidt, "Private Parts." *Civil War Medicine (and Writing)*. http://civil-warmed.blogspot.com/2009/02/medical-department-23-private-parts.html.

Brent Shaw, "The Age of Roman Girls at Marriage: Some Reconsiderations." *Journal of Roman Studies*, vol. 77 (1987), pp. 30–46.

——"The Family in Late Antiquity: The Experience of Augustine." *Past and Present*, vol. 115 (May 1987), pp. 3–51.

Jeanette Smith, "Katharina von Bora through Five Centuries: A Historiography." *The Sixteenth Century Journal*, vol. 30, no. 3 (Autumn 1999), pp. 745–74.

Pamela J. Smock, "Cohabitation in the United States: An Appraisal of Research Themes, Findings, and Implications." *Annual Review of Sociology*, vol. 26 (August 2000).

Status of Women Canada, "Polygamy in Canada: Legal and Social Implications for Women and Children: A Collection of Policy Research Reports." 2005.

Richard H. Steckel, "The Age at Leaving Home in the United States, 1850–1860." *Social Science History*, vol. 20, no. 4 (Winter 1996).

Fiona Harris Stoertz, "Young Women in France and England, 1050–1300." *Journal of Women's History*, vol. 12 (2001), pp. 22–46.

Lawrence Stone, "The Public and the Private in the Stately Homes of England, 1500–1990." *Social Research*, vol. 58, no. 1 (Spring 1991).

James Stribopoulos, "The Passing of the Honourable Bertha Wilson." The Court, May 1, 2007. www.thecourt.ca/2007/05/01/the-passing-of-the-honourable-bertha-wilson.

Alexis de Tocqueville, "Education of Young Women in the United States." Democracy In America. www.marxists.org/reference/archive/de-tocqueville/democracy-america/ch34.htm.

Andrea Tone, "Contraceptive Consumers: Gender and the Political Economy of Birth Control in the 1930s." *Journal of Social History*, vol. 29, no. 3 (1996).

Ana Veciana-Suarez, "She's Back! Face to Face with Celine Dion." *Reader's Digest*, April 2002.

Lynne Verbeek, "Dr. Spock's Last Interview." Parents' Press, 1994. www.parentspress.com/drspock.html.

Susan Cott Watkins, "Regional Patterns of Nuptiality in Europe, 1870–1960." *Population Studies*, vol. 35, no. 2 (July 1981), pp. 199–215.

Elizabeth C. Watson, "Home Work in the Tenements," Survey 25 (February 4,1911), pp. 772–81. www.tenant.net/Community/LES/watson8.html.

Kayla Webley, "Why Americans Are Adopting Fewer Kids from China." *Time*, April 28, 2009.

Bruce Western, "Incarceration, Marriage, and Family Life." Russell Sage Foundation, September 2004. www.russellsage.org/publications/workingpapers/ incarcerationmarriagefamilylife.

Denise L. Whitehead, "Policies Affecting Gay Fathers: Specific Issues and Policies." Father Involvement Research Alliance, University of Guelph, 2009. www.fira.ca/article.php?id=98.

Alison Wolfe, "Working Girls, Broken Society." *Toronto Star,* April 2, 2006.

Sylvia Wolfram, "Divorce in England 1700–1857." *Oxford Journal of Legal Studies*, vol. 5, no. 2 (Summer 1988), pp. 155–86.

Armine Yalnizyan, "The Rich and the Rest of Us: The Changing Face of Canada's Growing Gap." Canadian Centre for Policy Alternatives, March 2007. www.cjson-line.ca/pdf/rich.pdf.

Katherine Young and Paul Nathanson. "Marriage-a-la-mode: Answering Advocates of Gay Marriage." Paper presented at Emory University, Atlanta, Georgia, May 14, 2003.

Diane Zuckerman, "Welfare Reform in America: A Clash of Politics and Research." *Journal of Social Issues* (Winter 2000) pp. 587–99.

Index

Credits

Page 4: Courtesy of the author.

Page 7: Photo by Lewis Wickes Hine, 1910. Library of Congress LC-DIG-NCLC-04628. From the records of the National Child Labor Committee (U.S.).

Page 11: http://collectionscanada.gc.ca. *Landing of the Girls Sent Out as Brides in 1667 at Québec* by Arthur E. Elias. National Archives of Canada / C-029486. Arthur E. Elias fonds [graphic material] (R10619-0-X-E).

Page 13: Photograph by John H. Fouch, 1877. Courtesy Dr. James S. Brust, Azusa Publishing, CO.

Page 16: Library of Congress, Prints and Photographs Division, LC-USZ62-96089, LC-USZ62-72670. Copyright 1920, Meadville, PA, Keystone View Company.

Page 23: Library of Congress, Prints and Photographs Division, LC-USZ62-117487. Copyright 1899, Johnson Co., Salt Lake, UT.

Page 33: Wikimedia Commons, http://common.wikimedia.org. Scanned by H. Churchyard.

Page 36: Johannes Vermeer, 1673.

Page 44 (top): Library of Congress, Prints and Photographs Division, LC-USZ62-97817. Copyright between 1909 and 1932, National Photo Company Collection.

Page 44 (middle): Library of Congress, Prints and Photographs Division, LC-USZ62-85525. George Grantham Bain Collection. Copyright 1916, John Wanamaker.

Page 44 (bottom): Library of Congress, Prints and Photographs Division, LC-F8- 26779[P&P], Debutantes group. Dated October 8, 1923. Copyright between 1909 and 1932, National Photo Company Collection.

Page 48: Jan van Eyck, *The Arnolfini Portrait.* Currently located at the National Gallery, London, UK. The reproduction is part of a collection of reproductions compiled by The Yorck Project. The compilation copyright is held by Zenodot Verlagsgesellschaft mbH and licensed under the GNU Free Documentation License. Wikimedia Commons, http://commons.wikimedia.org.

Page 59: William Hogarth, 1734. *The Rake Marrying an Old Woman* is the fifth in the series of eight.

Page 61: *The Peasant Wedding* by Pieter Bruegel the Elder, 1568.

Page 63: Hans Bock the Elder, 1584. Wikimedia Commons, http://commons.wikimedia.org.

Page 68: BC Museum, Call Number A-01483. Photo by Stephen Allen Spencer, 1870s.

Page 75 (top): Vintage engraving of Queen Victoria of the United Kingdom of Great Britain and Ireland as a young woman, wearing her wedding dress. Engraving from 1860, photo by D. Walker.

Page 75 (bottom): *The Marriage of Queen Victoria, 10 February 1840,* by Sir George Hayter (1840–1842). Commissioned by Queen Victoria. Wikimedia Commons, http://commons.wikimedia.org.

Page 78 (top): Copyright 1850, Southworth & Hawes. George Eastman House Collection. Accession number 1974:0193:0251.

Page 78 (bottom): Godey's Fashions for December, 1861, Capewell & Kimmel. Library of Congress Prints and Photographs Division, LC-USZ62-69592.

Page 79: Courtesy of the author.

Page 82: Jane Austen, an engraving found in Evert Duyckinick, *A Portrait Gallery of Eminent Men and Women in Europe and America.* Johnson, Wilson and Company, New York, 1873. From www.lib.utexas.edu/exhibits/portraits/

index.php?img=23. This image comes
from the Portrait Gallery of the Perry-
Castañeda Library of the University of
Texas at Austin.

Page 88 (left): Lucas Cranach the Elder,
1529. Wikimedia Commons,
http://commons.wikimedia.org.

Page 88 (right): Lucas Cranach the Elder,
1530. Wikimedia Commons,
http://commons.wikimedia.org.

Page 99: Photographed by Evens, circa
1854. Library and Archives of Canada
/ C-0079115.

Page 103: Two sisters holding shuttles, QC,
about 1890. McCord Museum, MP-
1992.18.1. Copyright McCord
Museum.

Page 116: 0051766 Wellcome Library,
London. Demonstration using the
vibrator, 1891. (Engl. pat. 1890.
No. 4390) From *A Description of the
Vibrator and Directions for Use*, by
C. H. Liedbeck, published in
Stockholm by P.A. Norstedt & Söner,
1891.

Page 118: Lysol ad published in women's
magazines.

Page 122: Wm. Notman & Son, 1895,
Montreal. Purchase from Associated
Screen News Ltd. II-109867.
Copyright McCord Museum.

Page 127 (left): Martha Coffin Wright, n.d.
Photographer unknown. Courtesy
Sophia Smith Collection, Smith
College.

Page 127 (right): David Wright, n.d.
Photographer Thompson. Copyright
Thompson, Amesbury, MA. Courtesy
Sophia Smith Collection, Smith
College.

Page 130 (top): Library of Congress, Prints
and Photographs Division, Lot 7481,
no. 2986-A[P&P], LC-DIG-NCLC-
04253. Photographer Lewis Wickes
Hine, August 1912.

Page 130 (bottom): Photo by J.P. Soule,
1876, Boston, MA. Wellcome Library,
London from Iconographic
Collections, L0038392.

Page 140 (top): Happy Laundry Girls ad
for Kirkman's Borax Soap. Photo by
Falk, N.Y. Copyright 1891, Kirkman
& Son. Library of Congress, Prints and
Photographs Division, LC-USZ62-
52088.

Page 140 (bottom): Copyright 1901,
R.Y. Young; American Stereoscopic Co.
Library of Congress, Prints and
Photographs Division, LC-USZ62-
75653.

Page 142: Photographer William Notman,
1869. Purchase from Associated Screen
News Ltd., I-37457 by McCord
Museum. With permission from the
McCord Museum, Montreal.

Page 143: Thomas E. Askew, 1899 or
1900. Library of Congress Prints and
Photographs Division, LC-USZ62-
69915.

Page 148: Photographer Lewis Wickes
Hine, 1913. Library of Congress Prints
and Photographs Division,
LC-USZ62-42207.

Page 149: Photographer Lewis Wickes
Hine, 1911. Library of Congress Prints
and Photographs Division,
LC-DIG-NCLC-04105.

Page 150: Photographer Lewis Wickes
Hine, 1910. Library of Congress Prints
and Photographs Division,
LC-USZ62-93129.

Page 151: Detroit Publishing Co., 1907.
Library of Congress Prints and
Photographs Division, LC-DA-70118.

Page 154: Painter-engraver Bosselman-
Chasselat, p. 15, found in Archives
Nationales de France. Wikimedia
Commons, http://commons.
wikimedia.org.

Page 160: Charles Van Schaick, Black River
Falls, Wisconsin Collection. Image
appears in the book *Wisconsin Death
Trip* by Michael Lesy. WHS Image
ID 11994, Courtesy Wisconsin
Historical Society.

Page 166: "The arrest of abortionist Ann
Lohman (a.k.a. Madame Restell) by
Anthony Comstock." From the
February 23, 1878 edition of *The New
York Illustrated Times*. Scanned from
"The Wickedest Woman in New York:
Madame Restell, the Abortionist" by
Clifford Browde. Wikimedia
Commons, http://commons.
wikimedia.org.

Page 175: Mrs. Belcher's boys, Montreal,
QC, 1891. McCord Museum II-
95395.1. Courtesy McCord Museum.

Page 185: Marble time, by The Fellows
Photographic Co., 1891. Library of

Congress, Prints and Photographs Division, LC-USZ62-61810.

Page 188 (top): Lewis Wickes Hine, making dresses for Campbell Kid dolls in a dirty tenement room, 59 Thompson St., N.Y., 4th floor, front. February 1912. Library of Congress Prints and Photographs, LC-DIG-NCLC-04216.

Page 188 (bottom): Lewis Wickes Hine, Children playing with Campbell Kid dolls. New York City, March 1912. Library of Congress Prints and Photographs, LC-DIG-NCLC-04210.

Page 189: Lewis Wickes Hine, November 1908, On streets near Daniel Hill, Lincolnton, NC. Library of Congress Prints and Photographs LC-DIG-NCLC-01384.

Page 190: Lewis Wickes Hine, October 23, 1912, Bessemer City, NC. Library of Congress Prints and Photographs LC-DIG-NCLC-02655.

Page 191 (top): E. F. Brown, Photo #1050, North Pownal, VT, February 1910. Library of Congress Prints and Photographs LC-DIG-NCLC-05282.

Page 191 (bottom): Lewis Wickes Hine, April 1910. New York, NY. Library of Congress Prints and Photographs LC-DIG-NCLC-04637.

Page 198: Detail of *Maria-Louisa Phipps (née Campbell), Samuel Rogers, Caroline, Lady Stirling-Maxwell,* by Frank Stone, 1845, given to the National Portrait Gallery, London in 1921. Wikimedia Commons, http://commons.wikimedia.org.

Page 203: Catherine Hayes assisting Wood and Billings to cut off the head from her husband's corpse, from *Annals of Newgate,* in Project Gutenberg's EBook #13097 of Arthur L. Hayward's *Lives of the Most Notable Criminals Who Have Been Condemned and Executed for Murder, the Highway, Housebreaking, Street Robberies, Coining or Other Offences.*

Page 215: "Modern Persecution, or Married Woman's Liabilities," From *Modern Persecution,* by Elizabeth P. W. Packard, 1873. Copyright Disability History Museum.

Page 222: John F. Claghorn, 214 Gold St., Brooklyn. Digital ID: 1150166.

United States Sanitary Commission – 1861–1872. Formerly part of Medical Committee Archives, No. DCCLXXXII (782), Photographs, prints and drawings. The New York Public Library, Manuscripts and Archives.

Page 231: Ground for Divorce, 1889, Stereograph card copyrighted by Melander & Bro. Library of Congress Prints and Photographs Division, LC-USZ62-68473.

Page 247: John McCrae leaning against a sundial, circa 1912. Reference No. M983.5. Copyright M983.5.1, Courtesy of Guelph Museums.

Page 250: Project Gutenberg archives. Wikimedia Commons, http://commons.wikimedia.org.

Page 254: Personal photo from the Edna and Lois Greaves family. Courtesy of Colleen Miltenberger.

Page 259: GlA. Burkhardt, 1900. McCord Museum, MP-1982.15.8. Copyright McCord Museum.

Page 268: Photographer Lara Porzak via Getty Images. "Comedian Ellen DeGeneres and actress Portia de Rossi pose for photos celebrating their marriage in the backyard of their home on August 16, 2008 in Beverly Hills, California." Getty Images # 82518542. Copyright Getty Images.

Page 272: Photographer Fred W. McDarrah/Getty Images, 28 June 1969. Getty Images #83599295. Copyright Getty Images.

Page 285 (top): Photo by David McNew/Getty Images, Getty Images #81604764. "Gay Marriage Becomes Legal in California." Copyright Getty Images.

Page 285 (bottom): Elena Korenbaum at iStock.com. Copyright iStock.com.

Page 291: Library of Congress, Prints and Photographs Division, *Look* magazine Photograph Collection. Call number LOOK - Job 67-3538. (Wikimedia Commons, http://commons. wikimedia.org). All rights released per Instrument of Gift.

Page 300: Dionne Quints Museum Item Number 13070703: Dionne Quints/Childhood Museum Source. 1937, the Quints outside in the summer weather. N.E.A. Accession Number: 13070703. Found at Dionne Quints Digitization Project, Dionne Quints Museum, North Bay, Ontario.

Page 301: Family photograph courtesy of Dr. Michael Burslem.

Page 311: Personal photo courtesy of Pegi Dover and Philip Jessup.

Page 316: Getty Images #85621986, "Northwest Connecticut Hit Hard by Economic Slowdown." Copyright Getty Images.

Page 331: Bettmann U 1558136, "Richard and Mildred Loving in Washington, D.C., June 12, 1967." Copyright Bettmann/Corbis.

Page 334: Courtesy of the author.

Page 336: The General Synod Archives, Anglican Church of Canada, P7538-386. "School boys of St. Cyprian Residential School, Brocket, Alberta, 1920." Copyright The General Synod Archives, Anglican Church of Canada.

Page 337: Cheyenne woman named Woxie Haury in ceremonial dress and in wedding portrait with husband. Photograph negative number L94-52.78. Estelle Reel Collection. Copyright Northwest Museum of Arts and Culture/Eastern Washington State Historical Society, Spokane, WA.

Page 349: Undated photograph of immigrants arriving at the Immigration Station on Angel Island. National Archives, NARC Identifier 595673 / Local Identifier 90-G-152-2038, Item from Record Group 90: Records of the Public Health Service, 1794–1990.

Page 352: James Gillray, London, November 27, 1782. "Judge Thumb, or—patent sticks for family correction: warranted lawful!" Forms part of the British Cartoon Prints Collection (Library of Congress). LC-USZ62-114396.

Page 355: Currier & Ives, "Woman's holy war. Grand charge on the enemy's works," 1874. Library of Congress Prints and Photographs Division, LC-USZ62-683.

Page 357: Chase and Sanborn Coffee ad, mid-20th century.

Page 369: Photographer Alfred T. Palmer, February 1943, Transfer from U.S. Office of War Information, 1944. Library of Congress, Prints and Photographs Division, LC-USW361-295.

Page 382: Photographer Merna Forster, Women are Persons! Monument on Parliament Hill, Ottawa. Courtesy of Merna Forster.

Page 385: Michaels Photography, 2007.

Page 398: Personal photo from August 26, 2007, courtesy of Carol McPhee.